*The Manichaean Codices
of Medinet Madi*

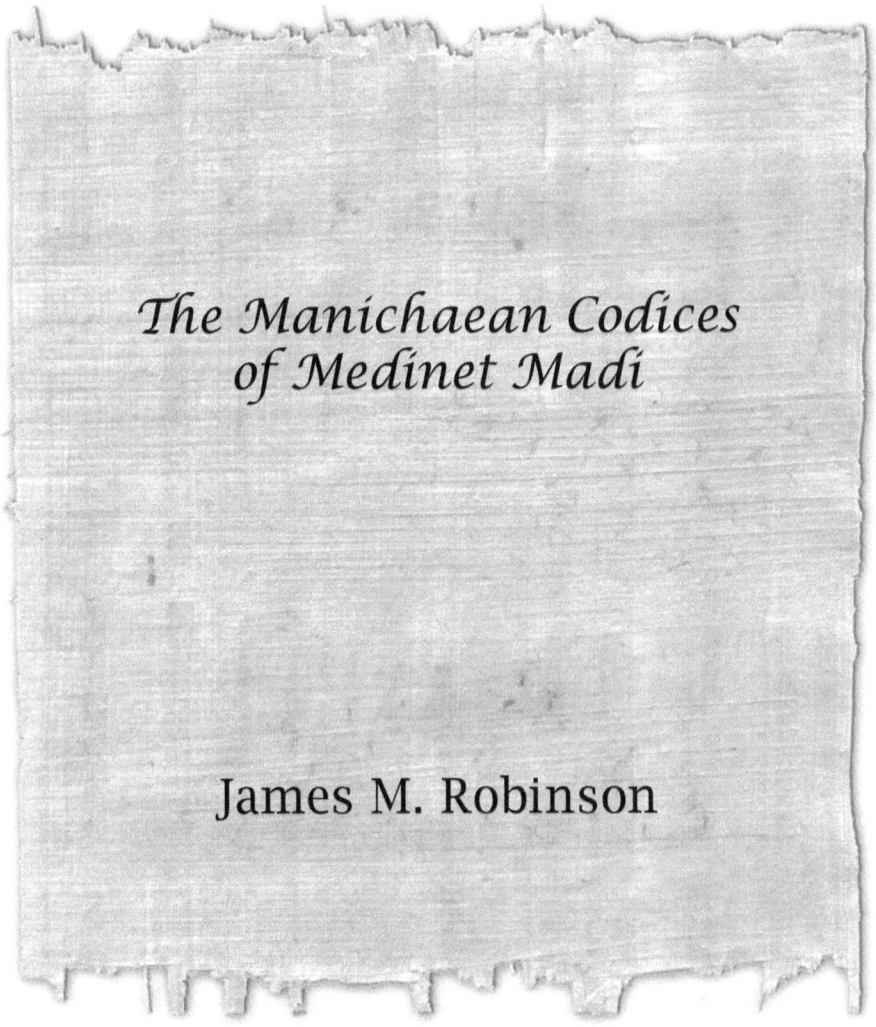

# The Manichaean Codices of Medinet Madi

## James M. Robinson

CASCADE Books • Eugene, Oregon

THE MANICHAEAN CODICES OF MEDINET MADI

Copyright © 2013 James M. Robinson. All rights reserved. Except for brief quotations in critical publications or reviews, no part of this book may be reproduced in any manner without prior written permission from the publisher. Write: Permissions, Wipf and Stock Publishers, 199 W. 8th Ave., Eugene, OR 97401.

Cascade Books
An Imprint of Wipf and Stock Publishers
199 W. 8th Ave., Suite 3
Eugene, OR 97401

ISBN 13: 978-1-59752-880-1

*Cataloging-in-Publication data:*

Robinson, James M. (James McConkey), 1924–.

The Manichaean codices of Medinet Madi / James M. Robinson.

ISBN 13: 978-1-59752-880-1

xvi + 326 p. ; 23 cm. —Includes bibliographic references and index.

1. Manichaeism—Manuscripts. 2. Manuscripts, Coptic (Papyri). 3. Manuscripts, Greek (Papyri). 4. Beatty, Alfred Chester, Sir, 1875–1968. 5. Schmidt, Carl, 1868–1938. 6. Ibscher, Hugo, 1874–1943. 7. Ibscher, Rolf, 1906–1967. 8. Polotsky, Hans Jakob, 1905–1991. 9. Chester Beatty Library. I. Title.

BT1410 R59 2013

Manufactured in the USA

## Contents

*Abbreviations / vii*
*Preface / ix*
*Abstract / xi*

Introduction: The Fate of the Manichaean Codices of Medinet Madi, 1929–1989 / 1

## Part 1: The Acquisition and Initial Conservation and Editing

1. The Acquisitions of Carl Schmidt / 51
2. The Acquisitions of Chester Beatty / 61
3. The Conservation by Hugo Ibscher / 80
4. Beatty, Ibscher, and Polotsky / 92
5. The Effects of World War II / 113

## Part 2: The Conservation by Rolf Ibscher

6. The Conservation of the Material in the State Museums of the Former East Berlin / 147
7. The Conservation of the Material in Schondorf/Göttingen/West Berlin / 163
8. The Conservation of the Material in London/Dublin / 182

Inventories of Individual Codices / 189

## Part 3: The Berlin Holdings

9 P$^{15995}$ *Synaxeis* / 193
10 P$^{15996}$ *Kephalaia*, Volume One / 198
11 P$^{15997}$ *Acts* / 225
12 P$^{15998}$ *Letters* / 248
13 P$^{15999}$ *Homilies* (Berlin Part) / 268

## Part 4: The Dublin Holdings

14 The Wooden Covers / 273
15 Codex A: *Psalms* / 282
16 Codex B: *Synaxeis* / 288
17 Codex C: *Kephalaia*, Volume Two / 303
18 Codex D: *Homilies* (Dublin Part) / 309

Collectors, Dealers, and Scholars / 313
Bibliography / 317
Index of Names / 323

# Abbreviations

| | |
|---|---|
| APF | *Archiv für Papyrusforschung* |
| BSAC | *Bulletin de la Société d'Archéologie Copte* |
| BSFE | *Bulletin de la Société française d'Égyptologie* |
| BZNW | Beihefte zur Zeitschrift für die neutestamentliche Wissenschaft und die Kunde der alten Kirche |
| JTS | *Journal of Theological Studies* |
| MPER | Mitteilungen aus der Sammlung der Papyrus Erzherzog Rainer |
| WUNT | Wissenschaftliche Unterschungen zum Neuen Testament |
| WZUH | *Wissenschaftliche Zeitschrift der Martin-Luther Universität-Halle-Wittenberg* |
| ZDMG | *Zeitschrift der deutschen morgenländischen Gesellschaft* |
| ZPE | *Zeitschrift für Papyrologie und Epigraphik* |

# Preface

THE PRESENT WORK, *The Manichaean Codices of Medinet Madi*, is primarily a mass of unpublished documentation I excerpted from the Manichaean archives in the main depositories, Berlin and Dublin, in 1984–1986, and from interviews with those directly involved. Copies were given to these two depositories in 1991, as well as to Wolf-Peter Funk of the University of Laval in Québec, Canada, the leading authority in this field, to whom I hence also gave my own Manichaean archives themselves. Hence the present publication does not continue the history of research up to the present, but leaves that for the next generation of scholarship.

The presentation contains very extensive—but often inconclusive—information; this uncertainty is indicated here, lest their publication give them a degree of certainty that is not appropriate. Yet the amount of otherwise inaccessible but reliable information, from interviews, correspondence, and unpublished documents, should not be lost from sight, but should be made available to the scholarship of the future.

To facilitate reading, indeed to keep the reader from being lost in detail, the extensive documentation is preceded by two already published summaries. First is a brief abstract prepared for the 18th International Congress of Byzantine Studies in Moscow, August 8–15, 1991. This then is followed by a more extensive introduction: "The Fate of the Manichaean Codices of Medinet Madi, 1929–1989." It was originally published in *International Kongress zum Manichäismus 6.-10. August 1989 St. Augustin/Bonn*, edited by Gernot Wiessner and Hans-Joachim

Klimkeit, in *Studies in Oriental Religions* 23 (Wiesbaden: Harrassowitz, 1992) 19–62.

The presentation of material is less complete for the material in the Chester Beatty Library, since the sorting and recording had to be done primarily for the scattered Berlin material. Yet the extensive archival material in Dublin makes it clear that considerably more detail could be added to the presentation of the return of the Chester Beatty codices after World War II, to the description of the work of Rolf Ibscher in London and Dublin, and to the analysis of the Dublin holdings.

James M. Robinson

# ABSTRACT

# The Manichaean Codices of Medinet Madi

THE SEVEN MANICHAEAN PAPYRUS codices of the fourth or fifth century were found in illicit excavation in 1929 in the desert in the ruins of Τερενοῦθις near Medinet Madi at the southern end of the Fayyum. They were acquired in about equal halves by A. Chester Beatty for his library then in London, now in Dublin, and by Carl Schmidt for the Papyrussammlung (papyrus collection) of the Staatliche Museen of Berlin. The status of the seven codices follows:

## CHESTER BEATTY LIBRARY CODEX A, *THE PSALMS*

Beatty acquired the front part of the codex from the Cairo dealer Maurice Nahman in 1931, and he had acquired the back part in 1930. The back part was conserved in Berlin by Hugo Ibscher and published by Charles R. C. Allberry in 1938. As Ibscher conserved each leaf of the front part, H. J. Polotsky transcribed each in Berlin. Copies went to both Beatty and W. E. Crum, for use in his *Coptic Dictionary*. Since the edition was never completed, it was not published, but in 1986/1988, Søren Giversen published a few lines of Psalm 119 he derived by Polotsky. The front part of the codex was put on loan at the Royal Library of Copenhagen in 1984 for Giversen to publish in facsimile and critical editions. He published both parts only in facsimile edition in 1988.

## CHESTER BEATTY LIBRARY CODEX B, *THE SYNAXEIS*

Beatty acquired this codex from a Fayyumic dealer in 1930 (except for 31 residual leaves that Schmidt acquired in 1931, P$^{15995}$). Beatty turned it over to Ibscher to conserve. By 1939 only thirteen leaves of Beatty's part had been conserved and returned to London. They moved with the library to Dublin in 1953 and to Copenhagen in 1984. Giversen published a facsimile edition in 1986. Beginning in 1934, the rest of Beatty's part of the codex was kept in Hugo Ibscher's home in Kleinmachnow, near Berlin, for conservation. But after Ibscher's death in 1943, his son Rolf Ibscher reported putting Beatty's parts of the codex in a reinforced concrete bunker at the Zoo Train Station of Berlin for safekeeping. After the bombing of that bunker in 1944, Rolf Ibscher reported having his assistant P. Seidel remove the codex so that Ibscher could take it to the home of his father-in-law, Wolf Henry Doering, in Schondorf on the Ammersee in Bavaria. From time to time Rolf Ibscher worked at conserving the leaves there. The West German authorities took control of the codex and engaged Carsten Colpe to edit it in 1956–1957. So the codex was taken to Göttingen. When he died in 1967, Rolf Ibscher had conserved only about half this material. When the Egyptian Museum was created in West Berlin in 1967, the material was deposited there. In 1985 the curator of the papyrus collection in that museum, William Brashear, asked me to investigate this material. There are 125 extant unpublished leaves plus the unconserved remainder of the book block. I reported on it to the Fachkommission Byzantinistik of the Historiker-Gesellschaft of the German Democratic Republic in Halle in 1986. Both museums authorized me to organize an edition of all the Manichaean material in Berlin. The transcription of the scarcely legible conserved leaves was begun in 1985. Gesine Schenke Robinson worked on the thirty-one leaves on the Museums-Insel of East Berlin, and others (especially Wolf-Peter Funk and Paul Mirecki) worked on those leaves in West Berlin. The photographing took place in Berlin in preparation for a facsimile edition of all the Manichaean material in Berlin, Vienna, and Warsaw, planned to be published by the Akademie-Verlag of Berlin.

## CHESTER BEATTY LIBRARY CODEX C, VOLUME TWO OF THE *KEPHALAIA*

Beatty acquired this codex from the Fayyumic dealer prior to Schmidt's talking to that dealer in the spring of 1931. It was conserved by Rolf Ibscher after World War II and published in facsimile edition by Giversen in 1986. A committee of Søren Giversen, Rodolphe Kasser, and Martin Krause held exclusive rights to publish a critical edition of the Dublin–Copenhagen material. Kasser was entrusted with organizing the publication of the critical edition of this codex.

## CHESTER BEATTY LIBRARY CODEX D, THE *HOMILIES*

Beatty acquired the bulk of this codex from Nahman with an option to buy in 1930. But Beatty released it to Carl Schmidt for Berlin in 1932 ($P^{15999}$). It was not considered conservable but was put on display as a showpiece for how impossible this task was. The unconserved book block is thought to have been among the materials stored in the bunker at the Zoo train station. From there it was thought to have been taken to the Soviet command post at the castle Friedrichsfelde in 1945–1946, and then to Leningrad in 1946, though it was not found when the material was returned to Berlin in 1958. A smaller part of the codex was acquired by Beatty in 1931, conserved by Ibscher, edited by Polotsky, and published in 1934. Giversen published a facsimile edition of the codex in 1987.

## BERLIN PAPYRUS COLLECTION $P^{15995}$, THE *SYNAXEIS*

See Chester Beatty Library Codex B above.

## BERLIN PAPYRUS COLLECTION $P^{15996}$, VOLUME ONE OF THE *KEPHALAIA*

Schmidt acquired this codex from Nahman in 1930. Ibscher conserved most of the leaves. H. J. Polotsky and Alexander Böhlig edited them. They were published in fascicles—by 1940, a first volume through page 244, line 20. Böhlig published through page 291 in 1966, and

through page 292 in 1985. Professor Grohmann of Prague acquired three unpublished remains for the Austrian National Library, where they are still extant. Five unpublished Berlin leaves are in Warsaw, where they were brought after having been lost in transit between Berlin and Leningrad in 1946. In Berlin there are some ninety extant unpublished leaves, equaling 180 pages.

The total of unpublished extant leaves then becomes $3 + 5 + 90 = 98$ leaves or $6 + 10 + 180 = 196$ pages. Wolf-Peter Funk is preparing a critical edition. Polotsky has put at Funk's disposal for the critical edition his transcriptions and translations located at the Academy of Sciences in Berlin, at the Griffith Institute of the Ashmoleon Museum in Oxford, and at the Chester Beatty Library in Dublin.

## BERLIN PAPYRUS COLLECTION $P^{15997}$, THE *ACTS*

This codex with its covers (which were photographed and published) was sold by a provincial dealer to Nahman, who sold the codex to Schmidt in 1931. One leaf that Ibscher conserved was returned to London, was moved with the library to Dublin, and was included in the material put on deposit in Copenhagen. Giversen published it in facsimile in 1987.

There are seven or eight unpublished leaves still in Berlin. Part of one unpublished leaf may be at the Institute for Papyrology of Warsaw University. There may thus be nine or ten extant leaves, eighteen or twenty pages. The unconserved book block and wooden covers did not return from Leningrad to Berlin in 1958. None of the leaves of this codex in Berlin or Warsaw have been published.

## BERLIN PAPYRUS COLLECTION $P^{15998}$, THE *LETTERS*

This codex was also sold by the provincial dealer to Nahman, who sold it to Schmidt in 1931. There are six unpublished leaves that were returned from Leningrad to Berlin in 1958 and three unpublished leaves in the National Museum in Warsaw. There are also fifteen containers with eighteen leaves (three secondarily assigned to the *Kephalaia*) among those that probably lay half-conserved in the Ibscher home throughout the war that may belong to this codex. A leaf originally

labeled as belonging to the Letters but reassigned to the Acts probably should be counted as belonging to the Letters. This would make a total of twenty-eight leaves or fifty-six pages. The book block did not return from Leningrad to Berlin in 1958. Hence none of the leaves of this codex were published.

# BERLIN PAPYRUS COLLECTION P$^{15999}$, THE *HOMILIES*

See Chester Beatty Library Codex D above.

# INTRODUCTION

# The Fate of the Manichaean Codices of Medinet Madi, 1929-1989

As you will remember Terentianus Maurus in *De litteris syllabic et metric*: "Pro captu lectoris habent sua fata libelli" [The fate of the books depends on the intelligence of the readers] which is often taken as said in the sense that books have their history. They have indeed, and also the Medinet Madi manuscripts have their fate as we all know. Some details, however, are still unknown to many although they are important in order for better understanding of the texts.

—Søren Giversen

THE SEVEN MANICHAEAN CODICES from Medinet Madi (Τερενούθις), whose ruins are still impressive (in the desert on the southern edge of the Fayyum), were made known to the scholarly community primarily through the essay of Carl Schmidt and H. J. Polotsky, "Ein Mani-Fund in Ägypten,"[1] although much information not included there has more recently become available from the Archives of the Chester Beatty Library in Dublin.[2]

1. Schmid and Polotsky, "Ein Mani-Fund," 4–90, with two plates and a contribution by Hugo Ibscher, "Die Handschriften," 82–85. Most of the information in that essay is not repeated here but is presupposed as generally known or readily available.

2. Copies of relevant archive documents were kindly supplied to the Manichaean archive of the Institute for Antiquity and Christianity, which provided a chronological history of the Manichaean archive. This inventory was then supplied to Søren Giversen, who, in August 1987, asked the Chester Beatty Library to supplement material he already had with copies of some material listed in the inventory. Dr. Pat Donlon, then Reference Librarian and Curator of the Western Collection, graciously honored this request.

# 2　THE MANICHAEAN CODICES OF MEDINET MADI

Schmidt narrated that he had been shown some of the material by antiquities dealers in Egypt on two trips, only the second of which is actually dated, to the spring of 1931. From this one has inferred that his first trip was in 1930,[3] which Schmidt has elsewhere stated to be the date of the discovery.[4] But Søren Giversen has reported that the Danish Egyptologist H. O. Lange was shown some of the material in Cairo on November 29, 1929, by Maurice Nahman, the leading Cairo antiquities dealer of the time, though he did not acquire anything.[5] Hence the date of the discovery, if one may assume such material tends to reach the market promptly, should be corrected to read 1929.[6]

## SIR CHESTER BEATTY'S ACQUISITIONS

On Schmidt's first trip he had been shown what he was able to identify on the spot as part of the *Kephalaia*, since he had just been reading proofs on Karl Holl's edition of Epiphanius's *Panarion* that refers to it! Yet he did not acquire it when first shown it, but continued on his trip to Jerusalem, with plans to secure authorization for its acquisition by the time he passed through Cairo on his return trip. But before that time,[7] or, now to be more specific, on March 23, 1930, Chester Beatty had obtained on approval from the same Cairo antiquities dealer Maurice Nahman two other manuscripts and two wooden covers.[8]

---

3. Beltz, "Katalog der koptischen Handschriften."

4. Schmidt, *Neue Originalquellen des Manichäismus aus Äegypten*, 4. Similarly Allberry, "Manichaean Studies," 337–49, especially 340, gives 1930 as the date when the "library was brought to light," as well as the date when Schmidt was shown the *Kephalaia* "by a Fayum dealer." The dealer in question was actually the Cairo dealer Maurice Nahman, who obviously had contacts with the Fayyum, but not the dealer located in the Fayyum whom Schmidt first visited with regard to these codices in 1931.

5. Giversen, *Psalm Book, Part 1*, 7–8. He points out that this date, which Lange's extant diary documents, was also confirmed by Schmidt in an extant letter of February 20, 1936. A similar report (Giversen, "Manichaean Texts from the Chester Beatty Collection," 265–72), especially 271–72, states that the antiquities dealer who showed "one of the manuscripts" to Lange was Maurice Nahman.

6. Giversen, *Manichaean Papyri of the Chester Beatty Library*, 1, speaks of "their rediscovery in 1929," in the quotation used as the motto at the beginning of this paper. This motto is repeated in somewhat different terms in Giversen, "Manichaean Texts from the Chester Beatty Collection," 271.

7. Schmidt and Polotsky, "Ein Mani-Fund," 6.

8. In the Archives of the Chester Beatty Library is a ledger sheet with the letterhead of Maurice Nahman, dated March 23, 1930. It was made out to Beatty and

At the end of May, Beatty had Hugo Ibscher, the Conservator of the Papyrus Collection of Berlin, who had worked periodically for him in London, assess the chances of conserving the material, since the leaves were stuck together by salt crystals resulting, one assumed, from lying in dampness over the centuries. Ibscher said the larger and more expensive manuscript, which only later was identified as the bulk of the *Homilies* codex (see below), could not be conserved.[9] Beatty apparently decided already then not to acquire it, for he did not send it along with the other to Berlin with Ibscher for conservation, but retained it in London for two years (see below).

## Chester Beatty Library Codex A, the *Psalms*, Part Two

The smaller of the manuscripts acquired by Beatty on March 23, 1930, with an option to buy was assessed by Ibscher as "very difficult" to conserve.[10] Beatty cabled Nahman on May 31, 1930, that he was willing to pay only £200, rather than the £500 that Nahman had asked. But on June 2, 1930, Nahman cabled that he would not accept the offer. Yet Beatty had already turned over the manuscript to Ibscher, who had just taken it back to Berlin with him to conserve. On or before June 9, 1930, while in New York on a business trip, Beatty agreed by transatlantic cable to pay £500. It turned out to be the latter part of the *Psalms* codex, which was published by Charles R. C. Allberry in 1938.[11] Photographic reproductions were published by Søren Giversen in 1988.[12]

---

listed fifteen items for sale with their prices, to which have been added annotations as to which are to be kept and which returned. A last item, offered for £1,200 reads: "Two Coptic manuscripts an[d] two binding[s] in wood." Underneath, notes were added that read:

> On approval
> £700 Mss
> £500 Mss
> £40 Binding

9. Hugo Ibscher arrived in London on May 26, 1930, according to Beatty's cable to an impatient Nahman on May 28, 1930. On May 31, 1930, Beatty cabled Nahman: "Doctor Ibscher thinks can do nothing with large book."

10. Quoted from Beatty's cable of May 31, 1930, to Nahman.

11. Allberry, *A Manichaean Psalm-Book, Part 2*.

12. Giversen, *Psalm Book, Part 2*, facsimile edition.

4   THE MANICHAEAN CODICES OF MEDINET MADI

### Chester Beatty Library Codex B, the *Synaxeis*

Schmidt reported that a Fayyumic dealer had explained to him in the Spring of 1931 that the discovery had been divided into eight parts among three dealers. The Fayyumic dealer himself had retained three parts, Nahman three, and a provincial dealer two. The Fayyumic dealer told Schmidt that he had already sold all three of his parts to Beatty.[13] Since there are apparently only two codices acquired by Beatty that he did not get from Nahman, the bulk of the *Synaxeis* and Volume Two of the *Kephalaia* (see below), one of these must have been dismembered by the time of the partition, a vandalism to which Schmidt referred in general, thereby producing three "codices" out of two codices. Since the *Synaxeis* codex is known to have been dismembered by this time (see below), one may assume that it was the one counted as two of the three "codices" acquired by Beatty from the Fayyumic dealer.

On November 27, 1930, Beatty turned over to Ibscher in London, to take back to Berlin for conservation, another "Coptic book."[14] Its acquisition is not otherwise documented, but it may be postulated to have been from the Fayyumic acquisition, which may have been cash and carry, without a written receipt. But the absence of documentation could be due merely to the incompleteness of the Archives or of our survey of them.[15]

Schmidt reported having acquired in the spring of 1931 for the sake of completeness "a few unimpressive piles" from a codex Beatty had acquired in the Fayyum.[16] Only two codices were shared between London and Berlin, the *Homilies* and the *Synaxeis*. This could not be the *Homilies*, since the Berlin part of this codex was later acquired from Nahman, once Beatty, who had it on approval, had decided not to acquire it (see below). Hence the *Synaxeis* must be for this reason also one of the codices Beatty acquired in the Fayyum, and indeed

---

13. Schmidt and Polotsky, "Ein Mani-Fund," 8.

14. In a letter of November 27, 1930, to Sir Alan Gardiner, Beatty speaks of sending Gardiner a Coptic book to have Ibscher put in his bag after verifying that it is satisfactorily packed.

15. The two manuscripts brought to London in April 1931 (see below) are recorded to have been brought that month, but a receipt from an antiquities dealer has not been located. The fact that the two manuscripts are in each case the other part of the two codices acquired from Nahman a year earlier supports the assumption that these came from Nahman.

16. Schmidt and Polotsky, "Ein Mani-Fund," 8.

prior to the spring of 1931.¹⁷ Thus it may be the book sent to Berlin for conservation at the end of November 1930, although this could also have been Volume Two of the *Kephalaia*. In fact, since both may have been unbound, and the *Synaxeis* was in more than one part, the "book" may have been a stack of papyrus pads without a clear distinction of where one codex began and another ended. In fact, someone had written in by hand on the typed letter of November 27, 1930, the word "Papyri" just before "Coptic Book," which might indicate that it looked less like a book than an amorphous stack of papyri.

Thirteen leaves of the *Synaxeis* codex were conserved by Hugo Ibscher and returned to London by the spring of 1939.¹⁸ They were moved with the Chester Beatty Library to Dublin in 1953 and in 1984 were put on loan at the Royal Library of Copenhagen for Søren Giversen to study.¹⁹ Giversen published photographic reproductions in 1986.²⁰ It is to be hoped that these thirteen leaves can be integrated fully in any future critical edition of the *Synaxeis* rather than being subjected to the either-or conditions announced by Rodolphe Kasser on behalf of an International Committee for the Publication of the Manichaean Coptic Papyri from Medinet Madi Belonging to the Chester Beatty Library (Søren Giversen, President; Rodolphe Kasser; Martin Krause), to the effect that persons editing Berlin materials

17. Ibid., 30, makes this explicit.

18. On April 22, 1939, Sir Alan Gardiner wrote Beatty that he had some Mani plates he would return soon. A day-book kept by Joan Kingford Wood of Beatty's library staff since 1927 recorded on May 3, 1939: "From Dr. G[ardiner]. Mani. Pap. Codex B.C. KEPHALAIA 49 in all (Cod. B. 51–62, 63–76 Cod. C. 1, 3, 4, 39–48, 49–58) = 49." An entry dated July 5, 1939, as "Fetched by Mr. A[llberry]" "Codex B KEPHALAIA pages 51–62, 63–76." Apparently two codices were distinguished, as B and C, yet both were on this occasion designated *Kephalaia*, whereas Beatty had only one *Kephalaia* codex, Codex C. Since Codex A, *Psalms*, is of a smaller format than the others (see below), and Codex D, the part of the *Homilies* owned by Beatty, had already been clearly identified and in fact published, the 13 leaves designated Codex B 51–76 must be from the only remaining codex acquired by Beatty, the *Synaxeis*.

19. Whereas Giversen had requested about 171 leaves on November 24, 1982, of Patrick Henchy, then librarian of the Chester Beatty Library, on November 7, 1983 he raised the figure to 184 in a request to the current director and librarian, Wilfrid Lockwood. The inventory dated January 13, 1984 and validated with the stamp of the Danish Royal Library lists as "Codex B" "13 glasses" numbered "51–76."

20. Giversen, *Homilies and Varia*, ix, states: "Pages 101–126 bear facsimiles of the leaves which Hugo Ibscher has labelled 'Codex B.' ... The sheets are marked from 51 to 76, the equivalent of this edition's 101–126."

(where the bulk of the *Synaxeis* codex is now located, see below) may not participate in editing Dublin materials.[21] Yet, as Alexander Böhlig has subsequently stated: "It is too onesided, when the Dublin team wishes to forbid simultaneous work on the two parts of the discovery, since, after all, overlappings of the material are present."[22] In fact the publication of the facsimile edition puts the facsimiles of these thirteen leaves in the public domain, free to the scholarly world to publish in critical editions as it sees fit. For, as Martin Krause, though a member of the committee advocating this segregation in the membership of the two teams, has said (with regard to the facsimile edition of the Nag Hammadi codices), the purpose of a facsimile edition is "so that the manuscripts after their publication in facsimile volumes stand avail-

---

21. At the meeting of the Association Francophone de Coptologie at the Louvre Museum in Paris on May 23, 1986, Rodolphe Kasser read and distributed an announcement entitled "Projet international pour la publication des manuscrits manichéens coptes de Medinet Madi appartenant à la Chester Beatty Library (premier communiqué)."

> Soon after this [the publication of a facsimile edition] the critical edition of the same texts will appear under the responsibility of the same committee [Søren Giversen, president; Rodolphe Kasser; Martin Krause], which will distribute this task between coptologists . . . only those persons will be invited to participate in the *editio princeps* of the Manichaean Coptic texts in the Chester Beatty Library who has [sic] not already obtained this possibility concerning the *editio princeps* of the Manichaean Coptic papyri of Berlin or Vienna.

This announcement followed directly upon my invitation to French-language Coptologists to participate in the work of an "International Committee for the Manichaean Codices of Medinet Madi" that was being planned. This invitation was published in *Newsletter* 19 of the International Association for Coptic Studies, August 1986, Annex 1, pp. 3–5, especially p. 4: ". . . qualified scholars are welcome to offer their services . . . For it is not the intention of the project to limit access to the material, but rather to facilitate access to it." The announcement by Kasser, president of the International Association for Coptic Studies, followed in French and English on pp. 6–9.

The Board of the International Association for Coptic Studies, at its meeting on June 12, 1986, "expressed its approval of both [projects], and hoped that there will be collaboration between the two projects," as published on page 1 of the same *Newsletter*.

22. Böhlig, "Neue Initiativen zur Erschliessung der koptisch-manichäischen Bibliothek von Medinet Madi," 245. "Es ist zu einseitig, wenn das Dublin-Team gleichzeitige Arbeit an beiden Fundgruppen verbieten will, sind doch Überkreuzungen des Materials vorhanden."

able to *all* scholars for study and work" (Krause's emphasis).²³ A transcription of the published facsimiles of the 13 *Synaxeis* leaves that has been prepared by Wolf-Peter Funk in conjunction with transcriptions of the leaves in Berlin that he is preparing should preferably be published together, for which purpose access to the papyri in Copenhagen should be granted to him and others working on the Berlin part of codices also represented in Dublin/Copenhagen. Negotiations during the conference at Bonn produced an agreement to at least a degree of cooperation:

> Persons participating in the *editio princeps* of material in Berlin can work together with persons participating in the *editio princeps* of material in Dublin / Copenhagen as a joint team to edit a shared text. In the naming of persons on such joint editorial teams Giversen will represent the Dublin group and Robinson the Berlin group. The person or persons named by each group will be primarily responsible for editing the leaves of that group, but members of such a joint team can study the papyri at both places, work in close collaboration with each other, and publish a joint edition.

A first step toward the implementation of this policy was a visit of Wolf-Peter Funk to Copenhagen, where he was permitted to study the 13 leaves of the *Synaxeis* codex. (Giversen has not approved subsequent plans to cooperate in editing the two volumes of the *Kephalaia*.)

Some of the material, while undergoing conservation, was not kept at the Papyrus Collection in Berlin, but in the Ibscher home, where Ibscher was permitted to work three days a week from the age of 60, i.e., from 1934 on.²⁴ Though Beatty himself went to Berlin before the war to bring back his papyri, he apparently brought back

---

23. Krause, review of *The Facsimile Edition of the Nag Hammadi Codices: Introduction*, 378.

24. Reported by Alexander Böhlig in a letter of February 10, 1986. A letter from Otto Firchow of October 28, 1960, had stated:

> In my opinion the papyri [Chester Beatty Library Codex B, the *Synaxeis*] ought to be found with Dr. Rolf Ibscher probably already mounted and glazed. Dr. Hugo Ibscher used to carry out this kind of work in his own home. If I were still in Berlin, or if I had known about the matter a few months ago, I could have offered you my help. I should suggest that you get in touch with Rolf Ibscher, who has no connection with the Berlin Museum. Let me say again that the papyri cannot be in the Berlin Museum but must have been in Hugo Ibscher's private possession.

only what had been conserved.[25] C. R. C. Allberry reported in May 1940 "that Dr. Ibscher had the remainder of Mr. Beatty's papyrus at his house in the country, at Kleinmachnow."[26] But there were in the home also materials belonging to Berlin, such as unconserved leaves of P[15996], the *Kephalaia*,[27] and P[15998], the *Letters*.[28] It would be to these Berlin holdings that Ibscher referred in 1949, to the effect that the remainder of the (Berlin) Papyrus Collection was in his home.[29]

25. Joan Kingford Wood wrote on February 7, 1960, her reminiscences:

> ... it must have been when things were boiling up in Germany against the Jews, before hostilities began with us, that Sir Chester went over to Berlin to fetch the remainder of the papyri, the Manichaean ... He went and brought back the papyri. But then Sir Chester has a way of overcoming difficulties with authority and persuasion.

26. The black loose-leaf folder in the Archives of the Chester Beatty Library entitled "Papyrus. Biblical Manichaean Hieratic Greek etc. General Catalogue," in the section "Manichaean Pap." presents this quotation, with the reference: "(see letter from Allberry)."

27. Böhlig, "Die Arbeit," 182: "Of the material in Berlin only a very small part has always remainded in Berlin. It was the last 20 leaves of the Berlin *Kephalaia* book."

28. Ibid., 184, 182:

> Of this book one finds in Berlin, put under glass already in the pre-war period, 6 leaves ... , and about 22 leaves in half-conserved condition. The folders in which they lay were numbered ...
>
> The urgently needed reglassing of all the pieces that had been glassed by Hugo Ibscher and that returned to Berlin in 1958 was undertaken by Rolf Ibscher beginning in June of this year (1960), along with the conservation of a few half-conserved leaves that Ibscher Sr. had at first put to one side as too difficult, doubtlessly correctly, for it had to do usually with double or triple leaves.

The half-conserved leaves are here distinguished as in folders rather than as glassed. And the reference to material being returned to Berlin is limited to the glassed material. This would indicate that the half-conserved material in folders had not been taken to Leningrad and returned in 1958 to Berlin. The Inventory Book of the Papyrus Collection of Berlin lists only 6 glassed leaves as going "to the East" and "back."

29. Ibscher wrote J. V. S. Wilkinson, the librarian of the Chester Beatty Library, on December 31, 1949: "The misfortune of our persecuted Museums with the destroyed rooms of the Papyrus Collection led after all to this, that the collection was stationed with me in [my] house, and that brought us many a convenience."

Actually the material was already in the Ibscher home; it is very doubtful (see below) if any papyri were still in the museum when it was very heavily damaged by air raids, or that Ibscher could have rescued any such material from the gutted Neues Museum to take to his home. There is a similar allusion to material in the home in a letter of January 9, 1949 from Ibscher to Beatty, of which only a translation of the

## Introduction: The Fate of the Manichaean Codices 9

The bulk of the Papyrus Collection not in the Ibscher home, along with other Museum holdings, was put for safekeeping during the war in a reinforced concrete bunker (removed after the war) at the Zoo Train Station, in what became West Berlin. The Museum was indeed very heavily damaged in a massive air raid on February 3, 1945, which left intact only the outer walls of the gutted Neues Museum, where the Papyrus Collection had been housed.

Rolf Ibscher reported that after his father's death on May 26, 1943, he added to the storage deposit in the Zoo bunker "the Manichaean papyrus books,"[30] presumably meaning the book blocks that had been in the home where his father had been conserving them, i.e., separating off the individual leaves. "But after 20 July 1944 [when the Zoo bunker was itself bombed[31]] this place too did not seem to me safe enough." Hence "with the approval of General Director Kümmel, in xi 1944."[32] Ibscher had an assistant, P. Seidel, get three book blocks from the bunker, in order to take them for safekeeping to Schondorf on the Ammer Lake in Bavaria, to the home of his father-in-law, the publisher Wolf Henry Doering. Rolf Ibscher maintained that he removed

---

relevant paragraph is in the Archives of the Chester Beatty Library: "We are grateful for one piece of good fortune which follows from my present situation in so far as it has been possible up to now to maintain our house properly heated on account of the fact that since the destruction of the Museums, I have continued to work at home and also harbour the remainder of the Papyrus collection which has not yet been transferred to West Germany."

None of the Berlin holdings of the Manichaean codices are known to have ever been taken to West Germany; the suggestion that some might already be in West Germany is no doubt a reference to the *Synaxeis*, which Ibscher mistakenly took to be the Berlin Codex, P[15998], the *Letters*, which he had taken to West Germany (see below).

30. Rolf, Ibscher. "Wiederaufnahme," 359–60 (abstract). The Archives of the Chester Beatty Library include Ibscher, "Zusammenfassung des auf dem Internationalen Orientalisten-Kongress gehaltenen Berichts," typescript, 4 pages; and the typescript of the complete paper, "Wiederaufnahme und neuester Stand der Konservierung der Manichäischen Papyruscodices," 12 pages, unpublished; the quotations come from p. 3.

31. On November 9, 1960, I. E. S. Edwards of the Department of Egyptian Antiquities of the British Museum wrote R. J. Hayes, then acting head of the Chester Beatty Library, that he had heard from Rudolf Anthes (director of the Papyrus Collection of Berlin 1935–1939, 1945–1950, but also enlisted during the war to move the objects from the Museum to safekeeping) that this was the reason for the removal of the material from the Zoo bunker.

32. Böhlig, "Die Arbeit," 181.

the material "on my own responsibility."[33] Böhlig has reconciled the divergence as to the person responsible as follows:[34]

> Rolf Ibscher had the authorization from General Director Kümmel to get the Dublin material from the anti-aircraft tower and take it to Bavaria. He did this in the company of the Museum worker P. Seidel, who has since died. In the process the idea came to him that it would perhaps be useful, in case worst came to worst, also to take along one of the Berlin codices. This decision was, as far as I know, spontaneous. That it was worth it, is shown by the success. These things remained completely preserved, in contrast to what the Soviets had "saved."

After the war, Beatty had sought with the help of Sir Alan Gardiner to establish contact with Rolf Ibscher so as to secure the return of his codices, but apparently without success. Rolf Ibscher himself seems to have been the first to establish contact, by writing to England on January 28, 1946, to the effect that he had saved Beatty's material, "together with a part of the Berlin Mani Codices," whereas the rest of the Berlin part had been taken East.[35]

Ibscher's initiative may have resulted from contact with the occupying forces, for it was at precisely the same time that these official channels seem to have located the material that had been kept at Schondorf. Alexander Böhlig has given 1946 as the date and Schondorf the place that two codices (Part 1 of the *Psalms* and Volume

33. Rolf Ibscher, "Das Konservierungswerk," unpublished typescript, 3: ". . . which on my own responsibility I had brought out of the danger zone of Berlin . . ."

34. Böhlig in a letter of February 10, 1986.

35. In a letter of November 16, 1946, Sir Alan Gardiner wrote to Joan Kingsford Wood, translating from a letter of Ibscher's of January 28, 1946 to him: "However much there is to say on this topic (his family affairs) it is more important to tranquilize you in the matter of the Mani MSS. or rather Codices. They are saved! After Father's death I took them, together with a part of the Berlin Mani Codices to Bavaria to my Father-in-law outside the danger zone; for also here in Kleinmachnow bombs often fell."
In a letter of May 17, 1946, from Gardiner to Wood, Gardiner reported that a letter of January 28, 1946, from Rolf Ibscher to Sir Herbert Thompson, who had died, had been forwarded to him. Gardiner quoted from Ibscher's letter: "You will know, perhaps through Dr. Gardiner or via the British Museum, that and how I could save the London possession from the effects and consequences of the war." Gardiner added: "He goes on to say that all the remainder of the MSS. belonging to the Berlin Museum had been taken East."

two of the *Kephalaia*) were released to Beatty,[36] information that is all the more reliable in view of the fact that it was Böhlig himself (who was in Munich at the end of the war) who had "separated them at Schondorf."[37] Böhlig considered it possible that, in view of inadequately marked parts, some material belonging to Berlin may have been released to London, and some belonging to London retained at Schondorf.[38] The 13 leaves that were in London (later in Dublin and then in Copenhagen), to which Böhlig here refers as perhaps belonging to Berlin but by mistake sent to England, do not, however, belong to the Berlin *Letters* codex $P^{15998}$, as he at the time conjectured (see below), but rather to the *Synaxeis* codex that belonged to Beatty; they had been quite appropriately returned to London before the war (see above). But regarding the converse possibility, that London material may have been retained in Schondorf: Böhlig himself was the first to publish, in 1957, the admission that by mistake the book block of Beatty's *Synaxeis* stayed at Schondorf rather than being returned to London (see below).

At the beginning of 1946 Sir John Forsdyke, director of the British Museum, received a vague report about Beatty's codices having been located in Germany, according to "the military authorities."[39] The

36. Böhlig, "Die Arbeit an den koptischen Manichaica," 180–81: "There [at the house of the father-in-law in Schondorf] Sir Chester Beatty had the parts of the Codices A and C picked up in the year 1946."

37. Rolf Ibscher reported in his broken English in a letter of October 6, 1955, to Beatty: "This wooden box [taken from the Zoo bunker] contained one Berlin manuscript (for which I had specially asked Mr. Seidel) to make certain, that at l[e]ast part of the Berlin collection also was saved, in addition those papyri which reached you in London in 1947 after Dr. Böhlig had separated them at Schondorf." In an interview on July 10, 1986, Prof. and Mrs. Böhlig confirmed the fact that they went to Schondorf in the absence of Rolf Ibscher and recalled having turned over the material after only a superficial examination of the contents.

38. Böhlig, in a letter of February 10, 1986: "Whether something was then confused when turned over to the emissaries of Chester Beatty, so that in the end result a Berlin part came to Dublin and an English part (the *Synaxeis* codex) to Göttingen / West Berlin, I consider to be quite possible. That the individual parts were not adequately marked I also consider possible."

39. From a letter of Forsdyke to Wilkinson of November 15, 1946: "The facts (so far as I have any) about Mr. Chester Beatty's papyri in Germany are that a box of papyri marked 'British Museum' but identified by us as his was found there and reported to me by the military authorities. I told them that I wished to receive them as soon as they could be released and despatched, and I have no doubt that this will ultimately be done in that order—if they are not in the Russian zone."

military authorities in this case would seem to have been Squadron Leader Christopher Norris, in charge of seeking "works of art, etc., in Germany that come from Britain."[40]

Forsdyke had written Norris as early as February 15, 1946, that the British Museum would receive Beatty's material if he could deliver it.[41] This suggests that Norris had just written Forsdyke that Beatty's material had been located. The timing of such a letter would thus fit that of Ibscher's letters of January 28, 1946, to London. From this, one may infer that the unpublished Part One of Beatty's *Psalms*, Codex A, and his Volume Two of the *Kephalaia*, Codex C, were probably turned over to the American forces in Schondorf about 1946, and were kept in the Fine Arts Repository that the Americans established in Munich in 1946.[42]

At the beginning of October 1947 Lieutenant Colonel Hugh Murray Baillie, of the Fine Arts Commission of the British Zone located in Düsseldorf, brought to Düsseldorf two codices thought to belong to the British Museum. Norris realized that the material was that of Beatty he had been expecting.[43] Baillie brought the manuscripts to

---

40. From a letter to Wilkinson dated July 16, 1946, whose author is not known: "... a British officer who was charged with the duty of investigating the whereabouts and present condition of works of art, etc., in Germany that come from Britain. The officer in question saw Forsdyke, and it was, I think, from Forsdyke that I got the most detailed information." References to Norris in this capacity recur in subsequent correspondence.

41. A letter of F. Francis, Secretary of the British Museum, to Wilkinson of July 25, 1946 reports this fact.

42. Wilkinson wrote Beatty on October 9, 1947, what Baillie (see also the following note) had reported (based on a rough memorandum also in the Chester Beatty Archives and dated the same day): "Dr. Ibscher handed the Papyri to a relative of his in Bavaria. (This corresponds more or less with what young Ibscher told Dr. Gardiner, i.e. that after old Ibscher's death, young Ibscher handed them to his father-in-law in Bavaria). This relation (i.e., apparently the father-in-law) handed the MSS. to the Fine Arts Repository which was established by the Americans last year, and they were held by the Americans together with other property which was to be sent back to the Allies, or other quarters."

43. Wilkinson's letter of October 9, 1947, to Beatty continued:

About a week ago Mr. Baillie was in Munich, arranging for the transfer of some fine arts property from the American to the British Zone, and these two parcels were handed to Mr. Baillie. He was told by the Americans that they thought it was British Museum property, and that it had been handed over by Dr. Gardiner to Dr. Ibscher. They handed it over readily, and were satisfied that it had come to Germany before the War. Mr. Baillie brought the parcels

London[44] and delivered them on October 8, 1947, to Joan Kingsford Wood[45] of the staff of the Chester Beatty Library, who commented:[46]

> Evidently untouched and as they were when handed to Dr. Ibscher, as far as it is possible to tell.

Part of the London concern to recover the material had involved an effort to determine just how much and which material belonging to Beatty was in Germany. It turned out that no one actually knew; the only documentation that could be turned up referred only to two manuscripts, the parts of the *Psalms* and of the *Homilies* brought to London in April 1931 (see below).[47] Since this part of the *Homilies*

---

back to his office in Düsseldorf, and informed Squadron-Leader Norris at the. Head Office; Norris recognized the parcels as your property about which I had had correspondence with him, i.e. Norris. Baillie was coming home on leave, and offered to bring the parcels to London himself. He had noticed that the Papyri, which he had opened, were very fragile.

44. Baillie's letter of October 5, 1947, to Beatty stated: "I have just brought over from Germany, on my return on leave, two codices, which I understand you sent to Dr. Ibscher of Berlin before the war. I collected them from Munich and it seemed the safest and quickest way of getting them back. Perhaps you would be good enough to let me know when it would be convenient for me to hand them over to you officially."

45. On October 8, 1947, Wood signed a receipt for "two parcels containing one labelled 'CODEX C' and the other 'MANICHEAN PSALM BOOKS.'"

46. Her note is not written on the receipt itself, but is handwritten by her on a letter of October 8, 1947 she received from John Wooderson, Beatty's secretary. In the note she refers to the "Psalm book "in the singular, thereby in effect correcting the receipt (see the preceding note).

47. On November 25, 1945,Wilkinson wrote Beatty asking "which MSS. were left with Ibscher." Beatty must have turned to Wood for information, for on November 28, 1945, she wrote him: "I have no note at all what Manichaean ms. or mss. were with Dr. Ibscher." The same day she wrote to Gardiner for assistance. On November 4, 1946, Wooderson wrote Wilkinson, asking him to inquire of Wood or Gardiner "exactly what were sent." Wilkinson talked to Wood, and on November 14, 1946, reported to Wooderson: "The MSS. were not, I should explain, dealt with by Mrs. Wood personally, in the first instance." She herself wrote Gardiner on November 14, 1946, "to ask if you happened to keep any note at all, of the number of Manichaean papyrus MSS. that were handed to Dr. Ibscher?"

He responded on November 16, 1946: "I am very sorry to say I cannot give you the information about the Manichaean papyri for which you ask. I never knew the number of rolls entrusted to Dr. Ibscher, but I believe his son to be perfectly honest and he will give Mr. Beatty the right information."

On November 16, 1946, she wrote to Wilkinson:

> There was one other source for details about the Mani MSS. which I fetched away yesterday morning, a day-book I used to keep. I found in it an entry

(like Part Two of the *Psalms* codex taken to Berlin the end of 1930) had long since been conserved, published, and returned to London, the only material that was actually identified as having gone to Germany and that was actually still in Germany was Part One of the *Psalms* codex. Overlooked were the materials in the Chester Beatty Library Archives (cited above) concerning Part Two of the *Psalms* codex being taken by Ibscher to Berlin at the end of May 1930, and the bulk of the *Synaxeis* codex and Volume Two of the *Kephalaia* being taken by Ibscher to Berlin—perhaps both November 27, 1930. Of the three items at Schondorf, the English team had been aware of only one as being in Germany. It is thus out of ignorance and oversight that the false conclusion was reached that everything had been returned from Germany.[48]

Inquiries were immediately begun as to who might be enlisted to conserve the two book blocks. No one in England could be recommended, but several recommended Rolf Ibscher. For this reason, and also no doubt in gratitude, Rolf Ibscher was offered employment to continue the conservation begun by his father. On May 27, 1948, he

---

for—

"May 8 1931 To Dr. Gardiner for Dr. Ibscher, the 2 Manichaean Coptic books, Hymns and Ritual Observances."

This is the only record I have found of ever having taken any Manichaean ms. in its original state to Dr. G.[ardiner] for Dr. I.[bscher]. The title 'Ritual Observances' may later have turned into 'Homilies' on examination? . . . As to whether these '2 Coptic books' later turned into 3 books, so-to-speak; or Mr. Beatty had one more afterwards, I cannot say.

This faint glimmer of awareness of there having been more than two that were turned over to Ibscher to conserve thus seems to have been dismissed. After the two codices had been returned from Germany, Wood appended a handwritten note to her file copy of her letter of November 28, 1945, to Beatty, to correct her comment to the effect that she had no notes about material going to Ibscher; she now quoted the note dated May 8, 1931, and added: "This date tallies fairly with that of 'April 1931,' written on one of the boxes returned Oct 8/47 from Munich." This must be the box containing the first part of the *Psalms*, since this was first brought to London April 1931 (see below) and was returned October 8, 1947.

48. Wilkinson wrote Wooderson on October 9, 1947: "the parcels appear to contain all the material which remained in Dr. Ibscher's hands. None of it has been mounted; it is still in its original condition. The two parcels contain (1) Codex C (2) The Psalm-books Papyri." In his letter the same day to Beatty, he also stated: "Further, a number of the mounted leaves marked 'Codex C,' at Baroda House, tally in size and appearance with the unmounted fragments of Codex C which have just arrived. The probability is, therefore, that we have got everything back at last."

## Introduction: The Fate of the Manichaean Codices 15

wrote Beatty accepting the offer, and incidentally covered himself by blaming careless American soldiers for whatever damages may have been suffered by the codices.[49] In the argosy from the Neues Museum to the Zoo bunker and on to Kleinmachnow, to Schondorf, to Munich, to Düsseldorf, and to London, American personnel of the Fine Arts Repository were responsible only for the approximately one-hour trip from Schondorf to Munich. Fortunately, a placing of blame was apparently not necessary.

Rolf Ibscher maintained as late as 1954 that all of Beatty's material thus survived,[50] though only a year later he explained to Beatty that the *Synaxeis* codex was among those taken to Leningrad.[51]

The other museum objects still stored in the Zoo bunker were taken by the Soviet forces to the Soviet sector of Berlin, before the Soviet forces vacated that part of Berlin in which the Zoo Station is located, which became the British sector. The loot from the Zoo bunker was deposited temporarily in a Soviet command post at the Friedrichsfelde Castle in the Soviet sector, as was indicated by a few glassed papyrus leaves turned in to the museum by persons reporting they found them there.[52] The hoard was then transported by train to

---

49. Ibscher wrote in his wooden English: "... I am not knowing how are the manuscripts being kept by the foolish way of acting of the American Military Service arbitrary, contrary to my entreaty. [Ibscher was not even in Schondorf when the codices were turned in. See note 37 above.] Surely the manuscripts were not treated carefully during the travelling over hedge and ditch. But how could this be expected by any soldier having not the slightest notion of the delicate material keeping in his hands!"

50. Rolf Ibscher, "Wiederaufnahme," 3.

51. Rolf Ibscher reported in his limited English to Beatty in a letter of October 6, 1955:

> The papyri were removed according to my arrangement from the bomb proof shelter (Zoo Bunker) in 1944 by my assistant at the Museum, Mr. Seidel, but Codex B [*Synaxeis*], sorry to say, seems to have been left behind. The reason being that the papyri had to be removed secretly in a frantic hurry, thus you can imagine how glad I *was*, when Mr. Seidel got past the SS-Guards with the invaluable little wooden box ...
>
> Thus Codex B [actually the Berlin codex P$^{15998}$, the *Letters*], together with 3 Berlin manuscripts [P$^{15996}$, P$^{15997}$, P$^{15999}$] and all other glazed [glassed] Berlin Manichaean Papyri of the Museum [P$^{15995}$ and leaves of P$^{15996}$, P$^{15997}$, and P$^{15998}$] were taken to Russia.

52. Wolfgang Müller, director emeritus of the Papyrus Collection in (East) Berlin, reported in 1986 that Rolf Ibscher told him this. Müller himself did not move to Berlin until 1951.

Leningrad in 1946 (see below) and in principle returned to Berlin in 1958. But none of the book blocks were returned.

Although Michel Tardieu has reported that the bulk of $P^{15997}$ and $P^{15998}$ had been "destroyed or lost during the Second World War,"[53] no evidence has emerged indicating any loss during the war, though the loss of the $P^{15997}$ and $P^{15998}$ book blocks (and of $P^{15999}$, the unconservable bulk of the *Homilies* that Tardieu overlooked) remains unexplained. Otto Firchow, director of the Papyrus Collection in (East) Berlin at the time, moved to the British sector of Berlin in August 1960, and commended himself to the British as a refugee by reporting that he had brought with him Beatty's missing codex.[54] But when the package finally reached the British Museum in October 1960, it turned out to contain "only blank leaves of papyrus and a few inscribed fragments."[55] Firchow maintained that the packet had been "packed by Dr. Ibscher" and that he himself was not involved.[56]

On May 23, 1985, I visited the British Museum to go through the files left behind in the office of the retired conservator of papyrus Stanley Baker, and came upon what seemed to be the box turned in by Firchow. My inventory of this item reads:

---

53. Tardieu, "Les Manichéens en Égypte," 5–19, especially 6. With regard to his estimate of 1,000 lost leaves as "that which would have been lost in Berlin at the time of the events of the Second War," (7), he refers to Rolf Ibscher, "Mani und kein Ende," 223, who, however, does not here date the loss to the time during the war.

54. In a letter of August 29, 1960, Otto Firchow, replying to a letter from I. E. S. Edwards, who had written to him at the Papyrus Collection inquiring about Beatty's material, described his move as follows: "I myself have been compelled to surrender during the past few days under political and personal pressure the Direction of the Berlin Museum, Egyptian Department, and to flee to West Berlin. I have used this opportunity to take the Mani Papyri with me. In the next few days I will hand them over to the British Military Authorities."

Johannes Irmscher, at the time director of the Institut für griechisch-römische Altertumskunde of the Academy of Sciences of the German Democratic Republic entrusted with editing the Manichaean codices, has in a letter of March 27, 1989, interpreted Firchow's move as not a "Politicum," but merely as an effort to improve his situation.

55. In a letter to Beatty dated October 26, 1960, Edwards reported that the package had arrived the preceding Sunday, was opened on Monday, and had the contents as quoted above.

56. In a letter of October 28, 1960, from Firchow to Edwards.

## Introduction: The Fate of the Manichaean Codices 17

> Flat wooden box. Contains vestiges of Mani codex without text. Sheets of paper presumably used in conservation contain German writing presumably by Ibscher.

There were in Baker's office also 15 large green folders containing remnants of the Mani material (as well as a German newspaper fragment dated May 15, 1931). I submitted the inventory to the director of the Chester Beatty Library, Wilfrid Lockwood, on May 26, 1985. On June 25, 1985, Lockwood wrote Giversen to the effect he might want to consult the items I had located at the British Museum. Giversen has identified the material turned in by Firchow as insignificant vestiges of the *Psalms* codex, which, however, Giversen did not include in the *Facsimile Edition*.[57] Perhaps it is from Part Two of the *Psalms* codex acquired March 23, 1930, since the box containing Part One of the *Psalms* acquired in April 1931 had already been returned to London in 1947 along with Part One of the *Psalms* (see note 47 above). Presumably Hugo Ibscher had not gone to the trouble to separate and put between glass what he considered insignificant unidentified vestiges (even though they may impress us as relatively large and numerous), but apparently had left them in the box in which the codex had been kept prior to its conservation.

---

57. Giversen, *Psalm-Book. Part 1*, vii, xi:

> Still remaining to be published are some fragmentary pages and small fragments of the Psalm Book which were entrusted to Hugo Ibscher for conservation by A. Chester Beatty in the 1930s. These remained unrestored at Ibscher's death in 1943 and in 1960 they were transferred to the British Museum by the German Egyptologist Otto Firchow.
>
> Since the material taken to the British Museum [actually only to the British Sector of Berlin] by Otto Firchow has not yet been conserved, it has not been included in this publication. It is to be hoped that the extremely difficult and tedious work of restoring this material will be carried out by a skilled expert.

It is apparently to this same situation that Giversen referred vaguely in his Lund essay, "The Manichaean Texts from the Chester Beatty Collection," 269:

> A few fragments and a couple of fragmentary pages also from the Psalm-Book, are not yet conserved as they were left in Hugo Ibschers [sic] home in Berlin. It cannot be doubted that they belong to the Chester Beatty effects but they were, in a strange way, brought to the British Museum in the 1960's.
>
> A now deceased scholar informed me some years ago that they were there, but since there are some problems attached to them I will not say more about them here.

Rolf Ibscher did not return the codex that he had kept in Schondorf to Berlin, to which he maintained it belonged, but rather, on his trips to and from London, worked at conserving the leaves while visiting his wife's family in Schondorf. Søren Giversen saw the material in Munich in 1955, by which time the West German authorities had taken control of the material.[58] He apparently did not identify it and presumably for that reason did not notify the Chester Beatty Library at the time. Carsten Colpe was engaged to edit it (from September 1, 1956, to November 30, 1957),[59] for which purpose it was moved to Göttingen. Böhlig was brought in as a consultant. In 1957 they noted running heads and chapter titles that identified the material as the *Synaxeis* codex.[60] Against this evidence, Rolf Ibscher's arguments that it must be the Berlin *Letters* codex $P^{15998}$ were in vain, and he ultimately somewhat grudgingly conceded the point.[61]

58. Mentioned by Giversen to P. Henchey, then librarian of the Chester Beatty Library, on May 8, 1980.

59. According to Carsten Colpe, in an interview on March 16, 1986.

60. Böhlig reported this discovery at the 24th International Orientalists' Congress in Munich in 1957. Böhlig published a summary, "Zu den Synaxeis des Lebendigen Evangeliums," 229–30. The full text was published in *Mysterion und Wahrheit*, 222–27, where Colpe's concurrence in this conclusion is expressly stated: "Thus one can assume, as C. Colpe also thinks, that the remainder of a Berlin codex discussed by C. Schmidt [$P^{15995}$] forms with this codex a content unity, but no unity in terms of ownership."

Regarding Böhlig's views on the *Synaxeis* codex, see also Böhlig, "Synaxies = Homilia?" 485–86, "Die Arbeit," and *Mysterion und Wahrheit*, 186, for the identification of the *Synaxeis* codex.

61. Rolf Ibscher, "Der Mani-Fund," 227, referred to the codex as "for the time being the only Mani manuscript that remains to Germany." He combined this claim with the concession that the codex was the *Synaxeis* by appeal to the 31 leaves of the *Synaxeis* that Schmidt had acquired for Berlin and that were inventoried as $P^{15995}$:

> ... our so-called Schondorf manuscript from the Berlin Museum holdings, and hence now stationed in Göttingen, does not contain the corpus of Mani's letters, as was assumed at first. Quite clearly however ... it belongs ... to the codex that was entered by my father still, with 31 leaves, under the old Berlin catalogue number 15995. That is to say, my father began among the Berlin holdings with the conservation of this codex, and then deferred further work on it in favor of the more important *Kephalaia* manuscript that bears the number 15996.

This special pleading ignores the fact that $P^{15995}$, according to the Inventory Book, consists only of 31 leaves, which is all that Schmidt purchased for Berlin. The rest of the codex had already been acquired by Beatty. Schmidt and Polotsky, "Ein Mani-Fund," 30, make this clear:

Colpe gave up the editing assignment as hardly possible and called for a suspension of further conservation of individual leaves until that process could be accompanied by photographic documentation of each stage, which in effect brought the conservation to an end in 1957.[62] This termination of the funding and of the work could also have to do with the recognition that it had to do with property that did not belong to Germany. Rolf Ibscher died February 5, 1967.

As a result of the transport of Egyptological artifacts stored in West Germany to West Berlin from Celle in 1957 and from Wiesbaden in 1958, the creation of an Egyptological Section there in 1962, and the opening of the Egyptian Museum in Berlin-Charlottenburg in 1967, the conserved leaves and book block that Rolf Ibscher had not lived to finish conserving were deposited there.

In 1985 William Brashear, the curator of the Papyrus Collection of the Egyptian Museum of Berlin-Charlottenburg, asked me to provide whatever information I could about this material there in storage (of which the present report is the outcome), and to activate interest in it. On November 18, 1985, Joachim Karig, acting director of the Egyptian Museum, wrote me that he had consulted with the general director of the State Museums, Prof. Dube, and his representative, the director of the Antiques Museum, Prof. Heilmeyer, and they approved my request, made orally August 2, 1985, and in writing October 5, 1985, for authorization to enlist scholars to prepare an edition. Similar discussions with Dr. Wolfgang Müller, director of the Egyptian Museum and Papyrus Collection, and with Dr. Gisela Holan, first representative of the general director of the State Museums of Berlin-Hauptstadt der DDR, led to a letter of authorization of August 14, 1987, from Müller, granting "approval for the scholarly work on

---

... a collection of 31 leaves that have been brought under glass, which were acquired in the Fayyum and without doubt belong to the London Mani pieces.

Ibscher made the same erroneous inference in his report, "Über den Stand," 50–64, especially 60. The meeting at which the paper was presented took place on December 14–15, 1964. Thus he never surrendered the claim to German ownership, upon which he no doubt considered his chances of employment as conservator depended, since by this time his working relationship with Beatty had dissolved.

62. Ibscher held Colpe thus responsible for terminating the conservation, "Über den Stand," 60. But in fact Colpe thus rescued something for more sophisticated procedures than those of Rolf Ibscher, if in fact such can be at least hoped for from the future.

and editing of the Coptic Mani texts of our Papyrus Collection according to the shared oral discussions." Wilfrid Lockwood, librarian and director of the Chester Beatty Library, who was kept abreast of the developments from 1985 on, also expressed himself willing to participate in such a cooperative plan, in such a way as to respect the commitment the Library had under his predecessor made with Søren Giversen (see below). I wrote Giversen proposing such cooperation on October 21, 1985 but received no reply.

I had invited scholars to participate, in announcements made at the 121st annual meeting of the Society of Biblical Literature in Anaheim, California, on October 19, 1985, at a conference of the Fachkommission Byzantinistik of the Historiker-Gesellschaft of the German Democratic Republic in Halle on February 21, 1986, at a conference of the Association Francophone de Coptologie at the Louvre in Paris on May 23, 1986, at the Second International Conference on Manichaeism in Bonn on August 9, 1989, and at the 18th International Congress of Byzantine Studies in Moscow on August 8–15, 1991.

During a sabbatical semester in Berlin the first half of 1986, I inventoried and organized for study the Manichaean material, and wrote the bulk of an extensive report, published below, of which the present paper is a summary. With regard to the *Synaxeis* codex, there are 125 conserved leaves (plus 5 glass frames of fragments) in Berlin-Charlottenburg, plus the remainder of the book block, where one page is exposed, making a total of 251 available pages that when added to the 31 leaves or 62 pages in East Berlin, makes a total of 156 conserved leaves and 313 accessible pages, with about 100 to 120 leaves unconserved in the book block.[63] The amount of legible ink is appallingly small, and the amount of text that can be recovered correspondingly minimal. Transcription efforts have been undertaken in West Berlin by Karen King, Stephen Patterson, Paul Allan Mirecki, and Wolf-Peter Funk. And 10 leaves were on loan for study in California from 1986 to 1988, where transcription work was done by Harold W. Attridge, Charles A. Bobertz, and Gesine Robinson, and in addition by Funk and Patterson. In 1988 these leaves were returned to Berlin, when 9 others plus 2 of the original leaves were brought to California for study; they were returned to Berlin the summer of 1989. In 1989 five

---

63. Ibscher estimated this number remaining in the book block after his work had come to an end, "Über den Stand," 60.

further leaves were brought to America and returned in 1991. Nothing from this Berlin-Charlottenburg part of the *Synaxeis* codex has been published, except transcriptions of ten chapters or *Synaxis* titles by Paul Allan Mirecki,[64] and English translations of some phrases and sentences prepared by Wolf-Peter Funk are being published.[65]

The material brought to California was photographed by Bruce Zuckerman, director of the West Semitic Research Project of the University of Southern California, and his brother, Kenneth, a professional photographer. They photographed the bulk of the material in Berlin from July through August 1991. They are already well known for their success in the photography of otherwise hardly legible sections of the Dead Sea Scrolls. The results of their photography seem very promising. This will be even more the case if the computer enhancement technology that is already available to them can be enlisted in this project. This involves what is called a microdensitometer: A photographic negative is scanned in units (called picture elements) as small as 5 microns (i.e., five thousandths of a millimeter), each of which is assigned a number in terms of its shade of gray, with more than a thousand grades of gray to choose from (the human eye can distinguish only some 22 shades). These numbers can then be entered into the computer so as to project the image on the screen. Then the numbers derived from the shades of gray can be changed at will, e.g., reducing the number of all picture elements with a shade of gray below a certain number, thus lightening the light gray, and increasing the number of all picture elements with a shade of gray above a certain number, thus darkening the dark gray—from which a picture of much higher contrast results. Or the shades of gray can be assigned any color or shade of color, which is a promising alternative, given the ability of the eye to detect more distinctions among colors and their shades than among shades of gray. And the picture can be enlarged on the screen at will, producing the added effect of microscopic examination. A demonstration by the Perkin-Elmer firm of Pomona, California, at the Ancient Biblical Manuscript Center in Claremont

64. Mirecki, "Coptic Manichaean *Synaxeis* Codex," 135–45, has transcribed and translated what remains of thirteen chapter or *Synaxis* titles, ten from the material in Berlin-Charlottenburg, three from the material in Berlin-Hauptstadt der DDR.

65. Funk has translated a number of phrases and sentences that he and other members of the Mani team transcribed. Karen King quoted these translations in King, "Progress Report."

on May 19, 1989, indicates that the technology is already functional, though still prohibitively expensive.

### Chester Beatty Library Codex C, Volume Two of the *Kephalaia*

Schmidt reported that the Fayyumic dealer had sold all three of his parts of the discovery to Beatty. As in the case of the *Synaxeis*, no definite reference to the acquisition of this codex has been located in the Dublin Archives, and yet one may assume that this material was acquired from the Fayyumic dealer. For since the *Psalms* and the *Homilies* may more probably have come from Nahman (see below), one may assume by the process of elimination that Volume 2 of the *Kephalaia* is from the Fayyumic dealer.[66] Since Schmidt talked to this dealer only in the spring of 1931, Beatty's acquisitions from him must have been earlier than that date.

In 1986 Søren Giversen published in the *Facsimile Edition* photographic reproductions of Volume 2 of the *Kephalaia*.[67] Though publication of a facsimile edition puts the facsimiles in the public domain, publication rights for an *editio princeps* are to be awarded by a committee consisting of Søren Giversen, president, Rodolphe Kasser, and Martin Krause.[68] Kasser was supposed to take administrative responsibility for editing this codex, but plans to involve Wolf-Peter Funk did not receive Giversen's approval.

In the Crum Archives (see below) there is a transcription (Crum Mss 11.30.10) of the page reproduced on plate 341 of the *Facsimile Edition*.

### Chester Beatty Library Codex A, the *Psalms*, Part One

In April 1931 Beatty brought from Egypt two further Manichaean manuscripts and three wooden covers (i.e., three front or back covers, out of an original total of fourteen such covers). The covers are at the Chester Beatty Library in a large envelope, on which is written:

---

66. Schmidt and Polotsky, "Ein Mani-Fund," 8. Hugo Ibscher, "Die Handschrift," ix, has referred to Beatty's acquiring three books "in the Cairo antiquities market" "in the year 1930," but this may have not been meant in any more precise sense than to say that beginning in 1930 he had been buying Manichaean texts in Egypt, i.e., the location may not have been intended to be any more precise than the inexact date.

67. Giversen, *Kephalaia*, facsimile edition.

68. See note 21.

"Purchased Spring 1931." Apparently, these are the only covers still extant today, since those that Beatty acquired in 1930, and those of P$^{15997}$ that Schmidt acquired in 1931 cannot be located at the Chester Beatty Library or at the Berlin Egyptian Museum.

No documentation has been located as to the dealer (or dealers) from whom Beatty acquired this material. The Fayyumic dealer is reported to have had three of the eight parts, and to have sold all his holdings to Beatty (except the scraps of P$^{15995}$ removed to make the codex look clean for Beatty—a codex that Schmidt subsequently acquired). Since only seven codices were involved in the discovery, one must assume that one codex had been divided. If the initially divided codex had belonged to the Fayyumic dealer, then in selling his three parts to Beatty he would in fact have only sold two codices, presumably the bulk of the *Synaxeis* in two parts, and Volume Two of the *Kephalaia* (see above). Thus the report that Beatty acquired three units from the Fayyumic dealer does not require that one postulate that he acquired Part One of the *Psalms* from that dealer. It may be more probable that he acquired it from Nahman, from whom he had acquired the other part a year earlier.

The "good manners" of leading Cairo antiquities dealers has to do with the fact that they have a vested interest in the goodwill of a regular client. Some such manners may be suspected in the case of Nahman. For he showed Volume 1 of the *Kephalaia* to Schmidt early in 1930 when Schmidt was on his way to Jerusalem, and, even though Schmidt did not acquire it then, Nahman did not proceed to sell it to Beatty shortly thereafter, when Nahman offered Beatty parts of other codices that Beatty took on approval. Thus Nahman was careful to offer Beatty other codices than what he had offered Schmidt, thereby avoiding offending Schmidt but, by informing him of Beatty's acquisitions (without making clear to Schmidt that they had only been taken on approval), also making clear to him that these were fast-selling items of which he should take advantage. Schmidt did in fact concede that Beatty's decision to acquire the material was one factor in persuading him on his return trip from Jerusalem, in spite of a lack of funding, to go ahead with the purchase of the *Kephalaia*. On subsequent trips he acquired other parts of the same codex— acquisitions that indicated the continuing practice, to which Schmidt referred, of subdividing codices to increase their value, making a total

of seven units of the one *Kephalaia* codex (see below), none of which seems to have been offered in the meantime to Beatty. It would have been in keeping with such an enlightened policy of self-interest that Nahman, having turned over to Beatty part of the *Psalms* codex and part of the *Homilies* codex in 1930, did not offer these to Schmidt, but held them for Beatty to acquire in 1931. Whereas Schmidt portrayed Nahman as "rejecting" Beatty after Schmidt got to him (see below), this fits much better the impression Nahman would have wanted to leave with Schmidt than the documented reality of his continuing business relationships with Beatty.

One of the two manuscripts brought to London in April 1931 was at the time designated "Manichaean Hymns" or "Manichaean MS. (Hymns) Psalms. Codex A,"[69] obviously the first and major part of the *Psalms* codex, of which Beatty had acquired the smaller concluding part the preceding year (see above).

Schmidt was eager to have access to the whole discovery. Ibscher informally broached in London cooperative procedures that Schmidt had envisaged; these procedures were incorporated in a letter of May 7, 1931, from Sir Alan Gardiner to his friend of long standing, Wilhelm Schubart, director of the Berlin Papyrus Collection. Beatty had initially sought to enlist his Egyptological friend Sir Alan H. Gardiner as his consultant and potential English coeditor. But Gardiner did not want to undertake such a large Coptic assignment, nor could Walter Ewing Crum, who was engrossed with completing his *Coptic Dictionary*. Hence Sir Herbert Thompson was settled upon as the British scholar to represent Beatty. On June 11, 1931, Thompson met with Schmidt in London, and they agreed formally on such a cooperative procedure:[70] Just as Ibscher had already been entrusted with conserving in Berlin

---

69. A two-ring binder that served as a kind of accessions book in the early years, now in the Archives of the Chester Beatty Library, lists for April 1931 Cairo "Manichaean Hymns," "Manichaean Ritual—Laws," "3 wooden covers." The black loose-leaf folder entitled "Papyrus: Biblical Manichaean Hieratic Greek etc. General Catalogue," in the section "Manichaean Pap.," p. 5ff., contains "DETAILS of when MANICHAEAN PAPYRUS were received and sent to Dr. Ibscher, for mounting." The first entry, dated April 1931, notes: "Brought by Mr. Beatty from Egypt," and itemizes: "Manichaean MS. (Hymns) Psalms. Codex A. *With Dr. Ibscher. May 8, 1931.*" "Manichaean Ms. Ritual Laws. *With Dr. Ibscher. May 8, 1931.*" "3 Covers." P. 6 reports "Entries from Day-Book." The first, dated May 8, 1931, reads: "*To Dr. G.*[ardiner] for *Dr. I.*[bscher] The 2 Mani Coptic books. Hymns and Ritual Observances."

70. Documented in letters of June 15, 1931, from Thompson to Beatty; of June 27, 1931, from Gardiner to Beatty, and of April 3, 1932, from Thompson to Beatty.

both collections, H. J. Polotsky would be entrusted with transcribing and translating the material in Berlin as it was conserved. He would be under the supervision of Schmidt and Thompson, to both of whom copies of his work on both the Berlin and London parts would be regularly sent, to be translated by Thompson into English and distributed to Crum (for the *Coptic Dictionary*) and to Beatty. Polotsky's work and salary would be divided equally between Berlin and London. As the leaves were conserved and transcribed, those belonging to Beatty would be brought back to London, usually by Ibscher on his annual London trips to conserve other materials owned by Beatty, but, as it turned out, at times also by C. R. C. Allberry, and once by Beatty himself.

Thompson was concerned that Beatty's codices be published in England, where he would be primarily involved. But on February 6, 1932, Schmidt wrote Thompson proposing that some of Polotsky's transcriptions and translations of material belonging to Beatty be published in the forthcoming essay for the Prussian Academy. Thompson appealed to Beatty to block what he considered to be a serious breach of the agreement. Beatty wrote Schmidt on March 21, 1932, forbidding him the right of even mentioning his codices in print. And on April 16, 1932, Beatty wrote Ibscher to stop all conservation work on his codices until the matter could be discussed on his forthcoming visit to London.

Thompson protested to Beatty on April 3, 1932, that terminating the arrangement completely would violate the valid agreements that had been made, which would be especially unfortunate with regard to Polotsky, whose high quality was recognized and whose livelihood depended largely upon this work.[71] Yet on May 2, 1932, Beatty wrote Thompson that "very difficult business conditions" made it necessary for him to terminate the arrangement, though some phase-out for Polotsky should be arranged. Polotsky was then instructed to concentrate his work for Beatty on the one manuscript nearest to completion,

---

71. Thompson wrote Beatty: "He is an extremely learned and able young man; but he is not a naturalized German (being a Russian) and hence has no prospect of an official or University post; and has to make a living. I believe he has nothing but these 270Rm. (orig. 300Rm.) per month, i.e., at par £180 p. ann." The letter explains that the ten percent reduction had been a German reduction of all salaries effective the first of that year. The Prussian Academy paid half the salary, and Beatty paid the other half.

the *Homilies*, with his salary terminating the end of May 1932. He was given until the end of June 1933 to edit it, with the right then to publish it in German, at no expense to Beatty, in Germany.[72] Thus Thompson's role, based on his assumption of an English edition, came abruptly to an end. The result was Polotsky's publication of the *Homilies* in 1934.[73]

The decisions not to acquire part of the *Homilies* and to terminate work on the Manichaean material, both of which were made by Beatty in the spring of 1932, seem to relate to each other in the sense that Beatty had decided not to engage further in the Manichaean venture. But he did later relent in part, permitting Schmidt and Polotsky in their article for the Prussian Academy to summarize Beatty's material though not to quote it. With regard to Ibscher, Beatty continued to use his valuable services to conserve his Manichaean and other papyrus holdings. Yet already on May 1, 1932, Thompson had quit in protest over Beatty's procedures, a move which facilitated the decision to permit Polotsky to publish in German. To judge by the exchange of correspondence, Beatty had really never fully accepted Thompson to replace his friend Gardiner as his representative in such negotiations.

The transcriptions and translations from various codices that Polotsky sent to Thompson for Beatty and Crum during this period of about a year of active collaboration are preserved at least in part in the Archives of the Chester Beatty Library in Dublin and in the Crum Archives at the Griffith Institute in the Ashmolean Museum in Oxford. The copies that Polotsky provided to Schmidt (and later some that Alexander Böhlig provided) were preserved by the Archives of the Academy of Sciences in Berlin. In view of the fact that what has survived is considerably less legible than it must have been half a century ago, and in view of the unusually high quality of Polotsky's work, these transcriptions and translations, a number of which were never

---

72. Documented in a memorandum of a conference between Beatty and Gardiner on May 8, 1932, and letters of May 12, 1932, from Gardiner to Beatty, May 13, 1932, from Beatty to Gardiner, May 20, 1932, from Beatty to Thompson, and May 24, 1932, from Thompson to Beatty. Alexander Böhlig, in a letter of February 5, 1989, has speculated that Polotsky's learning in the spring of 1932 that he would lose this employment may have led him already then to begin inquiries regarding a position at Hebrew University in Jerusalem to which he moved in the spring of 1933, in view of the fact that the kind of salary paid by the Prussian Academy was not in itself a living wage, as Böhlig, his successor, himself experienced.

73. Polotsky, *Manichäische Homilien*.

published, are among the most important material to have survived the tragic postwar story of the Manichaean codices of Medinet Madi.

In the Crum Archive are copies of Polotsky's transcriptions from Part One of the *Psalms*, corresponding to the facsimile edition, Volume 3 (see note 78 below), plates 140, 161, 162, 243, 313, and 314.

On June 16, 1980, Søren Giversen applied to the Chester Beatty Library for permission to publish their Manichaean papyri, both for a facsimile edition and for a critical edition. The Trustees granted permission on June 26, 1980.[74] On November 24, 1982, Giversen applied for permission to have about 171 leaves sent on loan to Denmark. On January 14, 1984, 184 leaves (his original request plus the 13 *Synaxeis* leaves, see above) were deposited at the Royal Library in Copenhagen.

On December 11, 1980, the librarian of the Chester Beatty Library at the time, Patrick Henchy, offered Giversen access to two files, one titled "Berlin Manichaean Papyrus Transcriptions," "From Sir H. Thompson July 1931 to May 18, 1932," obviously the transcriptions Polotsky had sent Thompson to pass on to Beatty during that time (see above); the other "A. Chester Beatty Manichaean Papyrus Codex A and B Translations," presumably Polotsky's translations and the English translations Thompson prepared for Beatty.

In 1984 Giversen presented, at the International Symposium on the Cologne Mani Codex, English translations of Psalms 136 and 119 that were published in 1986; and at the First International Conference on Manichaeism in 1987, he presented a Coptic transcription of the title and opening eight lines of Psalm 119 that was published in 1988. In the published form of the first speech, Giversen introduced his translation of Psalm 136 with a comment that apparently should actually have introduced Psalm 119, where the comment had in fact stood in the earlier transcript of his 1984 speech:[75]

74. Patrick Henchy, the librarian at the time, communicated this to Giversen on June 26, 1980.

75. Giversen, "Unedited Chester Beatty Mani Texts," 371–80, especially 376. Though in the published essay this statement comes immediately before the English translation of Psalm 136, this cannot be its correct place. For the opening of lines 30–33 in Giversen's translation of Psalm 136 is intact without lacunae, whereas Giversen's comment calls attention to something that has "gone lost." Furthermore Giversen had submitted to the trustees of the Chester Beatty Library on November 23, 1982, as a sample of his work, the transcription and translation of this same page, where lines 30–33 in his Coptic transcription have no lacunae at all. And there are no lacunae here in the *Facsimile Edition*, Volume 3, plate 189, where the text is unusually

From the notes and decipherment from 1931 I can see, that something has gone lost since then, especially at the beginning of lines 30–34.

Polotsky's name was not mentioned in connection with the reference to material of 1931, which was not clarified beyond the cryptic expression "notes and decipherment." In discussion during the 1989 conference at Bonn, Giversen explained that he had referred by name to Thompson and Polotsky, but that due to a typesetter's error, the names had fallen out; when I drew to his attention that in the typescript of his paper he had sent me prior to publication, the names were also absent, he said this must be due to a typist's error.

The publication of 1988 that contained the Coptic transcription made no reference to Polotsky's work at all. Polotsky had in 1931–1932 provided a Coptic transcription, a German translation, and notes to Psalm 119, each page of which concludes with his distinctive abbreviation of his name, "P-y." Since copies of Polotsky's transcriptions and translations were also forwarded by Thompson to Walter Ewing Crum, they are preserved in the Crum Archives in the Griffith Institution of the Ashmolean Museum in Oxford, where, according to records on file there, Giversen worked in August 1981.[76] Indeed Giversen's comment in 1986 in introducing his translation of Psalm 119 ("in fact it is possible that a new Psalm begins on page b, but unfortunately the upper part is almost illegible") would seem to reflect not only Polotsky's designation of the pages as a and b, but also his comment at the

---

legible. In fact, in the typescript of Giversen's lecture of 1984, the statement about the lacunae at the opening of lines 30–33 occurs immediately before the second English translation he presented—that of Psalm 119—where indeed the opening of the lines numbered 30–32 of his translation begins with lacunae, then with illegible material and a lacuna at the end of the English translation of line 33, as on p. 379 of the published lecture. In the *Facsimile Edition*, Volume 3, plate 162, the bottom left corner of the leaf (including text) is not extant. Thus one must assume that the statement has in view Psalm 119, rather than Psalm 136. Giversen confirmed this conjecture at the 1989 conference in Bonn.

76. In the Crum Archive, Polotsky's transcription and German translation of Psalm 119 occur on two pages each, since the Psalm straddles two pages of the codex. The first (Crum Mss 11.30.2 for the Coptic, Crum Mss 11.28.85 = Crum Mss 11.28.7 for the German = *Facsimile Edition*, Volume 3 [see note 78 below], plate 161) contains the first 8 lines of the chapter, which Giversen designates as "a." The second (Crum Mss 11.30.3 for the Coptic, Crum Mss 11.28.86 = Crum Ms 11.28.8 for the German = *Facsimile Edition*, Volume 3, plate 162) corresponds to what Giversen designates as "b," which ends with line 33. In Polotsky's Coptic transcription there are lacunae at the opening of lines 30–33.

*Introduction: The Fate of the Manichaean Codices* 29

opening of the second page: "[Beginning of new hymn]," since hardly more than the illegibility of the opening lines suggests this alternative. Indeed Giversen apparently later reached a quite different view on this point from that of Polotsky, for the *Facsimile Edition*, Volume 3, plates 162 no longer considers this page as Psalm 119, lines 9–33 (or as Psalm 120, lines 1–25), but rather has the note: "[Incipit psalmus XII in linea 13.]"

The Coptic transcription of the title and opening eight lines of Psalm 119 that Giversen published in 1988 agree completely (except for dots under a few letters on two lines) with the work produced but not published by Polotsky in 1931.[77] This is particularly striking in the case of the eighth, the last line on the page, which reads identically in Polotsky's and Giversen's transcriptions.

The facsimile published in the *Facsimile Edition*, Volume III, Plate 161, shows that this last line of the page is almost completely illegible, with perhaps three or four letters that with great difficulty could be read, a few dots of ink that could be taken to be any letter, and lacunae in the bulk of the line. Yet Giversen's transcription is complete except for three letters restored in square brackets and two letters dotted, just as in Polotsky's. This transcription could not possibly be derived from the papyrus in its present condition. It is hence hard to avoid the inference that it derives from the transcription of Polotsky, obviously made at a time when more of the papyrus was extant, perhaps even before the leaf was removed from the book block. This is in a different way suggested also in the case of lines 30–33, where Giversen had commented "that something has gone lost since then [1931], especially at the beginning of lines 30–33," since his own translation does not have more lacunae than Polotsky's transcription and translation, whereas the published facsimile does indeed indicate that much less is now legible on these four lines than is present in Polotsky's transcription and in Giversen's translation.[78]

---

77. Giversen, "Manichaean Texts from the Chester Beatty Collection," 271.

78. Giversen, *Psalm Book, Part 1*, facsimile edition, plate 62, the last 4 lines. Polotsky's translation:

> (Wir sind) freudig zum Kampf (ausgezogen) und haben mit unseren Feinden gekämpft. (. . .) uns, o unser Gott, dass Du uns nicht verlassen wirst . . . . . . .
> . . . wir haben sie empfangen. Du weisst, o unser Herr, dass unsere Freunde und unsere Feinde (?) alle mit uns.

Giversen's translation:

In the discussion at Bonn in 1989, Giversen explained that though he had worked in the Crum Archive more than once and had made use of Polotsky's transcription, this did not need to be mentioned in his article, since Giversen was not presenting a critical edition. He explained further that with the help of a microscope, he had been able to detect vestiges of ink from the top of the letters (the bulk of which are now in lacunae) that could fit the letters that Polotsky had read. Thus he could concur with Polotsky, though with dots under all these letters, though the dots disappeared due to typesetting errors—except for the two dots that are present, which happen to agree with those of Polotsky,—just as a typesetting error misplaced a diaeresis in another line.

Giversen published photographic reproductions of this major part of the *Psalms* codex in 1988, as volume 3 of the *Facsimile Edition*.[79] Publication rights for an *editio princeps* were to be awarded by the committee consisting of Søren Giversen, president; Rodolphe Kasser; and Martin Krause.

### Chester Beatty Library Codex D, the *Homilies*

The other manuscript that Beatty brought from Cairo to London in April 1931 is designated in the Chester Beatty Archives as "Ritual Laws," and "Ritual Observances" (see above), though it apparently was a minor part of the *Homilies* codex—the major part of which (Berlin's P[15999]) Beatty had acquired with an option to buy in 1930, an option that he decided in 1932 not to exercise (see below). Presumably Beatty did not realize that what he decided not to buy in 1932 as unconservable was part of the same codex that he had bought in 1931 and had

---

[rejoicing to the agony; we have contended with our enemies; [ ] us, our God, that you will not abandon us. [ ] have we received. You know, O Lord, that all our friends and our enemies . . .

79. Wood also suggested this identification in a letter of November 16, 1946 to Wilkinson (see note 44): "The title 'Ritual Observances' may later have turned into 'Homilies' on examination?"

Hugo Ibscher, "Die Handschrift," ix, confirmed the identification of the text acquired in 1931 with the *Homilies*: "The Mani text published here lay as a shapeless mass along with the Psalm Book when Mr. A. Chester Beatty turned this over to me in London to work on."

Alexander Böhlig, in a letter of February 5, 1989, has suggested that the designation "ritual laws" or "ritual observances" may have been due to the subscript title of the first text in the *Homilies* reading (7,7) "The Sermon of the Prayer Is Completed."

already paid to have conserved and edited. In view of the fact that the major part of this codex had been obtained on approval in 1930 from Nahman, one may assume that it was Nahman who sold Beatty the other part in 1931, perhaps in hopes thus to move Beatty actually to complete the transaction for the first part (whose price had already been reduced in 1930 from £700 to the same level of £500 that Beatty had paid in 1930 for part of the *Psalms* codex).

H. J. Polotsky has published this part of the codex, the first text from this discovery to be published.[80]

In 1987 Søren Giversen published photographic reproductions of the *Homilies* as Volume 2 of the *Facsimile Edition*.[81]

## CARL SCHMIDT'S ACQUISITIONS

One may now turn to the 5 holdings (three codices and parts of two others) in the Papyrus Collection of the State Museums of Berlin that were acquired by Carl Schmidt in a series of transactions from 1930 to 1932.

### Papyrus Collection, Berlin, P[15995], 31 leaves of the *Synaxeis*

Schmidt reported that in the spring of 1931 he had acquired in the Fayyum for the sake of completeness the remains of a codex, the bulk of which Beatty had already acquired, and that from this jumble 31 leaves could be conserved. This must be the 31 leaves of the *Synaxeis* codex in the Papyrus Collection of Berlin, inventoried as P[15995], since the only other codex shared between Beatty and Berlin was the *Homilies* codex, the Berlin part of which (P[15999]) was acquired from Nahman after Beatty had released his option (see below). The Inventory Book of the Papyrus Collection of the Berlin Museum's records in Wilhelm Schubart's hand concerning P[15995] (and also concerning P[15996-8]): "Acquired through Prof. Carl Schmidt, in Cairo, 1931. Gift of Mr. August Pfeffer 1933." These 31 leaves were taken with the other Berlin Museum holdings in 1946 to Leningrad, to be returned to Berlin with the other material in 1958 (see above). They went together with the other glassed Manichaean leaves in the Storage of the Papyrus Collection of (East) Berlin. Gesine Robinson prepared two

---

80. Polotsky, *Manichäische Homilien*.
81. Giversen, *Homilies and Varia*, facsimile edition.

draft transcriptions of the 62 pages in 1985 and 1986, but nothing has been published, except for three titles included among those that Paul Mirecki published.[82] The quality of the leaves varies considerably, but, as in the other cases, the amount of retrievable text is much less than the number of extant pages might lead one to expect.

**Papyrus Collection, Berlin, P[15996], Volume One of the *Kephalaia***

It was part of this codex that had been shown first to Carl Schmidt early in 1930 in Cairo, which he was able to identify from Epiphanius's reference to it. Schmidt, in transit to Jerusalem, did not acquire it, but on his return trip through Cairo he acquired it on credit. On his second trip early in 1931 and on his last visit to Cairo in the spring of 1932, Schmidt was shown each time two further lots, apparently from the same codex, which he also acquired.[83] Ultimately, Hugo Ibscher listed a total of 7 acquisitions by Schmidt of parts of this one codex.[84] A Prof. Grohmann of Prague acquired vestiges from the missing pages 311–30 for the Austrian National Library.[85]

82. See note 64 above.

83. Schmidt and Polotsky, "Ein Mani-Fund," 7–8.

84. Hugo Ibscher, "Die Handschrift," vi-vii:

> Hence the *Kephalaia* did not come to Berlin in one volume, but in two larger packets and five weaker layers. All of course nicely jumbled! . . . Purchase I is now pp. 1–18. Purchase II is now pp. 19–310. Purchase III is now pp. 331–56. Purchase IV is now pp. 357–76. Purchase V is now pp. 377–94. Purchase VI is now pp. 395–414. Purchase VII is now pp. 421 to the end.

What survived of the missing segment pages 415–20 are described as "paltry remains," "which can hardly be identified." What was considered the last extant leaf, though lacking pagination, was identified with the help of the chapter number 200 as being pages 501/502. A fragment with the pagination 514 stuck to this leaf indicates that the codex originally continued beyond the last extant leaf. Wolf-Peter Funk examined on August 11, 1986, the Warsaw leaf labeled pages 499/500 and detected there a chapter number in the 200s, which would require a pagination in the 500s, thus putting in question whether what was considered the last extant leaf is pages 501/502.

85. Schmidt and Polotsky, "Ein Mani-Fund," 8 n. 1. This material, forwarded from Vienna to Berlin for Ibscher to conserve , and then returned to Vienna (*Kephalaia*, 1. Hälfte, vii), is in four glass containers with the inventory number K 11010. Remains of three leaves labeled pages 311–16, but perhaps more likely pages 313–16, 319–20, have been identified, together with a dozen unidentified fragments. Schmidt and Polotsky refer only to fragments of two leaves having been "rescued," no doubt since the third is no more than a larger fragment hardly deserving the designation leaf. Gardner, *Coptic Theological Papyri*. "III. Unpublished pages from the Manichaean

## Introduction: The Fate of the Manichaean Codices 33

After World War II five of the Berlin *Kephalaia* leaves emerged in Warsaw, presumably the result of the looting of trains taking Berlin Museum holdings to Leningrad in 1946. Lothar Berfelde,[86] founder of the Gründerzeit Museum of turn-of-the-century furniture now in Mahlsdorf near Berlin, had lived for a brief time in the Friedrichsfelde Castle (with whose previous owners he was distantly related), after it was no longer used as a Soviet command post. During the period in which it was a command post (spring 1945 to spring 1946), he recalled libraries being stored there awaiting shipment to the Soviet Union, though he did not know the specific contents of the crates. German crews, even after the war, manned the trains from Germany through Poland (though different gauge tracks at the border to the Soviet Union called there for different trains and crews). Berfelde reported that a friend since childhood, who worked for the German railroads, told him that in the countryside Poles would stop these trains, disconnect the engine, and make the German crews drive away in the engine, leaving the freight cars in the fields unattended, for the Poles to loot.

Wincenty Myszor reported on July 14, 1986, concerning these leaves:

> The Manichaean manuscripts that are now in Warsaw surfaced shortly after the last war under not fully clarified circumstances. One always speaks about a place Brodnica, near Toruń (Thorn) ... The plates are said to have been at first in a private collection, then in some way (bought? acquired?) reached Prof. J. Manteuffel, the leader of the Institute for Papyrology of Warsaw University; he turned over a part of the manuscripts to the National Museum as a deposit. There are also rumors according to which the plates in the National Museum came directly from Brodnica to Warsaw, to Prof. Michalowski. Prof. J. Manteuffel and Prof. K. Michalowski wanted to return the leaves to Berlin. This did not succeed. In the '60s this matter is said to have almost landed in the Ministry.

Thus far H. J. Polotsky and Alexander Böhlig have published pp. 1–292 of the *Kephalaia*.[87] Of these, only pages 35/36 and 61/62 are missing from the boxes containing pp. 1–440.

---

*Kephalaia*," 53–55, gives a more detailed report.

86. Lothar Berfelde was interviewed on April 18, 1986, in Mahlsdorf and East Berlin.

87. Polotsky and Böhlig, *Kephalaia* (Manichäische Handschriften der Staatlichen

In Vienna there are three unpublished leaves, labeled pp. 311–316 (though they may be pages 313–16, 319–20, see note 85), as well as fragments.

In Warsaw there are five unpublished leaves, labeled pp. 447–54, 499–500. The pagination assigned to the last leaf may be inaccurate, since Wolf-Peter Funk has detected on it a chapter number beyond 200, which would require pagination in the 500s.

In Berlin 120 unpublished pages are in boxes: pages 293–310, 331–82, 387–414, 417–18, 421–40. Pages 455–56 are also present, making a total of 122 unpublished pages (61 leaves) that have been assigned pagination.

All that remains of pages 311–30 is in Vienna (see above). The absence of pp. 383–86, 415–16, and 419–20 is noted on cards in the relevant boxes in the hand of Rolf Ibscher's assistant, Otto Werner Luke. Since only the bottom half of pages 417–18 is extant, it is possible that it may be part of pages 413–14, of which only the top half is extant; the alignment of vertical fibers is inconclusive.

There are also 30 plates numbered not by pagination but by plate, 1–30, and 2 plates listed as "*Kephalaia* without number." Since item 23 is more a group of fragments than a leaf, there would be a total of

---

Museen Berlin), herausgegeben im Auftrage der Preussischen Akademie der Wissenschaften unter Leitung von Prof. Carl Schmidt, 1. Hälfte (Lieferung 1–10): v–xiv, "Die Handschrift," by Hugo Ibscher; pp. 1–102 by Polotsky, and pp. 103–244, 20 by Böhlig, according to p. iv (Stuttgart: Kohlhammer, 1940). Böhlig, in a letter of February 5, 1989, has confirmed that there were no draft transcriptions or translations by Polotsky of pp. 103ff. on which Böhlig's work was based, but that Böhlig edited them alone. Böhlig, *Kephalaia* (Manichäische Handschriften der Staatlichen Museen Berlin), herausgegeben im Auftrage der Deutschen Akademie der Wissenschaften zu Berlin, zweite Hälfte (Lieferungen 11-12 = Coptic pages 244, 21–291) (Stuttgart: Kohlhammer, 1966). Concerning the publication of these pages one may note the comment in the *Jahrbuch der Preussischen Akademie der Wissenschaften*, Jahrgang 1942 (Berlin: Akademie, 1943), 66–67 (see also n. 90 below):

> Since Dr. Böhlig was enlisted in the army from x 41 on, the first double fascicle of the second volume of the *Kephalaia* could not yet be completed, although already 4 quires had been sent in to the publisher ready to print. Besides, the printing house has been limited by the lack of specialists. But it hopes in a while to be able again to take up the work on the *Kephalaia*. In the second half of August work could begin again on the reading of quires 5 and 6. It was possible to improve them materially. But as a result of the bad condition of preservation, the manuscript could not be finally completed.

Böhlig has also published p. 292, "Ja und Amen in manichäischer Deutung," 59–70, reprinted in his *Gnosis und Synkretismus* 2:638–53, especially 2:640–41.

Introduction: The Fate of the Manichaean Codices   35

31 plates without assigned pagination but labeled as belonging to the *Kephalaia*. But since plate 30 contains 2 leaves, the figure rises again to 32 unpublished leaves numbered by leaf rather than by an assigned pagination.

The last reported page is page 501–2, but since a fragment with the pagination 514 was stuck to this last extant page (see note 84), one may assume the codex continued, perhaps to include as quire 22 pages 505–28. But if in fact the leaf 501–2 were the last extant leaf (it has not been identified), the extant leaves without assigned pagination would fall within the area of pages 441–46, 457–98, and 501–2, a total of at least 25 leaves. Since Rolf Ibscher, to illustrate how fragile the material was, admitted atomizing a leaf with a sneeze, one may assume there should be a total of at least 24 leaves (48 pages) without assigned pagination. Thus the 32 leaves labeled *Kephalaia* might include 8 more than one would minimally expect to be extant from the *Kephalaia*. But if in fact the Warsaw leaf labeled 499–500 should be renumbered in the 500s (see above), then all the leaves labeled *Kephalaia* could in fact belong to that codex. Otherwise one would need to assume that the excess 8 leaves belong to another codex, such as $P^{15998}$, the *Letters*. Plate 29 had originally had a printed label reading $P^{15998}$, and perhaps Plate 30 as well, though now the number is rubbed off, with 15996 written in by hand in both cases; these may hence be tentatively ascribed to $P^{15998}$. The two without numbers that had been stacked together with $P^{15998}$ are, however, tentatively included still with $P^{15996}$. Hence the number of unpublished leaves that have not been assigned pagination would tentatively stand at 29 equals 58 pages (those numbered plates 1–28, minus 1 that consists of fragments, equals 27; plus 2 leaves labeled "*Kephalaia* without number," equals 29 leaves).

Thus 122 unpublished pages with assigned pagination and some 58 pages without assigned pagination in Berlin, plus 6 pages in Vienna and 10 in Warsaw—a total of some 196 unpublished pages of Volume 1 of the *Kephalaia*—are still extant, although here, as in other cases, the amount of extant text is very much smaller than this figure would suggest.

Wolf-Peter Funk resumed transcription for a time (using P and a raised numeral to identify fragmentary pages), but it extended only from $P^{293}$ to $P^{295}$, line 11 (concluding with the title of chapter 123).

Hugo Ibscher had not completed the conservation of some leaves, and for this reason they lay unglassed in folders in his home during

the war. But his conservation had apparently left no book block of unconserved leaves of the *Kephalaia*.

On July 16, 1986, 8 additional plates of only temporarily sealed plates of fragments were located in the Storage of the Papyrus Collection of (East) Berlin, with a note on a piece of paper reading: "Defined and undefined Mani fragments (framed without color)— 8 plates." They contain largely unidentified fragments, presumably from the *Kephalaia*, including a few labels: "P$^{479}$ to *Kephalaia*," "459/60," "*Kephalaia* top right 503/4??," "*Kephalaia* 423–424." Plate 1 does contain a fragment with the pagination 479, but fragments with the other paginations were not found. The leaf 423/424 is extant in its proper box, though the pagination is not present.

Reinhold Merkelbach has remarked that chapter 138 is lost except for Polotsky's published German translation: "The Coptic text is lost, there still exists only the German translation."[88]

However, an examination of the papyri in the Papyrus Collection of (East) Berlin on December 13, 1988, tended to indicate that the papyri containing this chapter are in fact not lost.[89] Merkelbach has confirmed that he had no specific reason for postulating that the leaf or leaves containing this chapter were lost. (Polotsky's transcription has subsequently been located in Berlin; see note 90.)

Transcriptions of 51 unpublished pages of the Berlin *Kephalaia* preserved in the Archives of the Academy of Sciences in Berlin (42 by Polotsky and 9 probably by Böhlig)[90] may contain more text than

---

88. Merkelbach, *Mani und sein Religionssystem*, 18, n. 9.

89. Chapter 136 begins on page 337, chapter 137 on p. 338, chapter 138 on page 340, chapter 140 and 141 both on page 343. The leaf labeled 341/342 is also extant, on which the continuation and conclusion of chapter 138 (and the beginning of chapter 139) presumably take place. Yet the identity of the leaf in question seemed at first uncertain. For the labels reading 339/340, and with the chapter numeration 138, were affixed in such a way that when the labels were at the top of the page, the writing was upside down, so that the leaf needed to be returned to its upright position. Nor did the fiber directions conform to the pattern of like fiber directions on facing pages. But if the side labeled 339 is relabeled 340, and that labeled 340 relabeled 339, the fiber pattern becomes normal. Furthermore, only on the basis of these corrections do the profiles of this leaf and that of the preceding and following leaves conform to one another. Thus once I made these corrections, the codex seems at this part to be intact, though the text is less legible that it was half a century ago, to judge by the extant German translation.

90. Schenke, "Gnosis-Forschung 1984–1988," a paper read at the Fourth International Congress on Coptic Studies of the International Association for Coptic

the surviving unpublished papyrus itself, in view of the deterioration that the papyrus may have undergone during the intervening half century. Five of these same pages of transcriptions from the *Kephalaia* by Polotsky are also in the Archives in Dublin (pp. 343, 344, 353, 354, 366). There are also 2 pages of transcriptions from the *Kephalaia* by Polotsky in the Archives in Oxford; although they have not yet been definitely identified (they are right-hand and hence odd-numbered pages), the conventional numeration that Polotsky assigned would suggest that Crum Mss 11.30.23 is page 341 and Crum Mss 11.30.24 (= 11.30.27) is page 347, thus indicating they are also duplicates of those of the Academy in Berlin.

The transcriptions of half a century ago should be made promptly available to the public in some way, with due recognition to the scholar who actually did the work, and especially to Polotsky, in view of the fact that none of Polotsky's work on the *Kephalaia* published during the Nazi period could appear with his name on the title page.[91]

### Papyrus Collection, Berlin, P[15997], the *Acts*

According to Schmidt's report, the Fayyumic dealer had explained that the provincial dealer had sold his two parts to Nahman, who had sold them to Schmidt. By the process of elimination, it can be determined that P[15997] is one of these two: Nahman told Schmidt he acquired for Schmidt the two codices held by the provincial dealer after Nahman had "rejected" Beatty. This so-called rejection cannot be dated to a

---

Studies in Louvain-la-Neuve, Belgium, September 5–10, 1988, lists the following pages: 293, 301–7 (= chs. 125–29), 334, 337–57, 359–73 (= chs. 135–50), 395–99 (= chs. 157–60), 413. Alexander Böhlig, in a letter of February 5, 1989, reports that from samples that Schenke provided him of the script, he could ascribe pages 334, 337–57, 359–73, and 395–99 to Polotsky; and pages 293 (broken off), 301–7 (307 broken off), and 413 probably to himself. The *Jahrbuch der Preussichen Akademie der Wissenschaften, Jahrgang 1941* (Berlin: Akademie, 1942), 63, reported concerning Böhlig's work: "The fascicle 11/12 has been worked out apart from a few details (pages 244 to 292). Over and above that, transcriptions of the pages 300ff. could be carried out."

91. Böhlig, "Die Arbeit," 183 n. 1, stated: "The names of the real editors are missing from the title page for the following reason: The name of H. J. Polotsky was not supposed to appear on the title page in the Nazi time because of the racial legislation. But I turned down the naming of my name alone." It was in fact reported in *Kephalaia*, 1. Hälfte (1940), iv, at the conclusion of the preface: "The first two double fascicles Dr. H. J. Polotsky prepared. From p. 103 on Dr. A. Böhlig has taken his place."

time prior to Schmidt's seeing the *Kephalaia* on his first trip, for on his return from Jerusalem Nahman admitted having sold in the intervening time to Beatty. Thus it can hardly be the *Kephalaia* that belonged to the provincial dealer. Schmidt acquired the 31 leaves of the *Synaxeis* from the Fayyumic dealer. And he acquired the bulk of the *Homilies* codex from Nahman via Beatty (see below), when Beatty released the option that he had held on it since March 23, 1930. Thus the two codices in the hands of the provincial dealer must by the process of elimination have been the *Acts* and the *Letters* (see below). In fact the *Acts* must be the codex that Schmidt reported acquiring in the spring of 1931, when he said he had acquired a codex still in its original wooden covers.[92] For in describing $P^{15997}$, he reported that it was acquired in its covers, and a photograph of this codex in its covers was published. The covers cannot be found at the Egyptian Museum of (East) Berlin, according to Günter Poethke, Custos of Greek Manuscripts in the Papyrus Collection.

Apparently only a few leaves were conserved, just enough to identify the codex. Alexander Böhlig saw one in 1953, which hence must not have been taken to Leningrad (whence material was returned only in 1958), but must have stayed in Berlin in 1946, presumably in the Ibscher home, though the leaf had been conserved well before the war. When Böhlig could not relocate it in Berlin in 1960, he was told by Rolf Ibscher that Ibscher by mistake had taken it to London.[93] It was moved from London to Dublin, but was among those leaves put on deposit in Copenhagen. Facsimiles were published in 1987 in volume 2 of the *Facsimile Edition*, though the identification is there left open. When one compares Schmidt and Polotsky's summary with the segments that Giversen translated,[94] there can be little doubt that

---

92. Schmidt and Polotsky, "Ein Mani-Fund," 7, 8, 27, and Plate 2.

93. Böhlig reported this in an interview in Tübingen on July 10, 1986.

94. Giversen, "Manichaean Texts from the Chester Beatty Collection," 269: "This must either be a parallel text to that mentioned by C. Schmidt or physically be the same. I shall not say much more about this here, since I have dealt with it in the edition Vol. II pp. VIII–IX and I hope to return to it in connection with a preliminary critical edition and translation of the text." The plates are published in Giversen, *Homilies and Varia*, viii–ix, plates 99–100. On page viii Giversen states:

> The two pages have a text with some historical information, and this can be identified with similar information reported by C. Schmidt from a leaf in Berlin . . . Exactly the same persons are mentioned: Thadamor, Amarô, Sapores the hyparch, Narsaph, Hormezd, Innaios, Abiesus and others. This

## Introduction: The Fate of the Manichaean Codices 39

it is in fact the same text, and, since there is no second copy of the *Acts* among the codices from Medinet Madi,[95] it is no doubt the same copy.

> must either be a parallel text to that mentioned by C. Schmidt, or the leaf must physically be the same. Parallel texts are well known from other papyri, e.g., in the Nag Hammadi texts the two very close long versions of the Apocryphon of John, and the two versions of the Gospel of Truth.

The reference is to Schmidt and Polotsky, "Ein Mani-Fund," 28–29:

> Another piece leads us into a later time of Manichaeism. Here a mass of unknown persons come forward . . . Obviously it is here a matter of events that take place within the Persian Kingdom . . . It has to do further with the position assumed by provincial governments toward the Manichaean religion, some of which are disposed positively, especially Amara, who is designated as the "great patron" of the Manichaeans, since they enjoyed his support. Hence one of the heads of the Manichaeans turns to him with the request that he intervene for the persecuted believers in Persia with the king Narsaph, i.e., Narses (293–302). Amaro Innaios takes on this task and sends letters to the higher king that are crowned with success in that the persecutions cease. In these negotiations there occurs a certain, who is apparently the transmittor of the communication of Amaro Innaios to the king. He has an audience with King Narses, the result of which is that the suppressions and persecutions of the teachers and believers are suspended on the order of the king.

Giversen, "Unedited Chester Beatty Mani Texts," 379–80, republished in "Manichaean Texts from the Chester Beatty Collection," 269, has translated segments of this text:

> He told us that the king had arrived into the neighbourhood of our shepherd Innaios, together with the noble Persians who were his assistants. He spoke to him . . . He asked him to go to the king. He achieved mercy for us from him and stopped the (1986: our] destruction. The king together with the noblemen, who were many . . . Innaios, shall I raise Innaios went into . . . of the king [Sapores].

At the 1989 conference in Bonn, Giversen reported that after a visit to the Papyrus Collection in (East) Berlin he had decided that the relevant leaf is not there and that the leaf in Copenhagen is from this codex.

95. There is a *Kephalaia* codex in Dublin and one in Berlin, but they are not two copies of the same text, but rather a two-volume set. The *Homilies* material in Dublin and that (originally) in Berlin apparently belong to the same codex, rather than being two copies of the same text. With regard to Giversen's reference to duplicates in the Nag Hammadi library, all the duplicate texts within that collection of 13 codices prove on closer examination to belong to separate subgroups, only secondarily merged into a collection of collections. Of course in larger manuscript discoveries there are duplicates, e.g., among the Dishna Papers (as the discovery is referred to in Upper Egypt that the academic community has usually referred to as the Bodmer Papyri, since these form the largest block), the Gospel of John: in Greek, $P^{66}$ = P. Bodmer II, and $P^{75}$ = P. Bodmer XIV–XV; and in Coptic, P. Bodmer III, Chester Beatty ac. 1390, and perhaps P. Palau Ribes 182. Yet the Dishna Papers

There are 7 (or 8) leaves of this codex in the Papyrus Collection of (East) Berlin.[96] Thus there are extant 9 (or 10) unpublished leaves, 18 (or 20) unpublished pages.

Transcriptions of 3 pages that Schmidt and Polotsky used in their essay are preserved by the Archives of the Academy of Sciences in Berlin.[97]

Part of one leaf has perhaps turned up at the Institute for Papyrology of Warsaw University.[98]

---

also comprise a collection of collections or of individual codices and scrolls from a variety of provenances, whereas the Manichaean codices seem to be a set emanating from a single scriptorium.

96. The Inventory Book of the Papyrus Collection in (East) Berlin has penciled notes: "partially glassed," "8 leaves," and, initialed by Rolf Ibscher, "8 leaves are back." It is this reference in the Inventory Book that is no doubt responsible for the comment, "8 leaves in Berlin," in Müller's preliminary listing, "Die koptischen Handschriften," 65–85. This number was then repeated in Beltz's catalogue. But one of the 8 leaves there now has a printed label that reads $P^{15998}$; where the 8 has been marked out and a 7 written in by hand, a hand identified by Poethke as that of Luke. The leaf also has a separate label in ink reading 36, with the 6 marked out and replaced in pencil with 2. But the labels for the individual leaves of $P^{15997}$ use Roman numerals, with the highest IX, whereas $P^{15996}$ and $P^{15998}$ use Arabic numerals for individual leaves (and where some renumbering also occurs, see there). When one notes that the size of the glass panes in which the leaf in question is conserved is not the large format, used for $P^{15998}$, but a smaller format used for the 7 leaves of $P^{15997}$, one can wonder if one smaller leaf of $P^{15998}$ was packed for transport by size along with $P^{15997}$. When the material was returned from Leningrad, it may have been merely assumed that the eighth small leaf was part of the same codex with which it was packed, and the label "corrected" accordingly. Yet though the extant papyrus is indeed smaller in its dimensions than is usual for $P^{15998}$, the profile and the frayed edges are not what is characteristic of $P^{15997}$, though Stephen Patterson has noted a similarity in the scribal hands. The numeration attached to the leaves in Berlin does reach IX, which might suggest that nine leaves had been identified as belonging to $P^{15997}$. It could have been that the apparent contradiction of these 9 plates with the record in the Inventory Book of 8 having been conserved is what led Rolf Ibscher to "return" one to London. But there is also a leaf (actually only a narrow strip) in Warsaw (see note 98). The identity of the eighth leaf in Berlin thus remains uncertain.

97. Schenke, "Gnosis-Forschung 1984–1988" (see note 90 above).

98. Beltz, "Katalog der koptischen Handschriften," 97–98, states to I 605 = $P^{15997}$: "In Warsaw there is at present a leaf from this codex at the University." Inventories of July 12, 1986 by Wincenty Myszor and of August 11, 1986 by Wolf-Peter Funk indicate that there is a plate numbered 499/500 that is labeled $P^{15997}$, though it seems to belong (with 4 other leaves) to $P^{15996}$ (though Beltz does not list it at $P^{15996}$). But a sixth leaf, between much smaller panes of glass and taped with a different colored tape, has a label whose last digit is illegible ($P^{1599}$). Myszor read the last digit as 7 but added, it "is not quite clear—it can also be 6!" Funk could not read the digit, since part of

Stephen J. Patterson has made draft transcriptions of the seven leaves in Berlin and has as well transcribed the facsimiles of the one leaf in Copenhagen.

The unconserved book block is assumed to have been among the (East) Berlin Museum holdings that were taken to Leningrad in 1946, but when those holdings were returned in 1958, the book block was not present. What actually happened to it is not known. The missing wooden covers may have shared the same fate as the book block, from which they may never have been separated, since the conserved leaves may not have been the first and/or last leaves of the codex, but may have been exposed by the dealers breaking the codex open in the middle.

**Papyrus Collection, Berlin, P$^{15998}$, the *Letters***

The second of the two codices that the provincial dealer acquired, and passed on to Nahman to sell to Schmidt, can be determined by the same process of elimination to be P$^{15998}$.

As in the case of the *Acts*, only a sampling of leavings was conserved, to provide an initial identification. Six leaves are recorded in the Inventory Book of the Papyrus Collection of Berlin as having been taken to Leningrad and returned in 1958. They have been identified in a recent inventory of the material currently in the Papyrus Collection of Berlin as a separate stack with plates of a distinctive format numbered B 12, 13, 21, 23, 24, and 25. (Though 13 had lost its label, it could be identified by means of letters transcribed in Beltz's inventory; see note 3.) But 3 leaves, presumably also conserved by Hugo Ibscher, turned up after World War II in the National Museum in Warsaw.

Alexander Böhlig conjectured that 13 leaves of this codex were by mistake taken to London.[99] This conjecture is based in part on a comment by Rolf Ibscher that the 13 leaves in London were of "an unusually large format," a description that Böhlig thought singled out

---

the paper was broken off, but noted on the other side of the leaf a label of recent date reading "to P$^{15997}$." This "narrow strip of papyrus" that is scarcely legible (Funk) may hence come from P$^{15997}$, though this is far from certain. Whether it would be part of one of the leaves taken to Leningrad or counted as a separate leaf is unclear, and hence it is unclear whether it would have been a separate one of the nine leaves that the numeration system suggests, an ambivalence that would tend to obscure even further the identity of the uncertain leaf in Berlin.

99. Böhlig, "Die Arbeit," 186–87.

the *Letters* codex. Yet all the codices may have about the same dimensions, except for the smaller Psalms codex.[100] Böhlig's view is in part based on the absence from the leaves in Berlin of the running heads of 4 pages that Schmidt and Polotsky read, which suggested to Böhlig that these running heads might be on the leaves then in London. But, according to Wolf-Peter Funk's transcriptions, they have been located on the leaves in Warsaw. Böhlig concluded his argument with the comment that "a glance at the London leaves should suffice to solve all these problematic questions with one blow." It was not at the time possible for him to examine them in London. But the *Facsimile Edition* alone suffices:[101] The leaves are not unusually large and do not contain the running heads that Schmidt and Polotsky quoted. Hence these 13 Dublin leaves that Hugo Ibscher labeled as Codex B seem to belong to Chester Beatty Library Codex B, the *Synaxeis* codex, not to the *Letters*, though the 6 leaves of this codex conserved by Hugo Ibscher were also labeled B.

Rolf Ibscher kept half-conserved materials in the family home throughout the war (see above) and then returned them to the Papyrus Collection of (East) Berlin, where they are currently held. Among the 15 plates stacked together with Poethke's note to the effect that they belong to the *Letters*, 2 are labeled as "*Kephalaia* without number," 9 are numbered (8–12, 14–16, and 18), and 4 are unnumbered. One unnumbered plate, labeled by Rolf Ibscher "twin separated from number 8," does have the same profile as number 8. A second, labeled "twins" (in Rolf Ibscher's best English) does contain two leaves and has the same profile as number 9, on which a fragment of a second leaf is still stuck; the fragment seems to fit the location of a missing segment of the material labeled "twins." A third also contains two leaves. A fourth lacks the middle segment and was reglassed by Luke in 1970. Thus the 13 plates contain actually 15 leaves, in view of the two instances of "twins."

One plate that originally had the printed label $P^{15998}$ and was numbered 29 has the 8 marked out and replaced by 6; and the plate numbered 30 (which actually contains two leaves) has the printed

---

100. Hugo Ibscher, in Polotsky, *Manichäische Homilien*, xiii. The extant leaves of $P^{15997}$, the *Acts* codex, are also in a smaller format, but the book block, to which Ibscher may have had access but we do not, apparently had the larger format.

101. Giversen, *Homilies and Varia*, ix–x, plates 101–26.

label scraped off and replaced by 15996, thus shifting both to the *Kephalaia*, and in both cases perhaps from the *Letters*. Two others listed "*Kephalaia* without number" were stacked with the 13 leaves, making up the stack of 15 that Poethke ascribed to the *Letters*, which seems to suggest that these two leaves were thought to belong to the *Letters*. In fact as many as 8 leaves labeled as belonging to the *Kephalaia* could belong to another codex, such as the *Letters* (see above). One leaf with a printed label P$^{15998}$ has the 8 marked out and replaced by 7, thus suggesting it earlier was assigned not to the *Acts* but to the *Letters* (see above).

One may hence speak rather tentatively of 28 leaves or 56 pages of the *Letters* codex being extant today: the 6 leaves = 12 pages returned to Berlin that Hugo Ibscher conserved; the 3 leaves = 6 pages that emerged in Warsaw after the war; 15 leaves = 30 pages from among those that lay half conserved in the Ibscher home during the war and were put in 13 glass containers labelled by Rolf Ibscher; 3 leaves = 6 pages in 2 glass containers as belonging to the *Kephalaia*; and 1 leaf = 2 pages currently labeled as belonging to the *Acts* may actually come from the *Letters* codex. None of it has been published. The amount of text that survives is very much less than these figures suggest.

The unconserved book block is assumed to have been among the Berlin Museum holdings that were taken to Leningrad in 1946, but when those holdings were returned in 1958 the book block was not present. What actually happened to it is not known.

## Papyrus Collection, Berlin, P$^{15999}$, the Bulk of the *Homilies*

On March 23, 1930, Beatty received from Nahman with an option to buy for £700 the bulk of the *Homilies* codex, which Hugo Ibscher advised him could not be conserved.

At the beginning of 1932, Beatty learned that Schmidt had a second option to buy the manuscript if Beatty decided not to exercise his option.[102] On March 29, 1932, Beatty finally wrote Nahman that he would not make the purchase, and on May 10, 1932, the manuscript was turned over to Ibscher in London to take back with him to Berlin for Schmidt.[103] The publisher W. Kohlhammer purchased it for the

---

102. Sir Herbert Thompson wrote on January 4, 1932, this news that he had just received in a letter from Schmidt.

103. In the two-ring binder in the Archives of the Chester Beatty Library, there is

Papyrus Collection of Berlin for a price reported to have been 5,000 marks,[104] and it was inventoried as P[15999]. Though it was suspected to be the bulk of the *Homilies* codex, the rest of which Ibscher had in fact successfully conserved (Chester Beatty Library Codex D),[105] it was never considered to be conservable. Rather it was kept as a sort of showpiece of how impossible the conservation of these codices was.[106]

---

a note concerning this manuscript: "Given to Dr. Ibscher for Nahman." Technically speaking, the manuscript was released back to Nahman to dispose of as he saw fit. Yet Ibscher was not going to Cairo, but rather to Berlin. On May 14, 1932, before leaving London for Berlin, Ibscher wrote a receipt for Beatty, "to confirm that I have correctly received the Mani manuscript for Prof. Schmidt."

104. In a letter of August 29, 1957, from Rolf Ibscher to Carsten Colpe. The Inventory Book of the Papyrus Collection reports: "Acquired through Prof. Carl Schmidt in Cairo 1932. Gift of Dr. W. Kohlhammer." The reference to the acquisition in Cairo is literal only in the sense that Schmidt was in Egypt when Beatty released his option, and Schmidt exercised his option with Nahman in Cairo. But the manuscript itself had long since permanently left Egypt.

105. Hugo Ibscher, "Die Handschrift," in Polotsky, *Manichäische Homilien*, xii: "Whether the text published here is part of a lost Mani book, or belongs to one of the extant volumes not yet undertaken by me, can for the time being not be determined." This undecidedness corresponds to the statement of Schmidt and Polotsky, "Ein Mani-Fund," 30, concerning the Berlin part: "The papyrus book that has most recently been added to the corpus of the Berlin Manichaica could not yet be subjected to any further investigation. But this much seems to be certain, that it contains a collection of so-called λογοι (both the Coptic and the English use the same Greek loan word) of various authors. On the upper margins authors' names from the circle of Mani's disciples occur, such as Koustaios, Salmaios." But in the same essay, page 34, concerning the London part, the identification is affirmed: "A second papyrus book contains a collection of homilies (λογοι) of various contents and by various authors . . . Of this book, as I mentioned above [!], a voluminous part has come to Berlin." Alexander Böhlig, in a letter of February 3, 1989, has pointed out that in view of the frequent occurrence of homilies in Manichaean literature, one cannot be certain that this is part of the same codex of homilies as that of Beatty's that contains homilies. But then one would have to assume that the minor part of a codex of homilies that Beatty acquired in 1931 was part of an otherwise lost codex, whereas the homilies codex that Beatty obtained on approval from Nahman in 1930 would be a separate codex. It would seem simpler to assume that here, as in the case of the *Psalms* codex sold to Beatty in two installments, at the same time as were sold the two texts with homilies, and hence probably in the same two transactions, one has to do with two parts of the same codex. By marketing the two parts of a single codex in separate transactions, the dealer might assume a client would not notice that one had to do with two parts of the same codex—all the more so given the condition of the papyrus and Beatty's status as an amateur, not a scholar. Nahman probably had two codices that he succeeded in selling as four.

106. The Inventory Book of the Papyrus Collection of Berlin listed its location not, as in the case of the others, as a shelf in the work area, but as "displayed," i.e. on

Introduction: The Fate of the Manichaean Codices    45

The unconserved book block is assumed to have been among the Berlin Museum holdings that were taken to Leningrad in 1946, but when those holdings were returned in 1958 the book block was not present.[107] What actually happened to it is not known.

Few manuscript discoveries of the importance of the Manichaean codices of Medinet Madi have undergone such an ambivalent fate after their discovery. Since the leaves had been stuck together by salt crystals due to the dampness in which they were conjectured to have lain for a millennium and a half, their condition was such that the first scholar to see them, Lange, did not acquire them. Schmidt passed them up the first time he saw them; neither did Adolf von Harnack favor their acquisition; Schmidt's decision to acquire them was in part based upon his hearing that the famous bibliophile, Beatty, had acquired some. But Beatty at first acquired only with an option to buy, which he exercised only in part, and then only on receiving encouragement from Schmidt via Ibscher. Thus the material barely escaped being bypassed by the academic community.

The conservation and editing began under what might seem to be a lucky star, with two competing geniuses—Ibscher and Polotsky—working in collaboration,[108] so that each newly exposed leaf on the book block could be transcribed before being removed, thus producing a better transcription for at least the exposed side than might be possible after it had been removed and perhaps damaged in the process, and providing an aide memoire for reassembling the leaf after it was

---

exhibit. Rolf Ibscher, "Der Mani-Fund," 228: "Codex 15999, because of its unimpressive appearance, immediately wandered into the permanent display of the Berlin Museums, as a visible example of the terrible degeneration of the whole manuscript find." See Böhlig, "Die Arbeit," 157–61; and *Actes du XXVe Congrès International des Orientalistes, Moscou 9–16 août 1960*, 535–41; but here it is cited according to Böhlig's collected essays, *Mysterion und Wahrheit*, 177–87, especially 184: "The condition of the manuscript was so desolate that among the collaborators of the Papyrus Collection it was generally designated as the 'wig.'"

107. The Inventory Book of the Papyrus Collection of Berlin includes a note added in purple carbon reading, "at present in Moscow." Presumably this should read: Leningrad. This is the only indication in the Inventory Book as to the fate of any of the book blocks.

108. Böhlig, in a letter of February 5, 1989, recalls that the actual relationship was more nearly that of hostility. Polotsky was dependent on the speed, regularity, and success of Ibscher's conservation; Ibscher was dependent on Polotsky for the correct placement of fragments removed from the book block one by one, and may have been delayed by Polotsky's wishing to transcribe a surface before the leaf was removed from the book block.

peeled off the book block. Alexander Böhlig, who became Polotsky's assistant in 1933 and successor in 1934, himself was never so involved, though he might well have been, had the procedure in fact been functioning well. Efforts by the son, Rolf Ibscher, to reestablish such teamwork after the war, though several alternatives were envisaged, did not actually materialize in a way to produce comparably successful results, though Böhlig would have liked to have become more involved with Ibscher's work than an occasional visit to Göttingen made possible. After the material was returned from Leningrad to Berlin in 1958, he proposed in 1959 to the German Academy of Sciences in Berlin that it resume publication. In 1960 the Academy's Institut für griechisch-römische Altertumskunde (rather than the Academy's Orientalische Kommission, which, prior to the war, had been in charge), through the subdivision Kommission für spätantike Religionsgeschichte, commissioned Böhlig to prepare the publications. On July 5, 1960, Böhlig wrote T. C. Skeat of the British Museum for permission to see the conserved leaves there, expressing particular interest in the 13 unidentified leaves and leaves reported to have been found lying inside Beatty's *Kephalaia* codex. Böhlig proposed bringing Ibscher with him to remove opaque cellophane paper that lay between the papyrus and the glass, which would, if left in place, effectively prevent reading the text. On July 13, 1960, R. J. Hayes, honorary librarian of the Chester Beatty Library, replied that Böhlig could see the leaves, but that one could not remove the cellophane—a restriction apparently intended to insure that Rolf Ibscher, whose work had been terminated with some hard feelings, not return again.[109]

At the Twenty-Fifth Congress of Orientalists in Moscow in August of 1960, Böhlig presented the status of the Manichaean codices. A resolution was passed advocating international cooperation in publishing the codices.[110] On August 15, 1960, Johannes Irmscher, then director of the Institut für griechisch-römische Altertumskunde of the Deutsche Akademie der Wissenschaften in Berlin, wrote to Hayes informing him of this resolution and soliciting his cooperation, commending both Böhlig and Ibscher. Hayes responded on December

---

109. T. C. Skeat forwarded Böhlig's letter to Hayes on July 11, 1960, with the comment: "I must leave you to deal with the suggestion that he should bring Ibscher with him!"

110. See note 106 above.

5, 1960, that the restoration was being done at the British Museum, and that the Coptic experts there would converse with Böhlig on the occasion of a visit anticipated for 1961. Böhlig in fact did not go, since without Ibscher he could not remove the cellophane to make the leaves legible, and because of the impossibilities of his making such a trip at the time. The Berlin Wall was erected August 13, 1961. Böhlig hoped that Peter Nagel would take over his work in Berlin after he himself moved in 1963 to West Germany. Böhlig hoped that, for his part, he would be able to activate the English. But none of this materialized, and Coptological scholarship moved increasingly into Nag Hammadi studies.

The book blocks with the unconserved bulk of three codices (the *Acts*, the *Letters*, and the *Homilies*) have been lost. Of the four largely extant codices, half of one (the *Synaxeis*) has not been conserved but is extant as a currently unconservable book block. Of the leaves that have been conserved from all seven codices, about half have been published in critical editions; the unpublished half, most of which was conserved by Rolf Ibscher, is largely illegible, as the *Facsimile Edition* makes apparent.

This discovery was caught up to a very abnormal degree in the political disasters of the time: the departure of Polotsky for Jerusalem in 1933 to avoid the baneful auspices of the Third Reich; the death of C. R. C. Allberry through the shooting down of his plane over the Netherlands just before midnight on April 3, 1943;[111] the inaccessibility of the material in the Zoo bunker during the war and then in Leningrad for twelve years (1946–1958)—it actually became accessible again only in 1960, a hiatus of two decades. By this time Carl Schmidt and Hugo Ibscher had died, and the next generation simply did not succeed in carrying forward the work as it had been initiated so promisingly by the first generation, though Alexander Böhlig and Rolf Ibscher worked vigorously, though largely in isolation.[112] Alexander

---

111. Allberry's tragic life led a classmate C. P. Snow to write a novel, *Light and the Dark*, whose hero, Roy Calvert, is based largely on Allberry but also on the character Larry Darrell in Somerset Maugham's *The Razor's Edge*. When the novel was included in a series of television renderings of Snow's sequence of novels, *Strangers and Brothers*, Allberry's widow, Mrs. Patricia K. G. Lewis, felt called upon to clear Allberry's name by publishing privately a collection of testimonials and recollections: Lewis, *Charles Allberry: A Portrait*. See also Putt, "Charles Allberry and Roy Calvert," 70–76; see also Giversen, *Psalm-Book, Part 1*, viii.

112. See most recently, Böhlig, *Gnosis and Synkretismus*, especially, in vol. 1, 71–180; and, in vol. 2, the section "Manichäismus," 457–653.

Böhlig is the only member of the earlier team who has continued to be active and thus to provide some continuity in the current revival of interest in the Manichaean codices of Medinet Madi.

The plans worked out in 1931 for a complete coordination in the conservation, editing, and publication of the material, in spite of the plurality of ownership, began to be implemented successfully, as is evident from the publications between 1934 and 1966 by Polotsky, Böhlig, and Allberry from three codices in two parallel series at Kohlhammer in Stuttgart. Now, a generation or more later, the academic community has become aware that a salvage operation is urgently needed if the editing and publishing of this important manuscript discovery, which began so auspiciously, is not to end quite dismally.

The International Association for Coptic Studies expressed its approval of both the projects that have recently been proposed and hoped that there will be collaboration between them. This is a hope that we all, as participants in the Second International Conference on Manichaeism should heartily share, and that the newly founded International Association of Manichaean Studies might seek to implement.

Part One

The Acquisition and Initial Conservation and Editing

# — 1 —

# The Acquisitions of Carl Schmidt

THE BASIC PUBLICATION REPORTING on the circumstances of the acquisition of the Manichaean codices of Medinet Madi (Τερενοῦθις) is the report to the Berlin Academy of Sciences by Carl Schmidt and H. J. Polotsky, with a contribution by Hugo Ibscher, submitted July 28, 1932, and published the following year:[1]

| | |
|---|---|
| On the occasion of a research trip to Palestine [early in 1930] ... while passing through Cairo, I [Carl Schmidt] paid a visit to the various antiquities dealers I knew. Among other things, a papyrus book [P15996, *Kephalaia*] was put before me that was in an extremely desolate condition, so that I hardly dared to touch it. Fortunately I could decipher in the upper margin the word ⲚⲔⲈⲪⲀⲖⲀⲒⲞⲚ and in the text read the beginning of a section: "Again the Illuminator (ⲪⲰⲤⲦⲎⲢ) spoke" ... and the content must go back to an author who ascribed to himself the honorary title of an "Illuminator" or was honored as such by his followers, and who | Bei Gelegenheit einer Forschungsreise nach Palästina ... [early in 1930] stattete ich [Carl Schmidt] auf der Durchreise in Kairo den verschiedenen mir bekannten Antikenhändlern einen Besuch ab. Unter anderem wurde mir ein Papyrusbuch [P15996, *Kephalaia*]vorgelegt, das sich in einem höchst desolaten Zustande befand, daher ich es kaum zu berühren wagte. Zum Glück konnte ich auf dem oberen Rande das Wort ⲚⲔⲈⲪⲀⲖⲀⲒⲞⲚ entziffern und im Texte den Anfang eines Abschnittes lesen: "Wiederum sprach der Erleuchter (ⲪⲰⲤⲦⲎⲢ)" ... , und der Inhalt musste auf einen Verfassser zurückgehen, der sich selbst |

---

1. Schmidt and Polotsky, "Ein Mani-Fund," 4–90, with a contribution by Hugo Ibscher, "Die Handschriften," 82–85. The quotations here are from pp. 6–10.

had collected a circle of disciples around himself ... In happy excitement about this discovery I communicated information about it to his Excellency [Adolf] von Harnack and others whom I knew in Berlin, but I struck upon great skepticism, since no one wanted to believe in the discovery of original works of Mani. I was referred to anti-Manichaean writings from Egypt such as Alexander of Lycopolis or Serapion of Thmuis. So I drew back from an acquisition. Only on my return from Jerusalem was my attention led again to the papyrus, as I learned from the antiquities dealer that Mr. Chester Beatty, a well-known collector of manuscripts, had acquired [March 23, 1930] papyrus books similar to the one offered to me. This gave me the courage to acquire the papyrus at my own risk, especially since no downpayment was required of me. But I had not taken into account the fact that in the meantime a severe financial crisis had occurred in Germany, which also involved the museums and libraries too heavily for larger amounts to be provided for acquisitions. Hence all the efforts that were so kindly supported by my colleague Prof. Erich Seeberg seemed to be without success. Thus the danger was near that this valuable treasure might be lost to German scholarship. Then at the last minute a lucky star arose in the person of an unnamed Maecenas [August Pfeffer], who had been made aware of the significance of the

den Ehrentitel eines "Erleuchters" beigelegt hatte oder als solcher von den Anhängern verehrt wurde, und der einen Jüngerkreis um sich versammelt hatte ... In freudiger Erregung über diese Entdeckung machte ich Exzellenz [Adolf] von Harnack und anderen Bekannten in Berlin davon Mitteilung, stiess aber auf grosse Skepsis, da niemand an die Auffindung von Originalwerken des Mani glauben wollte. Ich wurde auf manichäische Gegenschriften aus Ägypten wie Alexander von Lycopolis oder Serapion von Thmuis hingewiesen. So trat ich von einer Erwerbung zurück. Erst bei meiner Rückkehr von Jerusalem wurde meine Aufmerksamkeit auf den Papyrus wieder gelenkt, als ich von dem Antikenhändler erfuhr, dass Mr. Chester Beatty, ein bekannter Sammler von Handschriften, ähnliche Papyrusbücher wie das mir angebotene erworben hätte [23 March 1930]. Dies gab mir den Mut, den Papyrus auf mein eigenes Risiko zu erwerben, zumal keine Anzahlung von mir verlangt wurde. Aber ich hatte nicht damit gerechnet, dass in Deutschland inzwischen eine schwere Finanzkrise ausgebrochen war, die auch die Museen und Bibliotheken zu stark in Mitleidenschaft zog, um grössere Summen für Ankäufe bereitstellen zu können. Daher schienen alle Bemühungen, die von meinem Kollegen Prof. Erich Seeberg in dankenswerter Weise unterstützt wurden, erfolglos zu sein und damit die Gefahr in die Nähe gerückt, dass dieser kostbare Schatz der deutschen Wissenschaft verlorenginge. Da tauchte im letzten Moment ein Rettungsstern in der Person eines ungenannten Mäzens [August Pfeffer] auf, der durch

find by my friend Dr. E. Lubowski. In great-hearted liberality he provided the Egyptian Museum with the purchase price, indeed he even expressed his willingness, in case further pieces of the papyrus book should come on the market in the Egyptian antiquities trade, to provide further means for their acquisition. German scholarship hence owes warm appreciation to this Maecenas, especially since such understanding patrons can be counted as rarities in the hard times of today.

So in the spring of 1931 I could again begin a trip to Egypt ... My trip had as its main purpose to investigate further the find as such, i.e. to collect more precise information about the site of the discovery, but especially to determine whether still further papyrus books from the same find had cropped up on the antiquities market. For anyone who is familiar with the antiquities trade knows very well that in the case of larger papyrus discoveries all the material is never brought to market at once, either by the discoverers or by the dealers, so as not to depress the price in offering larger quantities. My intuition had not deceived me, for already on my first visit to an antiquities dealer in Cairo he put before me two piles of papyrus [P$^{15996}$ Kephalaia] that outwardly recalled only too well those that had been earlier acquired. And again I could decipher on the upper margin the word ⲚⲔⲈⲪⲀⲖⲀⲒⲞⲚ. Thus it was proven that it belonged to

meinen Freund Dr. E. Lubowski auf die Bedeutung des Fundes aufmerksam gemacht war. In hochherziger Liberalität hat er den Kaufpreis für das Ägyptische Museum erstattet, ja, er erklärte sich bereit, sollten weitere Stücke des Papyrusbuches im ägyptischen Antikenhandel auf den Markt kommen, weitere Mittel zu deren Erwerbung zur Verfügung stellen zu wollen. Die deutsche Wissenschaft ist daher diesem Mäzen zu heissestem Dank verpflichtet, zumal in der heutigen Notzeit so verständnisvolle Mäzene zu den Seltenheiten zu rechnen sind.

So konnte ich im Frühjahr 1931 wiederum eine Reise nach Ägypten antreten ... Meine Reise hatte den Hauptzweck, dem Funde als solchem weiter nachzugehen, d.h. über den Fundort nähere Erkundigungen einzuziehen, insbesondere aber festzustellen, ob noch weitere Papyrusbücher aus demselben Funde auf dem Antikenmarkte auftauchen würden. Denn wer mit dem Antikenhandel vertraut ist, weiss zur Genüge, dass bei grösseren Papyrusfunden niemals das ganze Material, sei es von den Findern, sei es von den Händlern, auf einmal auf den Markt gebracht wird, um den Preis bei Angebot grösseren Umfangs nicht herabzudrücken. Meine Ahnung hatte mich nicht betrogen, denn gleich beim ersten Besuche eines Antikenhändlers in Kairo legte er mir zwei Papyrushaufen [P$^{15996}$, *Kephalaia*] vor, die dem Äussern nach nur zu sehr an jene früher erworbenen erinnerten. Und wieder konnte ich auf dem oberen Rande das Wort ⲚⲔⲈⲪⲀⲖⲀⲒⲞⲚ entziffern. Damit war die Zugehörigkeit zu dem Originalwerke erwiesen. Daneben kam ein Papyrusbuch [P$^{15997}$,

the original work. In the process, a papyrus book [P¹⁵⁹⁹⁷, *Acta*] emerged that lay in the original condition as when found, between two bare wooden covers, since one had risked no further handling. The whole was in such a condition of decomposition that even the dealer did not think he could recommend the acquisition to me, to spare me a later deception or a protest to him ...

Unfortunately, I was completely in the dark thus far about the site of the discovery. The dialect used in the text pointed to Upper Egypt, but many indications regarding the dealers spoke for the Fayyum. Hence my next visit, accompanied by Privy Councillor Moritz, was paid to an old business friend there. And again I had not been deceived, for he [p. 8] showed me a few unimpressive piles that on the first glance betrayed the fact that they belonged to the Mani discovery. So here the source was uncovered from which Mr. Chester Beatty had carried out his acquisition. And now there was no further difficulty in obtaining from the mouth of this well-versed dealer further information about the whole discovery. First of all, the news was important that three dealers had divided the discovery among themselves, and in fact there had been eight parts, of which he himself had gotten three parts, the dealer in Cairo also three parts, and a provincial dealer two parts. Of course this first partition was not the end of it, but each had carried out further divi-

*Acta*] zum Vorschein, das noch in dem ursprünglichen Zustande bei der Auffindung zwischen zwei kahlen Holzdeckeln lag, da man keine weitere Berührung gewagt hatte. Das Ganze befand sich in einem solchen Zerfall, dass selbst der Händler den Ankauf mir nicht empfehlen zu können glaubte, um mir eine spätere Enttäuschung bzw. Reklamation bei ihm zu ersparen ...

Leider war ich bis dahin über den Fundort ganz im unklaren. Der im Text gebotene Dialekt wies nach Oberägypten, aber manche Anzeichen in Rücksicht auf die Händler sprachen für das Fajum. Daher galt mein nächster Besuch in Begleitung von Hrn. Geheimrat Moritz einem dortigen alten Geschäftsfreunde. Und wieder hatte ich mich nicht getäuscht, denn er [p. 8] zeigte mir einige unansehnliche Haufen, die ihre Zugehörigkeit zu dem Mani-Funde auf den ersten Blick verrieten. Hier war also die Quelle entdeckt, aus der Mr. Chester Beatty seine Erwerbung getätigt hatte. Und nun machte es keine Schwierigkeit mehr, aus dem Munde dieses sehr versierten Händlers über den ganzen Fund nähere Kunde zu erhalten. Zunächst war von Wichtigkeit die Mitteilung, dass drei Händler den Fund unter sich geteilt hätten, und zwar wären es acht Teile gewesen, davon er selbst drei Teile, der Händler in Kairo ebenfalls drei Teile und ein Provinzhändler zwei Teile erhalten hätten. Natürlich war es bei dieser ersten Teilung nicht geblieben, sondern jeder hatte weitere Teilungen vorgenommen, um möglichst viel Geld herauszus-

sions in order to squeeze out of it as much money as possible. And what was even worse, one had removed the top and bottom layers of papyrus, which had suffered to an especial extent against the covers of the binding—a phenomenon that we experience in almost all codices—, to give the whole a better appearance. How much was lost in this manipulation one is not able now to judge. So I found such outwardly unimpressive remains, which doubtless belong to the papyrus books acquired by Mr. Chester Beatty in the Fayyum [only the *Synaxeis* was acquired in Egypt partly by Beatty, partly by Schmidt], and, for the sake of completeness, so as not to let the least bit get lost, acquired them for a cheap sum, since the dealer already had his great reward in his pocket. [Note 1: Prof (Adolf) Grohmann of Prague has acquired such rags for the papyrus section of the Vienna State Library from a dealer in Eshmunen (the remains of *Kephalaia*, 311–20)]. Ibscher recently saved fragments of two leaves from this junk heap. —On my last trip in the Spring of 1932 I found still two further piles [P$^{15996}$, *Kephalaia*] that had been peeled off, and brought them to Berlin.] I do not regret my decision, for in the conservation 31 leaves could be brought under glass in more or less fragmentary preservation [P$^{15995}$, *Synaxeis*]. Whereas the antiquities dealer in the Fayyum had sold his manuscripts exclusively to Mr. Chester Beatty, the Cairo one had divided his hold-

chlagen. Und was noch schlimmer war, man hatte die oberen und unteren Papyruslagen, die unter den Einbanddecken in besonderem Masse gelitten hatten—eine Erscheinung, die wir bei fast allen Kodizes erleben—abgehoben, um dem Ganzen ein besseres Aussehen zu geben. Wieviel bei dieser Manipulation zugrunde gegangen ist, entzieht sich jetzt der Beurteilung. So fand ich solche äusserlich unscheinbaren Reste, die ohne Zweifel zu den von Mr. Chester Beatty im Fajum erworbenen Papyrusbüchern gehören [only the *Synaxeis* was acquired in Egypt partly by Beatty, partly by Schmidt], und habe sie der Vollständigkeit halber, um nicht das geringste verlorengehen zu lassen, für billiges Geld erworben, da der Händler seinen grossen Verdienst bereits in der Tasche hatte. [Note 1: Derartige Fetzen hat Prof. (Adolf) Grohmann, Prag, für die Papyrusabteilung der Wiener Staatsbibliothek von einem Händler aus Eschmunen erworben [the remains of *Kephalaia*, pp. 311–20]. Ibscher hat jüngst Fragmente von zwei Blättern aus diesem Müllhaufen gerettet.—Bei meiner letzten Reise im Frühjahr 1932 fand ich noch zwei weitere abgehobene Haufen [P$^{15996}$, *Kephalaia*] vor und brachte sie nach Berlin.] Ich bereue meinen Entschluss nicht, denn bei der Konservierung konnten 31 Blätter in mehr oder weniger fragmentarischer Erhaltung unter Glas gebracht werden [P$^{15995}$, *Synaxeis*]. Hatte der Fajumer Antikenhändler

ings between Chester Beatty and myself, and, after he had turned him away, bought up the two pieces of the provincial, in order to offer them to me. But what was of the greatest importance: My man of confidence could give me a precise statement about the site of the discovery, which doubtless no one would have been able to guess. For the Mani books are written in the so-called Subachmimic dialect. Hence the translation must have originally been done in the region where this local dialect was at home. That was an Upper Egyptian dialect, which, as we will come to see in more detail, was spoken in the region of Assiut. According to what was told me, the site of the discovery was what is now called Medinet Madi, a place little known even to papyrologists . . . [p. 9]

My man of confidence must have had the whole discovery before his eyes, for, according to a passing comment that he just now made to me on my visit in March 1932, the papyrus books, each surrounded by bare covers in wood, lay in a wooden box that was found in what had been a dwelling house. The wooden box was said to have been rotten, so that saving it would not have been worthwhile. It seems as if the whole discovery had been offered by the Arabic discoverers to the antiquities dealer of the Fayyum, but the dealer had not risked putting his money alone in these unimpressive papyrus books, which is why he divided

seine Handschriften ausschliesslich an Mr. Chester Beatty verkauft, so hatte der Kairener seinen Besitz zwischen Chester Beatty und mir geteilt und hatte, nachdem er diesen abgestossen, die beiden Stücke des Provinzlers aufgekauft, um sie mir anzubieten. Aber was von höchster Wichtigkeit war: Mein Gewährsmann konnte mir auch eine genaue Angabe über den Fundort machen, den wohl niemand hätte erraten können. Denn die Mani-Bücher sind im sogenannten sub-achmimischen Dialekt abgefasst; die Übersetzung muss also ursprünglich in dem Gebiet stattgefunden haben, wo dieser Lokaldialekt heimisch war. Das war ein oberägyptischer Dialekt, der, wie wir noch näher erkennen werden, im Gebiete von Assiut gesprochen wurde. Den Mitteilungen zufolge war der Fundort das heutige Medinet Madi, ein selbst den Papyrologen wenig bekannter Ort . . . [p. 9]

Den gesamten Fund muss mein Gewährsmann noch vor Augen gehabt haben, denn nach beiläufiger Mitteilung, die er mir jetzt beim Besuch im März 1932 machte, lagen die Papyrusbücher, jedes von kahlen Deckeln in Holz umgeben, in einer Holzkiste, die in einem früheren Wohnhause aufgefunden wurde. Die Holzkiste soll zerfallen gewesen sein, so dass eine Aufbewahrung sich nicht lohnte. Es hat den Anschein, als ob dem Antikenhändler im Fajum der ganze Fund von den arabischen Findern angeboten wurde, dieser aber sich nicht getraute, sein Geld allein in diesen unansehnlichen Papyrusbüchern anzulegen, weshalb er den Fund mit anderen Händlern teilte. Damit wird auch eine Beobachtung von Dr. Ibscher bestätigt, dass die Mani-Handschriften infolge ihrer feuchten Lagerung in absehbarer

the discovery with other dealers. This also confirms an observation by Dr. Ibscher to the effect that the Mani manuscripts were near disintegration in the foreseeable future as a result of their damp storage; that is to say, they could not have been lying in the dry desert earth. For the basements of the houses of Medinet Madi were exposed to dampness from above and below, so that the papyri could be drenched through and through with salt crystals. The whole region is a swamp area, even if the old settlement was placed on the back of a hill ... [p. 10]

Meanwhile Dr. Ibscher has brought the Mani holdings of Chester Beatty from London to Berlin to put them under glass right here at his leisure. I myself had a conference in London with those interested in the discovery, Sir Herbert Thompson, Dr. W. E. Crum and Prof. Alan H. Gardiner, concerning some kind of collaboration with regard to a literary whole that basically belongs together, and it was agreed that expenses should be shared to interest a young collaborator. I could present such a one in the person of Dr. Polotsky, after my Maecenas [August Pfeffer] in the most generous way had assured his involvement for two years, so that the work could be begun seriously in July 1931.

Zeit dem Zerfall nahegebracht wären, also nicht in der trockenen Wüstenerde gelegen haben können. Denn die Keller der Häuser von Medinet Madi waren der Feuchtigkeit von oben und unten ausgesetzt, so dass die Papyri von Salzkristallen vollständig durchsetzt werden konnten. Die ganze Gegend ist Sumpfgebiet, wenn auch die alte Siedlung auf dem Hügelrücken angelegt war ... [p. 10]

Inzwischen hatte Dr. Ibscher den Mani-Besitz von Chester Beatty von London nach Berlin gebracht, um ihn hier an Ort und Stelle in aller Ruhe unter Glas zu bringen. Ich selbst hatte in London mit den Interessenten des Fundes, mit Sir Herbert Thompson, Dr. W. E. Crum und Prof. Alan H. Gardiner eine Konferenz betreffs einer gewissen Zusammenarbeit bei einem im Grunde zusammengehörenden Literaturganzen, und es wurde vereinbart, dass auf gemeinsame Kosten ein jüngerer Mitarbeiter angeworben werden sollte. Ich konnte diesen in der Person von Dr. Polotsky präsentieren, nachdem auch mein Mäzen [August Pfeffer] in hochherziger Weise seinen Anteil auf zwei Jahre sichergestellt hatte, so dass die Arbeit im Juli 1931 ernstlich in Angriff genommen werden konnte.

Schmidt published a more popularized summary of this lengthy article in a speech presented to the annual meeting of the *Gesellschaft für Kirchengeschichte* in Berlin on November 9, 1932. In general there is no new information in it, except for an occasional formulation that happens to be more precise or detailed than the equivalent section of the lengthier report. Thus the statement about the discovery and acquisition:[2]

In the year 1930 *fellahin*, so-called *sebachin*, who rummage through the junk heaps in old abandoned towns and settlements in search of salty earth to fertilize the ground as a substitute for expensive potash, discovered in Medinet Madi, in the ruins of a town in the southwest of the Fayyum, a wooden box in the ruins of a house. The wooden box disintegrated when brought out to the light, but its content remained intact. The box contained a series of papyrus books, each surrounded by rough wooden covers. The discoverers immediately offered their treasure to an antiquities dealer in the Fayyum, who acquired the whole, surely for a ridiculously low sum. Unfortunately the dealer divided the papyrus books with two other antiquities dealers, so that they surfaced at different places on the antiquities market . . . [p. 6]

Meanwhile the London private collector had enlarged his possession by new acquisitions, and I too could in the spring of 1932 add a new

Im Jahre 1930 haben nun Fellachen, sog. Sebachin, die in den verlassenen alten Städten und Siedlungen die Schutthügel durchwühlten nach salzhaltigen Erdmassen für die Bedüngung des Bodens als Ersatz für das zu teure Kali, in Medinet Madi, einer Ruinenstadt im Südwesten des Fajum, eine Holzkiste in den Ruinen eines Hauses aufgefunden. Die Holzkiste zerfiel beim Herausheben ans Tageslicht, erhalten blieb ihr Inhalt. Die Kiste enthielt eine Reihe Papyrusbücher, jedes von rohen Holzdeckeln umgeben. Sofort haben die Finder ihren Schatz einem Antikenhändler im Fajum angeboten, und das Ganze ist von ihm sicherlich für ein Spottgeld erworben wooden. Leider hat der Händler die Papyrusbücher noch auf zwei andere Antikenhändler verteilt, so dass sie an verschiedenen Stellen auf dem Antikenmarkt auftauchten . . . [p. 6]

Inzwischen hatte auch der Londoner Privatsammler seinen Besitz durch neue Ankäufe vermehrt, und auch ich konnte noch im Frühjahr 1932 ein neues Stück

---

2. Schmidt, *Neue Originalquellen des Manichäismus*, 4, 6.

piece to the Berlin Manichaica [P$^{15995}$, *Synaxeis*]. Thus, as far as one can now tell, the whole find is united in the London and Berlin collection; each possesses about a half.

Schmidt did not state the purchase price. Later Rolf Ibscher mentioned a price that seems very high:[3]

In acquiring the discovery, sold very expensively by the three dealers for about 80,000 gold marks, it was clear to C. Schmidt that, apart from skill at restoring that yielded to no difficulties, this terribly rotted papyrus discovery could never be made accessible to scholarship. But he took upon himself the risk.

The bulk of one codex, P$^{15999}$, was in so bad a condition that it was referred to as the wig, and its conservation was ruled to be impossible. Yet, according to Rolf Ibscher, it was purchased for five thousand marks through a gift by Dr. W. Kohlhammer, the publisher of the Manichaica, who was enthusiastic enough about them to produce a Coptic type font imitating one of the hands of these codices.[4] In the spring of 1932 an exchange rate of 18 Reichsmark = £1 was reported.[5] This would mean that 80,000 marks equaled £4,444, and that 5,000 marks = £347.

C. R. C. Allberry's article of 1938, based primarily on the published report by Schmidt and Polotsky, only added occasional details to what was already in print. He dated Schmidt's initial experience of

---

3. Ibscher, "Mani und kein Ende," 219.

4. Rolf Ibscher in a August 29, 1957 letter to Carston Colpe.

5. In a letter from Sir Herbert Thompson to Chester Beatty concerning Ibscher's salary.

being shown a codex that he was able to identify as *Kephalaia* to 1930, which the original report had not made explicit.⁶

Søren Giversen reported in 1988 that the discovery dates to 1929, since a Danish Egyptologist, H. O. Lange, saw some of the material in Cairo on November 29, 1929, a dating that Schmidt verified in 1936.⁷

---

6. Allberry, "Manichaean Studies," 340.

7. Giversen, *Manichaean Papyri*, 1, speaks of "their rediscovery in 1929," and explains on page 3: "The first European scholar to see them was the Danish Egyptologist H. O. Lange who saw them in November 1929, when parts of them were offered for sale in Cairo. At that time they had been split up into blocks; outer pages, which were not very nice, had been removed and the papyri had also been damaged in other ways." Giversen, *Manichaean Coptic Papyri*, 3:vii–viii, reports in more detail: "The first scholar to see one of the Manichaean Coptic papyri from Medinet Madi was the Danish Egyptologist H. O. Lange, who saw the papyrus on 29 November 1929. This was noted in Lange's diary on a journey to Egypt in 1929–30 (The diary is in The Royal Library in Copenhagen, Ny kgl. Samling 3919, 4o), and is verified by Carl Schmidt in a letter to H. O. Lange dated 20 February 1936 (The Royal Library, Copenhagen, Ny kgl. Samling 3736, 4o)."

— 2 —

# The Acquisitions of Chester Beatty

THE ARCHIVES OF THE Chester Beatty Library have made unpublished materials available that fill in many details omitted in the published German reports.

Sir Chester Beatty already had in place a procedure for the procurement and processing of Egyptian manuscripts when the Manichaean materials appeared on the market. As early as January 26, 1925, he purchased two Coptic manuscripts from the leading Cairo antiquities dealer of the day, whose ledger sheet on which the receipt was written had as its printed heading: Maurice Nahman Antiquaire, 27, Rue El-Madabegh, 27. Early in 1930, Beatty had Nahman send to Eric G. Millar of the Department of Manuscripts of the British Museum various manuscripts he acquired on approval. Beatty wrote from Cairo to J. W. Corble of his London staff to notify Millar to that effect. Beatty asked Corble to "cable his [Millar's] opinion," using a "code" in cables. The code consisted of "Copper Mine" for a Coptic manuscript, "Silver" for a Greek papyrus, and "Gold Mine" for "rare and valuable." In at least one instance Millar consulted Sir Harold I. Bell, whereupon John Wooderson, Beatty's secretary, cabled to Beatty the contents of a resultant phone conversation between Millar and himself, Wooderson. This content was also communicated orally to Edwards, a mutual friend, who must have been traveling just then from London to Cairo. Millar also wrote to Corble enclosing for Beatty a letter providing written confirmation of the oral telegraphed message. This letter graded as a "Silver Mine" a third-century Septuagint text of Daniel (Chester Beatty Biblical Papyrus X) and as a "Gold Mine" a fourth-century text of Genesis (Chester Beatty Biblical Papyrus IV).

Thus, Beatty, himself no expert in such matters, but a mining entrepreneur, had at his disposal the British Museum and its access to British scholarship.

As recently as January 23, 1930, Hugo Ibscher had sent from Berlin a bill for conservation work recently completed in London; he anticipated returning to London in June 1930 to resume this activity. Thus, Beatty had at his disposal the leading papyrus conservator of the day.

A ledger sheet with Nahman's letterhead dated March 23, 1930, and made out to Beatty, at the time in Cairo, listed prices alongside fifteen items for sale. There are also notes as to which are to be returned and which kept. A last item, offered for £1200, was separated from the rest by an empty space. It was described as follows: "Two Coptic manuscripts a[nd] two binding[s] in wood." Underneath, notes were added that read:

| On approval | £700 | Mss |
|---|---|---|
|  | £500 | Mss |
|  | £40 | Binding |

The figure 40 was written on top of "incl."

On the back of the ledger sheet is then a list of the items to be purchased, with their prices, and a total. The last in the list reads:

| Two Bindings | £80 |
|---|---|

Beside this entry is the note: "Can be returned if B[ritish] M[useum] says they are later than VI century." Apparently the two bindings had originally been included in the price of the two codices, then had been priced apart as £40, then sold at £40 each. There is then a second ledger sheet, where these purchased items are listed, with the concluding handwritten note: "Settled with thanks, M. Nahman." The last in this list of acquired objects reads: "Two binding[s] in wood. 80." Thus, it seems clear that the two bindings were acquired, that they were associated with the two Coptic manuscripts taken on approval without payment at the time of the transaction, and that the covers, paid for on the spot but with the option to return them if not satisfied, were thought to be no later than the sixth century, which would also indicate the assumed date of the manuscripts. The wooden bindings indicate that at least one of the Coptic manuscripts was a codex, or

part of a codex, although the fact that the bindings could come to be priced and acquired separately indicates they were no longer attached to the manuscript.

On May 26, 1930, Nahman cabled from Cairo to Beatty in London: "Am expecting your kind answer regarding the books please wire your decision I am leaving tenth June." On May 28, 1930, Beatty replied by cable: "Ibscher Berlin only arrived two days ago expect wire you few days."

On May 31, 1930, Beatty cabled again:

> Doctor Ibscher thinks can do nothing with large book [part of the *Homilies*] also smaller book for which you ask five hundred pounds [second part of the *Psalms*] will be very difficult. Prepared to give two hundred pounds for smaller manuscript which was the cheaper one otherwise prefer to return same.

If the difference in size is not merely that of thickness, but of height and breadth, then the *Psalms*, measuring 27 by 17.5 cm, is the smallest (with the possible exception of the *Acts*, whose no-longer extant book block is of unknown dimensions, but whose eight extant leaves are also small), the others being 31.5 by 18 cm.[1]

On May 31, 1930, Beatty also wrote Nahman a confirming letter:

> With regard to the two manuscripts in question, one of which I have the option to buy from you for £500 and the second for £700, Dr. Ibscher's opinion is that nothing can practically be done with the more expensive one as it was too difficult, but that there was a chance of doing something on the other though from what I could gather he thought the price is very high; therefore, I would not care to exercise either of the options. I would be willing however to pay £200 for the book for which you asked £500 and take the chance of making something out of it.

But on June 2, 1930, Nahman cabled Beatty, who was by then in New York, so that on June 5, 1930, Corble cabled its text to him there:

> Surprised cost too high cannot accept your kind offer Professor Schmidt bought damaged one [*Kephalaia*] five hundred please keep till my arrival.

---

1. Ibscher, "Die Handschrift," *Manichäische Homilien*, 1:xiii. Ibscher's statement that all except the *Psalms* have the larger dimension would presumably presuppose his having measured the book block of the *Acts*, though this is not made explicit.

Meanwhile Ibscher had returned to Berlin, taking with him the smaller manuscript [the second part of the *Psalms*] to conserve, as well as a report about the two manuscripts by Sir Alan H. Gardiner. On June 3, 1930, Ibscher wrote Gardiner (a letter extant only in English translation):

> In the Museum everybody was impatiently waiting for your report about the new discovery. Schubart is so glad that the beautiful papyri have gone to London. As I suspected, Prof. Schmidt has also bought a Coptic book [*Kephalaia*] from Nahman. I think it is better for everybody that no mystery should be made about it. When Schmidt showed me his purchase and I could see that it was an exactly similar book to the larger one which had been offered to Mr. Chester Beatty, I told him what I had seen in London. Upon this, Schmidt showed his bill for the book, from which I saw that he had paid for his book over £400. But I did not tell anybody about the London prices. As Schmidt is probably the greatest expert on such things, I showed him Mr. Chester Beatty's book [the second part of the *Psalms*]. He told me at once what it was, and when he called today he said that it was an exceedingly valuable purchase. The language according to him was "Achmimic II." He considers that the book originated from Assiut—at least so I understood. Mr. Beatty's book contained, from what Schmidt could see, songs about the original man. He considers the complete books are the works of the "Manichaeans," in other words, there is no other known example of this work in existence. For this reason alone Schmidt considers that it would be very advisable to buy if possible everything which can be bought. Schmidt considers the book which has been purchased by Mr. Beatty—that is to say, the book I have here—is the most valuable book of the whole lot. I am very pleased for Mr. Beatty that he has made such a lucky purchase. Since I have been told what valuable treasures these books are, I must of course put aside all my considerations and recommend him to complete the purchase.
>
> I should also like to save the badly preserved books. Of course, Mr. Beatty should try to get a lower price on account of the great expense incurred by the restoration.
>
> Where Schmidt's purchase will ultimately go, he does not know himself because the local collections and libraries here have no money and he will be forced to resell them very soon because he has purchased them on borrowed money. Perhaps it may be possible for this book also to be bought by Mr. Chester

Beatty. It is in better preservation than the large book which has been offered to him. Of course, this is only a suggestion of mine. Schmidt would probably be able to dispose of this book in Germany, only in case it should ultimately go to America I think it would be well if it went to its brothers in London.

Gardiner thereupon telephoned Wooderson on June 6, 1930, who passed on to Corble the phone conversation in typed form, which read in part as follows:

Dr. Alan H. Gardiner (Park 5109) rang up about the <u>COPTIC MANUSCRIPTS</u> for which Mr. Chester Beatty is negotiating with Mr. Maurice Nahman. He has received the MSS. from the little man (? Dr. Ibscher) who was working with the papyri in England, and who has now gone back to Berlin. This man thought at first that it was not desirable to purchase the better of these two manuscripts, but now he writes that, having found out what it is, he certainly does advise the purchase of it, as it is a very valuable MS. . . .

If he could not get it cheaper, he should pay the full price asked, i.e., £500 . . .

Of the series, it is by far the most important manuscript and of greater importance than the one Dr. Schmidt has bought. Dr. Ibscher writes very excitedly about it. The date is well known. It is the upper part of the one Mr. Beatty has already got. It was cut in two and Nahman is selling it as two manuscripts. Mr. Chester Beatty has bought one-half and it is the other half which Dr. Gardiner has in his house and is telephoning about.

The manuscript offered for £700 should be rejected.

The above is Dr. Gardiner's message verbatim.

In spite of the claim that the written text is the verbatim equivalent of Gardiner's oral report, there seems to be considerable garbling at some stage in the transmission. For Ibscher had all along advocated the purchase of the better of the two manuscripts (in terms of conservation), the one offered at £500 [the second part of the *Psalms*]. The purchase of this manuscript is considered a fait accompli: Ibscher in his letter called it "Mr. Chester Beatty's book," and referred to it as "the book which has been purchased by Mr. Beatty." The point at which Ibscher has changed his mind in the light of Schmidt's enthusiasm is, in Ibscher's letter, clearly the larger manuscript for which £700 was the

asking price and which Ibscher had initially described in London as not conservable and hence had left with Gardiner in London before returning to Berlin (part of the *Homilies*). The reversal of opinion is in the formulation "Schmidt considers that it would be very advisable to buy if possible everything which can be bought," and in Ibscher's resultant comment, "I should also like to save the badly preserved books."

When Ibscher continues, "Of course, Mr. Beatty should try to get a lower price on account of the great expense incurred by the restoration," this is not only motivated by a concern to protect funds from which his restoration work might be paid, but reflects his recognition that the manuscript Schmidt had purchased for "over £400" "was an exactly similar book to the larger one which had been offered to Mr. Chester Beatty," in that the dimensions of both were 31.5 by 18 cm, so that the price might well be negotiated down from £700 to something "over £400."

The second part of the *Psalms* had already begun to be conserved, as Schmidt's reference to a manuscript containing "songs about the original man" would indicate. For among the unpublished materials that H. J. Polotsky submitted to Sir Herbert Thompson for distribution to Beatty and Crum, there is (in the Crum Archives in the Griffith Institute of the Ashmolean Museum at Oxford) a leaf labeled by Polotsky "C.B.1," containing his Coptic transcription (Crum Mss. 11.30.1) together with another leaf containing his English (!) translation (Crum Mss. 11.28.84 and Crum Mss. 11.28.122). At the top of the transcription is written "Hymns to the Primal Man." The translation begins: "We praise our father, the Primal Man." The psalm is numbered 213. Beside the numeral in the Coptic transcription is the appended note: "(precedes Allberry p. 1)." We apparently have before us here the beginning of both Ibscher's and Polotsky's work for Beatty, as "C.B.1" may suggest.

This identification of the second part of the *Psalms* as the first thing conserved for Beatty was confirmed in its publication:[2]

| | |
|---|---|
| When I then succeeded in Berlin in detaching a leaf of the part acquired by Prof. C. Schmidt, he was able to conclude with certainty | Als es mir dann in Berlin gelang, eine Seite des von Herrn Prof. C. Schmidt erworbenen Teiles freizulegen, konnte dieser mit |

2. Ibscher, "Die Handschrift," *Manichaean Psalm Book*, 2:vii.

| | |
|---|---|
| that this discovery had to do with works of Mani. A few weeks later in London I succeeded in detaching a leaf from one of the volumes acquired by Mr. A. Chester Beatty, and the conclusion of Prof. C. Schmidt found a complete confirmation. | Sicherheit feststellen, dass es sich bei dem Funde tatsächlich um Werke des Mani handelte. Wenige Wochen später gelang es mir dann auch in London, von einem der von Mr. A. Chester Beatty erworbenen Bände ein Blatt abzuheben, und die Feststellung von Herrn Prof. C. Schmidt fand eine volle Bestätigung. |
| If the examination of the manuscript in Berlin showed that one had acquired here a part of the *Kephalaia*, the first separated leaf of the Chester Beatty possession showed us that here the *Psalms* of the Mani community lie before us. | Ergab die Prüfung der Handschrift in Berlin, dass man dort einen Teil der "Kephalaia" erworben hatte, so zeigte uns das erste losgelöste Blatt des Chester Beatty Besitzes, dass hier die Psalmen der Manigemeinde vorlagen. |

Hence the discussion was not about whether to acquire the second part of the *Psalms*, which was already being conserved as Beatty's property, but rather whether to acquire the unconservable larger codex which was in Gardiner's home (part of the *Homilies*). One might hope to get it for about the same price Schmidt had paid for a similar-sized manuscript. This was especially true since "Professor Schmidt's manuscript is better preserved than the one which is offered to Mr. Beatty," according to Ibscher's letter. This refers to the manuscript offered at £700 that Ibscher had ruled could not be conserved. However, Wooderson misunderstood Ibscher's comment to refer to the smaller and hence cheaper manuscript offered at £500: "Professor Schmidt's manuscript is better preserved than the one which is offered to Mr. Beatty . . . If he could not get it cheaper, he should pay the full price asked, i.e., £500."

This confusion is apparently responsible for the further inaccuracy in Wooderson's report:

> Prof. Schmidt thinks that it comes from Akhmim, and it contains poems about the first man. It is the upper part of the one Mr. Beatty has already got. It was cut in two and Nahman is selling it as two manuscripts. Mr. Chester Beatty has bought one-half and it is the other half which Dr. Gardiner has in his house and is telephoning about.

The grain of truth in this statement about two halves of a codex is that Nahman, or middlemen from whom he acquired the manuscripts, had broken in two the *Psalms* codex as well as the second codex (the *Homilies*, see below), no doubt to increase the profit. But Nahman intentionally or unintentionally offered Beatty part of each of two codices on March 23, 1930, and the other part of each of the same two codices in April 1931. The fact that the two offered in 1930 were from different books should have been clear from references to them as different sizes, but this detail seems here overlooked. At the time, one was in Berlin, the other in London, so that the difference in size was not immediately apparent.

The most reasonable assumption is that the manuscript in Gardiner's home is the one offered at £700, which Ibscher initially ruled was not conservable, and hence which he did not take to Berlin to conserve, and which, as a result, Beatty proposed not to buy, but which now Ibscher (and no doubt Gardiner, assuming the situation was clear to him) was recommending should be bought. Wooderson, misunderstanding the situation, would have inferred, based on his misunderstanding, that "the manuscript offered for £700 should be rejected." The whole point of Ibscher's letter (and Gardiner's phone conversation) was apparently just the reverse: to urge the purchase of the larger codex offered at £700, part of the *Homilies*, for whatever price it would take, but presumably about the amount Schmidt had paid for another manuscript of the same larger format, the *Kephalaia*, namely somewhat "over £400." This figure suggesting £500 may have in part led to the false identification of the manuscript in question with the one offered at £500.

On June 6, 1930, Corble cabled Beatty what was wrongly taken to be Ibscher's (and Gardiner's?) recommendation—that the smaller manuscript, the second part of the *Psalms*, be acquired "whatever the price."

> Doctor Gardiner hears from Ibscher that after further study he advises you purchase Coptic manuscript offered by Nahman five hundred pounds. Manuscript bought by Professor Schmidt better preserved but one offered by Nahman of greater importance and they think you should purchase it whatever the price. Schmidt thinks manuscript comes from Akhmim and contains poems about first man.

On June 9, 1930, Beatty cabled Corble ("have answered Nahman direct"), though the decision, much less the price offered, is not recorded, neither is the cable nor hence the price preserved (presumably "over £400"). Nahman cabled Beatty the same day: "Accept your offer for small manuscript many thanks if you are interested in large one will accept same price will be in London end June."

Nahman arrived in London July 9, 1930, and in the coming days settled his accounts with Beatty's staff. A sheet in Nahman's hand reads:

> Mr. Chester Beatty
>
> Two Coptic manuscripts on papyrus.
> Fayoumic language and two wood binding of a Coptic manuscript on approval in London £1200

An appended note reads, in another hand, "One purchased and paid for at £500-0-0." Other scrawled notes coordinating with other acquisitions of that time tend to indicate that Nahman submitted this document in July 1930, and hence that the acquisition of the smaller codex, the second part of the *Psalms*, was completed then. This would indicate that Beatty had not quibbled further about the price Nahman asked for the smaller codex, but had followed fully what was taken to be Ibscher's advice to "pay the full price asked, i.e., £500" (Ibscher had actually proposed negotiating down the price of the part of the *Homilies* for which Nahman had asked £700), and that Nahman had hence returned to his original asking price for the second, larger codex (£700), after having in fact come down to £500 in his cable to Beatty of June 9, 1930.

On July 16, 1930, Wooderson handed Nahman a letter from Beatty:

> I understand you wish to leave the damaged Coptic manuscript . . . with me so that I can study them further . . . If you decide to do this Miss Kingsford will give you a receipt for them and will hold them subject to your instructions.

A two-ring binder that seems to have served in the early years as a kind of accessions book at the Chester Beatty Library has a page dated "1930—July," that apparently refers to this manuscript and to one of the wooden covers:

> Sent by Nahman, belonging to him.
> Papyrus with 1 cover. Safe B.
> (Ibscher 1930)
>    Given to Dr. Ibscher for Nahman.

A similar entry is on another page, completely marked through, apparently when its contents were transferred to another filing system:

> —Coptic Ms. With 1 cover
> belonging to Nahman in Box. [Marked out: Study Safe B]
> —2 Magical vellum fragments,
> 10 pages in each (Marked out: BM]
> belonging to Nahman.    Both given to Dr. Ibscher
>            for Nahman, May 10, 1932

The cryptic reference to giving the material to Ibscher for Nahman on May 10, 1932, can be explained by tracing the story from 1930 to 1932 as follows: At about the end of June 1930, Ibscher wrote Gardiner from Turin (a letter conserved only in an undated English translation):

> I hope you received my letter from Berlin, when I wrote to you about the Coptic manuscripts. Schmidt's hope to dispose of his book in Berlin or Germany has become rather doubtful, after the death of Harnack [June 10, 1930], on whose support he counted a lot. The Berlin Library intended to buy the book, and Harnack's decision would have been the determining factor. Has Mr. Chester Beatty bought both books?

On May 19, 1931, Ibscher wrote Beatty from Berlin (with the English translation made at that time):

| | |
|---|---|
| The Berlin purchases are still in Egypt. Prof. Schmidt has brought with him only one very badly preserved volume which looked quite hopeless [part of the *Kephalaia*]. Nevertheless I have succeeded in saving some more or less complete pages. I therefore would still advise you to acquire the volume that is still at the British Museum. Certainly one should obtain more from this volume than from the indifferent purchase of Prof. Schmidt. | Die Berliner Ankäufe sind noch in Ägypten, nur einen sehr schlecht erhaltenen Band hat Prof. Schmidt mitgebracht, der hoffnungslos aussah [part of the *Kephalaia*]. Trotzdem ist es mir gelungen, auch daraus ziemlich vollständige Seiten zu gewinnen. Daher möchte ich doch raten, dass Sie den noch im British Museum befindlichen Band erwerben. Sicher muss daraus noch mehr zu holen sein, wie aus dem schlechten Ankauf von Prof. Schmidt. |

| | |
|---|---|
| Our Berlin volume which we already have here is 30 centimeters in height and 20 centimeters in width. As soon as the other purchases arrive I will let you know their dimensions.<br><br>I presume that the dealers have divided the individual books in order to obtain more money. Of course we shall only know the real position when we can compare all the volumes.<br><br>Meanwhile I have already been able to separate several pages of your papyri, but I must first arrange here the fibers and place pieces before I can put them under glass. | Unser Berliner Band, den wir bereits hier haben, ist 32 ctm. hoch and 20 ctm. breit. Sowie die übrigen Ankäufe eintreffen, teile ich Ihnen die Grösse mit.<br><br>Ich vermute, dass die Händler die einzelnen Bücher geteilt haben, um mehr Geld heraus zu schlagen. Genaues wird man darüber erst sagen können, wenn alle Bände beieinander sind.<br><br>In der Zwischenzeit habe ich bereits einige Blätter von Ihrem Papyrus wieder ablösen können, doch muss ich hier erst die Fasern in Ordnung bringen und Stücke ansetzen bevor ich sie verglasen kann. |

"The volume which is still at the British Museum" must be the part of the *Homilies* offered at £700 that had been in the home of Gardiner.

On January 4, 1932, Sir Herbert Thompson wrote Beatty:

> I have a rather urgent letter from Dr. Carl Schmidt in Berlin, asking me to send him some news as to the Mani papyrus, which you had, I believe, on approval, as scholars are very anxious—and not in Germany only—to have some public statement as to these "mysterious" Manichaean manuscripts. But Dr. Schmidt, rightly I think, wishes to defer any such statements till the fate of this outstanding papyrus of the Mani find is settled—either by its passing into your collection—or finding an assured home, perhaps at Copenhagen, or else in Berlin. The important point is that it should be in hands where it would be accessible for study in association with those in your hands and those in the Berlin Museum.
>
> So I venture again to trouble you with a question as to whether it is still in your custody—and if so, may I be allowed to see it? and also whether you still have any thought of acquiring it, or not? If you do not, Dr. Schmidt tells me that Nahman has given him the first option of purchase; but he fears that if the matter is delayed much longer, Nahman may change his mind, and the opportunity of fixing it in safe hands may be lost.

On January 26, 1932, Wooderson replied on behalf of Beatty to the effect "that the Mani Papyrus is still the property of Mons. Nahman and is being held in safekeeping by Mr. Beatty at Baroda House." Thus, the manuscript must have been moved again, from the British Museum to Beatty's home.

On March 15, 1932, Nahman wrote in his wooden English to Beatty in Cairo concerning it:

> The present is to inform you that I have sold the Coptic manuscript I left towards you in London. When you honoured me of your kind visit you told me that you are not interested in this manuscript neither the magical parchemins [sic] Coptic and I expected two years and with my regret I missed you in London and to-day I think you will not be angry with me if I have found a buyer. Then I beg of you, Dear Sir, to be as so kind to hand to Mr. Ibscher the manuscript and the magical Coptic parchemin [sic].
>
> Will you be as so kind to send the answer of this letter to me that you agree to hand the manuscript and the magical parchemin [sic] to Mr. Ibscher when he will be in London. Your letter will allow to me to prove to my buyer that the matter is settled.

On March 19, 1932, Schmidt, also in Cairo, wrote on his calling card a note to Beatty regretting that he had to leave the next day for Luxor and hence would not be able to see Beatty in Cairo as he had hoped. At this time in Cairo, he would have liked to have completed the transaction with Nahman.

On March 21, 1932, Beatty replied to Nahman: "I will be pleased to deliver the same to Dr. Ibscher when he comes to London." A handwritten note at the bottom of the letter states: "Taken to Dr. Gardiner's—May 10."

In the initial essay presented by Carl Schmidt and H. J. Polotsky to the Berlin Academy of Sciences, published in 1933, $P^{15999}$ is referred to as "the papyrus book very recently added to the corpus of Berlin Manichaica."[3] Such a designation tends to set this codex off from the others as the most recent acquisition. Wilhelm Schubart recorded in the Inventarbuch of the Papyrus-Sammlung: "Coptic Papyrus Codex. Acquired through Prof. Carl Schmidt in Cairo 1932. Gift of Dr. W. Kohlhammer." The *Inventarbuch* had recorded for $P^{15995}$–$P^{15998}$:

---

3. Schmidt and Polotsky, "Ein Mani-Fund," 30.

"Acquired through Prof. Carl Schmidt, in Cairo, 1931. Gift of Mr. August Pfeffer 1933." The disparity in time between the acquisition in 1931 and the gift of the purchase price in 1933 reflects the difficulties Schmidt had finding funding for his initial acquisitions, a procedure that seems to have been quite independent of the acquisition of $P^{15999}$ in 1932 through Kohlhammer's gift. Thus, even though in the cases of $P^{15995}$ through $P^{15998}$ more than a single transaction in Egypt was involved (as many as seven transactions in the case of $P^{15996}$), the manuscripts shared a common date and a common donor that set them apart from $P^{15999}$. This would tend to indicate that it was $P^{15999}$ that had been offered unsuccessfully to Beatty and was ultimately acquired by Schmidt for Berlin. The reference in the *Inventarbuch* to acquisition in Cairo is not contradicted by Ibscher's securing the manuscript in London and taking it directly to Berlin. For Schmidt and Nahman had completed their negotiation in Cairo in March 1932.

Schmidt knew that Ibscher planned to be in London in April 1932 (Ibscher had written to London already on February 19, 1932), and Schmidt would have proposed to Nahman that Ibscher deliver the manuscript to the new owner on Ibscher's return to Berlin. Ibscher's decidedly negative assessment of possibly conserving this manuscript for Beatty is the same as the assessment of the impossibility of conserving $P^{15999}$ that prevailed when the manuscript was in Berlin.

At the time Beatty released his option and thus let Schmidt exercise his option, it was not known that the manuscript was part of the *Homilies* of which Beatty by then had acquired a second, smaller part (see below), which was being actively conserved in Berlin by Ibscher and edited for Beatty by Polotsky.

Of the initial acquisition of two manuscripts on approval of March 23, 1930, we may hence conclude that one seems to have been acquired in July 1930 (the latter part of the *Psalms*, Codex A), the other to have been turned down on March 21, 1932, so that Schmidt could buy it for Berlin (part of the *Homilies*, $P^{15999}$).

At some time, Beatty also acquired the rest of the *Psalms*, Codex A; the *Synaxeis*, Codex B; volume two of the *Kephalaia*, Codex C; and the smaller part of the *Homilies*, Codex D. Documentation available is inadequate to identify the actual acquisition of each of these, but some information is available.

In a letter of November 27, 1930, from Beatty to Gardiner, a codex is to be entrusted to Ibscher to take to Berlin for conservation:

> I am sending you the tin box containing the [inserted by hand: Papyri] Coptic Book.
>
> I suggest, before Dr. Ibscher puts it into his bag, that he carefully looks at it to be sure it is satisfactorily packed.
>
> I hope this book will act in a more gentlemanly manner than the other, and respond to the treatment better.

On November 27, 1930, Ibscher also wrote Beatty a receipt for "the new treasures of your collection . . . handed over to me by Mr. Alan H. Gardiner," with the hope that he can complete the conservation of much of them before his expected return to London in March 1931.

This "new treasures" must refer to an otherwise undocumented acquisition after Ibscher's return to Berlin at the end of the spring of 1930, since at the end of May or the beginning of June Ibscher had already taken to Berlin the part of the *Psalms* codex acquired March 23, 1930, whereas the part of the *Homilies* acquired March 23, 1930, was kept on approval in London until Beatty decided on March 21, 1932, not to acquire it and turned it over to Ibscher for Schmidt on May 10, 1932.

On December 30, 1930, Beatty had £300 cabled to Nahman, no doubt the payment of a bill. A memo to Nahman while in London of July 16, 1930, confirmed a telephone conversation listing acquisitions ("the Greek Papyri and the bindings") with the stipulation that "the balance of £600 [be paid] on or before the 1st January, 1931." Thus the payment of £300 cannot be associated convincingly with a Manichaean purchase.

Another leaf in the two-ring binder that served as a kind of acquisitions notebook records:

> <u>1931</u>. April. Cairo.
> —Manichaean Hymns (box: 15 1/4 x 10 1/4 in.)
>      Ibscher.
> —Manichaean Ritual (box 14 5/8 x 9 1/2 in.)
>   Laws      Ibscher.
> —3 Wooden covers [Marked out: "<u>Safe B</u>." Added: "<u>IX</u>"]

The page with the marked-out entries reads similarly:

Brought by Mr. Beatty April 1931.
  —<u>Manichaean Ms. Hymns</u>
    [Added note: <u>With Dr. Ibscher May 8/31</u>] PSALMS. Codex A.
  —<u>Manichaean Ms. Ritual Laws</u>
  —3 Covers [Marked out: Safe B.]  Cup X.c

A handwritten note on a large paper envelope in which three wooden boards are presently stored at the Chester Beatty Library states: "purchased Spring 1931." This confirms that the reference "Brought by Mr. Beatty April 1931" is the date of this acquisition.

What is underlined in addition to a characterization of the contents is no doubt the reference to where the material was currently deposited. The words "Safe B" are marked through, and "IX" added, no doubt when the covers were removed from the safe. The "Manichaean Hymns" are no doubt the other part of Codex A, the *Psalms*, completing the acquisition of this codex, of which only a part had been acquired in 1930. But the identification of the manuscript referred to with the terms Ritual and Laws is less clear, as is the identify of another possible acquisition late in 1930 suggested by the following:

On May 19, 1931, Ibscher wrote Beatty from Berlin:

> According to your wish I have photographed your papyri, and I am sending you proofs thereof.
>
> Should you wish to have more proofs, I will gladly have several more made.
>
> Besides these three books I have another thinner one which certainly belongs to the smaller book. Should you wish to have the photograph of that I will also have it done. I have already taken a few leaves from the books which are already under glass.

It is unclear what the reference to three books in Berlin belonging to Beatty envisages. If the "smaller" book means the *Psalms*, the only codex with smaller dimensions, then what is referred to as "another thinner one" that "belongs to" that codex would be the part of the *Psalms* acquired in April 1931. Then the "three books" would be the *Psalms*, part of which was taken to Berlin in May and June of 1930 and the rest after its acquisition April 1931; the unidentified codex taken to Berlin November 27, 1930; and the part of the *Homilies* acquired in April 31 and taken to Berlin shortly thereafter.

On June 11, 1931, Thompson met with Schmidt, and on June 15, 1931, wrote to Beatty:

> He [Schmidt] has been recently in Egypt, making inquiries about the find, and he is satisfied that the whole find was divided into 8 parts, between 3 dealers, of which I understand 5 are coming to Berlin, and he declared you had two Mss. and one on approval, viz. your Hymn book, now in Ibscher's hands and another (?). Is this so? and if so, would you let me see it— and also the papyrus on approval? I should very much like to get some idea of its (their?) size and contents, if possible.

On January 4, 1932, Thompson again wrote Beatty inquiring whether Beatty still had in his custody the manuscript on which he had an option, and, if so, whether Thompson could see it. Apparently, Beatty did not respond to this part of either letter. In the same way that Beatty's unresponsiveness to Thompson is unintelligible, Thompson's identification of Schmidt's material is unclear. The two manuscripts Thompson writes about could be the two parts of the *Psalms*, counted as one or as two, and the part of the *Homilies* acquired in April 1931, without reference to the unidentified codex taken to Berlin on December 27, 1930; or it could be counted, but the part of the *Homilies* not counted as a separate book.

Ibscher's translation of a report of February 19, 1932, concerning the state of his conservation gives evidence that by then, Beatty had acquired the three and a half codices that were ultimately to be his part of the Manichaean discovery, in addition to the part of a codex that he held but finally did not acquire:

> Now as regards your question, how many leaves are still [to] be expected. From my Report herewith (draft of proposed paper for the Berlin Academy) on the Mani-books, you will see how many leaves I have been able to reckon on in the Berlin *Kephalaia*-book (viz. 498 pages—c. 250 leaves), and I expect that all the volumes were of approximately the same size. If we assume that the Hymnbook [Codex A, the *Psalms*] was so, as would appear from its external appearance, there should result from it a further 150–200 leaves. The other two volumes [Codex B, the *Synaxeis*; Codex C, volume two of the *Kephalaia*], which Mr. Beatty has purchased, may contain as much. If therefore fortune favours me, I may hope to get 450–600 leaves from the entire property of Mr. Chester Beatty, of which about 100 are already separated. The *Homilies* [the

part of the codex that Ibscher had left in London in 1930 as
not conservable] are not included in this calculation (?). It was
a hopeless-looking mass which lay beside the Hymn-book. At
first I did not think that anything could be done with it—and
yet you see what important things have come out of it. I am
proposing now first to finish up the 37 leaves which constitute
it, as that will exhaust it. These leaves do not belong to any of
the others here—nor I expect to the volume which is still in
Mr. Beatty's possession [actually they do belong to the same
codex: the *Homilies*]. Perhaps I shall be able to establish this
point, when I come to London in April and we may perhaps
be able to see the volume together. I shall certainly bring over
a number of the completed Homily leaves. I think you will also
agree that I had better finish up this portion of the collection
first; and the next work will be to complete the Hymnbook, at
the same time working on the two other books, from which it
may be that more important results will come.

The comment that the *Homilies* "lay beside the Hymn-book"
would tend to identify the second manuscript acquired in April 1931
("Manichaean Ritual Laws") as the *Homilies*. This would mean that
in March 1930 and in April 1931 Nahman offered Beatty parts of
the same two codices—the *Psalms* and the *Homilies*. The reason for
Beatty's not acquiring the part offered in 1930 was no doubt Ibscher's
initial opinion that it could not be conserved, and Ibscher's failure to
communicate his subsequent willingness to attempt it. This is much
the same reaction as that reported concerning the part acquired in
1931: "a hopeless-looking mass ... At first I did not think that anything could be done with it—and yet you see what important things
have come out of it." This would hence be an added confirmation that
one has to do in both cases with the same hopeless-looking codex. On
March 21, 1932, Beatty released his option on the second manuscript
of 1930; he no doubt did not yet realize that it completed a manuscript he had bought in 1931. For Ibscher was not yet aware of it on
February 19, 1932, but hoped to investigate the question when in
London in April that year. By this time Beatty had released his option,
and Schmidt had closed his deal with Nahman.

Ibscher's reference to "the two other volumes, which Mr. Beatty
has purchased," would seem to envisage complete codices, since they
are assumed to be the same size as the *Kephalaia*, yielding some 150–
200 leaves. They would then be Codex B, the *Synaxeis*, and Codex C,

volume two of the *Kephalaia*. The details of their acquisition are not known, beyond the reference to one being taken by Ibscher to Berlin in the autumn of 1930.

A document entitled "Notes of Conference Mr. A. C. B. had with Dr. Alan Gardiner on Sunday, 8th May, 1932" (in which, according to a letter of May 10, 1932, from Beatty to Thompson, Ibscher was also involved), confirms the identity of the manuscript not acquired by Beatty with the Berlin manuscript P$^{15999}$, in the context of an imprecise overview of all the holdings (no doubt a garbled version of Ibscher's view reported more accurately in his letter of February 19, 1932, quoted above):

> It seems that Berlin has four manuscripts; one is the epistles [P$^{15998}$], one seems to be about the life of Mani [P$^{15997}$], one seems to be of the principles of the Mani religion [P$^{15996}$]—this latter manuscript consists of two parts which were bought separately, and really represents one book of about 500 leaves [read: pages]. The other two are of about 200 leaves each. [P$^{15995}$ involves only thirty-one leaves; there is no further Berlin codex, other than P$^{15999}$ treated below. A handwritten note in the margin reads: "This makes five in all."]
>
> Schmidt has recently bought, I assume through Berlin, another manuscript [P$^{15999}$] from Nahman which was the one stored with Mr. A. B. C.
>
> The Manichean manuscripts owned by Mr. A. C. B. consist of four: one is in the form of homilies of about 200 pages; one seems to be an epistle of 200 pages; one is a book of travels and journeys of about 500 [above the figure is written by hand: 50] pages, and one which was in two parts of about 400 pages [added in hand: "? in the form of hymns;" hence Codex A, the *Psalms*].

Søren Giversen quoted the third paragraph above about Beatty's acquisitions and interpreted it as follows:

> The book of travels and journeys is apparently identical to the *Homilies*, later published by Polotsky, and in a letter of 12 May 1932 Alan H. Gardiner speaks of "the 50 leaves relating to the journeyings of Mani" which Polotsky was going to publish. In a formal letter of 13 May 1932 A. Chester Beatty writes: "I am to cede to Dr. Polotsky publication rights in the 50 leaves relating to the journeyings of Mani provided he produces his work within a reasonable time."[4]

---

4. Giverson, *Manichaean Coptic Papyri*, 2: ix.

This identification of the third item as the *Homilies* is in part based upon accepting the correction of "500 pages" to read "50." A page of handwritten notes on which the formal typed report is apparently based does in fact use the figure 50. This figure and the reference to travels are clearly used in the later quotations to refer to Codex D, the *Homilies*, Polotsky's first publication. This would mean that the first item listed in the Notes of May 5 1932 as belonging to Beatty, though described as "in the form of homilies," is not Codex D, the *Homilies*. It and the second item ("an epistle") would have to be, one, Codex B, the *Synaxeis*; and the other, Codex C, volume two of the *Kephalaia*. For the fourth item "in two parts" would be, as the handwritten note ("? in the form of hymns") would indicate, Codex A, the *Psalms*. Thus, between March 23, 1930 (when one part of Codex A, the *Psalms*, was acquired), and February 19, 1932 (the date of Ibscher's report mailed from Berlin), Beatty must have acquired four additional items: a second part of Codex A and Codices B–D. If the second part of Codex A and Codex D were acquired in April 1931, the details of the acquisition of Codices B and C remain unknown.

Rolf Ibscher has indicated that the nomenclature of Beatty's codices as A, B, and C was used by Hugo Ibscher, but that the designation of the *Homilies* with a letter D was first introduced by himself.

> Hence, up until 1938, of Sir Chester Beatty's part of the discovery, fully conserved were only the pack of the *Psalms* and the incomplete *Homilies* that lay beside it at the acquisition of the discovery, which also as the first publication could be presented by Polotsky to an expectant public.
>
> Of the three codices, which my father had designated A, B, C as working titles (whereby the independent *Homilies* should actually have been designated D), A, B, and C were only partially restored.[5]

This is a further reflection of the sense in which the minor part of the Homilies codex that Beatty actually purchased, though it was the first thing that Hugo Ibscher completely conserved and that Polotsky published, was not fully recognized as an entity in its own right but was associated with the *Psalms*, in light of the fact that the *Psalms* and the *Homilies* had been acquired together.

---

5. Ibscher, "Mani und kein Ende," 220.

# — 3 —

# The Conservation by Hugo Ibscher

THE ORIGINAL ESSAY OF Schmidt and Polotsky had been accompanied by a report from Hugo Ibscher, who had been entrusted with the conservation of the codices. Here he described their physical condition as follows:[1]

When the Mani manuscripts reached the Berlin Museum through the good offices of Prof. Schmidt, they were described by a few gentlemen as much-used foot mats, and by others as balls of peat. This is the best way to describe the state of preservation of these precious treasures. Surely every observer stood before these so-called books in doubt as to whether anything could ever be gotten out of them . . .

The bad state of preservation does not come from the age of the manuscripts, but must be attributed to the place of discovery, which, according to the information of Prof. Schmidt given above, is to be sought in a Coptic settlement not far from the south end of the Moris sea. Much older papyrus

Als die Mani-Handschriften durch Hrn. Prof. Schmidt in das Berliner Museum gelangten, wurden sie von einigen Herrn als vielbenutzte Fussmatten und von andern als Ballen Torf angesprochen. Hiermit ist die Erhaltung dieser kostbaren Schätze am besten gekennzeichnet. Zweifelnd stand wohl ein jeder Beschauer vor diesen sogenannten Büchern, ob sich jemals daraus etwas würde gewinnen lassen . . .

Der schlechte Erhaltungszustand liegt nicht am Alter der Handschriften, sondern muss auf den Fundort zurückzuführen sein, der nach den obigen Mitteilungen von Prof. Schmidt in einer koptischen Niederlassung unweit des Südendes des Mörissees zu suchen ist. Weit ältere Papyrusfunde, wie

---

1. Hugo Ibscher, "Die Handschriften," 81–82.

finds, such as, e.g., the large Bible discovery that I have worked on in the most recent past, and many others, even if they have fallen into numberless fragments, are much firmer in their structure and can readily be handled with a little caution. In the case of the Mani manuscripts, water must have exerted its destructive effect, for all the volumes have after all been brought rather near to disintegration by the effect of the dampness. Only a few decades would have sufficed to make of the extant treasures a pile of humus, if the fortunate though unknown finder had not preserved them from that fate. The greatest danger for the manuscripts lies in this, that they are shot through and through with salt crystals, which penetrated through the effect of the water. Unfortunately the disintegration has advanced so far, however, that one may not apply any kind of dampness, through which the salt could have been removed, if one does not wish to endanger the manuscripts. Yet with the prerequisite knowledge, patience and skill one will succeed in saving even this treasure for science, as the successes attained thus far show quite adequately.

z.B. der von mir in letzter Zeit bearbeitete grosse Bibelfund und viele andere, sind, wenn auch in unzählige Fragmente zerfallen, in der Struktur viel fester und lassen sich bei einiger Vorsicht leicht hantieren. Bei den Mani-Handschriften muss das Wasser seine zerstörende Wirkung ausgeübt haben, sind doch alle Bände durch die Einwirkung der Feuchtigkeit dem Zerfall recht nahe gebracht. Nur wenige Jahrzehnte hätten genügt, um aus den vorhandenen Schätzen einen Haufen Humuserde zu machen, wenn nicht der glückliche, unbekannte Finder sie davor bewahrt hätte. Die grösste Gefahr für die Handschriften liegt darin, dass dieselben vollständig von Salzkristallen, die durch die Einwirkung des Wassers hineingedrungen sind, durchsetzt sind. Leider ist der Zerfall aber schon so weit vorgeschritten, dass man keinerlei Feuchtigkeit anwenden darf, wodurch das Salz entzogen werden könnte, will man nicht die Handschriften gefährden. Mit der nötigen Sachkenntnis, Geduld und Geschicklichkeit wird es aber gelingen, auch diesen Schatz für die Wissenschaft zu retten, wie die bisher erzielten Erfolge zur Genüge beweisen.

In 1964–1965 Rolf Ibscher summarized in retrospect the conservation activity of his father, Hugo Ibscher, as follows:[2]

---

2. Rolf Ibscher, "Über den Stand," 50–51.

[p. 51] [The Dublin] *Homilies* and *Psalmbook* and the Berlin *Kephalaia*—that was the sequence to which he [Hugo Ibscher] adhered. The other codices were worked on from time to time, to make it possible for Carl Schmidt to dip into them and thus to provide an overview for him and for himself...

[p. 50] Actually already in 1937 my father had ... stopped exerting his over-taxed strength regularly on them.

[p. 51] [The Dublin] Homilien, Psalmbuch und Berliner Kephalaia—das war die Reihenfolge, bei der er [Hugo Ibscher] blieb. Die anderen Codices wurden zwischendurch ankonserviert, um Carl Schmidt ein Anlesen zu ermöglichen und damit einen Überblick ihm und sich zu verschaffen ...

[p. 50] Mein Vater hatte eigentlich ... schon 1937 aufgehört, regelmässig seine überforderte Kraft daran zu setzen ...

In 1965 Rolf Ibscher reported on his father's conservation as follows:[3]

The making accessible of the papyrus material that at first was put in motion with so much effort, since it was rotted, made into peat, with the leaves completely bonded together because of salt crystals that had soaked in, of which Hans Heinrich Schaeder wrote: "Ibscher is performing true miracles of meditation and concentration when confronted with the material," came after about seven years in 1938 [the year Schmidt died] to what amounted to a standstill, since this work overexerted excessively the eyes and the nerves.

A letter of my father to Sir Chester Beatty of 1938 expressed that clearly: "The tension is too great. I must for a while interpose smaller tasks in between that provide a great deal of variety. One cannot make marathon runs constantly without paying the price."

Die anfänglich mühsam in Gang kommende Aufschliessung des verrotteten, vertorften, durch eingeschwemmte Salzkristalle die Blätter miteinander völlig verfilzenden Papyrusmaterials, von der Hans Heinrich Schaeder schrieb: "Ibscher vollbringt wahre Wunder der Andacht und Konzentration vor dem Material," kam nach rund sieben Jahren 1938 [the year Schmidt died] so gut wie zum Stillstand, da diese Arbeit masslos die Augen und die Nerven überbeansprucht.

Ein Brief meines Vaters an Sir Chester Beatty 1938 drückt das klar aus: "Die Anspannung ist zu gross. Ich muss einmal eine Zeitlang [p. 220] abwechslungsreiche kleinere Arbeiten da zwischen schieben. Man kann nicht ungestraft dauernd Marathonläufe machen."

---

3. Rolf Ibscher, "Mani und kein Ende," 219–20.

Hence, up until 1938, of Sir Chester Beatty's part of the discovery, fully conserved were only the ball of the Psalms and the incomplete *Homilies* that lay beside it at the acquisition of the discovery, which also as the first publication could be presented by Polotsky to an expectant public.

Of the three codices, which my father had designated A, B, C as working titles (whereby the independent *Homilies* should actually have been designated D), A, B, and C were only partially restored.

Of the four Berlin codices, only the codex of the *Kephalaia* was being worked on, and was edited by Polotsky and from 1934 on by Böhlig.

In 1954 Rolf Ibscher had described the teamwork as follows:[4]

Dr. Polotsky functioned as coworker and the actual first editor both for parts of the London as well as for the Berlin manuscripts and, following him from 1934 on, when the awful political conditions in Germany forced a change, the young Charles Allberry for London and Dr. Böhlig for Berlin. From 1939 on, the continuation of the work for London stood still, and for Berlin too both the conservation [p. 3] and the editorial work came to a standstill in the

---

4. Rolf Ibscher, "Wiederaufnahme," 2–3. This unpublished lecture was presented at the twenty-third International Congress of Orientalists on August 23, 1954. The Chester Beatty Library supplied a typescript of this lecture to the Manichaean archives of the Institute for Antiquity and Christianity. The work is cited according to the typescript except where otherwise indicated. See also *Proceedings of the Twenty-Third*, 359–60.

course of the year 1940. My father no longer found inner repose for the minute detailed work on the Mani manuscripts.

torische [p. 3] als auch die editorische Arbeit zum Erliegen. Mein Vater fand keine innere Ruhe mehr für die minutiöse Feinarbeit an den Mani-Handschriften.

In 1955 Rolf Ibscher described as follows the way the project had finally ground to a halt:[5]

During the war this minutely detailed work, which could only be carried out in an atmosphere of the greatest repose, under secure conditions and with an absolute freedom from nervous strain, by the very nature of the case ultimately came to a complete halt. Also the scholarly work, handled at the end by Böhlig alone after the death of Schmidt in 1938, came to a standstill. The death of my father on May 26, 1943, marked a temporary end to all further conservation of the material.

Im Kriege kam diese minutiöse Feinstarbeit, die nur in einer Atmosphäre grösster Ruhe, gesicherter Verhältnisse und bei absoluter nervlicher Nichtbelastung geleistet werden kann, naturgemäss schliesslich zum völligen Erliegen. Auch die wissenschaftliche Erschliessung, zuletzt nach dem Tode von Schmidt 1938 von Böhlig allein bewältigt, kam zum Stilistand. Der Tod meines Vaters am 26. Mai 1943 setzte einen vorläufigen Schlussstrich unter jegliche weitere konservatorische Aufbereitung des Materials.

Rolf Ibscher itemized in 1954 what his father had conserved:[6]

For about 9 years my father had occupied himself almost without interruption with separating the leaves from the book blocks and impregnating and glassing the rescued material. His annual trips out of the country had become his recreation from this work that exhausted eyes and nerves.

Rund 9 Jahre hatte mein Vater fast ununterbrochen sich mit der Ablösung der Blätter von den Buchblöcken und der Imprägnierung des geretteten Materials und mit seiner Verglasung beschäftigt. Erholung von dieser die Augen und Nerven strapazierenden Arbeit

---

5. Rolf Ibscher, "Das Konservierungswerk," 2. This is an unpublished lecture presented at the Eighth International Papyrologists Congress in Vienna in 1955; Carsten Colpe supplied a typescript of this lecture to the Manichaean archives of the Institute for Antiquity and Christianity.

6. Rolf Ibscher, "Wiederaufnahme," 5–6.

# The Conservation by Hugo Ibscher

According to his last estimation my father hoped at the beginning of the war to be able to end the work in nine more years. But it was to come otherwise. Then what was the status of the whole undertaking when the fateful year 1945 created also for this discovery a completely new kind of situation. What was extant conserved, how much was edited, and what ended up behind a thick question mark?

I begin with the Berlin part of the discovery:

Since 1941 10 fascicles of the important *Kephalaia* manuscript were in print, i.e., 125 leaves or 250 pages of text. In addition 25 leaves or 50 pages were in manuscript form with Kohlhammer in Stuttgart.

There may have been 100 more leaves or 200 pages of text already glassed, but not yet read.

Except for a remainder of some 20 leaves, this manuscript in the original has not, or not yet, returned to German possession. Neither I nor anyone else can say more about it.

The remainder of the manuscript, designated by my father as no longer conservable, was conserved in 1951 in connection with my first stay in London.

The second important Berlin manuscript is the collection of Mani's *Letters*. It was taken by me in 1944 to Bavaria together with the British manuscripts, where it still is, and in the meantime is being worked on there.

waren ihm dabei seine jährlichen Auslandsreisen geworden. Nach seiner letzten Schätzung hoffte mein Vater zu Beginn des Krieges, das Werk in weiteren 9 Jahren beenden zu können. Aber es sollte anders kommen. Wie war nun der Stand des ganzen Unternehmens, als das schicksalsschwere Jahr 1945 auch für diesen Fund eine völlig neuartige Lage schuf. Was lag konserviert vor, wieviel war ediert und was endete hinter einem dicken Fragezeichen? —

Ich beginne mit dem Berliner Fundanteil:

Seit 1941 lagen 10 Lieferungen der wichtigen Kephalaia-Handschrift gedruckt vor, d.h. 125 Blatt oder 250 Seiten Text. Dazu kamen 25 Blatt oder 50 Seiten im Manuskript bei Kohlhammer in Stuttgart liegend.

Verglast schon, aber noch ungelesen mögen weitere 100 Blatt oder 200 Seiten Text vorgelegen haben.

Bis auf einen Rest von einigen 20 Blatt ist diese Handschrift im Original jetzt nicht mehr oder noch nicht wieder in deutschen Besitz zurückgekehrt. Mehr kann weder ich noch irgend jemand anderes darüber aussagen.

Der Rest der Handschrift, von meinem Vater als nicht weiter konservierbar bezeichnet, wurde 1951 im Anschluss an meinen ersten Londonaufenthalt konserviert.

Die zweite wichtige Berliner Handschrift ist die Briefsammlung Manis. Sie wurde zusammen mit den Britischen Handschriften von mir 1944 nach Bayern gebracht, wo sie noch liegt und inzwischen dort bearbeitet wird.

[Six] leaves of this collection of *Letters* separated by my father as well as 41 [31] leaves of another manuscript [P15995] still conserved by my father and two complete book units thus far unconserved [P15997 and P15998] have also not yet returned into German possession. That means ca. 500 leaves yet to be conserved or about 1,000 pages of text ...

[p. 6] The Chester Beatty part of the discovery was in the fortunate situation of having survived the war and its consequences complete and intact.

The book of *Homilies* is edited and conserved. It appeared in 1934 after four years of work, as the first publication of the discovery. It was followed in the autumn by the first fascicle of the Berlin *Kephalaia* manuscript. Hence 20 years have passed since it began to appear. The text of the *Homilies* embraces 48 leaves or 96 pages of text. Further, the second part of the *Psalms* was edited by Charles Allberry. In 1938 it appeared with 117 leaves or 234 pages of text. The first part is on hand with 53 leaves conserved, i.e., 106 pages of text. It too was edited by Allberry, but up to the present the manuscript has not yet been printed. To this one must add 47 leaves or 94 pages of text of Codex C of the Chester Beatty manuscripts, which alongside of another text is a continuation of the Berlin *Kephalaia*.

[Sechs] von meinem Vater abgelöste Blätter dieser Briefkollektion sowie 41 [31] Blätter einer anderen Handschrift [P15995], von meinem Vater noch konserviert und zwei vollständige bisher unkonservierte Bucheinheiten [P15997 und P15998] sind ebenfalls noch nicht in deutschen Besitz zurückgekehrt. Das bedeutet ca. 500 noch zu konservierende Blätter oder rund 1000 Seiten Text ...

[p. 6] Der Chester Beatty-Fundanteil ist in der glücklichen Lage gewesen, den Krieg und seine Folgeerscheinungen komplett und heil überstanden zu haben.

Konserviert und ediert ist das Homilienbuch. Es erschien im Jahre 1934 nach vierjähriger Arbeit als erste Veröffentlichung des Fundes. Ihm folgte im Herbst die erste Lieferung der Berliner Kephalaiahandschrift. [Zwanzig] Jahre sind also mithin seit diesem Ersterscheinen vergangen. Der Homilientext umfasst 48 Blatt oder 96 Seiten Text. Ferner wurde der zweite Teil des Psalmenbuches ediert durch Charles Allberry, im Jahre 1938 erscheinend mit 117 Blatt oder 234 Seiten Text. Der erste Teil liegt mit 53 Blatt konserviert vor, d.h. also 106 Seiten Text. Er wurde ebenfalls von Allberry ediert, aber bisher wurde das Manuskript noch nicht gedruckt. Dazu kommen 47 Blatt oder 94 Seiten Text des Codex C der Chester Beatty Handschriften, der neben einem anderen Text eine Fortsetzung der Berliner *Kephalaia* ist.

A typescript containing a summary of this speech presents somewhat different figures:

| The discovery as conserved and edited up until 1951: | Bis 1951 konservierter und edierter Fund: |
|---|---|
| A) Sir Chester Beatty | A) Sir Chester Beatty |
| 1. *Homilies*, 48 leaves or 96 pages of text | 1. Homilien 48 Blätter oder 96 Seiten Text |
| 2. *Psalms*, Part 2, 117 leaves or 234 pages of text | 2. Psalmbook Part II 117 Blätter oder 234 Seiten Text |
| 3. *Psalms*, Part 1, 53 leaves or 106 pages of text by Charles Allberry, extant only as a manuscript | 3. Psalmbook Part I 53 Blätter oder 106 Seiten Text durch Charles Allberry nur als Manuskript vorliegend |
| 4. Codex C, 47 leaves or 94 pages of text, thus far unpublished. | 4. Codex C 47 Blätter oder 94 Seiten Text unpubliziert bisher |
| B) Berlin part of the discovery | B) Berliner Fundanteil |
| 1. *Kephalaia*, 10 fascicles published | 1. Kephalaia 10 Lieferungen publiziert |

Ca. 100 further leaves were conserved, of which only 25 leaves have been read by Böhlig, extant as a manuscript with Kohlhammer. The remainder has not been read ...

Not yet returned, up to the present, are two unconserved manuscripts. According to the Berlin catalogue of accessions of what was then the Papyrus Collection, it is a matter of the numbers: 15995 and 15999 [read: P$^{15997}$ and P$^{15998}$]. Both books may produce ca. 500 leaves or 1,000 pages of text. Furthermore not yet returned are Codex No. 15996 *Kephalaia* as well as 31 leaves of Codex No. 15997 [read: P$^{15995}$] and 6 leaves of Codex 15998, which is identical with the codex that is in Bavaria.

Konserviert wurden ca. 100 Blätter mehr, davon nur 25 Blätter durch Böhlig gelesen, als Manuskript bei Kohlhammer liegend. Der Rest ungelesen ...

Bisher noch nicht zurückgekehrt sind zwei unkonservierte Handschriften, nach dem Berliner Standkatalog der früheren Papyrussammlung handelt es sich um die Nummern: 15995 und 15999 [read: P$^{15997}$ und P$^{15998}$]. Beide Bücher dürften ca. 500 Blätter oder 1.000 Seiten Text ergeben. Ferner sind noch nicht zurückgekehrt Codex Nr. 15996 *Kephalaia* sowie 31 Blätter von Codex Nr. 15997 [read: P$^{15995}$] und 6 Blätter des Codex 15998 der identisch ist mit dem in Bayern befindlichen Codex.

The full text and the summary present both garbled and conflicting information about the conservation carried out by Hugo Ibscher:

### P$^{15995}$: THE *SYNAXEIS*

The full text lists 41 leaves from an unidentified codex, which is presumably an inaccurate reference to the thirty-one leaves of this codex Hugo Ibscher conserved. The summary lists the figure correctly as 31, but identifies these leaves inaccurately as belonging to P$^{15997}$, the *Acts*. The rest of the *Synaxeis* codex was in Schondorf being conserved by Rolf Ibscher. However, he did not seem to know this but maintained inaccurately he was conserving P. 15998, the *Letters*.

### P$^{15996}$: THE *KEPHALAIA*

The full text lists 125 leaves published, twenty-five edited for publication, and a hundred conserved but not edited, for a total of 250 leaves or 500 pages The summary includes the 25 edited for publication within the 100, thus making a total of 225 leaves or 450 pages. A statistical table appended to the summary lists for the Berlin part "ca. 230 Blätter oder 460 Seiten," ["ca. 230 leaves or 460 pages"]. The following line reads, "*Kephalaia*," which may mean that these figures refer only to that codex. Perhaps only *Kephalaia* leaves are listed because the summary was designated "conserved and edited" material. For even though the statistical table lists its contents as what was "conserved," it probably is intended to be limited to what is conserved and edited. But even if the figure is intended to refer only to the *Kephalaia*, there is still a discrepancy between the three statements: 250, 225, or ca. 230 leaves. In addition, the full text listed "some 20 leaves" as still accessible in Berlin, and the summary listed as conserved by Rolf Ibscher: "Rest der *Kephalaia* ca. 25 Blätter oder ca. 50 Seiten Text" ["remainder of the *Kephalaia* ca. 25 leaves or ca. 50 pages of text"]. Both references, in spite of the discrepancy, are presumably to the same material (see below). Thus, the total number of the leaves of the *Kephalaia* that had been conserved could be variously calculated as 270, 275, 245, 250, or 255. In this data no distinction is made between the number of leaves originally in the codex, the number conserved, and the number extant.

## $P^{15997}$: THE *ACTS*

The full text refers to "two complete, thus far unconserved, book units" as not yet returned, one of which must, by a process of elimination, have been this codex. In the summary it is inaccurately ascribed the number $P^{15995}$ (just as, conversely, the 31 leaves of $P^{15995}$ are inaccurately given the number P. 15997). Since Hugo Ibscher had conserved at least eight leaves not mentioned by Rolf Ibscher, it was inaccurate to refer to this text simply as "thus far unconserved."

## $P^{15998}$: THE *LETTERS*

The full text and the summary list six leaves conserved by Hugo Ibscher. Both inaccurately identify the codex in Schondorf as the rest of $P^{15998}$, since in reality it was the rest of the *Synaxeis* codex. Some 22 leaves of $P^{15998}$, reported subsequently to have been in the Ibscher home throughout the war and immediate postwar period, are not mentioned (see below).

## $P^{15999}$: THE *HOMILIES* (BERLIN PART)

The full text apparently includes this codex among the "two complete books thus far unconserved," "ca. 500 leaves or 1,000 pages of text" that have not yet been returned. The summary stated that the two complete codices that had not yet been returned contained a total of "ca. 500 leaves or 1,000 pages of text." This reflects the standard estimate (based on the *Kephalaia*) of codices of about 250 leaves each. But the Berlin part of this codex was not a complete codex, but was part of the same codex as the *Homilies* text of Sir Chester Beatty, which consisted of forty-eight leaves. Hence, the Berlin part should have involved about 200 leaves.

It is clear that this list of what Hugo Ibscher had conserved is seriously imprecise and self-contradictory. It is obviously not based on well-organized records prepared during the conservation procedure. Nor is it based on a new inventory of the conserved leaves themselves, which had been taken to Leningrad after the war and had not yet been returned (see below). The list could have been based on published information and the *Inventarbuch* (inventory book) of the papyrus collection, to which it actually refers. But so many of its er-

rors would have been corrected by a careful study of such materials that one must assume that the list was based on such records only in a superficial way or on memory or on word of mouth. The list reads more as if it were heavily based on memory or oral tradition, whatever Rolf Ibscher could hurriedly put together, given the death or departure of the principals in the story. Alexander Böhlig, the only scholar still connecting the prewar and postwar periods, apparently did not have much clearer information than Rolf Ibscher. Thus, the postwar academic community began with fragmentary, very inexact, and often quite misleading information about each codex in the Berlin collection. It may be just as well that Rolf Ibscher's first public report was not published.

The amount of material that Hugo Ibscher conserved in the Berlin holdings cannot as a consequence be stated with precision, but can only be estimated as around 300 leaves, if one includes half-conserved material.

With regard to the London material, the situation may be less confused. For Rolf Ibscher's report is based on his having actually seen the material in London, none of which was lost. Thus the listed total of 265 leaves conserved by Hugo Ibscher may be accurate.

Such numbers would suggest that Hugo Ibscher succeeded in separating a total of about 565 leaves. This was no doubt a remarkable achievement, given the condition of the codices when entrusted to him, the degree of legibility of much of what he separated, and the fragile nature of his health at the time. His lifetime of conservation work meant that he represented the state of the art in the 1930s, which is one of the few fortunate dimensions of an otherwise misfortune-ridden story.

Alexander Böhlig has reported on the administrative dimensions of the original project:[7]

| | |
|---|---|
| In Germany the Berlin Academy of Sciences took over the task. As long as Carl Schmidt was an | In Deutschland nahm sich die Berliner Akademie der Wissenschaften der Aufgabe an. |

---

7. Böhlig, "Die Arbeit," 180ff. See also *WZUH* 10 (1961) 157–61; and *Actes du XXVe Congrès International des Orientalistes, Moscou 9–16 août 1960*, 1 (1962) 535–41. A typescript of the address of 1960 is in the Chester Beatty archives. The form published in *Mysterion und Wahrheit* has been copyedited but not substantively altered. Quotations are from *Mysterion und Wahrheit*.

official of the Kommission für spätantike Religionsgeschichte, the enterprise belonged to that area. After his departure, it was transferred to an enterprise under his leadership in the Orientalische Kommission. Meanwhile Hugo Ibscher had separated and put under glass rather large numbers of leaves, so that it was quite appropriate, after Polotsky had been called as full professor to Jerusalem, for each of the owners to engage one's own worker. For the Chester Beatty manuscripts C. R. C. Allberry was engaged, whose death in the war I would like also here bitterly to lament. The Berlin Academy commissioned me, and I am very happy that I had been introduced into this work and its problems back then by Polotsky himself. After Carl Schmidt's death in 1938 I took over the work on my own responsibility. Up to the war there were a total of 574 pages that were presented in print. W. Kohlhammer of Stuttgart, who had new Coptic letters cut just for this purpose based upon the hand of the *Kephalaia*, took over the printing and publishing.

Solange Carl Schmidt Beamter der Kommission für spätantike Religionsgeschichte war, gehörte das Unternehmen zu deren Bereich, um nach seinem Ausscheiden als ein unter seiner Leitung stehendes Unternehmen in die Orientalische Kommission überführt zu werden. Inzwischen hatte Hugo Ibscher grössere Mengen von Blättern abgelöst und unter Glas gebracht, so dass es durchaus angemessen war, nach der Berufung von Polotsky als Ordinarius nach Jerusalem für jeden der Besitzteile einen eigenen Bearbeiter zu bestellen. Für die Chester-Beatty-Handschriften wurde C. R. C. Allberry bestellt, dessen Tod im Kriege ich auch an dieser Stelle aufs tiefste beklagen möchte. Die Akademie Berlin beauftragte mich, und ich bin sehr froh, damals von Polotsky selbst in diese Arbeit und ihre Probleme eingeführt worden zu sein. Nach Carl Schmidts Tode im Jahre 1938 übernahm ich die Arbeit in eigener Verantwortung. Bis zum Kriege wurden von allen Beteiligten insgesamt 574 Seiten im Druck vorgelegt. Den Druck und Verlag hatte W. Kohlhammer, Stuttgart, übernommen, der eigens nach dem Schrifttyp der *Kephalaia* neue koptische Lettern schneiden liess.

# — 4 —

# Beatty, Ibscher, and Polotsky

On May 7, 1931, Sir Alan H. Gardiner wrote to Paul Schubart:

As you know, Coptic is not my immediate branch of study, but it appears that both Mr. Chester Beatty and Dr. [Hugo] Ibscher wish me to take a hand in negotiating the arrangements for the publication of the Manichaean books belonging to the former. Both Dr. [W. E.] Crum and Sir Herbert Thompson have been here and have discussed the matter fully with Ibscher and myself and this letter is intended to set forth Mr. Chester Beatty's wishes after hearing the results of our consultations. Crum's interest is confined to the lexicographic aspects of the books, which he wishes to utilize for his dictionary. Sir Herbert Thompson is too busy to devote any large part of his time to this work, but since Mr. Chester Beatty naturally desires an English editor for his publication, Thompson has declared himself ready to accept such an editorship, provided that the preliminary copying and translation are performed by someone else.

Everything points to the employment of Herr [H. J.] Polotsky for the purpose as an almost ideal solution, the more so if he is engaged, under Professor [Carl] Schmidt's direction, to copy the corresponding Berlin books. Mr. Chester Beatty would be ready to remunerate Herr Polotsky at the same rate of payment as is arranged for Polotsky in connection with the Berlin books, and would be most grateful if you would administer the requisite sum of money for the purpose. He would send you through me a preliminary sum of £50 for the beginning of the payments, but asks that when this sum is approaching its end he should receive (through me) an exact account of the work done and the payments made.

> Mr. Chester Beatty will be most glad to grant Professor Schmidt the right to study and utilize in a general way the books belonging to him, if Professor Schmidt is prepared to give to his English colleagues the same rights with regard to the Berlin books. As I have already said, Crum wishes merely to use the texts for his Dictionary, but it would be useful for Thompson to have copies of the Berlin books to utilize alongside the Chester Beatty books. If I might make a suggestion of my own, would it not be well for Polotsky to make these copies in copying ink, so that separate copies could be kept by Schmidt, Polotsky, Crum and Thompson? The existence of separate copies in the hands of each of the scholars interested would, I think, be of great value. A point on which Mr. Chester Beatty lays great stress is that he would like his books, after they have been unrolled by Ibscher, to be kept in the *Papyrusabteilung* of the Neues Museum and to be accessible for study by Professor Schmidt and Herr Polotsky only there. Mr. Chester Beatty would be most grateful if you would consent to take this matter up with the Director of the Museum and to obtain the latter's consent and authorization.
>
> I think that the most practical procedure would be if the copies for Crum and Thompson, as well as the accounts for Mr. Chester Beatty, could be sent to me from time to time. I would act as a sort of London agent, and distribute what is sent to the persons concerned.
>
> It is a wonderful discovery and also a wonderful opportunity for friendly and sensible international co-operation. That is one of the reasons, as you can imagine, why I personally am so much interested in it.

On June 6, 1931, Sir Herbert Thompson wrote to Miss Kingsford of Beatty's staff:

> I venture to trouble you with a question or two, as I know Mr. Beatty is an extremely busy man, and you can probably judge best when and how he can be approached on the side of his MSS. I dare say you have heard from Dr. A. H. Gardiner, that, owing to the impossibility of my friend, W. E. Crum, undertaking the supervision of the treatment of Mr. Beatty's new Coptic papyri, it has fallen to me—subject to Mr. Beatty's approval —to consider the questions of his relation to Berlin. Of course you know that these papyri relate to the Manichaean religion, and that part of the same find has gone to Berlin. Prof. Carl Schmidt (of Berlin University) is coming over here "early in June" to consider questions of joint dealing with this material.

My proposed attitude is somewhat as follows:—

1. Mutual communication of the material on both sides.

2. Working out of the material by a single editor, if possible—Polotsky being proposed—under supervision of C. Schmidt and myself.

    These two conditions are almost essential. It may be found that parts of the same MS are divided between the two collections. This cannot be settled till the whole mass has been taken to pieces and mounted under glass.

3. The question of publication. I feel that this is a subject which in the present state of affairs may, and should be, postponed. There is no hurry about it and I think it very desirable that Mr. Beatty should not be committed hastily to any scheme. I should not (nor, I fancy, would he) wish to see his MS appear as an appendix to a German publication. Such a publication would have to be a Government publication, and would almost necessarily be a slow—(also, *entre nous*, Prof. C. Schmidt has the reputation of being a very slow hand at producing things). At present, judging from the photographs I have seen of both Mr. Beatty's papyri and the German ones, they are distinct volumes, and there is no reason why the former should not be issued in a separate form. Of course if Polotsky is the sole editor of the texts, he would have to be allowed to take his own course in running the two sets of papyri side by side. But that is no reason why they should be one publication and I suggest that in any case, in the present state of affairs, no definite arrangement as to publication should be entered into.

I shall be very glad to hear how far these views have Mr. Beatty's approvation—and what he may have further to suggest. I may add that a joint publication would give rise to rather difficult questions on the financial side—besides details of printing, illustrations, etc.

On June 15, 1931, Thompson wrote Beatty following the meeting with Schmidt on June 11, 1931:

I met Dr. Carl Schmidt last Thursday, and had satisfactory discussions of the Mani-papyri question. I found him quite ready to take up a reasonable attitude. He quite agreed there is no need to consider any question of publication at present; and that, except as to any MS. that may be found to be divided

between your collection and Berlin, you would of course be free to publish in England and in any form you wished, and he did not press for any form of joint publication. As to any joint MS, that can be dealt with when the time arrives.

As far as possible, he agrees to Dr. Polotsky working alternate weeks for Berlin and yourself respectively—in detail, it would have to depend somewhat on the material supplied by Ibscher. He does not foresee any difficulty except as to the latter being able to keep his part of the work going at a sufficient rate, as it is difficult work and trying to his eyes—and also he can only work on your papyri out of his official hours. But the initial work on each papyrus is the most difficulty, and once the outer or more fragmentary portion is removed, the faster it proceeds . . .

He quite agreed about mutual interchange of material and nothing to be published on either side without consent, and I pressed him to keep the whole matter as quiet as possible. He told me he was being urged already to make a brief communication to the Berlin Academy, but I told him he must postpone it for the present till the material is separated and sifted. He has been recently in Egypt, making inquiries about the find, and he is satisfied that the whole find was divided into 8 parts, between 3 dealers, of which I understand 5 are coming to Berlin, and he declared you had two MSS. and one on approval, viz. your Hymn book, now in Ibscher's hands and another (?). Is this so? and if so, would you let me see it—and also the papyrus on approval? I should very much like to get some idea of its (their?) size and contents, if possible.

Thompson's English translation of a letter from Schubart to Thompson of July 19, 1931, reports:

Our common friend Gardiner wrote to me asking me to address myself directly to you in all that concerns the Mani-papyri . . . Dr. H. J. Polotsky, Berlin-Charlottenburg 4, Waitzstr. 20, has already worked on the Chester Beatty papyri during May and June so far that it is justifiable to pay him on June 30 the first of the monthly instalments [sic] of 150 Rm. How the payment shall be made is of course entirely a question for Mr. Chester Beatty; perhaps you would kindly speak to him about it. In future then Dr. Polotsky might expect the payment to be made always on the last day of the month. He binds himself to divide his work conscientiously between the Berlin and the Chester Beatty papyri, but it goes without saying that this can-

not be done mechanically and exactly according to the number of pages. I will see to it that both parts are carried forward evenly. Each month Dr. Polotsky shall send you copies of the Chester Beatty and Berlin pieces as far as possible with translation. It is understood that these copies are only provisional and that Dr. Polotksy will have to work on them further to improve them. I would ask you to write to Dr. Polotsky your idea as to the working out of the Chester Beatty papyri so that he may know how far he is also to occupy himself with the contents of the New Texts. Dr. Polotsky must also write to you thereon on his part.

I shall be very grateful to you if you will communicate to me any questions or doubts that may arise, and I am convinced that we shall be able to settle everything in an amicable manner. In any case it will be a pleasure to me to do anything I can to forward the great work without delay.

On June 23, 1931, Thompson wrote Miss Kingford inquiring if Beatty had received his unanswered letter of June 15, 1931, and forwarding his translation of Schubart's letter with the request that she ask Beatty "to act upon it:"

I am very glad to find that Prof. Schubart will keep the supervision in his own hands rather than leave it all to Dr. C. S.— Entre nous, I trust Schubart entirely—Dr. C. S. is apt to be dilatory and not to be depended on to the same extent.

Thereupon on June 26, 1931, Beatty sent Schubart's letter to Gardiner "and also the answer I propose to send," apparently proposing Ibscher as the intermediary in Berlin, with this request:

I shall be very glad if you will kindly look through this and let me know if you have any suggestion to make before I send the letter to Sir Herbert Thompson.

On June 27, 1931, Gardiner replied to Beatty as follows:

When I met Sir Herbert Thompson, Crum, and C. Schmidt about a fortnight ago, it was agreed between us that I had better retire from any concern with the Manichaean texts, because they belong to a province which is rather remote from my own. But since you are kind enough to ask me to comment upon your letter to Thompson here returned, I hope you will allow me to do so quite frankly. In my opinion, knowing as I do all the people concerned except Polotsky, I think it would

be the greatest possible mistake to entrust the controlling of Polotsky's work to Ibscher instead of to Schubart. Schubart is the head of the Papyrus Department, a distinguished man and Ibscher's chief. Ibscher, though a great friend of mine and a most splendid and trustworthy fellow, is an underling in the department and would not be regarded as able to exercise any authority over Polotsky except *through* Schubart, with whom he is on the best of terms.

I see through Schubart's letter to Thompson that he personally undertakes to see that both parts of the work are carried on evenly. If he says that, then in my opinion there is not the least doubt in the world that it would be done. If, after a month or two had passed, Thompson, who will be controlling the work, considered that your portion was being neglected in favor of C. Schmidt's the arrangement could at once be terminated. In a word, if the books were mine and I had to negotiate the matter on my own behalf, I should not hesitate to accept Schubart's offer without any reservation whatever.

I have written very frankly, because I think it is by so doing that I shall be of most help both to you and to this most important scientific undertaking...

P.S. I notice from your letter that you say you would rather prefer to deal with this business through Ibscher and not through Schmidt. I don't think that the latter course is proposed at all. Indeed, in taking charge of the matter himself doubtless Schubart's idea, like Ibscher's, is to keep the control out of Schmidt's hands.

On June 28, 1931, Thompson wrote Miss Kingsford inquiring whether the mail was functioning since he had still no reply from Beatty to his letters. On July 2, 1931, Beatty wrote Gardiner to the effect he was writing Thompson to work through Schubart rather than Schmidt or Ibscher. On July 7, 1931, Beatty wrote Thompson to arrange for Polotsky to be paid by Schubart not by the month but by the actual amount of work done, since he might work more for Berlin and Ibscher's work may move slowly.

On July 11, 1931, Thompson wrote Beatty, reporting on his implementation of the new arrangements Beatty proposed:

> However I have this morning received from Schubart the results viz. transcription (Coptic), translation and (occasionally) notes of 5 more leaves, of which 4 are from your papyri and 1 from the Berlin papyri.—He sent me 4 copies (mechanical) of

each and I enclose one copy of each of your 4 new pages. One copy will go to Crum for his Dictionary and the other two will remain with me for the present.

Schubart remarks in his letter: "This time the C.B. pages are the more numerous; another time it may be so with the Berlin pages. That naturally depends on the quality of the leaves [he means that as Ibscher divides his time equally on the two jobs, the number of each that he gets off depends on the condition of the papyrus]. But both parts, C.B. and Berlin, will be as far as possible carried forward equally." I feel sure that Schubart may be trusted to do his best to see this carried out. But we must await further results in due course . . .

I have not been able to go through these pages of Polotsky at present; but I see that he has got out the whole text and it looks very satisfactory as far as I can judge from a cursory glance.

On September 24, 1931, Thompson again wrote Beatty:

> I sent you on July 11th last the first results of Dr. Polotsky's work; but as I received no acknowledgement, I presumed, you were too busy to find time for giving attention to them. So I ceased troubling you with any more. They have been coming in regularly each month. Shall I send them all on to you now? He is doing most excellent, indeed remarkable work on them, and the results are of the highest interest—both in the contents—and philologically for the Coptic language in which they are written, and seems to have sprung up specially equipped for this particular job.

On October 12, 1931, Beatty wrote that he had been very busy, was leaving for New York, and would be glad to receive Polotsky's reports on his return in five or six weeks. On January 4, 1932, Thompson wrote him:

> I have a rather urgent letter from Dr. Carl Schmidt in Berlin, asking me to send him some news as to the Mani papyrus, which you had, I believe, on approval, as scholars are very anxious—and not in Germany only—to have some public statement as to these "mysterious" Manichaean manuscripts. But Dr. Schmidt, rightly I think, wishes to defer any such statement till the fate of this outstanding papyrus of the Mani find is settled—either by its passing into your collection—or finding an assured home, perhaps at Copenhagen, or else in Berlin. The important point is that it should be in hands where

it would be accessible for study in association with those in your hands and those in the Berlin Museum.

So I venture again to trouble you with a question as to whether it is still in your custody — and if so, may I be allowed to see it? and also whether you still have any thought of acquiring it, or not? If you do not, Dr. Schmidt tells me that Nahman has given him the first option of purchase; but he fears that if the matter is delayed much longer, Nahman may change his mind, and the opportunity of fixing it in safe hands may be lost.

On January 5, 1932, Beatty left for Egypt, but the letter was forwarded to him. On January 26, 1932, J. W. Corble, of Beatty's staff, replied to Thompson on Beatty's behalf that the papyrus was still the property of Nahman and Beatty had it in safekeeping.

Schmidt wrote Thompson on February 6, 1932, in a disturbing way, which Thompson reported to Beatty in a letter of February 14, 1932:

> I am sorry to have to trouble you with Mani matters again so soon, as I fear they are not very welcome. However, it is necessary that you should know that Prof. Carl Schmidt of Berlin, who is controlling Dr. Polotsky's work over there on behalf of the Berlin papyri, will very shortly be in Egypt, and purposes to call on you.
>
> He has prepared a Report which he purposes to lay before the Berlin Academy, relating to the find of Mani papyri. He first referred to it as a "Provisional report";—I assumed that he would give an account of the find—of the number of the papyri, their dates, their language and its dialect and some details of the nature of the contents. But about 10 days ago he wrote and informed me that he proposed to use 10 pages of your papyrus, i.e., publish in his report the Coptic texts and translations—and moreover 4 of those 10 pages have never been forwarded to me nor any account even of their contents. I at once protested, both to Prof. Schubart and to Dr. Schmidt. Schubart (head of the papyrus department of the Berlin Museum) mildly interposed and thought my point of view had not been considered sufficiently. But Schmidt is offended and wrote me an immensely long letter to show that—well, I was spoiling his game, but he was off to Egypt in a few days and would see you and hopes to get your permission for what he wants. He is one of those people to whom if you give him an inch, he will take an ell—and I have been warned of this by people who know

him much better than I do. He wants to publish your papyrus by driblets in successive reports to the Berlin Academy.

So I have written him today—it will catch him before he leaves—a very straight letter of which I enclose you a copy—so that you may know exactly what is the position I have taken up, and which I consider necessary, if you intend to keep any control over your exceedingly valuable papyrus.

I hope it will meet with your approval.

Thompson's blunt letter to Schmidt of February 14, 1932, is as follows:

... But with regard to the Beatty papyrus, you remark "es wäre mir sehr angenehm einmal Ihre Meinung angesichts der von mir geschilderten Lage zu hören" [it would be very agreeable to me to hear once your view regarding the situation portrayed by me"].

I am the more willing to do as you ask, because I fear that, in your anxiety to inform the Academy, you have overlooked certain fundamental conditions, which are these:—

1. The Ch. B. papyrus belongs to Mr. Chester Beatty.

2. The right of publication is vested in him solely.

3. He will decide when and how it is to be published.

4. His present intention is to publish it completely as soon as possible.

5. His publication will not form part of that of the Berlin papyri but will no doubt be made in England, as soon as Dr. Polotsky—on one-half of whose working time he has an exclusive claim—shall produce it in a condition fit for publication.

6. He objects to any piece-meal form of publication.

7. Your knowledge of the contents of the papyrus is confidential, and you have no right to the use of it, except by asking for, and receiving permission.

8. I have, as at present instructed, no authority to give you that permission.

I informed you, that you might "state in general terms["] the "contents of the Ch. B. papyrus." You answer, "Was will der Gelehrte mit *allgemeinen Bemerkungen anfangen*?" [What

does the scholar make of general comments?] But the "contents" include a great deal more than that and cover details: but not quotations.

I am very sorry to have to write to you in such unqualified terms. But you compel me to it. There is nothing in the above 8 points, which was not either common ground between us, or was stipulated for (especially—"no partial publication without common agreement") at our meeting in London.

I am fully aware of the immense difficulty of the work of decipherment on which you and Dr. Polotsky are engaged. I have a number of photographs of the Ch. B. papyrus by me, and can form a good judgment of it; and how necessarily slow it is.

But your calculations as to the length of time likely to be required for the Berlin papyri, do not apply to the Ch. B. papyrus, which I hope will be ready for publication much earlier.

Last autumn I wrote to Dr. Polotsky that my object was to have the *text*, with English translation, and such notes, philological and historical, as may be found necessary, printed, but it is not to include any elaborate commentary, as that cannot be adequately undertaken until the whole of the papyri have seen the light.

On February 22, 1932, Thompson wrote Miss Kingsford:

Shortly before Mr. Chester Beatty left for America, he asked me to hold back the results of Dr. Polotsky's work on the Mani papyrus till his expected return some weeks later from the U.S.A.

I fear I forgot that he had ever asked for them; but I have now been through the papers, and added a considerable number of translations, as I told Dr. Polotsky to cease making [English?] translations of the Beatty papyrus, so that he may have more time for deciphering. I send you the results up to the present date and will ask you kindly to keep them till Mr. Beatty's return from Egypt.

On March 19, 1932, Schmidt wrote on his calling card in Cairo a cryptic note to Beatty, also in Cairo, since he had failed to meet him there and was leaving the next day for Luxor. Later Thompson was to provide Beatty with an accurate translation of the relevant part of Schmidt's note:

I should like to discuss with you a report on the Mani find, which I wish to place before the Academy in Berlin. I have

already corresponded with Sir Herbert Thompson about it. The important point is as to your permission how far I may in my Report also make use of (the material in) your possession. I had proposed to give some examples in illustration from your most valuable Hymn-book so that scholars might be able to judge of the Hymn to Christ and to Mani. Perhaps you will be good enough to talk this over with Sir (H.) Thompson.

On March 21, 1932, Beatty wrote Schmidt already from Cairo, without awaiting an accurate translation, but responding in terms of what Thompson had already written him about Schmidt's proposals:

I beg to acknowledge the receipt of your note but unfortunately as I do not read German I have only been able to get a rough translation of it. I wish however to have it definitely understood that you are not to use in any way, shape or manner any of the material owned by me, in any article, lecture or quotation. Upon my return to London I will have a careful translation made of your note and will write you further, but in the meantime let there be no misunderstanding. You were allowed to see certain papyri as a matter of courtesy but anything you have seen is strictly confidential and you are not permitted to make any mention of it or make any use whatever of it, without either my consent or Sir Herbert Thompson's consent in writing.

On March 29, 1932, Beatty sent a copy of his sharp reply to Thompson, with the further comment:

I think the best solution is that I arrange with Ibscher for him to stop work on the thing, so that we will not have any further complications with Schmidt.

The same day Beatty wrote Nahman, agreeing to return the manuscript on which he had an option via Ibscher, knowing that this meant that Schmidt would acquire it. Apparently, Beatty had soured on the whole Mani enterprise. On April 3, 1932, Thompson wrote Beatty, quite annoyed that Beatty had gone too far:

Thank you for your letter of Mar. 29th, acknowledging mine of Feb. 10th. I could wish you had done so sooner, as you left me during my controversy with Prof. Schmidt in some doubt as to how far I was justified in maintaining so strict an attitude toward him as I did. But your letter to him of March 31 [21?] is so stiff that it rather puts me into fresh difficulty.

When Prof. Schmidt came over here in June of last year, I made certain arrangements with him as regards the common working out of the Berlin and your Mani papyri. The main points were:—

1. They were to be worked out by Dr. Polotsky under the supervision of Prof. Schmidt and myself, so far as I could control his work by photographs, or the originals when returned.

2. All the material, as worked out in Berlin, was to be sent to me.

3. Publication was reserved, to be dealt with by each party as they thought best; but no publication of any kind was to be permitted meanwhile without the consent of the other party.

4. I told Schmidt distinctly that Dr. Polotsky was to edit your papyrus for you, and that it would be published over here and not in Germany.

5. Dr. Polotsky was to divide his working time equally between the two parties and each party was to pay him 150 Rm. monthly. (This was before the gold standard was abandoned in England. Therefore, whereas 150 Rm. = £7.10.0 at par originally, it now, at 14 Rm. to the £ = £10.15.0. But, on the other hand, by German Govt. decree all salaries have been reduced by 10% since Jan. 1, so Dr. P.'s salary stands now at 135 Rm. per month).

6. It was agreed that some communication of the contents of these papyri should be made to the public as soon as it could reasonably be done; and that this should take the form of a Report by Prof. Schmidt to the Berlin Academy as to their nature and contents.

Accordingly, when Prof. Schmidt on Feb. 2 announced to me that he was preparing a Report to the Academy and that he intended to make large extracts from your papyrus, I protested at once that he was not entitled to do so, as this amounted to a part-publication. After many letters on both sides, Prof. Schmidt yielded on my writing to him the formal letter, of which I sent you a copy.

But I have given him permission to state the nature and contents of your papyrus with details as to names of persons

mentioned and places, and chronological references, provided he makes no quotation whatever; and so much I consider to be desirable in the public interest. This you have now withdrawn by the terms of your letter to him.

After our controversy, which I conducted, I hope, with due politeness, Prof. Schmidt, having conceded my points, gave in with a good grace, and we are again on excellent terms. As Prof. Schubart of the Berlin Museums, who has the custody and control of all the Mani-papyri, supported me throughout, I think it would be deplorable if you refused to sanction the further use of your papyrus, and withdrew from the agreed common work.

Further, with regard to your papyrus, I obtained from Dr. Ibscher on Feb. 22 a report as to his work on it, of which I enclose a translation. He will also make an appendix to Schmidt's Report, on the technical condition and treatment of the papyri. He has sent me a copy of his paper, and I see nothing whatever to object to in it.

In consequence of Ibscher's statement, (from which I learned for the first time that you own, not one papyrus only, but 3 or 4), I wrote to Dr. Polotsky that I advised him to concentrate on finishing up the shortest one of 37 leaves; and, as, if he were to wait till the whole 460–600 leaves were worked out, it would probably be some years before anything appeared, he should finish this short one up and you would arrange for a publication of it separately—which would bring him into prominence. He is an extremely learned and able young man; but he is not a naturalised German (being a Russian) and hence has no prospect of an official or University post; and has to make a living. I believe he has nothing but these 270 Rm. (orig. 300 Rm.) per month, i.e. at par £180 p. ann.

I hope very earnestly that you will not withdraw from the scheme as originally laid down. It cannot be carried out without the collaboration of Prof. Schmidt; and I have put matters on such a footing that I feel sure he will now act reasonably; as he has discovered that he has not a "man of straw" to deal with on this side. But if this is to be effected, I must ask you to back me up also in the concessions I have made both as regards Prof. Schmidt and Dr. Polotsky. They are no more than was allowed in the original agreement.

On April 16, 1932, Beatty wrote Ibscher:

*We have had a good deal of trouble and dispute with Professor Schmidt with reference to the Mani papyrus, and I understand*

from Dr. Gardiner that you are coming to London, so I wish you would stop all expenditure and work on the Mani papyrus and just leave the matter as it is until I can see you in London. We can then discuss the best policy to pursue, but at present I do not like Professor Schmidt's attitude; I feel the most satisfactory way is to stop all work in order not to have any complications.

Thompson wrote Beatty on April 22, 1932, on hearing from Berlin of Beatty's letter to Ibscher:

> I have this morning received a letter from Prof. Schubart telling me that you [have] written to Dr. Ibscher that he is to stop work on your Mani papyri in Berlin "on account of disagreement with Prof. Schmidt." As the latter is still in Egypt, Schubart naturally wishes to know what it means and applies to me for information.
>
> As you put the relations between you and Berlin into my hands, and as I had reminded Prof. Schmidt of his duty to you in respect of his use of your papyri, and replaced everything again on an amicable basis, after establishing a proper control over the use to be made of your property, I think it would have been better, had you continued to leave the matter to be conducted through me. Instead of which you have written letters of a very decisive import both to Prof. Schmidt and now to Dr. Ibscher without any reference to me whatever.
>
> Frankly, I cannot work for you on this double basis. Either you must leave the conduct of the business to me, or you take it all into your own hands. It is for you to choose.
>
> But I must remind you that you are under definite obligations to Dr. Polotsky, which cannot be suddenly cut short without notice.
>
> Will you kindly let me know what your intentions are as soon as possible, so that I may know where I stand in relation to the Berlin Museum authorities... I understand that Ibscher will be in London some time next week; and I shall be meeting him of course.

On May 1, 1932, Thompson again wrote Beatty:

> On April 22 I wrote you a letter in which I described the position in which you had placed me, and to which I asked for a speedy answer, but I have heard nothing from you.
>
> From the neglect with which you treat all my letters I can only conclude that you do not want me or my services any

> more. And so, much to my regret, I have to inform you that you must now find some one else to do the work, which, under more favourable circumstances I was so anxious to do in the interests of science.
>
> After three days, if I do not hear any further from you, I shall inform Prof. Schubart that, as far as I am concerned, I can take no further part in the working out of the Mani papyri.
>
> With regard to Dr. Polotsky, I have made certain engagements with him in your name, which I must see carried out, and if you repudiate them, then it will be a matter of honour to me to see that a proper compensation is made to him.

This bitter letter crossed in the mail with a more conciliatory letter from Beatty to Thompson of April 30, 1932:

> I am so sorry that there has been such a mix-up in the matter of the Schmidt business. I got your letter in Egypt, from which I gathered that Schmidt was not acting very well, and I got his letter and also a reprint in German apparently of a Biblical papyrus which he had been interfering with, and then I wrote to him. I thought in view of the dispute that the best way to bring him to terms was to stop the work absolutely. I quite understand that with reference to Dr. Polotsky we may have some work still to settle with him.
>
> I met Dr. Alan Gardiner the other day and understand that Dr. Ibscher is here, so that I will be seeing him within the next few days, and if you will let me know what days you expect to be in London I will try to call on you so that we can have a talk and straighten the matter out.
>
> I am sorry for any upset I have caused in your plans, but it was done with the best intentions.

On May 2, 1932, Thompson replied to Beatty:

> I have just received your letter of Apr. 30th and it has crossed mine, which was written to you yesterday. Your letter still gives me no answer as to your intentions in relation to the arrangements made through me with the authorities in Berlin. You speak of "stopping the work absolutely." If you have done so, or are doing so, you might have told me of it, before leaving me in the lurch. I have nothing to alter in my letter written to you yesterday; but if you think it worth while, I will come up to town and see you any day this week between 10:30 and 3 pm, that you like to name.

On the same day Beatty wrote a further conciliatory letter to Thompson, in which he nonetheless announced a formal closing down of the arrangements:

> I feel I owe you many apologies for my seeming discourtesy in not replying to your letters, but the fact is that since my return from Egypt I have been so engrossed with business matters that everything else had had to take a secondary place, and I have put off from day to day attending to my personal correspondence with the usual result that it has been entirely neglected. As a matter of fact, I did dictate a letter to you on Friday evening which was sent to my house for signature, but I had to go unexpectedly to the country and so unfortunately it was not dispatched at once.
>
> I quite understand that with regard to Dr. Polotsky and Professor Schubart there will be some settlement needed, and I am of course ready and willing to accept responsibility for this. I met Dr. Alan Gardiner the other day and understand that Dr. Ibscher is here, so I will be seeing him within the next few days.
>
> I regret very much any upset I may have caused in your arrangements, but it was done with the best intentions.
>
> In view of the very difficult business conditions which demand the whole of my time, I have decided to discontinue all work in regard to manuscripts at present. I do not want to offend my friends who have assisted me so much in the work on the library, and I feel I may inadvertently offend them if I try to continue the library work and at the same time have to look after business. I am Chairman of a number of Companies, and I feel that during these difficult times I must devote all my time to them; I am glad to say they are doing all right, but until we get through this world crisis I feel my first duty is to them, and so I cannot devote the time to manuscripts which I would like and would be able to in normal conditions.

A memorandum of a conference between Beatty and Gardiner on May 8, 1932, reported the following policy:

> Under the arrangement with Dr. Polotsky, he was to be paid 150 Rm. by each party monthly, and was to divide his working time equally between the two parties (Mr. A.C.B. and Berlin). Half of this is for Mr. A.C.B.'s account. Polotsky has now almost finished his work and has been working specially on the books of travels [*Homilies*] of which there are about ten pages

left; the idea is to dispense with Polotsky's time after he has finished these ten pages and to arrange through Dr. Schubart that he will finish the work by a certain time.

Then, if Sir Herbert Thompson approves, the idea would be to give Polotsky the right to publish it within a year at his own expense through some scientific paper.

Then in regard to the arrangement with Dr. Ibscher, who was to receive 50 marks (about £3) per page, he charges by the page and his work comes to about £200 a year. He has separated or has in process of separation about 100 leaves of which about 30 are under glass. The idea is that he will not separate any more leaves of the manuscript but gradually put the present leaves which he has separated under glass within the next year or so. He is not to undertake any new work on the remaining part of the manuscript without my approval.

On May 10, 1932, Thompson wrote Beatty:

The enclosed pages (7 of your MS. and 3 of the Berlin papyrus) reached me yesterday from Berlin, representing last month's contribution by Dr. Polotsky.

I have written to him to stop working on your papyri, since you wrote to me on the 2nd inst. that you decided to discontinue all work in regard to manuscripts at present. So this will be the last that he will send. I have not troubled (as with former sendings) to make a translation of them, as I do not suppose you will have time to read them, and it naturally takes a good deal of my time to do it.

On the same day Beatty wrote Thompson that he had "had a long talk with Dr. Alan Gardiner and Dr. Ibscher in reference to the Manichaean manuscripts and have taken some notes with regard to the matter," no doubt the memorandum of the meeting May 8, 1932, and inquiring if he could see Thompson in London. On May 11, 1932, Thompson responded, commenting "I wish you could have seen me when I offered it last week," and pointing out that the times Beatty now proposed were inconvenient. On May 12, 1932, Gardiner wrote Beatty:

I have had some further talks with Dr. Ibscher and Sir Herbert Thompson with regard to the best way of bringing the arrangement with Sir Herbert and Dr. Polotsky to a satisfactory conclusion. If I understand rightly, you are ready to cede to Dr. Polotsky publication rights in the 50 leaves relating to

the journeyings of Mani [*Homilies*] provided he produces his work within a reasonable time. I would suggest that, to treat Polotsky very liberally, you would allow him to retain those rights until this time next year, say the last day of June 1933. The publication would appear in Germany and no cost in connection with it would be incurred by you. Furthermore, after the end of this month, no further obligation for payments to Dr. Polotsky for his studies would rest upon you.

If this arrangement seems satisfactory, I should be grateful for a line at your earliest convenience. Ibscher is leaving for Germany on Saturday, and would like to go back bearing your consent with him.

On May 13, 1932, Beatty responded to Gardiner accepting his proposals.

On May 14, 1932, Ibscher wrote Beatty from London:

| | |
|---|---|
| Before I return again to Germany, I would not want to neglect to confirm that I have correctly received for Prof. Schmidt the Mani manuscript... | Bevor ich wieder nach Deutschland zurückfahre, möchte ich nicht versäumen zu bestätigen, dass ich das Mani-Manuskript für Herrn Prof. Schmidt richtig erhalten habe... |
| As agreed, I will continue treating the Mani text until the already unstuck 100 leaves are assured. I hope I can soon provide you more precise communications about this. | Die Manitexte werde ich wie verabredet weiter behandeln, bis die bereits losgelösten 100 Blätter gesichert sind. Ich hoffe Ihnen hierüber bald nähere Mitteilungen machen zu können. |

On May 20, 1932, Beatty wrote Thompson a summary of the situation, including a statement concerning Ibscher:

> Dr. Ibscher is just completing the work on the present pages he is doing which will probably take another six or nine months, and when he has finished this work I have promised to let him know whether I wish him to continue separating any more of the leaves.

On May 24, 1932, Thompson replied to Beatty:

> Thank you for your letter, which was forwarded to me here where I shall be nearly to the middle of next month. I have also heard from Dr. Gardiner with regard to the result of your conferences with him. It is quite satisfactory to me, but I note

that you write to me: "that he (Dr. Polotsky) would have the right for a certain period to publish an article on the pages (i.e. of the work he was lately doing) in a German publication." In your letter to Dr. Gardiner you said: "I am to cede to Dr. Pol. publication rights in the 50 leaves relating to the journeyings of Mani [*Homilies*], provided he produces his work within a reasonable time," defined as the end of June 1933. The difference is material and I have taken the latter as the more authoritative, and I have written to Dr. Polotsky that he has the right to publish the text of the short papyrus in question, with introduction, translation and notes, as an independent volume in Germany. That is what he was engaged to do in relation to your papyri before the matter came into my hands, with the difference that hitherto the stipulation was that the publication was to be in England. The difference now is that he is restricted to this short papyrus and the publication is to be in Germany. I hope this is quite clear; as also that he has no claim on you for future expenses either as to his work or the publication.

On May 30, 1932, Beatty acknowledged the correctness of Thompson's interpretation, which Thompson acknowledged on June 2, 1932. This seems to be the conclusion of this correspondence.

It would seem that Beatty's initial proposal of working through those with whom he already had good working relationships, Gardiner and Ibscher, was the procedure to which he had returned, after the relationship with Thompson repeatedly failed to become close, and Schmidt had come to be seen as a problem.

The conserved material has been partially published: Sir Chester Beatty's part of the *Homilies* by H. J. Polotsky in 1934; part two of Sir Chester Beatty's *Psalms* by C. R. C. Allberry in 1938; and the first part of the Berlin *Kephalaia* by H. J. Polotsky and Alexander Böhlig in double fascicles from 1935–1940, with fascicles 11–12 published by Böhlig in 1966, and the next page, 292, by Böhlig in 1985.[1]

---

1. Polotsky, *Manichäische Homilien*; Allberry, *Manichaean Psalm-Book, Part 2* (the preface reported that fascicles 1–8 had appeared in 1935–1937); Polotsky and Böhlig, *Kephalaia*. Manichäische Handschriften der staatlichen Museen Berlin, Band 1, herausgegeben im Auftrage der Preussischen Akademie der Wissenschaften unter Leitung von Prof. Carl Schmidt, 1. Hälfte (Lieferungen 1–10), pages 1–102 by Polotsky, pages 103–244 by Böhlig; *Kephalaia*. Manichäische Handschriften der Staatlichen Museen Berlin, Band 1, herausgegeben im Auftrag der Deutsche Akademie der Wissenschaften zu Berlin; zweite Hälfte (only Lieferungen 11/12 = pages 244–92), by Böhlig; Böhlig, "Ja und Amen," 59–70.

The unconserved book blocks belonging to Berlin are no longer extant, whereas three belonging to Sir Chester Beatty were saved and conserved after the war. The conserved leaves belonging to Berlin are largely extant (though the exact dividing line between what was ever conserved and what was still unconserved when the book blocks disappeared is not clear), and those belonging to Sir Chester Beatty are extant.

Some of the material transcribed by Polotsky but not published has been preserved, in the archives of the Chester Beatty Library, in the Crum Archives of the Griffith Institute at the Ashmolean Museum in Oxford, and at the Academy of Sciences in Berlin. None has survived at the Egyptian Museum in East Berlin or in the possession of H. J. Polotsky.

A ring binder at the Chester Beatty Library has two leaves that have the appearance of title pages, one reading: "A. CHESTER BEATTY. MANICHAEAN PAPYRUS. CODEX A. Psalms (Hymnbook). CODEX B. Homilies (Discourses). Transcriptions and Translations. From Sir H. Thompson. July, 1931—May 18, 1932." The other reads similarly: "BERLIN MANICHAEAN PAPYRUS. Transcriptions and Translations. From Sir H. Thompson. July, 1931—May 18, 1932."

In the Chester Beatty Library are to be found transcriptions of the published pages 25, 26, 30, 34–40, 51, and 54 of the *Kephalaia* and of pages 8, 11, 12, 27–30, 44, 60, 69, 76, 78, 79, 82–84, 91, and 93 of the *Homilies*, as well as two pages of the *Kephalaia* published only in the initial essay by Schmidt and Polotsky, pages 375–76.[2] Also to be found are five still unpublished pages of the *Kephalaia*: pages 343, 344, 353, 354, and 366.

In the preface to *A Coptic Dictionary* (1939), W. E. Crum referred to "copies of the unpublished portions [of the Manichaica] kindly sent by Dr. Polotsky and Mr. Allberry" that he was able to include "only since reaching the letter P." Among the "Abbreviations" are hence "Mani 1 = copies of Chester Beatty's unpublished Manichaean papyri by H. J. Polotsky and H. Thompson" and "Mani 2 = copies of similar papyri at Berlin by Polotsky." This reference to unpublished material would not include, at first glance, what had been published by 1939, which

---

2. Schmidt and Polotsky, "Ein Mani-Fund in Ägypten," 45, for the German translation and page 87 for the Coptic text from codex page 375; page 42 for the German translation and page 82 for the Coptic text of codex page 376. Schmidt and Polotsky did not give the page numeration in the codex.

consisted (according to the "Abbreviations," of the Dublin *Homilies*) of Part 2 of the Dublin *Psalms*, and the Berlin *Kephalaia*, presumably only fascicles 1–8, since they were published in 1935–1937; the first volume was published in 1940 with the appearance of fascicles 9–10. Thus, it is conceivable that some Berlin materials that Crum cites as unpublished are among those that have been subsequently published, whereas Dublin material cited as unpublished would still be unpublished, unless it was so listed in fascicles of Crum's *Dictionary* that appeared before Allberry published in 1938. Though the materials identified in the Dublin Archives include no unpublished Dublin material, there are in the Oxford Archives unidentified Dublin transcripts, though one (II, 30, 1) has the note "precedes Allberry p. 1," which must mean it comes from the unpublished first part of the *Psalms* codex. Two psalms published in English translation by Søren Giversen as derived from the unpublished first part of the *Psalms* are also present in the Crum Archives (see below).

— 5 —

# The Effects of World War II

THIS REMARKABLE STORY OF the discovery, acquisition, and initial conservation and publication of the Manichaica of Medinet Madi has as its sequel an equally remarkable story of the Manichaean codices in the aftermath of World War II.

In a guidebook, Joachim Selim Karig, acting director of the Ägyptisches Museum in Charlottenburg, West Berlin, until 1989, described precautions taken in wartime as follows:[1]

| | |
|---|---|
| *Rudolf Anthes*, the successor in office to Heinrich Schäfter from 1935 on, suffered a similar fate as well. [Similar to that of his predecessor's pupils: "Both were obliged, since they were not pleasing to the ruling powers, to give up their careers and later even their homeland."] Recognition was denied to him, for he had never hidden the fact when his personal political opinion stood in opposition to his superiors. He was not named director, though he had to bear the work and responsibility of the leader of the collection. Also the sad task rested on him of protecting the valuable objects of the collection from destruction by | Auch *Rudolf Anthes*, der Amtsnachfolger von Heinrich Schäfer seit 1935, erlitt ein ähnliches Schicksal. [Similar to that of his predecessor's pupils: "Beide mussten, da sie den herrschenden Machthabern nicht genehm waren, ihre Laufbahn, später sogar ihre Heimat verlassen."] Ihm, der nie ein Hehl daraus machte, wenn seine persönliche politische Meinung im Gegensatz zu seiner Obrigkeit stand, wurde die Anerkennung versagt. Er wurde nicht zum Direktor ernannt, obwohl er die Arbeit und Verantwortung des Sammlungsleiters zu tragen hatte. Ihm oblag auch die |

---

1. Karig, *Ägyptisches Museum Berlin*, 73–74.

war and bombing raids, of packing them up and carrying them to various places—an activity that he executed with the greatest conscientiousness in spite of all the impediments of the time.

traurige Aufgabe, die wertvollen Sammlungsgüter vor der Vernichtung durch Krieg und Bombenangriffe zu schützen, sie zu verpacken und an verschiedene Stellen abzutransportieren—eine Tätigkeit, die er mit der grössten Gewissenhaftigkeit, allen Behinderungen der Zeit zum Trotz, ausführte.

Jürgen Settgast, director of the Ägyptisches Museum in West Berlin, described the wartime and postwar period as follows:[2]

### Catastrophe

Already soon after the Second World War broke out, steps began to be taken also in the Egyptian Museum to put in safekeeping the objects of the collection. Storage places which one thought could offer them better protection than the museum in the center of Berlin had to be located and made ready to receive them. But statues and pieces of architecture that weighed tons remained at their place in the museum and were covered with protective walls.

The most valuable works of art were brought to the concrete bunker [removed after the war] in the Zoo. Many outstanding exhibition pieces wandered into the deep cellar of the Neue Münze; others remained on the Museum Island where they could find protection in the basements of the museums.

### Katastrophe

Schon bald nach Ausbruch des Zweiten Weltkrieges begannen auch im Ägyptischen Museum Massnahmen zur Sicherung des Sammlungsbestandes. Auslagerungsplätze, von denen man glaubte, dass sie besseren Schutz als das Museum im Berliner Zentrum bieten könnten, mussten gefunden und aufnahmebereit hergerichtet werden. Tonnenschwere Statuen und Architekturteile aber verblieben im Museum an Ort und Stelle und wurden mit Schutzmauern verkleidet.

Die wertvollsten Kunstwerke wurden in den Betonbunker [removed after the war] am Zoo gebracht. Viele hervorragende Ausstellungsstücke wanderten in den Tiefkeller der Neuen Münze, andere verblieben auf der Museumsinsel, konnten Schutz in den Kellern der Museen finden. Nahezu alle Objekte

---

2. Settgast, *Ägyptisches Museum Berlin*, 76. The hardback booklet published by the Ägyptisches Museum der Staatlichen Museen Preussicher Kulturbesitz, West Berlin, summarizes this report with more or less detail in three languages: Kniese and Robbel, *Ägyptisches Museum Berlin*, 8 (German); Fay, *Egyptian Museum Berlin*, 7–8 (English); and Alte, *Musée Égyptien Berlin*, 8 (French).

Almost all the objects of these three storage places survived the war intact, were transported into the Soviet Union in 1945–1946, and then returned to Berlin in 1958. These objects comprise today the core of the Egyptian Museum in the eastern part of Berlin.

Immediately after the end of the war the objects stored in the bunker of Friedrichshain became the victims of a large fire. However, the Egyptian Museum suffered its most serious losses in the total destruction of the depots of art objects in the castle Sophienhof in the region of Mecklenburg, which was heavily fought over in April 1945. Here almost 100 crates of small works of art, well over 500 stone objects, and the bulk of the collection of wooden coffins and mummy coverings were destroyed. The Berlin Egyptian Museum is still today marked by this catastrophe. What was stored in a mine near Grabsleben west of the Elbe fell into the hands of British troops in April 1945. They gave the 34 crates with objects from the reserves emergency asylum in Celle. Incomparably more important was what was given over to the American troops that pushed forward into Thüringen: ninety-seven crates, among them the one with the green head and another with the bust of Nofretete. That the best of the Berlin collections was rescued for us is also thanks to unknown railroad workers, who simply ignored Goebbel's

dieser drei Auslagerungsstätten haben den Krieg heil überdauert, sind 1945/46 in die Sowjetunion transportiert worden und kehrten 1958 nach Berlin zurück. Diese Stücke sind heute Kern des Ägyptischen Museums im Ostteil Berlins.

Die im Bunker Friedrichshain ausgelagerten Objekte wurden unmittelbar nach Kriegsende Opfer eines Grossfeuers. Die schwersten Verluste aber erlitt das Ägyptische Museum durch die totale Vernichtung des Kunstgutlagers in Schloss Sophienhof im Mecklenburgischen, das im April 1945 heftig umkämpft war. Hier wurden fast 100 Kisten mit Kleinkunst, weit über 500 Steinwerke und der grösste Teil der Sammlung von Holzsärgen und Mumienhüllen vernichtet. Von dieser Katastrophe ist das Berliner Ägyptische Museum noch heute gezeichnet. Was in einem Bergwerk bei Grabsleben westlich der Elbe ausgelagert war, fiel britischen Truppen im April 1945 in die Hände. Diese liessen die 34 Kisten mit Magazinbeständen in Celle Notasyl finden. Ungleich wichtiger war, was den bis nach Thüringen hinein vorgestossenen amerikanischen Truppen übergeben wurde: 97 Kisten, darunter die mit dem Grünen Kopf und eine andere mit der Büste der Nofretete. Dass das Spitzenstück der Berliner Sammlungen uns erhalten blieb, verdanken wir auch unbekannten Eisenbahnern, die den Goebbels Befehl, die Nofretete aber Ostern 1945 wieder nach

order to take Nofretete back to Berlin at Easter 1945. Instead, the Americans transferred the queen to Wiesbaden, where she resided for ten years before returning home to Berlin on June 23, 1956.

Berlin zu schaffen, einfach ignorierten. Statt dessen überführten die Amerikaner die Königin nach Wiesbaden, wo sie zehn Jahre residierte, bevor sie am 23. Juni 1956 nach Berlin heimkehrte.

Karig described the beginnings of the new Egyptian Museum just across the street from the castle in Charlottenburg:[3]

### New Beginning

One hundred and thirty-one wooden crates in the ballroom of the former troop casino, which with its emergency roof above the burnt-out and naked walls did not look at all festive any longer—that was the heritage that one had to use. A director, a secretary, and a conservator was the staff that from February 1, 1962, on, was supposed to produce from this an Egyptian Museum. Just the sifting and identifying of the objects of the collection already produced great difficulties. All the files about them, the Inventory Books and other records were in East Berlin, unavailable for our use, whereas the inventory numbers on the pieces themselves were often illegibly rubbed off, destroyed. Much was not published, but even if it was—also a specialized library had first to be built up out of nothing.

Nonetheless, a suitable house had already been found, which seemed to be remarkably suited to house in its relatively small rooms a collection containing many pieces of small format as a result of

### Neubegin

Einhundertundeinunddreissig Holzkisten im Festsaal des ehemaligen Landwehrkasinos, der mit seinem Notdach über den ausgebrannten and nackten Wänden keineswegs mehr festlich wirkte—das war das Erbe, das es zu nutzen galt; ein Direktor, eine Sekretärin und ein Restaurator die Mannschaft, die vom 1. Februar 1962 an hieraus ein Ägyptisches Museum schaffen sollte. Allein schon die Sichtung und Identifizierung der Sammlungsbestände brachte grosse Schwierigkeiten. Alle Akten hierüber, Inventarbücher und sonstigen Unterlagen waren in Ost-Berlin für uns nicht erreichbar, die Inventar-Nummern auf den Stücken selbst aber oftmals unleserlich abgerieben, zerstört. Vieles ist nicht publiziert worden, aber selbst wenn—auch eine Fachbibliothek musste erst aus dem Nichts aufgebaut werden.

Immerhin, ein passendes Haus war schon gefunden, das vorzüglich geeignet zu sein schien, in seinen relativ kleinen Räumen

---

3. Karig, *Ägpytisches Museum Beriln*, 78.

# The Effects of World War II 117

| | |
|---|---|
| the storage situation. The fact that the departure of the police from the eastern building constructed by Stüber was delayed by a further number of years was more nearly useful for the cause, since one could devote one's attention after all to the objects (now with the larger staff of colleagues), could restore them, and could also go at making the completely unstudied Papyrus Collection accessible. | eine Sammlung aufzunehmen, die, bedingt durch die Auslagerung, viele kleinformatige Stücke besitzt. Dass sich der Auszug der Polizei aus dem östlichen Stüberbau noch um Jahre verzögerte, war eher der Sache nach dienlich, konnte man sich doch, jetzt mit vergrössertem Mitarbeiterstab, den Denkmälern widmen und sie restaurieren und auch schon an die Erschliessung der noch gänzlich unbearbeiteten Papyrussammlung gehen. |

In an earlier guidebook, Karl-Theodor Zauzich had described the situation of the papyrus collection as follows:[4]

| | |
|---|---|
| In the Second World War the contents of the Papyrus Collection as well as of the Egyptian Museum had been stored in different parts of Germany to protect them from air raids. After the end of the war they remained in the relevant occupation zones, and, after some detours, were turned over to the papyrus collection of the Staatliche Museen in Berlin ([the former] DDR) and to the Ägyptisches Museum Preussischer Kulturbesitz. By the accident of the earlier storage, the papyri that reached West Berlin were almost exclusively those that had been worked on neither in terms of restoration nor in terms of scholarship, and still had no inventory numbers. By the very nature of the case, it was a matter of the papyrus leaves that were outwardly less appealing and especially of the | Im 2. Weltkrieg hat man die Bestände der Papyrussammlung sowie die des Ägyptischen Museums zu ihrem Schutz vor Bombenangriffen in verschiedene Teile Deutschlands ausgelagert. Nach Kriegsende verblieben sie in den jeweiligen Besatzungszonen und wurden nach einigen Umwegen der Papyrussammlung der Staatlichen Museen zu Berlin (DDR) und dem Ägyptischen Museum Preussischer Kulturbesitz übergeben. Durch die Zufälligkeit der seinerzeitigen Auslagerung sind nach West-Berlin fast ausschliesslich jene Papyri gelangt, die weder restauratorisch noch wissenschaftlich bearbeitet waren und auch noch keine Inventarnummern hatten. Das waren naturgemäss die äusserlich weniger ansprechenden und vor allem die stärker fragmentierten |

4. Zauzich, *Kunst der Welt in den Berliner Museen*, 11:

more fragmentary leaves, which, however, precisely because of their long neglect, are especially interesting from a scholarly point of view.

The guidebook of the Museum Island museums in Berlin portrays as follows the situation during and after the war:[5]

[p. 7] Fascism and war had also brought the State Museums to the edge of complete destruction. The first and most important task in 1945 was hence to save from the ruins what had survived Fascistic barbarism and war. Here began the inestimable help of the Soviet Union, which carried the works of art to the museums of Moscow, Leningrad, Kiev, and other cities, cared for them there, and gave them over to our people, when suitable prerequisites for caring for them had been created.

[p. 22] Then at the beginning of the Fascistic predatory war in 1939, all museums were closed. It lasted 10 years until an exhibit could again take place on the Berlin Museum Island.

A large part of the holdings were packed and put in storage outside [the museums], in basements, in crypts of banks, in the large bunkers at the Zoo and in Friedrichshain, in warehouses and mines. Numerous works of art and valuable books were ruined in these storage places during the war.

[p. 7] Faschismus und Krieg hatten auch die Staatlichen Museen an den Rand der völligen Vernichtung gebracht. Die erste und wichtigste Aufgabe war deshalb 1945, das aus den Trümmern zu bergen, was faschistische Barbarei und Krieg überstanden hatte. Hier setzte die unschätzbare Hilfe der Sowjetunion ein, die die Kunstwerke in die Museen Moskaus, Leningrads, Kiews und anderer Städte überführte, sie dort pflegte und unserem Volk übergab, als entsprechende Voraussetzungen für ihre Unterbringung geschaffen waren.

[p. 22] Bei Beginn des faschistischen Raubkrieges 1939 wurden dann alle Museen geschlossen, es dauerte 10 Jahre, ehe wieder eine Ausstellung auf der Berliner Museumsinsel stattfinden konnte.

Ein grosser Teil der Bestände wurde verpackt und ausgelagert, in Keller, Tresore von Banken, in die grossen Bunker am Zoo und im Friedrichshain, in Gutshäuser und Bergwerke. Zahlreiches Kunstgut und wertvolle Bücher gingen in diesen Auslagerungsorten während des Krieges zugrunde.

---

5. *Schätze der Weltkultur* (Berlin-Hauptstadt der DDR: Staatliche Museen zu Beriln, and Berlin-Information, 2. überarbeitete Auflage, 1981), "Vorwort," 7; and Hühns, "Zur Geschichte," 22, 23, 25.

The Museum Island was destroyed on February 3, 1945, by a massive attack. This barbaric air attack lies on the same level as the destroying of Dresden ten days later.

Fascism and war had destroyed a locale of world culture

To the Soviet troops that in May 1945 freed Berlin, a terrifying picture presented itself. All the buildings of the Museum Island were destroyed, only a few rooms in the basement floors were usable, but they too were without windows and [p. 23] endangered by water and cold, since all the houses' roofs were missing. Given the high degree of destruction in Berlin, it was not possible to find room for the rescued works of art, especially those from the places of storage outside, where they could be protected from further disintegration and theft. For the fact that we today can again admire these unique treasures of culture we are indebted to the Soviet soldiers, scholars, and restorers. They took to heart, as in the case of the Dresden paintings, also the Berlin art treasures. They were put in safekeeping and brought into the Soviet Union, where they were cared for and conserved in the museums in Leningrad, Moscow, and Kiev, until the possibility existed again in Berlin to receive the collections and care for and exhibit them in a professional way.

The holdings of the State Museums that were stored in the occupation zones of the Western allies were brought together by

Die Museumsinsel wurde am 3. Februar 1945 durch einen Grossangriff zerstört. Dieser barbarische Luftangriff liegt mit der Zerstörung Dresdens, 10 Tage später, auf einer Linie.

Faschismus und Krieg hatten eine Stätte der Weltkultur vernichtet.

Den sowjetischen Truppen, die im Mai 1945 Berlin befreiten, bot sich ein erschreckendes Bild. Alle Gebäude der Museumsinsel waren zerstört, nur in den Sockelgeschossen waren einige Räume brauchbar, aber auch sie ohne Fenster und [p. 23] von Wasser und Kälte gefährdet, da allen Häusern die Dächer fehlten. Bei dem hohen Grad von Zerstörung in Berlin gab es keine Möglichkeit, für die geretteten Kunstwerke, vor allem aus den Auslagerungsstätten, Raum zu finden, in denen sie vor weiterem Verfall und vor Diebstahl geschützt werden konnten. Dass wir heute diese einzigartigen Schätze der Kultur wieder bewundern können, verdanken wir den sowjetischen Soldaten, Wissenschaftlern und Restauratoren. Sie nahmen sich, wie der Dresdner Gemälde, auch der Berliner Kunstschätze an. Sie wurden sichergestellt und in die Sowjetunion gebracht, wo sie in den Museen in Leningrad, Moskau und Kiew gepflegt und konserviert wurden, bis in Berlin wieder die Möglichkeit bestand, die Sammlungen aufzunehmen, sachkundig zu betreuen und auszustellen.

Die in den Besatzungszonen der westlichen Alliierten untergebrachten Bestände der Staatlichen Museen wurden von den Besatzungstruppen zunächst in Wiesbaden und Celle

the occupation troops at first in Wiesbaden and Celle, and later taken to West Berlin, where they until today are denied to the State Museums as their owner ...

[p. 25] In 1958 the Soviet Union gave over to the [former] DDR the rest of the pieces from the collections of the museums that had been put in safe keeping in 1945. In several hundred railroad cars over a million museum objects arrived in Berlin, carefully folded in silk paper, wrapped in waxed paper and in upholstered boxes, along with the documentation that belonged with them. In the State Museums these treasures were then given back to the owners. Among them, holdings of the gallery of paintings and of the collection of sculptures, of the cabinet of etchings, the Pergamon frieze and many unique works, which since then are deposited and exhibited on the Museum Island. Tens of thousands of visitors saw at that time the exhibition "Treasures of World Culture Saved by the Soviet Union." A friendly, decades-long collaboration with the museums in Moscow and Leningrad dates from this time, to which we are indebted for many interesting exhibits and many a stimulus for our work.

zusammengeführt und später nach Westberlin gebracht, wo sie bis heute den Staatlichen Museen als ihrem Eigentümer vorenthalten werden ...

[p. 25] 1958 übergab die Sowjetunion die übrigen 1945 sichergestellten Stücke aus den Sammlungen der Museen an die DDR. In mehreren hundert Eisenbahnwagen trafen über eine Million Museumsexponate in Berlin ein; sorgsam in Seidenpapier gehüllt, in Wachstuch eingeschlagen und in gepolsterten Kisten, zusammen mit der dazugehörigen Dokumentation. In den Staatlichen Museen wurden diese Schätze dann den Eigentümern zurückgegeben. Unter ihnen Bestände der Gemäldegalerie und der Skulpturensammlung, des Kupferstichkabinetts, der Fries von Pergamon und viele einmalige Werke, die seitdem auf der Museumsinsel deponiert und ausgestellt werden. Zehntausende von Besuchern haben damals die Ausstellung "Schätze der Weltkultur von der Sowjetunion gerettet" gesehen. Von dieser Zeit an datiert nun eine schon Jahrzehnte währende freundschaftliche Zusammenarbeit mit den Museen in Moskau und Leningrad, denen wir viele interessante Ausstellungen und manche Anregungen für unsere Arbeit verdanken.

*The Effects of World War II*

In a small guidebook of the Ägyptisches Museum of Berlin, Wolfgang Müller has provided, as follows, more specific information about the papyrus collection:[6]

| | |
|---|---|
| At the end of the war in 1945, the New Museum was a ruin. Parts of the collection stored outside and taken over by the West's occupation troops are today unlawfully in (West) Berlin and have not yet been given back to their original place of storage on the Museum Island. Many works of art saved in destroyed Berlin were taken for safekeeping to the Soviet Union. Already in 1953, after years of rebuilding, the first Egyptian exhibit could be opened on the Museum Island. After the return of the art holdings preserved in the Soviet Union, the Egyptian Museum had been showing since 1959 in the Bode Museum a large number of works of art of the highest quality, from the early period down to the Hellenistic age, papyrus manuscripts, selected finds from daily life, and mummies. This chronologically arranged exhibit was enlarged in 1964 with new rooms, and since 1973 has been basically rearranged. | Bei Kriegsende 1945 war das Neue Museum eine Ruine. Ausgelagerte and von den westlichen Besatzungstruppen übernommene Sammlungsteile befinden sich heute widerrechtlich in Berlin [West] und sind noch nicht an ihren ursprünglichen Aufbewahrungsort auf der Museumsinsel zurückgegeben worden. Viele im zerstörten Berlin gerettete Kunstwerke wurden zur Sicherung in die Sowjetunion überführt. Nach Jahren des Aufbaus konnte bereits 1953 auf der Museumsinsel die erste ägyptische Ausstellung eröffnet werden. Nach Übergabe des in der Sowjetunion bewahrten Kunstbesitzes zeigt das Ägyptische Museum seit 1959 im Bode-Museum eine grosse Zahl von Kunstwerken ersten Ranges von der Frühzeit bis zum Hellenismus, Papyrushandschriften, ausgewählte Funde aus dem täglichen Leben und Mumien. Diese chronologisch aufgebaute Ausstellung wurde 1964 durch neue Räume erweitert und seit 1973 grundlegend umgestaltet. |

In 1954 Rolf Ibscher narrated, as follows, the course of events during the war, relative to the Manichaean codices:[7]

---

6. Müller, "Einleitung," 6.
7. Ibscher, Rolf. "Wiederaufnahme," 3.

After the passing of my father on May 26, 1943, I took the Manichaean papyrus books for reasons of security into the repository, safe from bombs, that had received the papyri of the Berlin Museums. But after July 20, 1944, this place too did not seem to me safe enough, especially since the remainder of the not yet conserved Mani books of Sir Chester Beatty was in Berlin, and I removed them, together with a Berlin manuscript, to Bavaria, into the house of my father-in-law in the country. Thence, after the war, the parts belonging to Chester Beatty returned to London.

The Berlin manuscript remained in Bavaria.

Nach dem am 26. Mai 1943 erfolgten Ableben meines Vaters brachte ich die Mani-chäischen Papyrusbücher aus Sicherheitsgründen in das bombensichere Verliess, das die Papyri der Berliner Museen aufgenommen hatte. Aber nach dem 20. Juli 1944 erschien mir auch dieser Platz nicht mehr sicker genug, besonders, da ja der Rest der noch nicht aufgearbeiteten Manibücher von Sir Chester Beatty in Berlin war, und ich entführte diese zusammen mit einer Berliner Handschrift nach Bayern in das Haus meines Schwiegervaters auf dem Lande. Dort kehrten nach Kriegsende die Teile des Chester Beatty-Besitzes nach London zurück.

Die Berliner Handschrift blieb in Bayern.

Alexander Böhlig has summarized what happened to the Manichaean codices as follows:[8]

The war brought the thriving editorial activity to an abrupt end. Besides, the air attacks brought with them an unusual endangering of the manuscript material. As a result, one went at moving them outside. The glassed pieces of the Chester Beatty collection were already by and large in London. The Berlin collection was, to the extent it was glassed, brought into one of the anti-aircraft towers at the Zoo train station, together with the not-yet-restored Mani manuscripts. In fact, at that time there were in the Berlin Papyrus Collection the not yet restored pieces from both the English and

Der Krieg machte der regen Editionstätigkeit ein jähes Ende. Die Luftangriffe brachten ausserdem eine ausserordentliche Gefährdung für das Handschriftenmaterial mit sich. Infolgedessen machte man sich an die Auslagerung. Die verglasten Stücke der Chester-Beatty-Sammlung waren bereits im wesentlichen in London. Die Berliner Sammlung wurde, soweit sie verglast war, in einen der Flaktürme am Bahnhof Zoo gebracht, zusammen mit den noch nicht restaurierten Mani-Handschriften; es befanden sich damals nämlich die noch nicht restaurierten Stücke

---

8. Böhlig, "Die Arbeit," 180–81.

the German holdings. Rolf Ibscher had already in 1940 taken the place of his father, who then died in 1943. Concern for the safekeeping of the manuscripts moved him, with the approval of General Director Kümmel, in November 1944 to bring the remainder of Sir Chester Beatty's Codices A and C (the *Psalms* and the *Kephalaia*), as well as a further manuscript, to Schondorf on the Ammers Lake in Upper Bavaria, into the house of his father-in-law. There Sir Chester Beatty had the parts of the Codices A and C picked up in the year 1946. The Manichaean texts that had been brought into the USSR, in connection with the action of the Soviet armed forces to make things secure, were given back to Berlin in the year 1958.

sowohl aus englischem wie aus deutschem Besitz in der Berliner Papyrussammlung. Die Sorge um die Sicherung der Handschriften bewog Dr. Rolf Ibscher, der schon 1940 an die Stelle seines dann 1943 verstorbenen Vaters getreten war, mit Genehmigung von Generaldirektor Kümmel im November 1944 die Sir Chester Beatty gehörigen Reste der Codices A und C (Psalmbuch und Kephalaia) sowie eine weitere Handschrift nach Schondorf am Ammersee in Oberbayern in das Haus seines Schwiegervaters zu bringen. Dort liess Sir Chester Beatty die Teile der Codices A und C im Jahre 1946 abholen. Die bei der Sicherstellungsaktion der sowjetischen Streitkräfte in die UdSSR geschafften manichäischen Texte wurden im Jahre 1958 nach Berlin zurückgegeben.

Rolf Ibscher had reported in 1955 about the fate of Sir Chester Beatty's codices:[9]

which on my own responsibility I had brought out of the danger zone of Berlin at the end of 1944 for the final phase of the war together with a Berlin manuscript (Codex No. 15998 [actually Sir Chester Beatty's *Synaxeis* Codex B] on the shrewd advise of my father-in-law, the publisher Wolf Henry Doering, into his secure house on the quiet Ammer Lake in Schondorf, a good hour from Munich.

die ich Ende 1944 auf den klugen Rat meines Schwiegervaters, des Verlegers Wolf Henry Doering, zusammen mit einer Berliner Handschrift (Codex Nr. 15998 [actually Sir Chester Beatty's *Synaxeis* Codex B]) auf eigene Verantwortung aus der Gefahrenzone Berlins für die Endphase des Krieges in sein sicheres Haus am stillen Ammersee in Schondorf, eine gute Stunde von München entfernt, gebracht hatte.

9. Ibscher, Rolf, "Das Konservierungswerk," 3.

Ibscher's phrase, "on my own responsibility," presents a different emphasis from Böhlig's phrase, "with the approval of General Director Kümmel." In any case, Kümmel would have difficulty retaining responsibility for a codex of the Berlin Papyrus Collection that was far away in Bavaria. If Kümmel had been informed of the plan to remove the codices of Sir Chester Beatty, he could well have taken the position that these materials were not formally under his control, hence he would not like to bear the responsibility for them, either in war-torn Berlin or elsewhere, and Ibscher could assume that responsibility and could act according to his own discretion. But it is hard to see how Kümmel could have formally approved of hiding Berlin Museum and Papyrus Collection holdings quite unofficially in Schondorf and at the invitation of a person neither on the museum staff nor otherwise officially involved in the safekeeping of the Museum's holdings.

Böhlig has similarly interpreted this rescue operation:[10]

| | |
|---|---|
| Rolf Ibscher had the authorization from General Director Kümmel to get the Dublin material from the anti-aircraft tower and take it to Bavaria. He did this in the company of the Museum worker P. Seidel, who has since died. In the process the idea came to him that it would perhaps be useful, in case worst came to worst, also to take along one of the Berlin codices. This decision was, as far as I know, spontaneous. That it was worth it, is shown by the success. These things remained completely preserved, in contrast to what | Rolf Ibscher hatte von Generaldirektor Kümmel die Genehmigung, die Dubliner Materialien aus dem Flakturm zu holen und nach Bayern zu bringen. Er tat das in Begleitung des inzwischen verstorbenen Museumsarbeiters P. Seidel. Dabei kam ihm der Gedanke, es wäre vielleicht nützlich für den Notfall, auch einen der Berliner Codices mitzunehmen. Dieser Entschluss war meines Wissens spontan. Dass es sich gelohnt hat, zeigt der Erfolg. Diese Dinge blieben vollständig erhalten im |

---

10. Böhlig, in a letter of February 10, 1986. For his concluding comment he refers to Søren Giversen's paper, "The Unedited Chester Beatty Mani Texts," 371, where Giversen listed the following extant material as belonging to the Chester Beatty Library: "The whole CB collection consists of somewhat 1040 pages of which only 334 have been published so far. I said somewhat 1040 pages—the exact number depends on how some very fragmented pages or remnants of pages are counted. These 1040 pages are: A) Psalmbook 546 pages, B) Unidentified codex 20 pages, C) 'Kephalaia' 358 pages, D) Homilies 98 pages, E) Addenda et Varia 20 pages." This makes a total of 1048 pages, of which he lists 334 as published, leaving 714 yet to be published.

| the Soviets had "saved." Whether something was then confused when turned over to the emissaries of Chester Beatty, so that in the end result a Berlin part came to | Gegensatz zu dem, was die Sowjets "gerettet" haben. Ob dann bei der übergabe an die Abgesandten von Chester Beatty etwas verwechselt worden ist, so dass im Endeffekt |
|---|---|

Rolf Ibscher described to Sir Chester Beatty the rescue operation in his broken English as follows:[11]

> The papyri were removed according to my arrangement from the bomb proof shelter (Zoo Bunker) in 1944 by my assistant at the Museum, Mr. Seidel, but Codex B [*Synaxeis*], sorry to say, seems to have been left behind. The reason being that the papyri had to be removed secretly in a frantic hurry, thus you can imagine how glad I was, when Mr. Seidel got past the SS-Guards with the invaluable little wooden box.
>
> This wooden box contained one Berlin manuscript [actually Sir Chester Beatty's Codex B, the *Synaxeis*] (for which I had specially asked Mr. Seidel) to make certain, that at l[e]ast part of the Berlin collection also was saved, in addition those papyri which reached you in London in 1947 after Dr. Böhlig had separated them at Schondorf.
>
> Thus Codex B [actually the Berlin Codex $P^{15998}$, the *Letters*], together with 3 Berlin manuscripts [$P^{15996}$, $P^{15997}$, $P^{15999}$] and all other glazed Berlin Manichaean Papyri of the Museum [$P^{15995}$ and leaves of $P^{15996}$, $P^{15997}$, $P^{15998}$] were taken to Russia.

On November 1, 1960, I. E. S. Edwards of the British Museum's Department of Egyptian Antiquities wrote to Rudolf Anthes, then in Philadelphia, who had been assistant keeper of the Egyptian Department of the Berlin Museums in 1939, inquiring about the whereabouts of Beatty's papyri:

> I should like to know in particular whether there were many pages or few, and also whether Hugo Ibscher would have worked on them in the Museum or at home.

On November 9, 1960, Edwards wrote to R. J. Hayes, then head of the Chester Beatty Library:

> I have had a reply from Anthes who confirms what Böhlig says about Rolf Ibscher taking the Chester Beatty material to

---

11. Rolf Ibscher in a letter of October 6, 1955, to Sir Chester Beatty.

Schondorf when the Flakturm was bombed (p. 5 [of the transcript of Böhlig's paper]).

In the archives of the Chester Beatty Library there is a black loose-leaf folder titled "Papyrus. Biblical Manichaean Hieratic. Greek etc. General Catalogue." In the section entitled "Manichaean Pap." there is a note dated May 1940:

> Mr. Allberry said that Dr. Ibscher had the remainder of Mr. Beatty's papyrus at his house in the country, at Klein Machnow (*see* letter from Allberry).

Böhlig has subsequently reported similarly concerning half-conserved *Kephalaia* material belonging to Berlin:[12]

| | |
|---|---|
| Of the material in Berlin only a very small part has always remained in Berlin. It was the last 20 leaves of the Berlin *Kephalaia* book. They were conserved by Rolf Ibscher in the years 1952 and 1953. | Von dem in Berlin befindlichen Material war nur der kleinste Teil immer in Berlin geblieben; es waren die letzten 20 Blätter des Berliner Kephalaiabuches; sie wurden von Rolf Ibscher in den Jahren 1952 and 1953 konserviert. |

Rolf Ibscher then reported similarly about the half-conserved remainder of the Berlin *Kephalaia*:[13]

| | |
|---|---|
| The remains of the Berlin *Kephalaia* had escaped destruction by being stored in my house after 1945. The degree of difficulty in conserving them, which I overcame between 1951 and 1955, was worse than that which the Chester Beatty papyri displayed. | Der Schwierigkeitsgrad der Konservierung für die Reste der Berliner Kephalaia, die der Vernichtung durch die Aufbewahrung in meinem Haus nach 1945 entgangen waren und die ich zwischen 1951 und 1955 bewältigte, war schlimmer als ihn die Chester Beatty Papyri aufwiesen. |

It would seem probable that what was stored in his house after 1945 had already been stored in his house during the war, a conjecture confirmed by Böhlig:[14]

12. Böhlig, "Die Arbeit," 182.
13. Rolf Ibscher, "Über den Stand," 52.
14. Böhlig, in a letter of February 10, 1986, to the author.

# The Effects of World War II 127

If half-conserved leaves of the Berlin *Kephalaia*, the material belonging to Sir Chester Beatty, and perhaps other book blocks or half-conserved leaves had been taken to the Ibscher home to be worked on there, it is unclear what of this material Rolf Ibscher took to the Zoo Bunker after his father's death of on May 26, 1943. At least some material remained in the Ibscher home throughout the war (cf. Böhlig's comment, "only a very small part," "the last 20 leaves of the Berlin *Kephalaia* book"). P$^{15999}$, referred to pejoratively as the wig, was apparently classified by itself, in that it was put on display as hopeless rather than as classified with the other Manichaean codices to be conserved. Thus it may well not have been in the Ibscher home for conservation. If Hugo Ibscher still worked some days in the museum, some unconserved or half-conserved material may have been still there for him to work on. Thus, it is indeterminate just what material stayed in Berlin throughout the war and postwar periods (or what was taken from the

| | |
|---|---|
| Why did Rolf Ibscher also have material at home? He, like his father, always had material at home, since his father at his sixtieth birthday had received the right to work at home three days a week. When the papyri came into the Zoo bunker, the material on which he was working naturally remained in Ibscher's residence. That bombs would fall in the region of his residence—Kleinmachnow is incidentally not part of Berlin, but rather belongs to the district of Potsdam—was not exactly probable and in fact did not happen. | Warum Rolf Ibscher auch zuhause Material hatte? Er hatte wie sein Vater immer Material zuhause, weil sein Vater bei seinem 60. Geburtstag das Recht erhalten hatte, 3 Tage der Woche zuhause zu arbeiten. Als die Papyri in den Zoobunker kamen, blieb natürlich das Material in Ibschers Wohnung, an dem er arbeitete. Dass in die Gegend seiner Wohnung (Kleinmachnow ist übrigens kein Teil von Berlin, sondern gehört zum Bezirk Potsdam) Bomben fallen würden, war nicht gerade wahrscheinlich und ist ja auch nicht geschehen. |

Ibscher home in Kleinmachnow to Schondorf on the Ammer Lake), what material went to the Zoo bunker and from there to Schondorf (no doubt via the Ibscher home in Kleinmachnow), and what material went to the Zoo bunker and from there to Leningrad (or at least in the direction of Leningrad) but did not return to Berlin in 1958. The major losses were the unconserved book blocks of P$^{15997}$, P$^{15998}$, and P$^{15999}$.

One can only postulate that all the conserved leaves of P$^{15997}$ and P$^{15998}$ and all the half-conserved leaves of P$^{15996}$ and P$^{15998}$ are all accounted for; four conserved leaves of P$^{15996}$ do seem to be missing (see below).

Michel Tardieu describes the loss of the bulk of P$^{15997}$ and P$^{15998}$ as "detruit ou perdu durant la seconde guerre mondiale" ["destroyed or lost during the second world war."][15] Apparently, there was no loss during the war but only after the war.

Rolf Ibscher described what happened to the material taken to Leningrad:[16]

On August 29, 1960, Otto Firchow, director of the Egyptian Museum and Papyrus Collection in East Berlin, responded as follows to an inquiry about Beatty's codices from I. E. S. Edwards of the British Museum's Department of Egyptian Antiquities (according to the English translation preserved in the Chester Beatty Library archives):

> The papyri which Sir Chester Beatty sent to Dr. Ibscher shortly before the war were taken by the Russians to Leningrad together with the Berlin collection of papyri. I am however glad to be able to tell you that they were among those which came back safely. Only I and my wife, who has hitherto been Conservator of Papyri in the Museum, knew about their existence. To return them at the present moment would probably require considerable diplomatic intervention on the part of the British Foreign Office with the East German Government.
>
> I myself have been compelled to surrender during the past few days under political and personal pressure the Direction of the Berlin Musuem, Egyptian Department, and to flee to West Berlin. I have used this opportunity to take the Mani Papyri with me. In the next few days I will hand them over to the British Military Authorities. I consider that in this way this valuable material will eventually reach your hands.

| | |
|---|---|
| Three Berlin codices [the unconserved book blocks of P$^{15997}$, P$^{15998}$, and P$^{15999}$] and Codex B of Sir Chester Beatty [which in fact did not go into "exile"] have not reemerged thus far after the return of the Berlin papyrus col- | Drei Berliner Codices [the unconserved book blocks of P$^{15997}$, P$^{15998}$, and P$^{15999}$] und Codex B von Sir Chester Beatty [which in fact did not go into "exile"] tauchten bisher nach Rückführung der Berliner Papyrussammlung aus dem Exil |

---

15. Tardieu, "Les Manichéens en Égypte," 6.
16. Rolf Ibscher, "Mani und kein Ende," 220.

lection from exile. In the case of such extensive objects something can always be overlooked and still be peacefully slumbering somewhere, or these very brittle codices crumbled into dust when transported, before they could be registered into the very conscientious protection with the very exactly executed salvage lists. Hence there are certainly hopes, and miracles are always taking place at all times, if one believes in them. I spoke about this with Professors Guber and Diakonov in 1954 in Cambridge and later also with Prof. Struve in Moscow in 1960.

noch nicht wieder auf. Bei so umfänglichen Objekten kann immer etwas übersehen werden und noch friedlich irgendwo schlummern, oder diese sehr mürben Codices sind beim Abtransport zerstäubt, bevor sie noch in die sehr gewissenhafte Obhut mit den sehr genau geführten Bergungslisten eingetragen werden konnten. Es bestehen also noch durchaus Hoffnungen, und Wunder geschehen immer zu allen Zeiten, wenn man an sie glaubt. Ich sprach darüber mit den Professoren Guber und Diakonov 1954 in Cambridge und später auch mit Prof. Struve in Moskau, 1960.

In September 1960 Edwards reported this to Beatty:

> Clearly Dr. Firchow found himself in an awkward position. I am sure that he will not part with the papyri unless he is satisfied that the military authorities will convey them safely, but there is always the risk that they will not agree to help. On the whole I should feel happier if he had left them in the Museum and I could have started negotiations with the Foreign Office. I am writing to him to ask him to let me know how matters stand at present and I shall also ask him to hold his hand unless he is absolutely sure that the military authorities can be trusted to deliver them safely. If he runs into difficulties I shall suggest that he takes them to Professor Grapow an old friend of mine in the Berlin Acadamy. We can then review the courses open to us.

The same day Edwards also wrote to R. J. Hayes, honorary director of the Chester Beatty Library:

> I have written to Sir Chester to let him know that the missing portion of his Mani codex has been traced in the Berlin Museum...
> As you will see events have taken a rather disconcerting turn and I shall write immediately to Firchow and urge him

> to exercise the greatest care. Personally, I mistrust military authorities. However, it is quite clear that he cannot now return the papyri to the Museum and, if he runs into difficulties, I think his best course will be to deposit them with Grapow in the Berlin Academy. If there were any alternative I should not have chosen him, although I have known him for twenty-five years and I saw him last month in Moscow, but it is rather a case of faute de mieux [lack of better].

The Berlin Academy was in the Soviet sector, where Firchow probably would not have wanted to return to visit Grapow. Nor would Grapow have felt comfortable going to West Berlin to bring back to the Academy or to the Museum (also in East Berlin) what Firchow had secretly carried to West Berlin. There was a customs check between sectors, even if the wall became official only on August 13, 1961.

On September 15, 1960, Hayes replied to Edwards:

> It is great news about the Mani Papyri. I hope they will come through safely, but I would feel they were safer in British than in any German hands. Do you think I should ask a man I know in M. I. 5 to hold a watching brief? . . .
>
> Is the Russian returned material between glass or an unopened roll?

On September 20, 1960, Edwards replied to Hayes:

> I do not know whether the Russian returned material is between glass or if it is still in a pack. I saw Ibscher senior working on one pack when I was in Berlin in 1934, but I think that one belonged to the Berlin Museum. It was a large pack and must have contained at least 100 sheets. I cannot imagine that Firchow has removed as much glass as that from the Museum. My guess is therefore that it is still unglazed, but I may be wrong . . .
>
> The part remaining in Berlin is an unknown quantity, except to Firchow.
>
> Perhaps it would be better to leave an approach to your friend in M. I. 5 until we know exactly what we can ask him to do.

On September 26, 1960, Edwards wrote again to Hayes:

> I am delighted to be able to tell you that I have heard from Firchow that he has handed what he describes as "das Paket mit den Mani-Papyri" ["the packet with the Mani papyri"] to the British consul in Berlin.

I am getting in touch with him and I hope we shall have the papyri safely here very soon. [An appended hand-written note: "The Bag Room at the F{oreign}.O{ffice}. reports that nothing has yet arrived."] Since he refers to a packet it seems to me unlikely that the papyri are already between glass.

On October 21, 1960, Edwards wrote again to Hayes:

I heard yesterday that the Berlin Mani package will be arriving at London Airport next Sunday. I shall go and meet the bearer myself and I hope to be able to write on Monday saying that it has arrived safely.

On October 26, 1960, Edwards wrote to Beatty with a copy to Hayes:

I am writing to let you know the result of our quest for the Mani papyri in Berlin.

The operation, which I now realise is only the first round, did not turn out to be much of a success, I am sorry to say. Our Consul-General in Berlin and the Foreign Office were most helpful. The package was brought by a member of the diplomatic staff and I took delivery at London Airport last Sunday. By previous arrangement with the Customs it was opened at the Museum on Monday.

Up to that point everything seemed to be running our way, but alas, on opening the package we found it contained only blank leaves of papyrus and a few inscribed fragments. It was most disappointing. [Papyrus Conservator Stanley] Baker will deal with the pages, but they will not yield very much, I fear.

My guess is that we have received no more than the outermost leaves which Dr. Ibscher probably abstracted from the main body of the codex. The latter is, I suspect, still in Berlin and was overlooked by our friend, Dr. Firchow. I have written to him at the refugee camp in Hamburg, where he is now domiciled, and have told him my suspicions. Perhaps he will be able to suggest an explanation.

For the present I feel the only course is to lie low and see who is appointed to the Berlin Museum as Dr. Firchow's successor. Obviously we do not want to do anything to embarrass either Dr. Firchow or the Consul-General. If the new Keeper of the Berlin Museum is someone whom I know and feel I can trust I can take up the problem anew without reference to the first attempt. I shall, however, have a better idea of what can be done when I have heard from Dr. Firchow whether he has left my letters in the files of the Museum.

It is very sad that a quest which looked so promising should have suffered such an anticlimax, but I have not lost hope that we shall succeed in the end. However, I wish I could report that we had done so already.

On October 28, 1960, Firchow wrote Edwards; a translation of this letter is in the archives of the Chester Beatty Library:

I received your letter with real dismay. I am so sorry that the important papyri have not reached you, but only material of relatively little value. Unfortunately, I did not know anything about the circumstances in which Sir Chester Beatty handed over the papyri to Dr. Hugo Ibscher, and in consequence, I supposed that they consisted only of those which my wife and I found in the packet. We alone have examined the packet—very hastily—since it was packed by Dr. Ibscher. Under the prevailing conditions we were unable to make a thorough examination of such fragmentary material; I did however recognize that it consisted of Mani fragments and I believed that I had found confirmation of this identification in your letter. We last saw the papyri in the office of the British Council General, Mr. Weymes. I can only remember one hieratic fragment.

I agree that the material was not substantial and I hoped that the most important part had already been mounted by Ibscher before the war and had been sent back to Sir Chester Beatty. You are certainly right in supposing that the packet contained only odds and ends. But I am certain that the main body (of the papyri) is *not* in Berlin.

In my opinion the papyri ought to be found with Dr. Rolf Ibscher probably already mounted and glazed. Dr. Hugo Ibscher used to carry out this kind of work in his own home. If I were still in Berlin, or if I had known about the matter a few months ago, I could have offered you my help. I should suggest that you get in touch with Rolf Ibscher, who has no connection with the Berlin Museum. Let me say again that the papyri cannot be in the Berlin Museum but must have been in Hugo Ibscher's private possession.

While writing this letter my wife has told me that she actually remembered Dr. Ibscher speaking to her once about material belonging to Sir Chester Beatty which he had in his possession.

It would certainly be better not to mention your personal correspondence with me. I have kept your letter among my personal papers. I sincerely hope that the affair will soon be satisfactorily settled. Please keep me in touch with developments.

Edwards wrote on November 1, 1960, to Hayes and Beatty in support of Rolf Ibscher's ignorance in the matter. To Hayes he wrote:

> I cannot myself think that Rolf Ibscher could have known anything about these papyri. He was working for Sir Chester Beatty for about four years and he would surely have told one of us if he had known of their existence. I feel we should regard him as a last resource.

To Beatty he wrote:

> Personally I do not think Rolf Ibscher would have kept quiet about these papyri if they had been in his possession when he was working for you. So, for the present anyhow, I do not intend to follow Firchow's advice to write to Rolf Ibscher. Instead I am writing to-day to Dr. Rudolf Anthes in Philadelphia and to Dr. [Günther] Roeder in Hildesheim to ask them if they can tell me anything helpful. Dr. Roeder was the Keeper of the Egyptian Department in the Berlin Museum when the war broke out and Dr. Anthes was Assistant Keeper. They are both good friends of mine and I am sure they will tell me all they know. I shall write again when I have heard from them.
>
> What I find so perplexing at present is to understand why Hugo Ibscher should have put the odds and ends in a packet in the Berlin Museum and have kept the main body of the papyri in his home. I should have thought that he would have taken all of them to the Museum when the war broke out.
>
> One difficulty, of course, is that we do not know exactly what we are looking for. Until the pages had been mounted no one could know anything about the contents. Another problem is the bulk of the missing material; was it large or small?

In the letter to Roeder the same day he explained:

> Some weeks ago Sir Chester Beatty happened to tell me that he had sent some of his Mani codex before the war to Dr. Hugo Ibscher in Berlin for mounting between glass. I told him that I knew that the Berlin papyri were back in the Museum and I promised to write to Dr. Firchow and ask whether the portions of Mani in question had come to light. The result of the inquiry was not satisfactory and Dr. Firchow has, he tells me, now left the Museum and Berlin.
>
> I wonder whether you have any recollection of having seen these papyri at any stage either in Dr. Ibscher's possession or in the Museum. It is possible that Dr. Ibscher had them in his home and if so the only one who could help would be Rolf

Ibscher. If possible, however, I do not want Rolf Ibscher to be involved in this matter because he and Sir Chester Beatty have had some differences over the mounting of the Mani papyri which were not sent to Dr. Hugo Ibscher.

I realize that Dr. Ibscher probably received these papyri in the days when you were still at Hildesheim, but perhaps he told you something about them at the beginning of the war which would help now in recovering them.

In the letter to Anthes the same day he explained:

Some time before the war Sir Chester Beatty sent to the Berlin Museum some of his Mani papyri for Dr. Hugo Ibscher to disentangle and to mount. In an attempt to trace these papyri I wrote to Firchow who was most helpful and sent me what he could find in Berlin, but it amounted to no more than a few blank pages and some fragments.

As you know, Firchow has left the Museum and gone to Western Germany so he can do no more. However he says that he is certain that there are no more of Sir Chester's Mani papyri in the Museum.

This is my question. Do you remember anything about these papyri? I should like to know in particular whether there were many pages or a few, and also whether Hugo Ibscher would have worked on them in the Museum or at home.

I must mention that I think it would perhaps be a disservice to Firchow to let his part in this matter be known; I am sure you will regard it as confidential. I must also add that—at least at present—I do not want Rolf Ibscher to know that I am trying to trace these documents. He has been rather troublesome to Sir Chester Beatty and I am not very sure that I can count on his good will.

On November 9, 1960, Edwards again wrote Hayes his confidence in Rolf Ibscher:

However, it does not seem likely that Rolf Ibscher would be working consciously on Chester Beatty material, even in Berlin, without obtaining Sir Chester's consent.

I have a reply from Anthes who confirms what Böhlig says about Rolf Ibscher taking the Chester Beatty material to Schondorf when the Flakturm was bombed (p. 5 [of the typescript of Böhlig's Moscow speech]).

On November 14, 1960, Hayes wrote Edwards:

> I also enclose another page of typescript (keep it also) that seems to me to be of great significance. There are so many mistakes in spelling in the German that I think it must be something Miss McGilligan typed from a manuscript note by Ibscher. I found it with the 13 leaves of Codex B [*Synaxeis*]. The words "Hauptmasse mit ca. 200 Blättern in Russland" ["the main mass with about 200 leaves in Russia"] seem to be just what we are seeking.

In 1957 and again in 1960, in the paper circulating among the English, Böhlig had identified the book block in Schondorf as the *Synaxeis* belonging to Beatty, but the English did not locate this identification. Thus, the search for the missing codex was gradually given up. I drew the attention of the staff of the Chester Beatty Library to this situation in 1985 and again in 1988.

Böhlig has provided further details about the material during and after the war:[17]

| | |
|---|---|
| They were stored splendidly and securely in the anti-aircraft tower at the Zoo train station and, just before the division of Berlin went into effect, were taken by the Soviets quickly from the Zoo (English Sector!) to Friedrichsfelde Castle in the Russian part and were then put in storage in the USSR. And in this process not only papyri, but also other things got lost. Hence Warsaw too has its Mani leaves—someone found along the railroad tracks glassed papyrus leaves that had fallen out from the transport into the USSR. | Sie waren im Flakturm am Bahnhof Zoo glänzend und sicher aufbewahrt und wurden ganz kurz vor Inkrafttreten der Teilung Berlins von den Sowjets schnell vom Zoo (englischer Sektor!) ins Schloss Friedrichsfelde im russischen Teil gebracht und dann in die UdSSR ausgelagert. Und dabei sind nicht nur Papyri, sondern auch andere Dinge verlorengegangen. Daher hat auch Warschau seine Mani-Blätter (man hat an der Bahnstrecke verglaste Papyrusblätter gefunden, die aus dem Transport in die UdSSR herausgefallen waren). |

Friedrichsfelde Schloss is a small castle, privately owned until 1945. Dr. sc. Wolfgang Müller, director emeritus of the Egyptian Museum and of the Papyrus Collection in East Berlin, has reported

---

17. Böhlig in a letter of February 5, 1986.

that Rolf Ibscher told him that a few papyri were found near the castle and returned to the Papyrus Collection. Ibscher's report to Müller is the basis for the assumption that the crates were temporarily housed there.

The castle has subsequently been heavily restored, with a new roof and new inner construction throughout. But what necessitated the rebuilding seems not to have been war damage, but rather a general process of deterioration and in 1948–1949 reuse of the building as an adult education center for Berlin city government functionaries (according to Lothar Berfelde, see below). The castle's current guide-booklet reports on the restoration in the preface but without making clear the castle's condition in 1945:[18]

| | |
|---|---|
| Immeasurable are the losses in monuments of history and culture in our city that were caused by the Second World War launched by German Fascism. Many valuable historical buildings were lost beyond recovery or were severely damaged. Other witnesses to our cultural heritage among buildings that were not directly affected by the war showed clear signs of deterioration due to long neglect under the domination of capitalism. From the very beginning it required the greatest exertions of our workers-and-peasant power to restore the substance of monuments thus destroyed. In spite of magnificent achievements of restoration and reconstruction in the center of our capital city, maintenance and restoration projects in the care of monuments must also be effectively carried out, in connection with the augmentation of measures for the reconstruction and modernization of the | Unermesslich sind die Verluste an Denkmalen der Geschichte und Kultur in unserer Stadt, die durch den vom deutschen Faschismus ausgelösten zweiten Weltkrieg verursacht wurden. Viele wertvolle historische Bauten gingen unwiederbringlich verloren oder wurden stark beschädigt. Andere nicht unmittelbar vom Krieg betroffene Zeugnisse unseres baulichen Kulturerbes zeigten durch lange Vernachlässigung unter der Herrschaft des Kapitalismus deutliche Spuren des Verfalls. Es bedurfte von Beginn an grosser Anstrengungen unserer Arbeiter- und Bauern-Macht zur Wiederherstellung der auf diese Weise zerstörten Denkmalsubstanz. Trotz grossartiger Restaurierungs- und Rekrukturleistungen im Zentrum unserer Hauptstadt müssen im Zusammenhang mit der Erhöhung der Baumassnahmen für die Rekonstruktion und die |

---

18. Dathe, Schunchardt et al., "Vorwort."

substance of old buildings, as was called for by the Tenth Party Congress of the Socialistic Union Party of Germany.

The completion of the Berlin Friedrichsfelde Castle is a worthy contribution to this, in demonstrating the continuous culture politics of our socialist state, directed toward the care of the cultural heritage and toward actively rendering it accessible. Thanks to the magnanimous support of the party of the working class and of the government of the German Democratic Republic, with its politics directed toward the well-being of the people, our capital city has become richer by an appealing tourist attraction, on the eve of the elections to the Volkskammer of the German Democratic Republic and of the Assembly of the city government of Berlin.

The extent of the restoration activities, as well as of measures to refinish and refurbish the interiors, was considerable. The difficult tasks in the care of monuments could only be undertaken in stages. The results attained, however, justify this special course, and will certainly instigate further initiatives for the maintenance of monuments and for making them accessible to society.

Modernisierung der Altbausubstanz, die der X. Parteitag der SED fordert, auch die denkmalpflegerischen Erhaltungs- und Wiederherstellungsarbeiten wirksam fortgesetzt werden.

Die Fertigstellung des Schlosses Berlin-Friedrichsfelde ist dazu ein würdiger Beitrag, der die kontinuierliche, auf die Pflege und lebendige Erschliessung des kulturellen Erbes gerichtete Kulturpolitik unseres sozialistischen Staates beweist. Dank der grosszügigen Unterstützung der Partei der Arbeiterklasse und der Regierung der Deutschen Demokratischen Republik mit ihrer auf das Wohl des Volkes gerichteten Politik ist unsere Hauptstadt am Vorabend der Wahlen zur Volkskammer der DDR und der Stadtverordnetenversammlung von Berlin um eine attraktive Sehenswürdigkeit reicher geworden.

Der Umfang der Wiederherstellungsarbeiten sowie der Ausgestaltungs- und Ausstattungsaufgaben für die Innenräume war beträchtlich. Nur schrittweise konnten die schwierigen denkmalpflegerischen Aufgaben in Angriff genommen werden. Die erreichten Ergebnisse jedoch rechtfertigen diesen besonderen Weg und werden sicher weitere Initiativen zur Erhaltung und gesellschaftlichen Erschliessung von Denkmalen auslösen.

In the introduction of the guide, the details of the cause of the damage to the building become more specific:

Meanwhile it was possible to restore the castle as an important part of this significant ensemble of monuments of building and gardening art. Due to the deficient care of buildings before and during the Second World War, the Friedrichsfelde Castle had suffered severe damages. Nonetheless, ever-increasing deteriorations, whose cause was not known back then, were even more grave. Whereas the original five-part building had only field stone foundations, the side parts added in 1719 were in addition erected on wooden piles. As a result of the lowering of the water table after the construction of a waterworks directly in the neighborhood of the park at the beginning of our century, the wooden parts, no longer resting in the area of the ground water, gradually rotted and increasingly led to considerable settlings of the building and severe cracking.

The restoration, as part of the maintenance of monuments, began with comprehensive measures to eliminate the dangers and secure the building, and thus began the new history of the Castle. The main interest was at first directed to the retaining or restoring of the exterior.

Als wichtiger Bestandteil dieses bedeutenden Denkmalensembles der Bau- und Gartenkunst konnte das Schloss inzwischen wiederhergestellt werden. Durch mangelnde Baupflege vor und während des zweiten Weltkrieges hatte das Friedrichsfelder Schloss beträchtliche Schäden erlitten. Schwerwiegender waren jedoch fortschreitende Zerstörungen, deren Ursache damals noch nicht bekannt war. Während der fünfachsige Ursprungsbau lediglich Feldsteinfundamente besass, waren die 1719 angefügten Seitenteile ausserdem noch auf Holzpfählen errichtet. Infolge der Grundwasserabsenkung nach dem Bau eines Wasserwerkes in unmittelbarer Nähe des Parkes zu Beginn unseres Jahrhunderts verrotteten die nicht mehr im Grundwasserbereich liegenden Holzteile allmählich und führten zunehmend zu erheblichen Bausetzungen und starker Rissbildung.

Mit umfassenden Massnahmen zur Gefahrenbeseitigung und Sicherung des Gebäudes begann die denkmalpflegerische Wiederherstellung und damit die neuere Geschichte des Schlosses. Das Hauptinteresse galt zunächst der Erhaltung bzw. Wiederherstellung des Aussenbaus.

In the description of the Historical Staircase:

The main staircase was restored in its early classicistic room arrangement. Whereas the reconstruction of the ceiling paintings had to be executed largely on the basis of fotos, there stood at our disposal in addition to the illusionistic wall paintings, in varying degrees of conservation, a part of the original wallpaper removed in 1947, as well as segments of wall paintings that had remained partially intact on the ground floor.

Regarding the Garden Room:

In 1947 there were pieces of the interior decoration dating back to the Biedermeier period still intact. However, at the commencement of the comprehensive restoration of the castle there were no longer any historical decorative elements or objects of interior decorating.

In the section titled "Dates on the History of the Castle" one reads:

1945 [actually 1948, according to Lothar Berfelde (see below)]: The Castle and park were taken over by the city government of Berlin.

1948–49: The castle was renovated into a home for school purposes.

August 27, 1954: The city government decided to develop a Zoo in Friedrichsfelde.

July 2, 1955: The opening of the Berlin Zoo.

| | |
|---|---|
| 1966: The commencement of the first work to secure and restore the heavily destroyed castle. | 1966: Beginn von ersten Sicherungs-arbeiten zur Wiederherstellung des stark zerstörten Schlosses. |
| Until 1971: The securing of the foundations. | bis 1971: Unterfangung der Fundamente. |
| 1973: The erection of a new roof of steel construction with large triangular gables. | 1973: Aufbringen eines neuen Mansardendaches (Stahlkon-struktion) mit grossen Dreieckgiebeln. |

The guide of the conducted tour on March 9, 1986, explained that a Soviet command post ("Kommandantur") was housed in the castle in 1945, and that a distant relative of the former owner of the castle was afterwards permitted to use three rooms for a private museum for a few years.

Lothar Berfelde has moved his Gründerzeit-Museum to Mahlsdorf near Berlin in another building he restored. It has been put under governmental protection as a "collection," since private "museums" are not legal. He reported on April 18, 1986, that a Soviet command post occupied the castle from the spring of 1945 to the spring of 1946. Then when the castle was vacated, he was able to block a proposal to raze it, and was permitted to occupy part of it with the beginnings of his Museum for a couple of years. During the year that it was used as a command post he was aware of libraries being stored there until they could be transported to the Soviet Union, but he had no specific information about holdings of the state museums being stored there.

Thus, one may suppose that the museum objects were brought to the Friedrichsfelde Castle when it was a Soviet command post. At that time the building was apparently run down, but the dismantling of the interior would seem to have taken place beginning 1947, no doubt especially in 1948–1949 when the building was adapted into a school for city employees; the roof was first removed when the restoration was undertaken and a new roof installed in 1973. Thus, the building was sufficiently intact in 1945–1946 to have served as a temporary repository for crates moved from the Zoo bunker to await shipment to Leningrad, before the education center was installed. For 1947 seems to mark the date of the dismantling of interior architecture and the removal of antique furniture for this new purpose, and 1966 the

beginning of the restoration that involved strengthening the foundations, replacing the roof, and completely redoing and refurbishing the interior. The building could presumably have housed the museum objects in 1945 without undue risk.

Joachim Karig has reported that the retreating German army had removed all railroad tracks east of Berlin and had cut all the ties in 1944–1945. During 1945 and 1946, this action no doubt made rail transportation of museum objects from Berlin to Leningrad bumpy, congested, and insecure. When whole factories and other movable objects moved east, works of art (which required several hundred railroad cars for the return to Berlin in 1958) might have had a lower priority. Karig recalled, e.g., a report that a quantity of grand pianos were seen beside the railroad tracks, exposed to the elements, apparently having been temporarily unloaded to provide boxcars for higher-priority transports to the east, or awaiting their turn for shipment east.

Berfelde reported further, from a childhood friend who worked for the German railroads, that the German railroad crews continued to operate the trains even after the end of the war. These crews were aboard German trains as far as the eastern border of Poland, where the Soviet railroads, with different gauges, began. Crossing Poland, trains laden with German items were at times stopped by train robbers. In a robbery, freight cars would be separated from the engine, in which the German crew was told to proceed down the tracks, leaving the freight cars unguarded in the countryside. There the freight cars would be looted before the authorities could be notified and police or soldiers sent to stop the looting. The one reporting this story attributed the practice of robbery to Poles resentful of the Soviet Union for not returning, at the end of the war, land the Soviets had occupied since 1939, when the Germans had invaded Poland. No doubt avarice also accounted for a Polish desire to share in the war booty.

Alexander Böhlig has reported:[19]

| | |
|---|---|
| As a result of a rumor that papyri had been found on the rail line, the rail line was combed with success at the instigation of Prof. von Manteuffel. | Auf ein Gerücht hin, dass an der Bahnlinie Papyri gefunden worden seien, wurde auf Veranlassung von Professor von Manteuffel die Bahnlinie mit Erfolg abgesucht. |

---

19. Böhlig, in a letter of February 10, 1986.

Böhlig has further clarified his initial comment:[20]

| | |
|---|---|
| Professor von Manteuffel, responsible for papyrology before and after the war, was known to me personally. I went on a walk with him in London after the International Papyrologists' Congress in Oxford in 1937. I do not know whether he had a chair for ancient history or for classical philology in Warsaw; for papyrology alone there are hardly professorships. He was always a Pole with a well-formed national consciousness. | Der vor und nach dem Krieg für Papyrologie zuständige Professor von Manteuffel ist mir persönlich bekannt gewesen. Ich bin mit ihm im Anschluss an den internationalen Papyrologenkongress in Oxford 1937 in London spazierengegangen. Ob er etwa einen Lehrstuhl für Alte Geschichte oder Klassische Philologie in Warschau innehatte, weiss ich nicht; für Papyrologie allein gibt es ja kaum Professuren. Er ist immer ein ausgesprochen nationalbewusster Pole gewesen. |

On July 12, 1986, Wincenty Myszor sent a report of his inquiries into what took place as follows:

| | |
|---|---|
| The Manichaean manuscripts that are now in Warsaw cropped up shortly after the last war under circumstances that have not been fully clarified. There is always talk of a place Brodnica, near Torun [Thorn]. I have thus far received no answer to my letter of April 21, 1986, to the regional museum in Brodnica. There are also no documents in the archive of the Warsaw University and in the National Museum. The plates are thought to have been first in a private collection, then in some way [sold? acquired?] to have reached Prof. J. Manteuffel, the leader of the Institute for Papyrology of Warsaw University, and a part of the manuscripts turned over to | Die manichäischen Handschriften, die sich jetzt in Warschau befinden, sind kurz nach dem letzten Krieg unter nicht ganz aufgeklärten Umständen aufgetaucht. Es wird immer über einen Ort Brodnica, bei Torun [Thorn], gesprochen. Auf meinen Brief an das Regional-Museum in Brodnica von 21. April 1986 habe ich bis heute keine Antwort bekommen. Es gibt auch keine Dokumente im Archiv der Warschauer Universität und im National-Museum. Die Platten sollen sich zuerst in einer Privatsammlung befunden haben, dann in irgendeiner Weise [gekauft? bekommen?] zu Prof. J. Manteuffel, dem Leiter des Instituts für Papyrologie der |

20. Böhlig, in a letter of March 7, 1986.

the National Museum on deposit. There are also rumors according to which the plates in the National Museum came directly from Brodnica to Warsaw, to Prof. Michalowski. Prof. J. Manteuffel and Prof. K. Michalowski wanted to give the leaves back to Berlin. But they did not succeed in that. In the sixties the issue almost reached the Ministry. In any case there are still many questions that probably can no longer be answered. Thus one cannot say why the manuscripts are today preserved at two places. There is the view that this has to do with an exhibition in the National Museum. But there are in the National Museum also other manuscripts from the Berlin collection that Dr. Poethke from Berlin has once already seen. These manuscripts could have come to the Museum from a private collection.

Warschauer Universität gelangt und ein Teil der Handschriften dem National-Museum als Depot übergeben worden sein. Es gibt auch Gerüchte, nach denen die Platten im National-Museum direkt aus Brodnica nach Warschau, zu Prof. Michalowski gekommen seien. Prof. J. Manteuffel und Prof. K. Michalowski wollten die Blätter nach Berlin zurückgeben. Das ist ihnen nicht gelungen. In den 60er Jahren wäre diese Sache fast im Ministerium gelandet. Jedenfalls gibt es noch viele Fragen, die wahrscheinlich schon nicht mehr beantwortet werden können. So kann man nicht beantworten, warum die Handschriften heute an zwei Stellen aufbewahrt sind. Es gibt die Ansicht, dass dieses mit einer Ausstellung im National-Museum zusammenhinge. Es gibt aber im National-Museum auch andere Handschriften aus der Berliner Sammlung, die Dr. Poethke aus Berlin schon einmal gesehen hat. Diese Handschriften könnten direkt von einem Privatbesitz zum Museum gekommen sein.

Since there is no list of how many leaves Hugo Ibscher had actually conserved from Berlin's part of the Manichaean codices of Medinet Madi, it is unclear whether those in Warsaw are actually the only leaves not included in the return with other German museum holdings to East Berlin in 1958. No book blocks were returned, and hence, if in fact they had been included in those left in the zoo concrete bunker and taken to the Friedrichsfelde Castle and from there to Leningrad, they would be the only clear instance of material still completely missing.

Once the material was back in East Berlin, plans were initiated to resume its publication. Böhlig has reported on the steps leading to his being reassigned after the war to publish the Manichaean material, while he was still in East Germany.[21] He moved in 1963 to Munich and then to Tübingen, where he lived until his death in 1996:

| | |
|---|---|
| In the year 1959 I then submitted to the German Academy of Sciences in Berlin a memorandum in which I pointed out how urgently the resumption of the editing of the Manichaean texts is. The Academy responded positively to this initiative and entrusted the undertaking to the Institut für griechisch-römische Altertumskunde, in order that its working group "Kommission für spätantike Religionsgeschichte" could assume responsibility for the continuation of the edition. At the session of the commission on May 13, 1960, this task was entrusted to me. | Im Jahre 1959 reichte ich daraufhin der Deutschen Akademie der Wissenschaften zu Berlin eine Denkschrift ein, in der ich darauf hinwies, wie dringlich die Wiederaufnahme der Editionsarbeit an den manichäischen Texten sei. Die Akademie nahm zu dieser Anregung positiv Stellung and übergab das Unternehmen an das Institut für griechisch-römische Altertumskunde, damit dessen Arbeitsgruppe Kommission für spätantike Religionsgeschichte die Weiterführung der Edition in ihren Aufgabenbereich aufnehmen sollte. In der Kommissionssitzung vom 13. Mai 1960 wurde diese Aufgabe mir übertragen. |

---

21. Böhlig, "Die Arbeit," 181.

Part Two

The Conservation
by Rolf Ibscher

— 6 —

# The Conservation of the Material in the State Museums of the Former East Berlin

THE POST-WAR ACTIVITY HAS until recently consisted almost exclusively of Rolf Ibscher's conservation work. Ibscher made every effort to present himself in unbroken continuity with his father, and thus to build a career on his father's reputation. As he phrased it typically, "die Kunde von der Wunderleistung der konservatorischen Rettung durch meinen Vater" ["the report of the miraculous performance of the conservation rescue by my father"].[1] But it is rather clear that Rolf Ibscher began with fuzzy information and lack of experience. The former is indicated by his summary of the material cited above from 1954 and his revised summary in 1955:[2]

At the beginning of the 1930s the codices were purchased: three bundles and a vestige came to London into the possession of Sir Chester Beatty (*Psalms*, Codex B, Codex C, and the *Homilies*), and four bundles and a vestige to Berlin into the possession of the state museums (*Kephalaia*, Codex 15995, Codex 15998, Codex 15999, and 31 leaves of Codex

Anfang der dreissiger Jahre kamen durch Ankauf die Codices mit drei Konvoluten und einem Rest nach London in den Besitz von Sir Chester Beatty (Psalmbuch, Codex B, Codex C und die *Homilien*) und mit vier Konvoluten und einem Rest nach Berlin in den Besitz der Staatlichen Museen (*Kephalaia*, Codex Nr. 15995, Codex Nr. 15998, Codex Nr. 15999 und 31

---

1. Ibscher, "Das Konservierungswerk," 1.
2. Ibid.

15997). The remainder of a quire acquired for Vienna by Grohmann could be added to the *Kephalaia*, Berlin's main text alongside of Codex 15998, containing the corpus of *Letters* and now in Schondorf in Upper Bavaria on Ammer Lake. It [the remainder in Vienna] comprises pp. 311–30.

Blätter des Codex Nr. 15997). Der durch Grohmann für Wien erworbene Lagenrest konnte der Kephalaia, Berlins Hauptschrift neben Codex Nr. 15998, das Briefcorpus enthaltend und jetzt in Schondorf/Obb in Oberbayern am Ammersee liegend, zugeführt werden. Er umfasst die Seiten 311–30.

Here the information available in Schmidt and Polotsky's published report is identified confusedly with the information in the *Inventarbuch* of the Ägyptisches Museum in Berlin-Hauptstadt der DDR. The Berlin holdings themselves, except for some partially conserved leaves of $P^{15996}$ and $P^{15998}$ in the Ibscher home, were in Leningrad, inaccessible to Ibscher. One need merely enumerate the needed corrections of this summary, along with those itemized in the preceding chapter, to assess the fuzziness of the information with which Rolf Ibscher began: $P^{15995}$ consists only of 31 leaves (which are not $P^{15997}$) and hence are not a bundle but only a vestige; $P^{15996}$ should be listed as the inventory number of the *Kephalaia*; $P^{15997}$ consists not merely of 31 leaves, hence it was not acquired as a vestige but was a complete codex, from which only some eight or nine leaves seem to have been removed by Hugo Ibscher before the war; Codex 15998 was among the material taken east rather than to Schondorf; $P^{15999}$, the other half of the London *Homilies* and hence to be designated a vestige, also went east. What was in Schondorf was actually Sir Chester Beatty's Codex B, the *Synaxeis*.

Hence, it is not surprising that material left half conserved and hence inadequately labeled by Hugo Ibscher in his home, should have been variously and unreliably identified by Rolf Ibscher.

Rolf Ibscher's inexperience becomes clear from a passing remark of 1954: "here in London I began with this work that my father had designated as the most difficult task of his life as a conservator, a life rich in difficult tasks. It was a task that I could entrust to myself since one expected it of me, although never before had I separated a leaf as a test under the supervision of my father. It was a risk, but a successful one."[3]

3. Ibscher, Rolf, "Wiederaufnahme," 11: "... hier in London begann ich mit dieser

That is to say, Sir Chester Beatty, no doubt grateful to Rolf Ibscher for having rescued his codices from the ruin of the war, quite unaware that Ibscher was still withholding one in Schondorf, and in response to Rolf Ibscher's appeals, engaged the son on the assumption he was, in the craft tradition of Europe, the father's only understudy and hence his qualified successor, whereas the son had in fact had no experience in the conservation of the Manichaean codices. Under permissive supervision at the British Museum, he inductively learned his trade. Rather jeopardize the codices than his own future!

On his return trip from London, Rolf Ibscher began conservation on the *Synaxeis* codex in Schondorf (see below), and in Berlin began to work at completing the conservation work of his father, on what had been in his home throughout the war.

In 1954 Rolf Ibscher himself had referred as follows to the beginnings of his conservation work on this material:[4]

| | |
|---|---|
| Between my first [Oct–Dec 1951] and second [June–Oct 1952] London trips I succeeded in saving in Berlin the remainder of the Berlin *Kephalaia* manuscript. So some 20 leaves and leaf fragments came from it. The state of preservation of this outside pad of the codex was even more desolate than that of the remaining pads of the *Psalms* book I had worked on previously in London. I can understand that my father deferred again and again the separating off of these leaves and considered the possibility of giving up this part of the manuscript as unconservable. The leaves and fragments of leaves have meanwhile been impregnated and are awaiting the collaboration of the scholarly colleague, | Zwischen meiner ersten x–xii 51 [Oct–Dec 1951] und zweiten vi–x 52 [June–Oct 1952] Londoner Reise gelang es mir in Berlin den Rest der Berliner Kephalaiahandschrift zu retten. Es kamen dabei einige 20 Blätter und Blattfragmente heraus. Der Erhaltungszustand dieser Aussenlage des Codex war noch desolater als derjenige der Restlagen des zuvor von mir in London bearbeiteten Psalmenbuchs und ich kann verstehen, dass mein Vater immer wieder die Ablösung dieser Blätter hinausgeschoben und die Möglichkeit in Aussicht gestellt hatte, diesen Teil der Handschrift als unkonservierbar aufzugeben. Die Blätter und Blattfragmente |

---

Arbeit, die mein Vater als die schwierigste Aufgabe seines an schweren Aufgaben reichen Konservatorenlebens bezeichnet hatte. Es war eine Aufgabe, die ich mir zutraute, weil man sie von mir erwartete, obgleich ich niemals je zuvor ein Blatt als Probe unter der Leitung meines Vaters abgelöst hatte. Es war ein Risiko, aber es gelang."

4. Rolf Ibscher, "Wiederaufnahme," 10–11.

| since from the material alone the arrangement and sequence of the leaves and fragments cannot [p. 11] be guaranteed with certainty. | sind inzwischen imprägniert und harren der Mithilfe des wissenschaftlichen Bearbeiters, da vom Material allein aus mit Sicherheit die Einordnung und Anordnung der Blätter und Fragmente nicht garan- [p. 11] tiert werden kann. |
|---|---|

In his report in 1955, Rolf Ibscher summarized his work as follows: "Following the experimental separation of a few leaves of the Schondorf manuscript from Berlin, I attempted on my return home to Berlin in the winter months [of 1952] to separate and impregnate a residue of very fragmented leaves of the *Kephalaia*, which my father had also designated as 'inoperable.' These leaves should be definitively glassed this winter, at the beginning of 1956."[5]

Rolf Ibscher did in fact develop his own conservation techniques, which he considered vastly superior to those of his father.[6]

| In September I could ... see in the beautiful library of Sir Chester Beatty in Dublin the leaves of the *Homilies* and of the *Psalms* conserved by my father and reassure myself as to whether his method of impregnating them had proven itself over a period of 15 or 20 years. Nevertheless I have now decided to follow a proposal of Dr. Plenderleith of the laboratory of the British Museum and use a fixative recommended by him to strengthen the brittle papyrus weave. | Im September konnte ich ... in der schönen Bibliothek Sir Chester Beatty's in Dublin die von meinem Vater konservierten Blätter der Homilien und des Psalmenbuches sehen und mich vergewissern, ob seine Imprägnierungsmethode über fast 15 bis 20 Jahre hin sich bewährt hatte. Dennoch habe ich mich jetzt entschlossen, dabei einem Vorschlag von Dr. Plenderleith vom Laboratorium des Britischen Museums zu folgen und ein von ihm empfohlenes Fixativ zur Festigung der mürben Papyrusgewebe zu benutzen. |
|---|---|

5. Rolf Ibscher, "Das Konservierugswerk," 5: "Der probeweisen Ablösung von einigen Blättern der Schondorfer Handschrift aus Berlin folgte dann bei meiner Heimkehr nach Berlin in den Wintermonaten [of 1952] der Versuch, einen Restbestand sehr fragmentarisierter Blätter der Kephalaia abzulösen und zu imprägnieren, den mein Vater auch als "unauflösbar" bezeichnet hatte. Diese Blätter sollen im Winter Anfang 1956 definitiv verglast werden."

6. Rolf Ibscher, "Wiederaufnahme," 7–10.

The conservation thus moves in completely new paths. I have been able to develop a new procedure for separating the leaves, which permits one to separate intact also such leaves as dissolved into their component parts according to the method used by my father. On August 22, 1936, he suspended work on Codex C after he had been able to separate 47 leaves, and wrote in this regard: "The papyrus dissolves completely into its component parts in separating the individual leaves, and was held together only in the whole mass. Further investigation of the book block showed that already in antiquity the book had been very damaged. After one place that readily separated there followed at first 2 blank leaves and then very faded text of another hand, so that it appeared as if here another work began. Of course I think I have seen at one place a chapter title. In any case it was hardly worth working on the block after the empty leaves, since the writing will be able to be figured out only in a few places."—This turned out in the course of the work in 1952 and in this summer to be an error. I obtained 136 usable and in part very beautiful leaves. The few leaves with very faded handwriting can no doubt be made visible given the state of our modern photography. The Berlin manuscript in Schondorf displays the same deficiencies. But I hope that Pater Dolt of the Palimpsest Institute in the Cloister Beuron will help me to develop a

Die Konservierung geht damit völlig neue Wege. Ich habe ein neues Verfahren zur Ablösung der Blätter entwickeln können, das auch solche Blätter im Zusammenhang ablösen lässt, die nach der von meinem Vater geübten Methode sich in ihre Bestandteile auflösten. Am 22. August 1936 stellte er die Arbeit am Codex C ein, nachdem er 47 Blätter abheben konnte, und schreibt dazu: "Der Papyrus löste sich beim Abheben der einzelnen Blätter vollständig in seine Bestandteile auf und wurde nur in der ganzen Masse zusammengehalten. Bei weiterer Untersuchung des Buchblockes ergab sich, dass das Buch bereits im Altertum sehr zerstört war. An einer Stelle, die sich leicht löste, folgten zunächst 2 leere Blätter und dann sehr verblasster Text von anderer Hand, sodass es den Anschein hat, als wenn hier ein andres Werk begann. Allerdings glaube ich an einer Stelle eine Kapitelüberschrift gesehen zu haben. Jedenfalls lohnt es sich kaum, den Block von den leeren Blättern an zu bearbeiten, da die Schrift nur an wenigen Stellen zu entziffern sein wird."—Das stellte sich im Verlauf der Arbeit 1952 und in diesem Sommer als ein Irrtum heraus. Ich gewann 136 brauchbare und zum Teil sehr schöne Blätter. Die wenigen Blätter mit sehr verblasster Handschrift dürften beim Stande unserer modernen Photographie sichtbar gemacht werden können. Gleiche Mängel weist die Berliner Handschrift in Schondorf auf. Ich hoffe aber, dass Pater Dolt vom Palimpzest-Institut an Kloster Beuron mir helfen wird, ein brauchbares fotografisches

usable photographical procedure to balance out this deficiency.

My procedure for separating the individual leaves from the book blocks is characterized as the adjustable sloping plane. The leaf is compelled to draw itself off as it were by its own weight, over a very smooth parchment paper, that presents no resistance to the papyrus fiber, laid above on the book block. With tweezers and a thin scalpel only a bit of supplemental help is provided in pushing the leaf in front of them over the slanting plane and carefully separating the fibers ruined by pressure and salt crystals. I would like to name this procedure "the extremely freewheeling method."

My father, on the other hand, lifted off the individual leaf without such a slanted support. He lifted the individual fragments separated from each other onto a paper support lying next to the book block and attempted to advance the leaf with extreme carefulness in its entirety from the book block off onto this support. This procedure presupposed an incredibly sure hand and an equally unimaginable gift of recollection, to transfer the fragmentary splinters with absolute certainty into the right arrangement. The individual fragment would have to come immediately with certainty into its right place, since every grasping with the tweezers in the case of especially rotted leaves immediately led such small fragments to break down into dust. I would like to name this procedure

Verfahren zu entwickeln, um diesen Nachteil auszugleichen.

Mein Verfahren, die einzelnen Blätter von den Buchblöcken abzuheben, wird durch die verstellbare schiefe Ebene gekenn-zeichnet. Das Blatt wird genötigt, sich gleichsam durch sein eigenes Gewicht über ein sehr glattes, der Papyrusfaser gar keinen Widerstand entgegensetzendes Pergaminpapier, das auf den Buchblock oben aufgelegt wird, abzuziehen. Mit Pinzette und dünnen Skalpells wird lediglich nachgeholfen, das Blatt vor ihnen her über die schiefe Ebene zu schieben und die durch Pressung und Salzkristalle verbackenen Fasern vorsichtig zu trennen. Ich möchte dieses Verfahren "the extremely freewheeling method" bezeichnen.

Mein Vater hob dagegen das einzelne Blatt ohne solche schräge Unterlage ab. Er hob die einzelnen Fragmente getrennt auf eine neben dem Buchblock liegende Papierunterlage und versuchte, mit äusserster Behutsamkeit das Blatt in seiner Gesamtheit vom Buchblock weg auf diese Unterlage zu befördern. Dieses Verfahren setzte eine unvorstellbar ruhige Hand voraus und eine ebenso unvorstellbare Gabe des Erinnerungsvermögens, die Fragmentsplitter mit absoluter Sicherheit in der richtigen Anordnung zu übertragen. Das einzelne Fragment musste sofort sicher an seinen richtigen Platz kommen, da jedes Anpacken mit den Pinzetten bei besonders vermorschten Blättern sofort dazu führte solche kleinen Fragmente zu Staub zerbröckeln zu lassen. Ich möchte dieses Verfahren "the very delicately compelling method" nennen.

"the very delicately compelling method."

To the new method of separating leaves and the handling of the separated leaves with a new fixative, in order to impede or eliminate the inner decomposition of the very degenerated material, will be associated the new glassing of the impregnated leaves, in that, instead of simple glass, now plexiglass will be used. To be sure it is very expensive, but it does not break and is very light and permits one to photograph the individual leaf even through the glass with infrared or ultraviolet light in order to entice out the faded writing. The electric effect can unfortunately thus far be eliminated only for a brief time by means of a special substance, so that laying the leaf between the glass panes is not difficult. The magnetic effect proves to be very unpleasant and dangerous when one is compelled to take the leaf out of the glasses again. Equally disagreeable is the fact that plexiglass, in distinction from simple glass, is very sensitive and gets abrasions or scratches immediately with careless handling. And it is a risk, how plexiglass in the course of decades reacts to climatic conditions and whether it darkens or not.

Whether the disadvantages or advantages in using plexiglass over conserving the leaves between simple glass panes will dominate will become clear after a few years, when it becomes necessary to reconserve the leaves again. And this necessity will emerge, even if the

Der neuen Ablösungsmethode und Behandlung der abgelösten Blätter mit einem neuen Fixativ, um den inneren Zerfall des sehr angegriffenen Materials aufzuhalten bzw. zu beseitigen, wird sich die neuartige Unterbringung der imprägnierten Blätter gesellen, indem anstelle des einfachen Glases jetzt das Perspexglas treten wird, das zwar sehr teuer, aber unzerbrechlich und sehr leicht ist und gestattet, das einzelne Blatt auch durch das Glas hindurch mit infrarotem oder ultraviolettem Licht zwecks Hervorzauberung der verblassten Schrift zu fotografieren. Der elektrische Effekt geht leider bisher nur für kurze Zeit durch ein Spezialmittel zu entfernen, sodass das Zwischenlegen zwischen die Glasscheiben keine Mühe verursacht. Sehr unangenehm und gefährlich erweist sich die magnetische Wirkung, wenn man genötigt ist, das Blatt noch einmal aus den Gläsern herauszunehmen. Ebenfalls unangenehm ist es, dass Perspexglas im Gegensatz zu einfachem Glas sehr empfindlich ist und Schrammen oder Kratzer sofort bei unpfleglicher Behandlung erhält. Und ein Risiko ist es, wie sich Perspexglas im Laufe von Jahrzehnten verhält gegen Witterungseinflüsse und ob es blind wird oder nicht.

Ob die Nachteile oder Vorteile bei der Benutzung von Perspexglas gegenüber der Unterbringung der Blätter zwischen einfachem Glas dominieren werden, wird sich nach einigen Jahren herausstellen, wenn die Notwendigkeit sich ergibt, die Blätter aufs neue umzuglasen. Und

rescued leaves are stored carefully and with constant temperature and protected from climatic influences, since the papyrus material between the glasses begins to work in the course of time, in spite of the impregnation, which only serves to strengthen the rotted papyrus substance and slow down further decomposition, just as did the earlier treatment of the leaves, the dusting with zapon lacquer applied by my father.

Subterranean water and inundation water has in the course of the centuries soaked through the book block. The salt residue cannot be soaked out in conservation by means of baths. Every additional dampness would inescapably dissolve the papyrus substance between the papyrus fibers into a sticky soupy mess. But the infiltration with salty elements, this enrichment of the papyrus substance with ingredients containing salt, produces in the course of time, and especially with changes of temperature, a blue-like film on the glass panes, because of which seeing through the glass is disturbed and the traces of writing, often only weakly distinguishable from the very darkened papyrus material, is hardly still perceptible. In such a case the only thing that helps is to take the leaves out of the glasses and, after cleaning the glasses of this blue-like film to reglass them.

For this reason too there emerges for photography here a special task, not only for reasons of security, as the most recent sad

diese Notwendigkeit wird sich ergeben, auch wenn die geretteten Blätter sorgsam und bei gleichmässiger Temperatur und geschützt vor Witterungseinflüssen aufbewahrt werden, weil trotz der Imprägnierung, die ja nur der Festigung der morschen Papyrussubstanz dient und den weiteren Zerfallsprozess aufhalten soll, ebenso wie die frühere Behandlung der Blätter durch die von meinem Vater angewandte Bestäubung mit Zaponlack, das Papyrusmaterial zwischen den Gläsern im Laufe der Zeit zu arbeiten beginnt.

Grund- und Überschwemmungswasser hat im Laufe der Jahrhunderte die Buchblöcke durchtränkt. Die salzigen Rückstände können bei der Konservierung nicht durch Bäder ausgelaugt werden. Jede zusätzliche Feuchtigkeit würde die Papyrussubstanz zwischen den Papyrusfasern unweigerlich sofort in eine schmierige breiige Masse auflösen. Aber das Infiltrat von salzhaltigen Elementen, diese Anreicherung der Papyrussubstanz mit salzhaltigen Ingredienzien bewirkt im Laufe der Zeit und ganz besonders bei Temperaturschwankungen einen bläulichen Niederschlag auf den Glasscheiben, wodurch die Sicht durch das Glas getrübt wird und die oft sich nur schwach vom stark gebräunten Papyrusmaterial abhebenden Schriftspuren kaum noch wahrnehmbar werden. In solchem Fall hilft da das Eine, die Blätter aus den Gläsern herauszunehmen und sie nach Reinigung der Gläser von diesem bläulichen Scheibenbelag von neuem zu verglasen.

Aus diesem Grunde erwächst auch der Fotographie hier eine besondere Aufgabe, nicht nur aus Sicherheitsgründen, wie die jüngste traurige Vergangenheit es gelehrt hat,

past has taught us, and as an indispensable supplement and help for the reader. One should, preferably immediately after conservation, or, if that is not possible, very soon after the definitive glassing, photograph each individual leaf without imperfection before any impediment to legibility can emerge. I concede that no photography, no matter how perfect it may be technically, even if it exceeds the most demanding requirements, can replace the unimpeded work on the direct original, but at some time the time will arrive that in future times, even if we leave catastrophes completely out of view, a repeated reglassing of the Manichaean papyri will simply no longer be possible, since this most sensitive of all papyrus materials that have emerged will no longer permit such a procedure of reglassing even with the most careful handling.

Hence the problem of the best possible photographic recording of each of these precious leaves must be solved now, as an aid for the reader, the interpreter, and precisely as a prophylactic means that can endure over the centuries.

und als unentbehrliches Ergänzungs- und Hilfsmittel für den Leser, dass es hier gelingt, sofort nach der Konservierung am besten oder wenn das noch nicht möglich werden sollte, sehr bald nach der definitiven Verglasung, jedes einzelne Blatt einwandfrei im Bild aufzunehmen, bevor irgendwelche Sichtbehinderungen auftreten. Ich gebe zu, dass keine Fotografie, und mag sie technisch noch so einwandfrei sein, mag sie anspruchsvollste Forderungen überbieten, die einwandfreie Arbeit am direkten Original ersetzen kann, aber einmal wird der Zeitpunkt eintreten, dass in künftigen Zeiten, wenn wir Katastrophen dabei völlig ausser Acht lassen, eine mehrmalige Umglasung der Manichäischen Papyri einfach nicht mehr möglich sein wird, da dieses empfindlichste aller bisher aufgetretenen Papyrusmaterial die Prozedur des Umglasens bei sorgsamster Handhabung nicht mehr zulassen wird.

Daher muss das Problem der bestmöglichen fotografischen Bestandaufnahme jedes einzelnen dieser kostbaren Blätter jetzt gelöst werden als Hilfsmittel für den Leser, den Interpreten und eben als prophylaktisches Mittel, das die Jahrhunderte überdauern kann.

In 1960 Böhlig then reported as follows on Rolf Ibscher's work on this material:[7]

---

7. Böhlig, "Die Arbeit," 182.

... the last 20 leaves of the Berlin *Kephalaia* book ... were conserved by Rolf Ibscher in the years 1952 and 1953. The urgently needed reglassing of all the pieces that had been glassed by Hugo Ibscher and returned to Berlin in 1958 was undertaken by Rolf Ibscher beginning in June of this year (1960), along with the conservation of a few half-conserved leaves that Ibscher Sr. had at first put to one side as too difficult, doubtlessly correctly, for it has to do usually with double or triple leaves.

... die letzten 20 Blätter des Berliner Kephalaiabuches ... wurden von Rolf Ibscher in den Jahren 1952 und 1953 konserviert. Die dringend notwendige Umglasung aller von Hugo Ibscher verglasten und 1958 nach Berlin zurückgekehrten Stücke hat Rolf Ibscher seit Juni dieses Jahres (1960) in Angriff genommen, ebenso die Konservierung einiger halbkonservierter Blätter, die Ibscher sen. zunächst—sicher mit Recht, handelt es sich doch dabei meist um Zwillings- oder Drillingsblätter—als zu schwierig beiseite gelegt hatte.

Rolf Ibscher reported as follows in 1964–1965 on the final conservation of this material and on the reglassing of the material returned from Leningrad:[8]

[p. 52] The remains of the Berlin *Kephalaia* had escaped destruction by being stored in my house after 1945. The degree of difficulty in conserving them, which I overcame between 1951 and 1955, was worse than that which the Chester Beatty papyri displayed. Unfortunately a marvellous leaf, after being separated [from the book block], was lost, completely atomized. I had to sneeze, but could not turn away with lightening speed—and all had disappeared without a trace.

[p. 62] One has to do here with the reglassing of the *Kephalaia*. More than half has been accomplished ... [p. 63] After the

[p. 52] Der Schwierigkeitsgrad der Konservierung für die Reste der Berliner Kephalaia, die der Vernichtung durch die Aufbewahrung in meinem Hause nach 1945 entgangen waren und die ich zwischen 1951 und 1955 bewaltigte, war schlimmer als ihn die Chester Beatty-Papyri aufwiesen. Leider ging mir ein wundervolles Blatt nach seiner Ablösung restlos atomisiert verloren. Ich musste niesen, konnte mich nicht blitzschnell abwenden—und alles war spurlos verschwunden.—

[p. 62] Es geht da um die Umglasung der Kephalaia. Sie ist über die Hälfte gediehen ...
[p. 63] Nach den Kephalaia

---

8. Rolf Ibscher, "Über den Stand," 52, 62, 63.

# The Conservation of the Material in the State Museum 157

| | |
|---|---|
| *Kephalaia*, groups of the codices Nr. 15[9]95, 15[9]97 and 15[9]98 still must be reglassed, along with a sizable number of leaves separated last, quite provisionally, by my father, with an entry on the paper cover that protected them which really creates puzzles: "from the codex B," i.e. then Chester Beatty [*Synaxeis*] or ?—and with the addition put in parentheses "*Letters*," i.e. then again Codex Nr. 15[9]98. What is one to make of that? But there is also among these leaves one with the number 361. To what does this belong? | müssen noch Gruppen der Codices Nr. 15[9]95, 15[9]97 und 15[9]98 umgeglast werden, sowie eine stattliche Anzahl zuletzt ganz provisorisch von meinem Vater abgelöster Blätter mit einer wahrlich Rätsel schaffenden Eintragung auf der sie bergenden Papierhülle: "aus dem Codex B", d.h. also Chester Beatty oder ? und mit dem in Klammern gesetzten Zusatz "Briefe", d.h. dann wieder Codex Nr. 15[9]98. Was soll das? Aber auch unter diesen Blättern ist eines mit der Nummer 361. Wozu gehört dieses? |

Ibscher's situation with regard to the material in East Berlin was rendered all the more serious by the departure for Tübingen in 1963 of Alexander Böhlig, the scholar commissioned to edit the material; Böhlig hence terminated his involvement:[9]

| | |
|---|---|
| [p. 54] And even Alexander Böhlig suddenly bailed out, when the resolution [of the twenty-fifth International Congress of Orientalists in Moscow in August 1960 favoring the publication of the Manichaica], with its confidently sounding tone, remained unnoted on all sides, and turned to a new illustrious task, possibly more suited to him. | Und gar Alexander Böhlig sprang plötzlich ab, als die Resolution [of the twenty-fifth International Congress of Orientalists in Moscow in August 1960 favoring the publication of the Manichaica] mit ihrem zuversichtlich stimmenden Klange allenthalben unbeachtet blieb und wandte sich einer neuen möglicherweise ihm mehr gemässen illustren Aufgabe zu. |

In Rolf Ibscher's last article of 1965 he described his reconservation experience:[10]

---

10. Ibscher, "Mani und kein Ende," 221–22.

9. Rolf Ibscher, "Über den Stand," 54.

The difficulties that emerge in reglassing vary, just as in separating off individual leaves from the book blocks. But here no "inclined plane" helps, my method for simplifying the separating of leaves, over against the procedure used by my father, this discovery of mine in the last moment before failure, thanks to desperation and the grace of the moment, or of luck. What would a restorer be when confronted with the unusual, the unique object, in the right moment, *en kairo*, without the igniting spark of genius! To sense this magical impulse in all creative realms and vocations would be worth a carefully interpretive investigation!

But the inflexible glass required extreme care in disengaging the leaves from the panes, which split the papyrus layers that lie at right angles to each other. The fixing down of the fragment parts also naturally called for great effort after reglassing. The slightest unevenness in the glass causes bad slippage when taping the edges, and often the glass plates must be reopened two or three times, even in the case of the old smooth glasses that my father had tested. Even in my father's time that happened often enough. Then if the material lies for a while, it settles down on its own.

Probably, after this first basic total reglassing, one has the assurance that now, with correct, consistently climatized storing of the restored discovery, no new

Die Schwierigkeiten, die sich bei einer Umglasung ergeben, variieren, genau wie beim Ablösen der einzelnen Blätter von den Buchblöcken. Hier hilft aber keine "Schiefe Ebene," meine Erleichterungsmethode des Ablösens, gegenüber dem von meinem Vater geübten Verfahren, diese meine Erfindung in letzter Minute vor dem Scheitern aus Verzweiflung und Gnade des Augenblicks oder Glücks. Was wäre ein Restaurator vor dem seltenen einmaligen Objekt im rechten Augenblick *en kairo* ohne den zündenden Funken des Genius. Diesem magischen Impuls in allen schöpferischen Bereichen und Berufen nachzuspüren wäre schon wert einer vorsichtig deutenden Untersuchung!

Das unflexible Glas aber verlangt äusserste Vorsicht beim Ablösen der Blätter von den mitunter die kreuzweisen Papyruslagen spaltenden Scheiben. Grosse Mühe bereitet natürlich auch nach dem Umglasen das Festigen von Fragmentteilen. Die geringste Unebenheit im Glas verursacht böses Verrutschen beim Rändeln, und oft müssen selbst bei den alten planen Gläsern, die mein Vater erprobt hatte, die Glasplatten zwei- und dreimal nochmals geöffnet werden. Auch zu meines Vaters Zeit kam das oft genug vor. Liegt das Material dann erst eine Weile, so beruhigt es sich ganz von selbst.

Wahrscheinlich wird nach dieser ersten grundlegenden totalen Umglasung die Gewähr bestehen, dass nun bei richtiger, konsequent wohltemperierter Lagerung des restaurierten Fundes keine neuen

condensations will occur between the glass panes.

[p. 222] The Berlin part of the discovery, with the exception of the codex that is in West Berlin, has been for some time undergoing reglassing, and, if no new illness puts me out of action, should be completed by the fall of 1966. A remainder of provisionally rescued material that my father had separated off last and that is still in the first stage of conservation should then follow. Dr. Dr. Nagel of the Institut für Byzantinistik in Halle, successor to Böhlig, has taken over the still unread leaves energetically and with devoted care and love. Also this deserves to be mentioned, that the important problem of the photographability is in the process of being well solved thanks to his tireless activity.

Kondensationen zwischen den Gläsern auftreten werden.

[p. 222] Der Berliner Fundanteil, mit Ausnahme des in Westdeutschland befindlichen Codex, wird seit geraumer Zeit umgeglast und dürfte, wenn keine neue Erkrankung mich ausser Gefecht setzt, bis Herbst 1966 abgeschlossen sein. Ein Rest provisorisch gesicherten Materials, das mein Vater zuletzt ablöste und das sich noch im ersten Stadium der Konservierung befindet, soll dann folgen. Der noch ungelesenen Blätter nimmt sich Dr. D. Nagel vom Institut für Byzantinistik in Halle in Nachfolge von Böhlig tatkräftig, mit hingebender Umsicht und Liebe an. Auch das verdient genannt zu werden, dass das wichtige Problem der Fotografierbarkeit dank seiner unermüdlichen Tatkraft auf dem besten Wege ist gelöst zu werden.

Wolfgang Müller's obituary for Rolf Ibscher reported his death on February 5, 1967, with the following relevant information:[11]

Chosen by the world-renowned "papyrus doctor," Hugo Ibscher, to be his successor, the graduate of the humanistic gymnasium in Berlin-Charlottenburg in 1928 began the study of classical philology at the University of Berlin, which he completed in 1938, after an interruption and temporary activity as assistant restorer in the Papyrus Collection, with graduation in Munich. Again apprentice years followed, in which Rolf

Vom weltbekannten "Papyrusdoktor" Hugo Ibscher zu seinem Nachfolger bestimmt, begann der Abiturient des humanistischen Gymnasiums in Berlin-Charlottenburg 1928 das Studium der klassischen Philologie an der Universität zu Berlin, das er nach Unterbrechung und zeitweiliger Tätigkeit als Hilfsrestaurator in der Papyrus-Sammlung 1938 in München mit der Promotion abschloss. Wieder folgten

---

11. Müller, "In memoriam Rolf Ibscher," 207.

Ibscher, under the critical eyes of his father, gained the technical assurance of all stages of the work, until he accredited himself more and more after the Second World War with significant achievements of his own, as a conservator of international stature in his own right. Thus he succeeded largely in completing the conservation of the famous Coptic papyrus codices with Manichaean texts in Berlin and Dublin, whose restoration had been interrupted by the death of his father in 1943 ...

Lehrjahre, in denen Rolf Ibscher unter den kritischen Augen des Vaters die technische Sicherheit aller Arbeitsgänge erwarb, bis er sich in zunehmendem Masse nach dem zweiten Weltkriege mit bedeutenden eigenen Leistungen als selbständiger Konservator von internationalem Rang erwies. So gelang es ihm, die Konservierung der berühmten koptischen Papyruscodices mit manichäischen Texten in Berlin und Dublin, deren Wiederherstellung durch den Tod des Vaters 1943 unterbrochen war, weitgehend zu vollenden ...

Otto Werner Luke, Rolf Ibscher's assistant, completed the reconservation of the *Kephalaia* after Ibscher's death:[12]

He could not complete the work by the time of his death, so that the continuation was entrusted to me. [p. 152] Ca. 70 leaves still had to be freed of the milky film and reconserved.

The difficult technical procedure should be briefly described. The individual papyrus leaves lie, as has been already mentioned, between glass panes that a strip on the edges holds together. This has first to be cut open on three sides, in order to lift up one of the glass panes. Here it became clear that the fine papyrus material in many cases, as a result of the early handling with laquer, was so firmly stuck to the glass panes that it could be separated off only with the greatest care with a spatula.

Er konnte die Arbeit bis zu seinem Tode nicht vollenden, so dass mir die Weiterführung anvertraut wurde. Es mussten [p. 152] noch ca. 70 Blätter von der milchigen Eintrübung befreit und umgebettet werden.

Der schwierige technische Vorgang soll in Kürze dargestellt werden. Die einzelnen Papyrusblätter liegen, wie erwähnt, zwischen Glasplatten, die ein Randstreifen zusammenhält. Dieser muss zunächst an drei Seiten aufgeschnitten werden, um eine der Glasplatten anheben zu können. Dabei stellte es sich heraus, dass das feine Papyrusmaterial in vielen Fällen infolge der früheren Behandlung mit Lack an den Gläsern so fest haftete, dass es nur

---

12. Luke, "Die Umkonservierung," 151–52.

This had to be done with full concentration, since the papyrus came loose only centimeter by centimeter and the work on one side often called for hours of work. Any careless movement of the hand endangered the object, since the papyrus fiber is so fine that it can be rubbed into powder without difficulty.

The papyrus loosened from a glass plate was, in order to prevent new sticking, covered with parchment paper and a pane of glass. In this way it was possible to turn the leaf on this firm foundation and to work on the second side in the same way. Finally the papyrus, now lying between parchment paper, was taken from the glass plates, which were to undergo a basic cleansing. The papyrus preserved between the parchment paper, by reversing the work procedure, again comes between the glass plates, that then were attached anew. The strips used here then received, to make them hold better, a stroke of color and lacquer.

The papyrus itself is held only by means of the pressure of the glass panes. No adhesive may come into contact with the fine papyrus material. Whereas an individual complete papyrus leaf is held in its position well by the pressure, the holding in place of fragments is especially difficult, since with the slightest unevenness in the glass and any shaking, it can slide and be destroyed. For this reason, the completed plates

unter grösster Vorsicht mit einem Spachtel abzuheben war. Dies musste mit aller Konzentration geschehen, da der Papyrus nur zentimeterweise sich löste und die Arbeit an einer Seite oft Stunden in Anspruch nahm. Jede unvorsichtige Handbewegung gefährdete das Objekt, da die Papyrusfaser so fein ist, dass sie sich ohne Schwierigkeit zu Pulver verreiben lässt.

Der von einer Glasplatte gelöste Papyrus wurde, um erneutes Ankleben zu verhüten, mit Pergaminpapier und einer Glasscheibe bedeckt. Damit war es möglich, das Blatt auf dieser festen Unterlage zu wenden und die zweite Seite auf gleiche Weise zu bearbeiten. Schliesslich wurde der Papyrus, jetzt zwischen Pergaminpapier liegend, von den Glasplatten genommen, die einer gründlichen Reinigung zu unterziehen waren. Der zwischen dem Pergaminpapier aufbewahrte Papyrus gelangte durch Umkehrung des Arbeitsvorganges wieder zwischen die Glasplatten, die dann neu verklebt wurden. Die hierbei verwendeten Streifen erhielten anschliessend zur besseren Haltbarkeit einen Farb- und Lackanstrich.

Der Papyrus selbst wird nur durch den Druck der Glasplatten gehalten, irgendwelche Klebstoffe dürfen mit dem feinen Papyrusmaterial nicht in Berührung kommen. Während ein einzelnes vollständiges Papyrusblatt durch den Druck gut in seiner Lage gehalten wird, gestaltet sich die Festlegung von Fragmenten besonders schwierig, da sie durch die geringsten Unebenheiten im Glas

| | |
|---|---|
| are stored in boxes horizontally. Thus the reconservation of the *Kephalaia* codex is completed, which is to be hoped will prevent a new cloudiness on the papyrus material. | und durch Erschütterungen verrutschen und zerstört werden können. Aus diesem Grunde werden die fertigen Platten horizontal in Kästen aufbewahrt. Damit ist die Umkonservierung des Kephalaia-Kodex abgeschlossen, die hoffentlich eine Neueintrübung des Papyrusmaterials verhindern wird. |

Plans for Peter Nagel to complete the editing of the *Kephalaia* were not realized, and Rolf Ibscher died without a scholar as colleague to guide him.

## — 7 —

# The Conservation of the Material in Schondorf/Göttingen/West Berlin

In 1954 Rolf Ibscher described as follows his work on the codex then in Schondorf:[1]

[p. 6] On the trip home [from London in December 1951], prevented by fog from continuing the flight, I began in Schondorf on Ammer Lake with the work of separating the leaves of the Berlin manuscript that contains the letters of Mani. This work I continued in May 1952 before flying on to Berlin, and did about 20 leaves . . .
[p. 10] In October and November 1952, on the trip home from London, I continued my work on the Berlin manuscript in Bavaria, and could remove 20 more leaves. Hence, together with the leaves separated there in the spring, there are now in all 40 legible leaves, which I impregnated in the fall of 1953.

[p. 6] Auf der Heimreise [from London in December 1951], durch Nebel am Weiterflug behindert begann ich in Schondorf am Ammersee mit der Blätterablösungsarbeit der Berliner Handschrift, die die Briefe Manis enthält. Diese Arbeit setzte ich im Mai 1952 vor dem Weiterflug nach London fort und schaffte rund 20 Blatt . . .
[p. 10] Im Oktober und November 1952 setzte ich auf der Rückreise von London meine Arbeit an der Berliner Handschrift in Bayern fort und konnte weitere 20 Blätter abheben. Zusammen mit den im Frühjahr dort abgelösten Blättern liegen jetzt also insgesamt dort 40 lesbare Blätter vor, die ich im Herbst 1953 imprägnierte.

---

1. Rolf Ibscher, "Wiederaufnahme," 6, 10.

In 1955 Rolf Ibscher gave a much fuller report on his work up to that time:[2]

[p.3] At Christmastime 1951, returning from London and delayed at the airport by fog that lasted for days, I could inform myself there right away thoroughly about the condition of the Berlin manuscript, which I had not seen since 1944. I used the time to separate a few leaves by way of experiment, after my hands had become unusually sensitive in their touch for beginning a new manuscript through the work in London that had gone on for weeks...

[p. 5] Since the Schondorf manuscript certainly must be photographed, in hopes that the faded traces of writing may possibly stand out better from the dark papyrus background, one must either use plexiglass also in Germany for our Mani leaves, or distance oneself from definitive glassing until the photography problem that has been initiated has been solved. But I must here too insist that finally this intermediate task reach a conclusion, since it is now time, in the case of the leaves that I separated in 1952 and 1953 and in part already impregnated, that they [p. 6] can be sealed off hermetically from atmospheric influences. The problem could have been solved if the Deutsche Forschungsgemeinschaft, which took over the financial supervision of the Schondorf manuscript, had followed my recommendations...

[p. 3] In den Weihnachtstagen 1951, von London kommend und durch tagelang anhaltenden Nebel am Heimflug verhindert, konnte ich mich dort gleich über den Erhaltungszustand der Berliner Handschrift eingehend informieren, die ich seit 1944 nicht mehr gesehen hatte, und nutzte die Zeit, einige Blätter probeweise abzulösen, nachdem die Hände durch die wochenlange Arbeit in London für den Beginn an einer neuen Handschrift ausserordentlich fühlfähig geworden waren...

[p. 5] Da die Schondorfer Handschrift unbedingt fotografiert werden muss, in der Hoffnung, dass die verblassten Schriftzüge eventuell besser aus dem dunklen Papyrushintergrund hervortreten, so müsste man entweder auch Plexiglas in Deutschland für unsere Maniblätter verwenden oder solange vom definitiven Verglasen Abstand nehmen, bis das in Angriff genommene fotografische Problem gelöst worden ist. Aber ich muss auch hier darauf dringen, dass endlich diese Zwischenaufgabe zum Abschluss gelangt, da es nun für die Blätter, die ich 1952 und 1953 ablöste und zum Teil schon imprägnierte, Zeit wird, dass sie hermetisch gegen atmosphärische Einflüsse abgeschlossen werden [p. 6] können. Das Problem hätte gelöst sein können, wenn man seitens der Deutschen Forschungsgemeinschaft, die finanzielle Betreuung der Schondorfer Handschrift übernahm, meine Ratschläge befolgt hätte...

2. Rolf Ibscher, "Das Konservierungswerk," 3, 5, 7–11.

Since in those days, after the currency reform and the establishing of two governmental systems in Germany, the financing of such a massive work, extending over years across zone frontiers, would have to strike upon insurpassable difficulties from Berlin, especially since in Berlin one had serious reservations about the task of the Manichaean conservation, I was most deeply grateful that a personal acquaintance with a person of broad connections, whom I had often seen in Berlin in the house of his son-in-law, Prof. Schellenberg, and who would have been glad to transplant me to West Germany, brought to the Mani undertaking insightful aid. It was Professor Geiler, formerly the minister president of Hesse after the collapse, and rector of Heidelberg University and temporary president of the *Deutsche Forschungsgemeinschaft*. His point of departure was the correct insight that this work should not be in arrears behind the work called to life by Sir Chester Beatty in London. When I came from London shortly before Christmas in 1951, he invited me to him in Heidelberg and promised me to mediate the help of the *Deutsche Forschungsgemeinschaft*. A clear-headed spirit seemed to radiate over the Mani enterprise that was getting moving also on German soil. Overjoyed, I travelled to Berlin. Since the president of the German Academy of Sciences in Berlin, Professor Stroux, recognized the same necessity not to

Da in jenen Tagen nach der Währungsreform und der Etablierung zweier Regierungssysteme in Deutschland die Finanzierung einer solchen umfangreichen über Jahre sich erstreckenden Arbeit über Zonengrenzen hinweg von Berlin aus auf unüberbrückbare Schwierigkeiten stossen musste, zumal man in Berlin der Manichäischen Konservierungsaufgabe noch reichlich fremd gegenüberstand, war ich zutiefst dankbar, dass eine persönliche Bekanntschaft mit einem Manne von weitreichenden Beziehungen, den ich im Hause seines Schwiegersohnes, Prof. Schellenberg, in Berlin des öfteren gesehen hatte und der mich gern nach Westdeutschland verpflanzt hätte, dem Maniunternehmen eine [ein]sichtige Hilfe zuführte. Es war Professor Geiler, der frühere Ministerpräsident von Hessen nach dem Zusammenbruch und Rektor der Heidelberger Universität und zeitweilige Präsident der Deutschen Forschungsgemeinschaft. Er ging von der richtigen Erkenntnis aus, dass diese Arbeit nicht im Rückstand hinter der von Sir Chester Beatty ins Leben gerufenen Arbeit in London bleiben dürfte. Als ich von London kurz vor Weihnachten 1951 kam, lud er mich zu sich nach Heidelberg und versprach mir, die Hilfe der Deutschen Forschungsgemeinschaft zu vermitteln. Ein lichter Geist schien über dem nun auch auf deutschem Boden in Gang kommenden Maniunternehmen zu erstrahlen. Beglückt fuhr ich nach Berlin. Da der Präsident der Deutschen Akademie der Wissenschaften zu Berlin, Herr Professor Stroux, die gleiche Notwendigkeit erkannte, die

leave to its own fate the Berlin manuscript and, in view of the creeping inner disintegration, not to let the rescue become illusory, I laid hold thankfully of the help that was actually coming forward, but which could become effective first in the fall of 1953, just at the moment when special difficulties blocked for me the way from Schondorf to London.

[p. 7] But for the work in Bavaria a temporary contract was created, as it had been arranged for my stays in England on the part of Sir Chester Beatty. But it must be decidedly brought to expression that the material reimbursement of this exceptional work by Sir Chester Beatty shows that he had a much greater esteem for the performance of the conservator.

In order not to let the time until this help came into force go by unused, I had to finance the work in Schondorf on the Berlin Mani manuscript in 1952 by my own means. In union with the generous help by my nearest relatives, the publisher Wolf H. Döring and my brother-in-law, the co-publisher Ernst Günther Vockrodt, who immediately introduced first steps for solving the photographical problem by means of Perutz and later Agfa-Leverkusen and Prof. Hellwich of Darmstadt, and himself undertook experiments, it succeeded that prior to my second trip to London and immediately thereafter for weeks on end I found free asylum in Schondorf and could work undisturbed.

Berliner Handschrift nicht sich selbst zu überlassen und bei dem inneren schleichenden Verfall die Rettung nicht illusorisch werden zu lassen, griff ich die tatsächlich erfolgende Hilfe, die aber erst im Herbst 1953 wirksam werden konnte, dankbar auf, just in dem Moment, als besondere Schwierigkeiten mir den Weg von Schondorf aus nach London blockierten.

[p. 7] Für die Arbeit in Bayern aber wurde ein temporäres Vertragsverhältnis geschaffen, wie es für meine Aufenthalte in England seitens Sir Chester Beatty eingerichtet wurde. Es muss aber entschieden zum Ausdruck gebracht werden, dass die materielle Vergütung dieser aussergewöhnlichen Arbeit durch Sir Chester Beatty zeigt, dass er eine weitaus grössere Hochachtung vor der Leistung des Konservators hat.

Um die Zeit aber bis zum Inkrafttreten dieser Hilfe nicht ungenutzt verstreichen zu lassen, musste ich die Arbeit in Schondorf an der Berliner Manihandschrift 1952 noch aus eigenen Mitteln finanzieren. Im Verein mit der grosszügigen Hilfe durch meine nächsten Verwandten, den Verleger Wolf H. Döring und meinen Schwager, den Mitverleger Ernst Günther Vockrodt, der sofort erste Schritte für die Lösung des fotografischen Problems über Perutz und später über Agfa-Leverkusen und Prof. Hellwich-Darmstadt einleitete und selbst Versuche anstellte, gelang es, dass ich vor meiner zweiten Reise nach London und unmittelbar danach wochenlang ein gastfreies Asyl in Schondorf fand und ungestört arbeiten konnte.

By this time 84 leaves of the Schondorf Mani manuscript, which contain, at least in large parts of the outer strata, the corpus of letters of Mani to his heads of congregations, have now been detached and provisionally laid between protective paper and glass. The first 6 leaves, which my father before the war had loosened as an experiment, were identified by C. Schmidt as letters of Mani. An examination of the leaves that I disengaged in 1952 was carried out by Böhlig, who came to the same result. The kernel or inner strata of the manuscript seem however parts of a still unknown manuscript. And it will have to do here with the same case as with the Chester Beatty manuscript, Codex C.

In this manuscript too I will proceed according to the proven London method of working: It has in view that all leaves are loosened with one effort, but that, in between, the work on the individual leaves takes place. That means that for each individual leaf there must repeatedly be undertaken a sort of reading to correct the fibers. Especially [p.8] the texts must be searched again and again for remaining splinters of fibers and small chips of papyrus, and entangled fibers straightened out.

After these proceedures, the impregnating of the leaves can then be begun. It will be, and remain, the same proven procedure of my father, as I applied already in Berlin and on a series of Schondorf leaves. It has to do with

Bisher liegen nunmehr 84 Blätter der Schondorfer Manihandschrift, die zumindest in weiten Partien der Aussenlagen das Briefcorpus Manis an seine Gemeindeoberhäupter enthält, abgelöst und provisorisch zwischen Schutzpapier und Glas gelegt, vor. Die ersten 6 Blätter, die mein Vater vor dem Kriege probeweise abgelöst hatte, waren von C. Schmidt als Briefe Manis identifiziert worden. Eine Überprüfung der Blätter, die ich 1952 ablöste, erfolgte durch Böhlig, der zu gleichem Resultat kam. Der Kern oder Innenlagen der Handschrift scheinen aber Teile einer noch unbekannten Handschrift zu sein. Und es wird hier ein gleicher Fall vorliegen wie bei der Chester Beatty Handschrift, Codex C.

Auch bei dieser Handschrift werde ich nach dem bewährten Londoner Arbeitsprinzip vorgehen: Es sieht vor, dass alle Blätter in einem Zuge abgelöst werden; dass zwischendurch aber die Arbeit an den einzelnen Blättern erfolgt. Das heisst, wiederholt muss bei jedem einzelnen Blatt eine Art Faserkorrekturlesung vorgenommen werden. Speziell [p. 8] die Texte müssen immer erneut nach restlichen Fasersplittern und kleinen Papyrusabsprengseln abgesucht und verworrene Fasern gestreckt werden.

Nach diesen Arbeitsvorgängen kann dann mit dem Imprägnieren der Blätter begonnen werden. Es wird das gleiche bewährte Verfahren meines Vaters sein und bleiben, wie ich es schon in Berlin und an einer Reihe Schondorfer Blätter anwandte. Es handelt sich um das Besprühen

spraying the leaves with a weak solution of zapon lacquer.

The London fixative, recommended by Dr. Plenderleith, did not pan out, since it made the papyrus too dark. It effected exactly what in London was said of the use of zapon lacquer, but does not correspond to the facts. For all the leaves handled in this way by my father more than 20 years ago show no darkening, whereas the new fixative indeed consolidates excellently, but develops traits of tanning and darkening the papyrus.

Furthermore it is my wish and will that the photographic problem be solved before the definitive glassing, since photographing through glass, except for plexiglas, is a dubious thing.

Now if all attempts fail, then I hope that the Beuron Palimpsest Institute knows a solution. Since my brother-in-law as a specialist in photography is very interested in this problem, and knows all previous results of the attempts at Perutz and Agfa-Leverkusen, it will be necessary that as soon as possible he goes with me to Beuron, so that, through his professional information, unnecessary attempts are avoided.

Also, in the section of work before the definitive glassing, there belongs the exact determination of the individual quires in the manuscripts. It reassures me to read in the introductions to the [p. 9] individual editions, especially to the "Manichaean Homilies," what efforts and how much time this

der Blätter mit einer schwachen Lösung von Zaponlack.

Das Londoner Fixativ, von Dr. Plenderleith empfohlen, hat sich nicht bewährt, indem es den Papyrus zu sehr dunkel machte. Es hat genau das bewirkt, was in London der Verwendung von Zaponlack nachgesagt wurde, aber nicht den Tatsachen entspricht; denn alle vor über 20 Jahren in dieser Weise von meinem Vater behandelten Blätter zeigen keine Nachdunklung, indessen das neue Fixativ zwar ausgezeichnet festigende, aber zu stark gerbende und den Papyrus dunkel färbende Eigenschaften entwickelt.

Ferner ist es mein Wunsch und Wille, dass das fotografische Problem vor dem definitiven Verglasen gelöst wird, da das Fotografieren durch Glas, ausgenommen bei Plexiglas oder Perspexglas, ein missliches Ding ist.

Sollten alle Versuche jetzt scheitern, so hoffe ich, dass das Beuroner Palimpzest-Institut vielleicht eine Hilfe kennt. Da mein Schwager als Fotofachmann an der Lösung dieses Problems sehr interessiert ist und alle bisherigen Resultate der Versuche bei Perutz und Agfa-Leverkusen kennt, wird es nötig sein, dass er mit mir, sobald als möglich, nach Beuron geht, um dort durch seine fachmännischen Informationen zu verhindern, dass unnötige Versuchsreihen angestellt werden.

Ebenfalls in den Arbeitsabschnitt vor dem definitiven Verglasen gehört die exakte Feststellung der einzelnen Buchlagen in den Handschriften. Es beruhigt mich, in den Einleitungen zu den [p. 9] einzelnen Editionen, speziell den "Manichäischen Homilien," zu lesen, welche Mühen und welche Zeit meinem Vater diese Ordnung der Blätter

arranging of the leaves has cost my father. For it becomes apparent that, as a result of the mixing up by the dealers, and especially also by the owners of this small Manichaean library, losses within the seequence of leaves have taken place. But since the fibers, often due to the high degree of loss and decay of key fibers decisive for determining by the eye, often do not provide an irreproachable guide, the identification of double leaves that belong together, out of which the quires consis, is made very difficult and often is put in question.

All such newly emerging problems, within a work procedure that is new for me, must hold me up and bring delays in estimates of time unexpectedly and unavoidably. One must accept them, and only be glad that my new technique for separating leaves … shortens amazingly this difficult and very awkward procedure, while at the same time providing a more certain guarantee of being able to lift off leaves in a whole piece that previously could not be removed at all, or survived this new birth only in fragments. All other techniques cannot be speeded up on tempo. They need their time.

It would be a further important help if also, before the final putting under glass, the person working on the text stood by my side, in the same way that this immeasurable help stood by my father already at the beginning of the conservation task by

gekostet hat. Denn es zeigt sich, dass infolge der Vertauschungen durch die Händler und besonders auch durch den Eigentümer dieser manichäischen Handbibliothek innerhalb der Blätterfolge Verluste eingetreten sind. Dadurch aber, dass die Fasern oft bei dem hochgradigen Ausfall und Verfall entscheidender Leitfasern für die Bestimmung durch das Auge oft keine einwandfreie Handhabe bieten, wird die Identifizierung zusammengehöriger Doppelblätter, aus denen die Buchlagen bestehen, sehr erschwert und oft in Frage gestellt.

Alle solche innerhalb eines für mich neuartigen Arbeitsprozesses neu auftretenden Probleme halten auf und bringen Zeittermine für veranschlagte Teilabschnitte unvermutet und unvermeidbar ins Gleiten. Man muss sie hinnehmen, und kann nur froh sein, dass meine neuartige Ablösetechnik … gerade diesen schwierigen und sehr heiklen Vorgang erstaunlich verkürzt und zugleich relativ doch eine sicherere Gewähr bietet, auch Blätter in einem Stück abzuheben, die früher garnicht ablösbar waren oder nur fragmentarisiert diese Neugeburt überstanden. Alle anderen Vorgänge können nicht im Tempo beschleunigt werden. Sie brauchen ihre Zeit.

Eine weitere wichtige Hilfe wäre es, wenn gleichfalls vor dem definitiven Verglasen mir in gleicher Weise der Textbearbeiter zur Seite stande, wie diese unschätzbare Hilfe meinem Vater schon zu Beginn der Konservierungsaufgabe durch

Schmidt and Polotsky, and later by Schmidt, Allberry and Böhlig.

This collaboration achieved, that really every fragment is proven by the text as to its correct placement and that overlooked fiber inexactitudes, which could seriously distort the text, are eliminated with the highest possible probability.

Unfortuanteley these legitimate wishes, which after all had as their goal the reestablishment of the really proven method of teamwork during the lifetime [p. 10] of my Father, led to incomprehensible tensions with the Deutsche Forshungsgemeinschaft.

The hope that with the departure of the curator of the Mani undertaking, Prof. Scheel, and under the new Curator, Prof. Hengstenberg, who is an expert aware of the goal, is not yet really fulfilled, since also over against this area of research he stands too unfamiliar and new.

After a fully absurd and unnecessary time-consuming episode which finally, in addition, ended quite unpleasantly, since, on bad advice, instead of Prof. Böhlig, as proven editor for 9 years from 1934 to 1943, one entrusted an absolute beginner [Rudnitzki] with the deciphering and reading of these difficult texts, who, in a grotesque way, also still had to give an evaluation, upon which the further financing of the work was to be made dependent, where of course nothing came of it other than an invalid false judgment, since he thus far had no experi-

Schmidt-Polotsky und später durch Schmidt, Allberry und Böhlig dauernd zur Verfügung gestanden hat.

Diese Zusammenarbeit gewährleistet, dass wirklich ein jedes Fragment auch vom Text überprüft auf seine richtige Anordnung am richtigen Platz untergebracht werden kann und dass übersehene Faserungenauigkeiten, die das Textbild empfindlich entstellen können, mit grösstmöglicher Wahr-scheinlichkeit ausgeschaltet werden.

Leider führten diese berechtigten Wünsche, die doch nur die Neuetablierung der wirklich bewährten Arbeitsteammethode zu Lebzeiten [p. 10] meines Vaters zum Ziel hatten, zu unbegreiflichen Spannungen mit der Deutschen Forschungsgemeinschaft.

Die Hoffnung, dass mit dem Ausscheiden des Kurators des Maniunternehmens, Professor Scheel, unter dem neuen Kurator, Professor Hengstenberg, ein zielbewusster Fachmann mir zur Seite träte, will sich bisher nicht recht erfüllen, da auch er diesem Arbeitsbereich zu fremd und neu gegenübersteht.

Nach einer völlig absurden und unnötigen, Zeit vergeudenden und schliesslich obendrein noch unerquicklich verlaufenden Episode, weil man schlecht beraten anstelle von Professor Böhlig, als bewährtem Editor über 9 Jahre von 1934 bis 1943, einen absoluten Anfänger [Rudnitzki] mit dem Entziffern und Lesen dieser schwierigen Texte betraute, der grotesker Weise auch noch ein Werturteil zu fällen hatte, wovon die weitere Arbeitsfinanzierung abhängig gemacht werden sollte, wobei natürlich nichts dabei herauskam als ein unmassgebliches Fehlurteil, da er noch keine Erfahrung mit Papyrusoriginalen hatte

ence with papyrus originals and stood there completely helpless and unprepared. After checking with Böhlig and the Vice-President of the German Academy of Sciences in Berlin, Prof. Steinitz, I now received the agreement that Böhlig could be put immediately at my side at Berlin's expense. I made this information known without delay to the German Forschungsgemeinschaft, so that it can hence make contact with the German Academy of Sciences in Berlin to the extent it was really serious with the view that this undertaking advance "promptly and continually," which last year it had called for precisely regarding my period of work in Bavaria.

The German Academy of Sciences has taken this desire into account in that they arranged my employment so that I was to devote myself completely to working up this scattered discovery.

The German Academy of Sciences, the work on the text, at first deferred for lack of funds [p. 11] could now, as is desirable, take place at the same time, which provided a firm assurance that the work of conservation could, not only one-sidedly on the more technical side, reach completion in the foreseeable future.

Now it will become clear whether the bright spirit of Prof. Geiler, under whom the great work was initiated, will hopefully give its renewed blessing to the task.

A rejection would be incomprehensible; it would find the

und gänzlich hilflos und unvorbereitet dastand, habe ich nach Rücksprache mit Böhlig und dem Vizepräsidenten der Deutschen Akademie der Wissenschaften zu Berlin, Professor Steinitz, nun die Zusage erhalten, dass Böhlig sofort mir auf Kosten Berlins zur Seite gestellt werden kann; ich gab diese Mitteilung unverzüglich der Deutschen Forschungsgemeinschaft bekannt, damit sie deswegen mit der Deutschen Akademie der Wissenschaften zu Berlin Fühlung nehmen kann, sofern es ihr wirklich ernst damit ist, dass dies Unternehmen "zügig und kontinuierlich" vorankommt, was sie im vorigen Jahr gerade hinsichtlich meiner Arbeitsaufenthalte in Bayern gefordert hatte.

Die Deutsche Akademie der Wissenschaften hat diesem Wunsch Rechnung getragen, indem sie mein Arbeitsverhältnis so regelte, dass ich weitgehend mich der Aufarbeitung dieses verstreut liegenden Fundes ausschliesslich widmen sollte.

Durch das Angebot der Deutschen Akademie der Wissenschaften würde die von der Deutschen Forschungsgemeinschaft aus Geldmangel vorerst [p. 11] zurückgestellte Textbearbeitung, nunmehr, wie es wünschenswert ist, gleichzeitig erfolgen können, was eine sichere Gewähr gäbe, das das Konservierungswerk nicht nur einseitig nach der mehr technischen Seite hin zur Vollendung in absehbarer Zeit gelangen könnte.

Es wird sich jetzt zeigen, ob der lichte Geist Prof. Geilers, unter dem das grosse Werk eingeleitet wurde,

disapproval of all scholars who again take inner satisfaction at the progress and success, and would bring a storm of resentment.

But the work in Schondorf had developed well in terms of work, especially since it is possible from this year on, thanks to the agreement of the German Academy of Sciences of Berlin, for me to work in Schondorf for longer periods of time. Such work on material this obstinate requires very extended work periods, especially what the eye has to perform, is dependent very much also on good weather, since artificial light overworks the eyes too much, and not least of all from the absolute reliability and relaxation of the hands.

But after the conclusion of the conservation of Sir Chester Beatty's Manichaica, the main effort will automatically go to the Schondorf manuscript, to the extent that a surprising return to London or Dublin of the three Berlin codices that wandered to Russia and of Codex B from the possession of Sir Chester Beatty not create a new turning point.

hoffnungsvoll erneut der Aufgabe seinen Segen spenden wird.

Eine Zurückweisung wäre unverständlich und würde die Missbilligung aller Wissenschaftler finden, die an dem Fortgang und Gelingen nun wieder innigen Anteil nehmen, und müsste einen Sturm der Entrüstung heraufbeschwören.

Die Arbeit in Schondorf aber hat sich arbeitsmässig gut eingespielt, besonders, nachdem es mir nun seit diesem Jahr auch möglich ist, dank dem Entgegenkommen der Deutschen Akademie der Wissenschaften zu Berlin in längeren Zeitabschnitten in Schondorf zu arbeiten. Eine solche Arbeit an derartig aufsässigem Material bedarf durchaus ausgedehnterer Arbeitsfolgen, zumal sie auch, besonders was das Auge dabei zu leisten hat, sehr von der Gunst des Wetters abhängig ist, da künstliches Licht zu sehr die Augen überanstrengt, und nicht zuletzt von der absoluten Sicherheit und Ruhe der Hände.

Nach dem Abschluss der Konservierung der Sir Chester Beatty Manichaika aber wird automatisch der Hauptakzent auf die Schondorfer Handschrift übergehen, sofern nicht eine überraschende Rückkehr der drei nach Russland gewanderten Berliner Codices und von Codex B aus dem Besitze von Sir Chester Beatty nach London oder Dublin eine neue Wende schafft.

The current status of papyrus conservation theory indicates a reversal of Rolf Ibscher's conservation theory:[3][4]

---

3. Fackelmann, *Resaurierung*, 60–61.
4. Ibid., 21, 60–61.

[p. 21] *Zapon lacquer polishing:*
Zapon is a self-polishing protection for the surface. Originally used for the protection of the top surface of metals, it was used in modified form for the conservation of library material—with the use of saltpeter acid, nitrated cellulose was dissolved in amyl acetate and carbonated hydrogen and mixed with a softening mixture of oil and camphor. coatings on paper as well as papyrus showed devastating results: Yellowing, splits, brittleness of the material, along side of the danger of fire that existed for objects treated in such a way, were the negative effects...
*Glassing:*
All too eager glassing and supplemental closing off from air of the glass plates with sealing lacquer led to the emergence of a small climate inside the plates that favors the microscopic organisms.
Result: Strong decomposition of the cellulose in the papyrus—rapid degeneration—film on the glass plates.
[p. 60] 2. *Glassing with the Elimination of Air:*
Hundreds of papyri were mounted without padding, presumably for their better [p. 61] protection, between two glass panes, which were pasted with strips of paper and finally sealed with zapon lacquer. Yet this intentional protection from the outside world had terrible consequences: Because of the lack of the interchange of air there emerged within the glass plates a miniature climate, which was ad-

[p. 21] *Zaponlacküberzuge:*
Zapon ist ein selbstglättender Oberflächenschutz. Ursprünglich für den Oberflächenschutz von Metallen verwendet, wurde er in abgewandelter Form zur Konservierung von Bibliotheksgut benützt—mit Salpetersäure nitrerte Cellulose wurde in Amylacetat und Kohlenwasserstoff gelöst und mit einem Weichmachergemisch von Öl und Kampfer versetzt. Überzüge auf Papier sowie Papyrus zeigten niederschmetternde Ergebnisse: Vergilben, Risse, Versproden des Materials waren neben der Feuergefahr, die für solchermassen behandelte Objekte bestand, die negativen Auswirkungen...
*Verglasen:*
Allzu bereitwilliges Verglasen und zusätzliches luftdichtes Verschliessen der Glasplatten mit Siegellack führte zum Entstehen eines die Mikroorganismen begüstigenden Kleinklimas innerhalb der Platten.
Folge: starker Abbau der Cellulose im Papyrus—rascher Verfalls Beschlag auf der Glasplatte.

[p. 60] 2. *Verglasung unter Luftabschluss:*
Hunderte Papyri wurden zum vermeintlich bes- [p. 61] seren Schutz ohne Einlage zwischen zwei Glasplatten montiert, welche mit Papierstreifen umklebt und letztlich mit Zaponlack versiegelt wurden. Dieser beabsichtigte Schutz vor der Aussenwelt hatte jedoch erschreckende Folgen: durch den fehlenden Luftaustausch entstand innerhalb der Glasplatten ein Kleinklima, das dem Wachstum von Pilzen förderlich war.

vantageous to the growth of fungus. The cellulose molecules gave up their necessary water constitution onto the glass plates pressed on it (according to the principle of osmotic pressure), as a result of which the degeneration of the cellulose proceeded more rapidly. Access to air and the circulation of air are a necessity for the existence of organic materials.

Die Cellulosemoleküle gaben ihr notwendiges Konstitutionswasser an die angepressten Glasplatten (nach dem Prinzip des osmotischen Druckes) ab, wodurch der Abbau der Cellulose rascher vor sich ging. Luftzufuhr und Luftzirkulation sind eine Notwendigkeit für den Bestand organischer Materialien.

In 1960/68, Böhlig summarized efforts to conserve and copy the codex after it had been moved from Schondorf to Göttingen:[5]

The manuscript that had come to West Germany and remained there after the war is at present in Göttingen and is cared for by the *Deutsche Forschungsgemeinschaft* ... I was able to see the manuscript in Göttingen through the cooperation of the *Deutsche Forschungsgemeinschaft* in the year 1957.

Rolf Ibscher repeatedly undertook conservation work on the codex in Göttingen, funded by the *Deutsche Forschungsgemeinschaft*; C. Colpe prepared the transcriptions. But at present the work has come to a halt and urgently needs to be carried forward.

Die nach Westdeutschland gekommene und nach dem Kriege dort verbliebene Handschrift befindet sich gegenwärtig in Göttingen und wird von der Deutschen Forschungsgemeinschaft betreut ... Die Handschrift in Göttingen konnte ich durch Entgegenkommen der Deutschen Forschungsgemeinschaft im Jahre 1957 besichtigen.

An dem in Göttingen befindlichen Codex wurden auf Kosten der Deutschen Forschungsgemeinschaft mehrfach von Rolf Ibscher Konservierungsarbeiten vorgenommen und von C. Colpe Abschriften angefertigt; die Arbeit ist aber gegenwärtig ins Stocken gekommen und bedarf dringend der Weiterführung.

In 1965 Rolf Ibscher described as follows the work on this codex:[6]

---

5. Böhlig, "Die Arbeit," 181–82.
6. Rolf Ibscher, "Über den Stand," 54, 58–61.

[p. 54] Charles Allberry, the great hope in the younger generation, fell as a victim of the anti-aircraft defense over Berlin. Rudnitzki quickly turned out to be not up to the job on the Berlin manuscript in Schondorf, and endangered the help that had been attained, precisely thanks to Prof. Geiler, from the Deutsche Forschungsgemeinschaft in Bad Godesberg. In his place entered Carsten Colpe in Göttingen. Colpe's joy to collaborate, at first unbounded, burned out in a rapid straw fire. From him too there resulted an endangering that still continues to persist.

[p. 58] The situation is no different [than the discouraging report about the Dublin Manichaica] with the codex in Göttingen. Carsten Colpe, who worked for a time on the leaves that had been won up until then, brought into play in Munich at the International Orientalists' Congress [1957] the thesis that the manuscript does not belong to Berlin at all but is identical with the 13 leaves of Codex B in Dublin (or again now in London, since all the Mani material was shipped back to the British Museum by Sir Chester Beatty, without the Museum's being able to administer it). Böhlig, on the other hand, maintained that, in view of the shared titles on the pages (*Synaxis*), the 31 leaves of the Berlin codex Nr. 15[9]95 belong together with [p. 59] the Göttingen codex, whereas he had earlier held it to be codex Nr. 15[9]98 (collection of *Letters*). Böhlig's cautious, but nonetheless quite fixed thesis

[p. 54] Charles Allberry, die grosse Nachwuchshoffnung, fiel der Flugabwehr über Berlin zum Opfer. Rudnitzki erwies sich sehr schnell nicht gewachsen der Aufgabe an der Berliner Handschrift in Schondorf und gefährdete die gerade dank Professor Geiler gewonnene Hilfe seitens der DFG Godesberg. An seine Stelle trat Carsten Colpe in Göttingen. Seine zuerst unbändige Freude am Mitwirken verflog in schnellem Strohfeuer. Auch von ihm ging Gefährdung aus und wirkt noch nachhaltend an . . .

[p. 58] Nicht anders [than the discouraging report about the Dublin Manichaica] steht es mit dem Codex in Göttingen. Carsten Colpe, der eine Zeitlang an den bisher gewonnenen Blättern arbeitete, warf in München auf dem Internationalen Orientalistenkongress [1957] die These ins Spiel, die Handschrift gehöre gar nicht Berlin, sondern sei identisch mit den 13 Blättern des Codex B in Dublin oder jetzt London wieder, da alles Manimaterial an das Britische Museum von Sir Chester Beatty zurückverlagert wurde, ohne dass das Museum darüber verfügen kann. Böhlig hingegen erklärt, die 31 Blätter des Berliner Codex Nr. 15[9]95 gehören wegen der gemeinsamen Überschriften auf den Seiten (SYNAXIS) zusammen mit [p. 59] dem Göttinger Codex, währehd er ihn früher für Codex Nr. 15[9]98 (Briefkollektion) gehalten hatte. Böhligs vorsichtige,

was that, possibly *by error*, my father had brought to London the 13 leaves of the Codex B of Sir Chester Beatty, *once* they were glassed, as the result of which a dilemma again emerges. What is then the situation with the 31 leaves in Berlin, that, after all, are identical with those of the codex in Göttingen? When these leaves of Codex B came back to London, Carl Schmidt was still alive. At that time, in all probability, Charles Allberry was very clearly informed about the shares in the find. I.e., probably three minds and six eyes were at work as a control. But anyone who knew my father knows that he was inerrant, unconfusable, infallible, yes, that he possessed a phenomenal ability of memory.

Again and again I must come back to my conclusions, which came to me simply from the familiarity with, the eyewitnessing of, the glassed Mani papyri that are in Dublin. At the time, I inferred therefrom that Sir Chester Beatty's Codex B had remained in Berlin (that is to say, before the termination of the war's activities) and had shared the fate, then still uncertain, of all the rest of the papyri in the Zoo bunker. The format of these leaves of Codex B was very different for me from that of the manuscript that at the time was still in Schondorf on the Ammer Lake. The first embraced 7 leaves, the second 6 leaves [per quire?].

Accordingly, in view of my calculations, *three* Berlin codi-

aber doch eben fixierte These war, mein Vater hätte möglicherweise die 13 Blätter des Codex B von Sir Chester Beatty *irrtümlich einst* verglast nach London'gebracht, wodurch wieder ein Dilemma entsteht. Was ist dann mit den 31 Blättern in Berlin, die doch identisch sind mit denen des Codex in Göttingen? Als diese Blätter des Codex B nach London zurückkamen, lebte Carl Schmidt noch. Dann war aller Wahrscheinlichkeit nach Charles Allberry sehr klar informiert über die Fundanteile. D.h. wahrscheinlich waren drei Hirne und sechs Augen als Kontrolle am Werk. Aber wer meinen Vater kannte, weiss, dass er unbeirrbar war, unverwirrbar und unfehlbar, ja, dass er ein phänomenales Erinnerungsvermögen besass.

Immer wieder muss ich auf meine Ergebnisse zurückkommen, die sich mir einfach aus der Kenntnis, aus der Autopsie der in Dublin befindlichen verglasten Manipapyri ergaben. Ich folgerte daraus damals, dass Sir Chester Beattys Codex B in Berlin verblieben war (also vor Einstellung der Kriegshandlungen) und das damals noch ungewisse Schicksal aller übrigen im Zoobunker verbliebenen Papyri geteilt hatte. Das Format dieser Codex-B-Blätter unterschied sich mir sehr von dem der damals noch in Schondorf am Ammersee befindlichen Handschrift. Die erste umfasste 7, die zweite 6 Blätter [per quire?].

ces [*Acts*, P[15997]; *Letters*, P[15998]; *Homilies*, P[15999]]—and *one* codex from the possession of Sir Chester Beatty [*Synaxeis*, Codex B] must not have returned from their odyssey. Likewise six leaves of the *Kephalaia* are missing, as has now become apparent from the reglassing. I do not believe in carelessness and destruction resulting from it, since the return lists show damages correctly noted in each case. In the case of a few papyri whose glasses were cracked, someone even carried out primitive first-aid conservations. So one was very concerned not to let anything fall victim to destruction, as well as it could be achieved. I explain the six missed *Kephalaia* leaves as still slumbering somewhere in a drawer, [p. 60] having missing the return trip. Forgetfulness is after all something very human. One will hence still have to request an inquiry. Sir Chester Beatty said to me in the summer of 1956, when we were talking about my discovering the absence of Codex B, that after all it would be a while before all Berlin papyri had returned to Berlin. It would be easier for him then to occupy himself in Berlin with a return.

The Berlin Codex Nr. 15[9]95 that is now in Göttingen still has about 100 to 120 unseparated leaves, which become more and more brittle under the climate's influence, in spite of good storage thus far. It already gave me very great difficulties at the time of my work between Christmas 1951 until 1958 in Göttingen. This work

Nach meinen Berechnungen müssen demnach *drei* Berliner Codices [*Acts*, P15997; *Letters*, P15998; *Homilies*, P15999] und *ein* Codex aus dem Besitz von Sir Chester Beatty [*Synaxeis*, Codex B] von ihrer Odyssee nicht zurückgekehrt sein. Ebenfalls fehlen sechs Blätter der Kephalaia, wie sich jetzt bei der Umglasung ergibt. Ich glaube nicht an Fahrlässigkeit und damit verbundene Vernichtung, weil die Rückkehrlisten Beschädigungen jeweils korrekt vermerkt anzeigen. Man hat ja auch bei einigen Papyri, deren Gläser zersprungen waren, sogar primitive Notkonservierungen gemacht, war also sehr bedacht, alles so gut es eben gehen wollte, nicht der Vernichtung anheim fallen zu lassen. Die sechs fehlenden Kephalaia-Blätter erkläre ich mir damit, dass sie irgendwo noch in einem Fache schlummern [p. 60] und die Rückreise verpasst haben. Vergesslichkeit ist schliesslich etwas sehr Menschliches. Man wird also noch einmal um eine Ermittlung ersuchen müssen. Sir Chester Beatty sagte mir im Sommer 1956, als wir über meine Entdeckung des Fehlens von Codex B sprachen, dass das ja Zeit hätte, bis alle Berliner Papyri wieder nach Berlin zurückgekehrt seien. Es würde für ihn einfacher sein, dann um eine Rückgabe in Berlin sich zu bemühen.

Da der Berliner, jetzt in Göttingen befindliche Codex Nr. 15[9]95 noch ca. 100 bis 120 nicht abgelöste Blätter hat, die unter der klimatischen Einwirkung, trotz guter Lagerung bisher, immer mürber werden und schon zur Zeit meiner

of a provisional safeguarding, undoubtedly most important, must be carried forward, after having been interrupted for six years. For otherwise the same thing can happen that happened to my father with Codex C [Chester Beatty's *Kephalaia*], that it was no longer possible to save it, not even with the tricky method of the Inclined Plane ... My desire was that one should also see to it that photography must go hand in hand with the conservation and editing. But this has ballooned into such a mania that precious time is wasted in search of some open-sesame formula for photography, to the detriment of the codex. This is something Mr. Colpe may perhaps secretly already regret, but this will not remove the original evil from the world.

The writing is often very rubbed off, since here we again have to do precisely with soot ink, with the exception of the writing in the parts of the codex "stored" inside, as in the case of Codex C. Here ultraviolet rays can hardly conjure up anything. Since there are large lacunae in the text in many of the ca. 145 leaves, [p. 61] photography can perhaps perform a certain supplemental help in the case of individual leaves, more in the sense of an "aid in collation" for the editor after a first transcription, in case he, as in the case of Charles Allberry, must carry on his work on the text in a different location, where he cannot have the original papyrus before him. Without "strong eyes,"

Bearbeitung zwischen Weihnachten 1951 bis 1958 in Göttingen sehr grosse Schwierigkeiten mir bereiteten, muss jetzt unbedingt diese vorerst wichtigste Arbeit der provisorischen Sicherung nach sechs Jahren ihrer Unterbrechung vorangebracht werden, weil sonst das eintreten kann, was meinem Vater mit Codex C [Chester Beatty's *Kephalaia*] passierte, dass eine Rettung nicht mehr möglich ist, auch nicht mit der überlistungsmethode der Schiefen Ebene ... Dass mein Wunsch, man sollte auch dafür sorgen, dass Hand in Hand mit dem Konservieren und dem Edieren das Fotografieren gehen möge, sich zu einer solchen *Manie* jetzt ausgewachsen hat, indem kostbare Zeit mit der Suche nach einer "Sesam-öffne-dich-Fotografierformel" zu Ungunsten des Codex vergeudet wird, mag Herrn Colpe vielleicht insgeheim schon reuen, aber damit wird das Urübel nicht aus der Welt geschafft.

Da die Schrift oft sehr abgerieben ist, weil wir es hier wieder gerade mit Ausnahme der bei den Partien des ebenso wie in Codex C "eingelagerten Codex" mit Russtinte zu tun haben, wo ultraviolette Strahlen kaum etwas hervorzaubern können, und da grosse Lücken im Text bei vielen der ca. 145 Blätter bestehen, kann [p. 61] die Fotografie bei einzelnen Blättern vielleicht eine gewisse zusätzliche Hilfe leisten, mehr im Sinne einer "Repetierhilfe" nach erster Lesung für den Editor, falls er, wie im Falle von Charles Allberry, an einem anderen Ort, wo er eben den Papyrus nicht als Original vor sich sehen kann, am Text weiterarbeiten muss. Ohne die "starken Augen," wie es Carl Schmidt im ersten Akademiebericht nennt,

| | |
|---|---|
| as Carl Schmidt puts it in the first Academy report, it will not work. Also not without a tremendous ability to make combinations, and not without the often quite odd positionings of the correct angle for the light to fall, by each individual editor, and the often amazing necessity to decipher each individual leaf—for each one it is different, according to the degree of rotting—with quite specific lighting, but never by making use of artificial light, since the papyrus, as a result of very great darkening, almost already lets one perceive hardly any more writing. | geht es nicht; ohne ein immenses Kombinierungsvermögen auch nicht und ohne die von jedem einzelnen Editor vorzunehmenden, oft wunderlichen, Einstellungen des rechten Lichteinfallwinkels und der oft frappierenden Nötigung, das jeweilige Blatt—bei jedem ist es anders, je nach dem Grade der Verrottung unter ganz bestimmter Beleuchtung, aber niemals unter Zuhilfenahme künstlichen Lichtes, zu entziffern, da der Papyrus, infolge sehr starker Nachdunklung, fast schon nicht mehr Schrift wahrnehmen lässt. |
| It should not lead to the situation that photography is elevated to a rigid doctrine for something, where nothing lies behind it except an excuse. With or without photography, Mr. Colpe can hardly find a stronger interest again in this quite difficult codex, after he has once learned to recognize very quickly that editorial work on such a Mani manuscript, in the area of editing, is among the most demanding. | Es darf jetzt nicht dazu führen, dass die Fotografie als eine starre Doktrin für etwas erhoben wird, wo nichts anderes dahinter steht als eine Ausflucht. Mit oder ohne Fotografie dürfte Herr Colpe kaum ein stärkeres Interesse wieder an diesem recht schwierigen Codex finden, nachdem er einst sehr schnell erkennen lernte, dass editorische Arbeit an einer solchen Manihandschrift zum Schwersten auf editorischem Gebiet gehört. |

Böhlig has explained, as follows, the possibility that thirteen leaves could have been taken by mistake to London: "Various individual leaves . . . were at various times also transported by both Ibschers between England and Berlin back and forth."[7]

Böhlig also has clarified Rolf Ibscher's statement that Böhlig "had earlier held it to be codex Nr. 15[9]98 (collection of *Letters*)":[8]

---

7. Böhlig, in a letter of February 5, 1986: "Verschiedene einzelne Blätter . . . sind zu verschiedenen Zeiten von beiden Ibschers auch zwischen England und Berlin hin und her transportiert worden."

8. Böhlig, in a letter of June 1, 1986.

| | |
|---|---|
| When Ibscher claimed that it has to do with a German manuscript, then it of course first of all only about the historical book or the letters of Mani, since the third German manuscirpt, the so-called "wig," would have exerted no motivation for speical security... Since apparently statements in the first and second person occur, it could less likely be the historical book, so only the letters remained. Yet what today is completely incomprehensibile... is that the codices after all were apparently so inadequately characterized that even a doubt could ever arise as to their identity. | Wenn Ibscher behauptete, es handel sich um eine deutsche Handschrift, dann konnte es sich ja zunächst einmal nur um das historische Buch oder die Briefe Manis handeln, weil die 3. deutsche Handschrift, die sog. "Perücke," keinen Reiz für eine besondere Sicherstellung ausgeübt hätte... Da anscheinend Aussagen in der 1. und 2. Person vorkammen, konnte es weniger gut das histor-ische Buch sein; also blieben, konnte es weniger gut das historische Buch sein; also blieben nur die Briefe übrig. Was nur heute völlig unbegreiflich ist ..., ist, dass die Codices doch offenkundig so mangelhaft gekennzeichnet waren, dass überhaupt ein Zweifel über ihre Identität entstehen konnte. |

Presumably, when Böhlig went to Schondorf to sort out the book blocks to be turned over to the Allied authorities, he was simply following Ibscher's instructions to keep one in Schondorf on the assumption it was one of the Berlin codices.

In the first version of his essay on the *Synaxeis* in 1957 Böhlig wrote: "In the war one of the codices belonging to the Berlin holdings was stored outside, in the region of what is now the Federal Republic."[9] In the second edition of that essay in 1968, the formulation was left open, in that the codex is no longer said to belong to Berlin and yet is said to be stored along with those of Sir Chester Beatty, as if it were not itself one of them: "In the war a manuscript was stored outside in the region of what is now the Federal Republic, along with the codices belonging to Sir Chester Beatty; this text is at present in Göttingen

---

9. Böhlig, "Synaxis = Homilia?" 485–86, especially 485: "Im Kriege wurde einer der zum Berliner Bestand gehörigen Codices ins Gebiet der jetzigen Bundesrepublik ausgelagert." Böhlig published a revised and expanded version as "Zu den Synaxeis," 222–27, especially 222–23.

to be conserved."[10] But a further insertion into the second edition of the essay makes it clear that Böhlig no longer assumed the codex belonged to Germany, in that he clearly identified it as the bulk of the codex of which Berlin owned only a vestige: "Thus one can assume, as C. Colpe also thinks, that the remainder of a Berlin codex discussed by C. Schmidt [P$^{15995}$] forms with this codex a unity of contents, but not of ownership."[11]

Here it is clear, even if cautiously and then only obliquely expressed, that Böhlig with Colpe had reached the conclusion that the codex then in Göttingen is not a codex belonging to Berlin but rather a codex belonging to Sir Chester Beatty, since from the very beginning all agreed that the *Synaxeis* belonged to Sir Chester Beatty (except for the 31 leaves of this codex that Carl Schmidt had purchased in Egypt for Berlin). Although the Göttingen codex had already been identified as the *Synaxeis* codex at the time the first edition of this essay was published, Böhlig did not in the first edition state the inescapable inference that it was hence not a codex belonging to Berlin.

---

10. "Im Kriege wurde zusammen mit den Sir Chester Beatty gehörigen Codices eine Handschrift in das jetzige Gebiet der Bundesrepublik ausgelagert; dieser Text befindet sich gegenwärtig in Göttingen zur Konservierung."

11. "Damit kann man annehmen, wie auch C. Colpe meint, dass der von C. Schmidt besprochene Berliner Restcodex [P$^{15995}$] mit diesem Codex eine inhaltliche, aber keine besitzmässige Einheit bildet."

## — 8 —

## The Conservation of the Material in London/Dublin

Regarding the London/Dublin material, Ibscher wrote in 1955:[1]

[p. 2] Thanks to the initiative of Sir Chester Beatty, events took a turn after the war . . .

[p. 3] At the suggestion of Sir Alan H. Gardiner, Sir Harold I. Bell, and Professor Glanville, Sir Chester Beatty engaged me in 1948 to carry forward the conservation work that had been orphaned. Difficult circumstances of the time put me at a disadvantage, so that it was only in x 51 that I could reach London and begin with the conservation of the Chester Beatty papyri, which at the end of 1944, on the smart advice of my father-in-law, the publisher Wolf Henry Doering, together with a Berlin manuscript (Codex No. 15998), I on my own responsibility had brought from the danger zone of Berlin for the final phase of the war into his safe

[p. 2] Dank der Initiative von Sir Chester Beatty trat nach dem Kriege eine Wende ein . . .

[p. 3] Auf Vorschlag von Sir Alan H. Gardiner, Sir Harold I. Bell und Professor Glanville engagierte mich Sir Chester Beatty 1948 zur Fortführung der verwaisten Konservierungsarbeit. Widrige Zeitverhältnisse benachteiligten mich, sodass ich erst Oktober 1951 nach London gelangen und mit dem Konservieren der Chester Beatty Papyri beginnen konnte, die ich Ende 1944 auf den klugen Rat meines Schwiegervaters hin, des Verlegers Wolf Henry Doering, zusammen mit einer Berliner Handschrift (Codex Nr. 15998) auf eigene Verantwortung aus der Gefahrenzone Berlins für die Endphase des Krieges in sein

---

1. Rolf Ibscher, "Das Konservierungswerk," 2–3.

| | |
|---|---|
| house on the quiet Ammer Lake in Schondorf, a good hour away from Munich… <br><br> In London I had begun with three residual pads (not identical with quires in the sense of codicology) of the *Psalms* book, which my father some time before the war had put to one side, for, as he had written to Sir Chester Beatty, "the unremitting difficult work of separating the leaves was too exhausting over a period of time," and separated 49 well-preserved leaves and a few very fragmentary remains of leaves. | sicheres Haus am stillen Ammersee in Schondorf, eine gute Stunde von München entfernt, gebracht hatte… <br><br> In London hatte ich mit drei Restlagen (sie Sind nicht identisch mit den buchtechnischen Buchlageneinheiten) des Psalmenbuches begonnen, die mein Vater einige Zeit vor dem Kriege zurückgestellt hatte, da ihn, wie er an Sir Chester Beatty geschrieben hatte, "die unentwegte schwere Ablösearbeit zu sehr auf die Dauer anstrengte," und 49 gut erhaltene Blätter und einige sehr fragmentarische Blätterreste abgehoben. |

Already in 1954 Rolf Ibscher had described the beginning of his work in London in somewhat more detail:[2]

| | |
|---|---|
| In 1951, after three years of persistent waiting, I obtained the exit permit from East Germany and began on October 5, not without a pounding heart, the difficult work of separating the leaves from the remains of the *Psalms* book. It was three quires that I, shortly before Christmas, was able to bring provisionally under glass. It became 49 leaves or 98 pages of text, and, in addition to that, fragmentary leaves of probably 12 leaves. | 1951, nach dreijährigem beharrlichem Warten, erlangte ich die Ausreisegenehmigung aus Ostdeutschland und begann am 5. Oktober nicht ohne einiges Herzklopfen mit der schwierigen Arbeit des Ablösens der Blätter von Resten des Psalmenbuches. Es waren drei Lagen, die ich bis kurz vor Weihnachten provisorisch zwischen Glas bringen konnte. Es sind 49 Blatt oder 98 Seiten Text geworden, dazu noch Fragmentblätter von wahrscheinlich 12 Blättern. |

In 1955 Ibscher also reported on his continuing work up to 1955:[3]

---

2. Rolf Ibscher, "Wiederaufnahme," 6.
3. Rolf Ibscher, "Das Konservierungswerk," 4–5.

[p. 4] In 1952 I began with Codex C, which, as my father too had already ascertained by separating 34 leaves, contains in large parts valuable *Kephalaia* text.

It was good luck that I did not let myself be led astray by a report of my father about the condition of the codex preservation. He had given up the work after a certain number of leaves by pointing out that each further leaf, peeled from the block of the manuscript, dissolved completely, and it seemed that one could hardly expect still useful and legible text, since practically no writing would be still recognizable.

But my new outsmarting technique, which had proven so successful on the seemingly hopelessly brittle leaves of the *Psalms* book, made it in fact possible for me to clear this hurdle.

It soon became clear that, after a series of leaves with very faded writing, suddenly quite visible *Kephalaia* text with ca. 75 leaves came to light.

It was part of the discordant accompanying music of this truly ideal task, and the false decisions that one would hope by now would belong forever to a legendary past, that in 1953 I could not continue my London work in spite of daring efforts.

But in 1954, thanks to the intervention of many good forces on the part of the German Academy of Sciences in Berlin and especially of Sir Chester Beatty, all impediments were overcome, so

[p. 4] 1952 begann ich mit Codex C, der in weiten Partien, wie auch mein Vater schon durch Abheben von 34 Blättern ermittelt hatte, wertvollen Kephalaia-Text enthält.

Es war ein dass ich mich nicht durch einen Bericht meines Vaters über den Erhaltungszustand des Codex hatte beirren lassen. Er hatte nach einer gewissen Anzahl von Blättern die Arbeit unter dem Hinweis aufgegeben, dass jedes weitere Blatt, aus dem Verbande der Handschrift geschält, sich völlig auflöste und es den Anschein hätte, kaum noch brauchbaren und lesbaren Text erwarten zu können, da so gut wie keine Schrift mehr erkennbar wäre.

Aber meine neue überlistungstechnik, die sich so gut an den hoffnungslos scheinenden mürben Psalmenbuchblättern bewahrt hatte, liess mich tatsächlich diese Hürde nehmen.

Es zeigte sich bald, dass nach einer Serie von Blättern mit Behr verblasster Schrift plötzlich guttsichtbarer Kephalaia-Text mit ca. 75 Blättern zutage kam.

Es gehörte zu der misstönenden Begleitmusik dieser wahrhaft idealen Aufgabe und den hoffentlich nunmehr für immer einer legendarischen Vergangenheit angehörenden Fehlentscheidungen, dass ich 1953 meine Londoner Arbeit trotz waghalsiger Bemühungen nicht fortsetzen konnte.

Aber 1954 waren dank dem Eingreifen vieler guter Kräfte seitens der Deutschen Akademie der Wissenschaften zu Berlin und vornehmlich Sir Chester Beatty's alle

that I could now impregnate the *Psalms* codex and in July separate the last leaf of Codex C, with a deep breath and yet with some melancholy. The most beautiful work on the Mani discovery is the separating of a leaf.

Thus, however, the most difficult partial task had been completed for the papyri belonging to Sir Chester Beatty. Codex C had produced in all about 140 partially quite good leaves. They also were all impregnated in 1954.

[p.5] The definitive glassing should have taken place in this year [1955], but since thus far the special glass perspex, or, as it is called in Germany, plexiglass, had not yet arrived, one can hardly any longer hope that more than a fourth of this also ticklish work can be performed...

Since the writing [of the "Schondorf" codex] is relatively clear, the glassing can be justified. For this reason Sir Chester Beatty also decided for the use of plexiglass, since one can also photograph through this with infrared, if it should prove to be necessary.

Hemmnisse beseitigt, sodass ich jetzt das Psalmenbuch imprägnieren und im Judi das letzte Blatt des Codex C aufatmend und doch ein wenig melancholisch abheben konnte. Die schönste Arbeit am Manifund ist das Abheben eines Blattes.

Damit aber war die schwierigste Teilaufgabe an den Sir Chester Beatty Papyri abgeschlossen worden. Codex C hatte insgesamt rund 140 zum Teil recht gute Blätter hergegeben. Sie wurden ebenfalls 1954 imprägniert.

[p. 5] Die definitive Verglasung sollte in diesem Jahre [1955] erfolgen, da aber bisher noch nicht das Spezialglas Perspex oder, wie es in Deutschland heisst: Plexiglas eingetroffen ist, bleibt kaum zu erwarten, dass mehr als ein Viert el dieser ebenfalls heiklen Arbeit geleistet werden kann...

Da die Schrift [of the "Schondorf" codex] relativ deutlich ist, lässt sich das Verglasen rechtfertigen. Aus diesem Grunde entschied sich Sir Chester Beatty auch für die Verwendung von Perspexglas, da durch dieses auch mit Infrarot, wenn es sich als nötig erweisen sollte, hindurchfotografiert werden kann.

In 1954 Ibscher had given a slightly different figure for the number of leaves he had conserved from Codex C, the *Kephalaia*:[4] "136 leaves or 272 pages of text of partially very good condition are separated and thus available."

In 1964/65 Rolf Ibscher also presented a much more disillusioned report:[5]

---

4. Rolf Ibscher, "Wiederaufnahme," 11: "136 Blätter oder 272 Seiten Text von zum Teil sehr guter Verfassung liegen abgelöst damit vor."

5. Rolf Ibscher, "Über den Stand," 55–57.

| | |
|---|---|
| [p. 55] The annoyance is and remains that the work that had advanced so energetically on the Chester Beatty part of the find has come to a complete standstill since 1956, when I was for the last time in Dublin. This is due to the death of the librarian Mr. Wilkinson and that of Mr. Merton, both of whom alone knew what still needed to be mastered. Until 1962 I had hoped [p. 56] to be able to complete the work in Dublin . . . [p. 57] The death of Mr. Wilkinson, the librarian of the Chester Beatty Library in Dublin, and just so that of Mr. Merton, led to the situation that Sir Chester Beatty, now standing under the influence of other advisors, stopped the undertaking, with the explanation that the most important part—*nota bene* the most important for him—the separating of the remaining leaves of the codex, had been completed,—whereby he was not stingy with praise—, but he said he had many other important projects in view and he was no longer the youngest. | [p. 55] Das Ärgernis ist und bleibt, dass die so stürmisch vorangekommene Arbeit am Chester Beatty-Fundanteil in völliges Stocken seit 1956 geraten ist, als ich das letzte Mal in Dublin gewesen war, durch den Tod des Bibliothekars Mr. Wilkinson und Mr. Merton's, die beide allein um das noch zu Bewältigende wussten. Bis 1962 hatte ich gehofft, in Dublin vollenden zu [p. 56] können . . . [p. 57] Der Tod Mr. Wllkinson's, des Bibliothekars der Chester-Beatty-Library in Dublin und ebenso der von Mr. Merton führte dazu, dass Sir Chester Beatty nun unter dem Einfluss anderer Berater stehend, das Unternehmen mit der Begründung abstoppte, der wichtigste—wohlgemerkt für ihn wichtigste—Teil, die Ablösung der restlichen Codicesblätter sei abgeschlossen,—wobei er mit Lob nicht kargte—, aber er habe noch viele andere wichtige Projekte vor und er sei nicht mehr der Jüngste. |

One may recall (see above) the comment that I. E. S. Edwards made in a letter to R. J. Hayes on November 1, 1960: "I cannot myself think that Rolf Ibscher could have known anything about these papyri. He was working for Sir Chester Beatty for about four years and he would surely have told one of us if he had known of their existence. I feel we should regard him as a last resource." Edwards wrote to Günther Roeder on the same day:

> I wonder whether you have any recollection of having seen these papyri at any stage either in Dr. Ibscher's possession or in the Museum. It is possible that Dr. Ibscher had them in his home and if so the only one who could help would be Rolf

Ibscher. If possible, however, I do not want Rolf Ibscher to be involved in this matter because he and Sir Chester Beatty have had some differences over the mounting of the Mani papyri which were not sent to Dr. Hugo Ibscher.

On the same day Edwards wrote to Rudolf Anthes: "I must also add that—at least at present—I do not want Rolf Ibscher to know that I am trying to trace these documents. He has been rather troublesome to Sir Chester Beatty and I am not very sure that I can count on his good will."

Thus, Ibscher stood alone, a technician dependent for employment on nonexistent scholars and patrons. He had sought in vain to persuade Polotsky to resume the collaboration that had been so effective with his father, but by 1964–1965 no scholar was available:[6]

[p. 61] Walter Till wrote me on June 6, 1957: "Of course I was in the Chester Beatty collection. But there was no talk of a continuation of the publication. That is indeed a difficult chapter. When you say that one should draw on no young forces, I must agree with you, if you mean by that beginners. This is of course not for beginners. But it is also not for old people; for one must have for it good young eyes. Young forces would be quite acceptable, but not mere beginners. People with some experience, who have worked on other things. After all, one must reflect that Polotsky, Böhlig and Allberry were also young when they tried their hands at the *Manichaica*. If now a young person goes at it, he would have the great advantage over the three I have named that indeed three volumes lie before us published, on which he [p. 62] can train himself. This possibility is some-

[p. 61] Walter Till schrieb mir am 6. Juni 1957: "Natürlich war ich in der Chester-Beatty-Sammlung. Aber über eine Weiterführung der Publikation wurde nicht gesprochen. Das ist ja ein schwieriges Kapitel. Wenn Sie sagen, man sollte keine jungen Kräfte heranziehen, so muss ich Ihnen dann recht geben, wenn Sie darunter Anfänger verstehen. Das ist natürlich nichts für Anfänger. Es ist aber auch nichts für Alte; denn man muss gute junge Augen dazu haben. Junge Kräfte wären schon recht, aber nicht gerade Anfänger. Leute mit etwas Erfahrung, die schon andere Dinge bearbeitet haben. Schliesslich muss man bedenken, dass auch Polotsky, Böhlig und Allberry jung waren, als sie sich an den Manichaika versuchten. Wenn jetzt ein Junger Baran herangeht, hat er vor den drei genannten den grossen Vorteil, dass eben schon drei

---

6. Ibid., 61.

thing the three I have named did not have. Of course there stood perhaps Carl Schmidt by their side with his great experience."

Bände publiziert vorliegen, an denen er [p. 62] sich schulen kann. Diese Möglichkeit hatten die drei Genannten nicht. Allerdings stand ihnen vielleicht Carl Schmidt mit seiner grossen Erfahrung zur Seite."

# Inventories of Individual Codices

THIS SERIES OF MISADVENTURES of the Manichaean codices as a result of the war and the postwar period means that to a certain extent, the material must be, as it were, rediscovered. For the information Schmidt and Polotsky provided more than a half a century ago, incomplete though it was, provided a picture of what there was, where it was, and what was being done with it at the time, which stands in sharp contrast to the absence of any comparable published information today. The present study hence seeks to clarify such questions as of today, so that the current generation of scholars can know what can be ascertained about the present status of this important manuscript discovery.

Schmidt and Polotsky's article proceeded to discuss in a preliminary way the Manichaean codices one by one. That initial information is cited here as a point of departure. It is then supplemented first by the official entry made in the *Inventarbuch* by Wilhelm Schubart, director of the Ägyptisches Museum and of the Papyrussammlung, together with whatever subsequent unofficial notes were added to the entries. (The *Inventarbuch* is now kept in the administration offices beneath the Pergamonmuseum on the Museumsinsel of Berlin.) This is then updated from the *editiones principes*, to the extent the codices have been published. For each codex there is added the information that Rolf Ibscher and Alexander Böhlig provided in various articles and lectures presented over the subsequent years. Then recorded for each codex is the information found in a preliminary catalog of Coptic manuscripts in the Berlin papyrus collection, a catalog presented by Wolfgang Müller to a workshop held at the Institut für Byzantinistik of

the Martin-Luther-Universität Halle-Wittenberg on December 14 and 15, 1964.[1] Then the entry is excerpted from a more detailed catalog published by Walter Beltz in 1978.[2] Finally, this secondary literature is updated with an inventory of the actual papyri themselves.

---

1. Müller, "Die koptischen Handschriften der Berliner Papyrussammlung," 67-68.

2. Beltz, "Katalog der koptischen Handschriften," APF (1978) 57-119; (1980) 121-222. The Manichaean codices are catalogued on pp. 97-98.

Part Three

The Berlin Holdings

# — 9 —

# 𝑃¹⁵⁹⁹⁵ *Synaxeis (Berlin Part)*

SCHMIDT AND POLOTSKY REPORTED as follows:[1]

And with equal brevity we must report on a collection of 31 leaves brought under glass, which were acquired in the Fayyum and without doubt belong to the London Mani pieces. It also has to do with individual treatises, as the remains of titles show. We read there: ⲦⲘⲀ2ⲤⲚⲦⲈ ⲚⲤⲨⲚⲀⲌⲒⲤ, "the second σύναξις [a chapter superscription on lines 14–15 of the side with vertical fibers of the leaf labeled 18, and a running head at the top of the side with vertical fibers of the leaf labeled 17], and beside this the number ⲖⲄ, which indicates the 33rd treatise, or ⲦⲘⲀ2ⲰⲀⲘⲦⲈ ⲚⲤⲨⲚⲀⲌⲒⲤ ⲘⲠⲀ2ⲰⲀⲘⲦ ⲚⲖⲞⲄⲞⲤ ⲘⲠⲈⲨⲀⲄⲄⲈⲖⲒⲞⲚ ⲈⲦⲀⲚⲤ = "The Third σύναξις of the Third λόγος of the Living Gospel" [a chapter superscription on lines 10-11 of the side with the horizontal fibers of the leaf labeled 16]. What is meant by σύναξις, "assembly,"

Und ebenso kurz müssen wir referieren über eine Sammlung von 31 unter Glas gebrachten Blättern, die im Fajum erworben sind und unbedingt zu den Londoner Manistücken gehören. Es sind ebenfalls einzelne Abhandlungen, wie die Reste der Überschriften zeigen. Wir lesen dort: ⲦⲘⲀ2ⲤⲚⲦⲈ ⲚⲤⲨⲚⲀⲌⲒⲤ "die zweite σύναξις" [a chapter superscription on lines 14–15 of the side with vertical fibers of the leaf labeled 18, and a running head at the top of the side with vertical fibers of the leaf labeled 17], daneben die Zahl ⲖⲄ, die die 33. Abhandlung anzeigt, oder ⲦⲘⲀ2ⲰⲀⲘⲦⲈ ⲚⲤⲨⲚⲀⲚⲒⲤ ⲘⲠⲀ2ⲰⲀⲘⲦ ⲚⲖⲞⲄⲞⲤ ⲘⲠⲈⲨⲀⲄⲄⲈⲖⲒⲞⲚ ⲈⲦⲀⲚⲤ = "die dritte σύναξις des dritten λόγος des lebendigen Evangeliums" [a chapter superscription on lines 10-11 of the side with the horizontal fibers of the leaf

---

1. Schmidt and Polotsky, "Ein Mani-Fund," 30.

still remains unclear. A hint is provided by the mention of the "Living Gospel," the well-known original work of Mani. It seems to have to do with some kind of commentary to this text, from the pen of a later Manichaean.

labeled 16]. Was unter σύναξις "Versammlung" zu verstehen ist, bleibt noch unklar. Ein Fingerzeig gibt die Erwähnung des "lebendigen Evangeliums," des bekannten Originalwerkes des Mani. Es scheint sich um eine Art von Kommentar zu diesem aus der Feder eines späteren Manichäers zu handeln.

Schmidt and Polotsky's report about the rest of the *Synaxeis* codex is included in their report among the codices belonging to Sir Chester Beatty (see Codex B *Synaxeis* below).

In their original report (see above), Schmidt and Polotsky had stated: "The antiquities dealer in the Fayyum had sold his manuscripts exclusively to Mr. Chester Beatty." The 31 leaves are an exception, for "one had removed the top and bottom layers of papyrus, which had suffered to an especial extent against the covers of the binding . . . , to give the whole a better appearance." In the spring of 1931, after Sir Chester Beatty had acquired the three codices of the Fayyum dealer, Schmidt "found such outwardly unimpressive remains, which doubtlessly belong to the papyrus books acquired by Mr. Chester Beatty in the Fayyum, and . . . acquired them for a cheap price, since the dealer already had his great reward in his pocket. I do not regret my decision, for in the conservation 31 leaves could be brought under glass in more or less fragmentary preservation." Thus, only 31 leaves of this codex belong to the Papyrus-Sammlung of the Ägyptische Abteilung of the Staatliche Museen of Berlin.

Volume 15 of the *Inventarbuch* of the Papyrus-Sammlung, titled on the spine "Staatl. Museen Ägyptische Abteilung $P^{15001-16000}$" ("State Museums, Egyptian Section, $P^{15001-16000}$"), records on facing pages both numbered 2294, each of the Manichaean manuscripts, under the numbers $P^{15995-15999}$. The hand of the initial entry in black ink Wolfgang Müller has identified as that of Wilhelm Schubart, under whom he had studied, and who was his predecessor (several times removed) as director of the Papyrus-Sammlung and the Ägyptische Abteilung.[2]

---

2. In letters of May 7, 1957, and May 14 and 15, 1957, from Rolf Ibscher to Carsten Colpe, these entries are ascribed, apparently erroneously, to Hugo Ibscher.

At P$^{15995}$ there is the following entry, apparently made before the identification of the leaves as deriving from the *Synaxeis* codex:

| | |
|---|---|
| Coptic Papyrus Codex, 31 leaves, partially damaged. Manuscript of about the fifth century A.D. Content: Manichaean writing about theogony. Acquired through Prof. Carl Schmidt, in Cairo, 1931. Gift of Mr. August Pfeffer 1933. The leaves are on the average 22 cm high, 15 cm wide. | Koptischer Papyruskodex, 31 Blätter, z. T. beschädigt. Handschrift etwa des 5. Jh. n. Chr. Inhalt: Manichäische Schrift über Theogonie. Erworben durch Herrn Prof. Carl Schmidt, in Cairo, 1931. Geschenk des Herrn August Pfeffer 1933. Die Blätter sind im Durchschnitt 22 cm hoch 15 cm breit. |

To this basic entry have been added in pencil: "Schrank 5" ["cupboard 5"] and "z. Zt. Papyrus-Sammlung Regal" ["at present Papyrus Collection shelves."] A rubber stamp reading "1958 vorhanden" ["1958 present"] records the return of the material from Leningrad, after which 31 counting marks record the presence of all 31 leaves, which is also stated explicitly: "31 Blätter zurück" ["31 leaves back"]. A second line in the same hand records: "Codex in Göttingen! [Rolf] Ib[scher]." A stamp reading "1972 vorhanden" ["1972 present"] confirms that the material was present at the time of the inventory of holdings made that year by Ulrich Luft, then of the Museum staff.

The *Vorwort* of 1940 to the *Kephalaia* provides more information, though still cryptic, about the patron who made possible the Museum's acquisition of the Manichaica:

| | |
|---|---|
| Professor Schmidt sought to gain the rest of the papyri for Germany. That was possible for him only thanks to the financial support of Director August Pfeffer, who acquired the texts and in a very generous way gave them to the State Museums in Berlin. | Den Rest der Papyri suchte Professor Schmidt für Deutschland zu gewinnen. Das wurde ihm nur möglich durch die finanzielle Unterstützung des Herrn Direktor August Pfeffer, der die Texte erwarb und in hochherziger Weise den Staatlichen Museen zu Berlin schenkte. |

Alexander Böhlig has explained (during a visit to his Tübingen home on May 8, 1986) that Schmidt cultivated a circle of well-to-do patrons, to which Pfeffer must have belonged. The title *director* does not refer to a position with, e.g., the museum or the publishing house, but the title apparently reflects a business relationship.

The possibility that there are in Berlin more leaves of the *Synaxeis* than the 31 Schmidt acquired was raised by Rolf Ibscher[3] with regard to

> a sizable number of leaves separated last, quite provisionally, by my father, with an entry on the paper cover that protected them which really creates puzzles: "from Codex B," i.e., then Chester Beatty [*Synaxeis*] or ?—and with the addition put in parentheses "Letters," i.e., then again Codex Nr. 15[9]98. What is one to make of that?

These additional leaves that puzzled Rolf Ibscher are currently in the Papyrus-Abteilung of Berlin, now classified unambiguously as belonging to $P^{15998}$.

Wolfgang Müller's preliminary inventory of 1964–1965 reported: "*Synaxeis* = sermons, 31 leaves in Berlin, the rest in Göttingen, here 145 leaf units separated, about 100–120 leaves still on the book block."[4]

Beltz catalogued the 31 leaves as follows:

| | |
|---|---|
| I 603 $P^{15995}$. 31 leaves of a codex, $P^{15995}$, averaging 18–20 cm in height and 11–16 cm in width. There are about 26–28 lines per page. It is very poorly preserved. It is hardly legible. The codex belongs to the discoveries of Medinet Madi and was acquired by Schmidt for Berlin in 1928 [read: 1931]. The remainder of the codex is to be found for the time being in West Berlin. Since 1945, 145 new leaf units have been separated and conserved there. The remainder of the book block is not yet conserved. A. Böhlig and C. Colpe have defined the codex as "*Synaxeis* to the *Living Gospel* of Mani." On the text see Schmidt and Polotsky, "Ein Mani-Fund in Ägypten," Berlin 1933, and W. | I 603 $P^{15995}$; 31 Blätter eines Codex, $P^{15995}$, durchschnittliche H. 18–20 und durchschnittliche B. 11–16. Pro S. etwa 26–28 Z. Sehr schlecht erhalten. Kaum lesbar. Codex gehört zu den Funden von Medinet Mandi und wurde von Schmidt für Berlin 1928 [read: 1931] erworben. Der Rest des Codex befindet sich z. Z. in Berlin-West. Seit 1945 sind dort 145 neue Blatteinheiten abgelöst und konserviert. Der Rest des Buchblockes noch nicht konserviert. A. Böhlig und C. Colpe haben den Codex bestimmt als "Synaxeis zu dem Lebendigen Evangelium des Mani." Zum Text siehe Schmidt-Polotsky, Ein Manifund in |

---

3. Rolf Ibscher, "Über den Stand," 62.

4. *Synaxeis* = Predigten, 31 Bl. in Berlin, Rest in Göttingen, hier 145 Blatteinheiten abgelöst, etwa 100–120 Bl. noch auf dem Buchblock.

| | |
|---|---|
| Müller, "Koptologische Studien in der DDR," *Wissenschaftliche Zeitschrift der Universität Halle-Wittenberg* 1965, Sonderheft, pp. 67–68. | Ägypten, Berlin 1933, und W. Müller, Kopt. Studien in der DDR, WZU Halle-Wittenberg 1965, Sonderheft, S. 67–68. |

Photographs of both sides of leaf 20 are on file at the Papyrus-Sammlung in Berlin. One copy of each side was donated to the Manichaean archives of the Institute for Antiquity and Christianity, which were turned over to Wolf-Peter Funk.

Gesine Schenke Robinson transcribed the thirty-one leaves in 1985–1986. Wolf-Peter Funk provided a partial draft translation in April 1988.

This codex has not been published.

# — 10 —

## 𝑃¹⁵⁹⁹⁶ *Kephalaia, Volume One*

SCHMIDT AND POLOTSKY'S BASIC report cited above noted that it was part of the *Kephalaia* that was first shown to Schmidt in 1930 and acquired on his return trip from Jerusalem, and that it was this codex that was then supplemented by two further piles of papyrus acquired from the same dealer in the spring of 1931. Schmidt and Polotsky added specific information about this codex as follows:[1]

[p. 18] In first place among the present papyrus books stands a work whose parts came to Berlin in individual stages and whose conservation was begun immediately by Ibscher, so that already rather large connected portions have been brought under glass. It has to do here with a work that was counted among the original writings of Mani and once bore the name Κεφάλαια in the Greek tradition.

[p. 19]... With regard to externals, the work must have embraced an unusually large size, in that Ibscher has already been able to identify the number ΦΙΔ = 514 on one of the leaves. For a fortunate circumstance comes to

[p. 18] Unter den vorliegenden Papyrusbüchern tritt an erste Stelle ein Werk, dessen Teile in einzelnen Etappen nach Berlin gekommen sind und dessen Konservierung sofort von Ibscher in Angriff genommen ist, so dass bereits grössere zusammenhängende Stücke unter Glas gebracht worden sind. Es handelt sich hier um ein Werk, das zu den Originalschriften des Mani gerechnet wurde und einst den Namen Κεφάλαια in der griechischen überlieferung trug.

[p. 19]... Was das Äussere anbetrifft, so muss das Werk einen ungemein grossen Umfang gehabt haben, wenn Ibscher bereits die Ziffer ΦΙΔ = 514 auf einem der Blätter feststellen konnte. Denn als günstiger Umstand kommt uns zur Hilfe, dass die einzel-

---

1. Schmidt and Polotsky, "Ein Mani-Fund," 18–24. The quotations are from 18–19.

| our help, in that the individual pages were numbered and thus an arrangement of the separated parts becomes possible. In any case the work must have included in the papyrus codex more than 520 pages = 260 leaves. | nen Seiten numeriert waren und dadurch eine Anordnung der auseinandergefallenen Teile ermöglicht wird. Jedenfalls muss das Werk in dem Papyruscodex mehr als 520 Seiten = 260 Blätter umfasst haben. |
|---|---|

Quire 21 would have consisted of pages 481–504, quire 22 of pages 505–28.

Wilhelm Schubart recorded in the *Inventarbuch* of the Papyrussammlung of the Ägyptisches Museum of Berlin-Hauptstadt der DDR in black ink for P[15996] the following entry: "Koptischer Papyruskodex." ["Coptic Papyrus Codex."] The column regarding "Art der Erwerblung" ["Nature of the Acquisition"] reports "dsgl." ["the same"] as P[15995], i.e.: "Acquired through Prof Carl Schmidt, in Cairo, 1931. Gift of Mr. August Pfeffer 1933." An added penciled note reports "NKEFALAION." A rubber stamp "Phot." may mean the material was photographed. The original report contained a photograph of p. 33, and the publication of Volume 1 contained a photograph of p. 31 as the frontispiece. In the Papyrus-Sammlung there are on file glossy prints of p. 295 (with a black background) and of pp. 167–68 (on a white background), presumably resulting from such photography. Glossy prints of pages 259, 261, 262, 265–74, 277, 278, 281–91, 297–99 (on a white background), prepared under the supervision of Peter Nagel for his work on the codex in the 1960s, are also present. Duplicates of pages 167, 168, 282 and 295 were given to the Manichaean Archives of the Institute for Antiquity and Christianity, and from there to Wolf-Peter Funk. A purple carbon note reports "ca. 200 Blätter, Rest in Berlin, übr. in Mo[skau]." ["ca. 200 leaves, a remainder in Berlin, the rest in Moskow]." A rubber stamp reading "1958 vorhanden" ["1958 present"] records the return of the material (presumably not from Moscow but) from Leningrad, and a rubber stamp reading "1972 vorhanden" ["1972 present"] records that the material was present at the time of the inventory of holdings made that year by Ulrich Luft, then of the museum staff.

In 1940 Hugo Ibscher reported:[2]

---

2. *Kephalaia* (see following note), Ibscher, "Die Handschrift," v–xiv, especially vi–vii.

[p. vi] Hence the *Kephalaia* did not come to Berlin in one volume, but in two larger packets and five weaker layers. All of course nicely jumbled! However, after five years of hard work, we have succeeded in saving from the *Kephalaia* over 400 pages for scientific work and in defining with certainty and almost without a gap the sequence of the leaves.

| Purchase Number | Page Range |
|---|---|
| 1 | 1–18 |
| 2 | 19–310 |
| 3 | 331–56 |
| 4 | 357–76 |
| 5 | 377–94 |
| 6 | 395–414 |
| 7 | 421–end |

[p. vii] I could identify the pages that are missing in the list, 311-30, in a quite small find which had come to the Vienna collection along with other papyri. This acquisition was in such a bad condition that the administration of the Vienna collection at first did not even want to send it to me, since the whole appeared to be only a confusion of fibers. I succeeded in gaining from it a few more pages, even though they were quite incomplete, and on one page deciphered the chapter [number] 132, by means of which then it could be established that we had to do here with remains of pp. 311–30. Also at the other places where the leaves had been ripped

[p. vi] Die Kephalaia kamen daher auch nicht in einem Volumen nach Berlin, sondern in zwei stärkeren Packen und fünf schwächeren Lagen. Alles natürlich hübsch durcheinander! Nach fünfjähriger angestrengter Arbeit ist es aber gelungen, allein von den Kephalaia über 400 Seiten für die wissenschaftliche Bearbeitung zu retten und die Reihenfolge der Blätter fast lückenlos sicher zu bestimmen. Die einzelnen Ankäufe ergeben folgende Seiten:

| Ankauf | jetzt Seite |
|---|---|
| I | 1–18 |
| II | 19–310 |
| III | 331–56 |
| IV | 357–76 |
| V | 377–94 |
| VI | 395–414 |
| VII | 421–Schluss |

[p. vii] Die in der Aufstellung fehlenden Seiten 311-330 konnte ich in einem winzigen Funde feststellen, der mit andern Papyri in die Wiener Sammlung gekommen war. Dieser Ankauf war so schlecht erhalten, dass die Direktion der Wiener Sammlung ihn mir erst gar nicht schicken wollte, weil das Ganze nur ein Gewirr von Fasern zu sein schien. Es gelang mir, daraus noch einige, wenn auch unvollständige Seiten zu gewinnen und auf einer Seite das Kapitel 132 zu entziffern, wodurch dann festgestellt werden konnte, dass es sich hier um Reste der Seiten 311–30 handelt. Auch an den anderen Stellen, wo die Blätter mit Gewalt voneinandergerissen worden sind, sind stets die betref-

apart by force, the leaves in question have always been more or less destroyed. Thus between the pp. 414–21 there are only paltry remains of the missing leaves, which can hardly be identified. [Pages 415/16 and 419/20 are missing from the box listing pages 401–20. Only the bottom half of pages 417/18 is extant, and only the top half of pages 413/14 is extant. They complement each other well, and hence could be halves of the same leaf, though vertical fiber continuity is inconclusive.] Also the pages after 421 have suffered very much. By means of the circumstances of the find I was able to identify the last leaf that survives, in spite of the missing pagination, as bearing the page number 501/02. It shows the chapter [number] c = 200.

But whether the Berlin *Kephalaia* have come down to us complete, or whether at the end further pages will be missing, is difficult to determine. But one may conjecture that a rather large number of leaves is lost. For I was able to identify a further *Kephalaia* book among the Mani books in the possession of Chester Beatty. Whereas the last discernible chapter number in the Berlin *Kephalaia* is 200, on a page of the London *Kephalaia* I could clearly read the chapter [number] 333. Since a number of pages still preceded it, which I have not yet been able to conserve, one can with certainty assume that the London *Kephalaia* in the present condition began with chapter 300. Thus there are missing between the Berlin and

fenden Blätter mehr oder weniger zerstört worden. So befinden sich zwischen den Seiten 414–21 nur noch kümmerliche Reste der fehlenden Blätter, die sich kaum werden bestimmen lassen. [Pages 415/16 and 419/20 are missing from the box listing pages 401–20. Only the bottom half of page 417/18 is extant, and only the top half of page 413/14 is extant. They complement each other well, and hence could be halves of the same leaf, though vertical-fiber continuity is inconclusive.] Auch die auf 421 folgenden Seiten haben noch sehr gelitten. Das letzte erhaltene Blatt liess sich durch die Fundumstände, trotz der fehlenden Paginierung, von mir als Träger der Seitenzahl 501/502 bestimmen. Es zeigt das Kapitel c – 200.

Ob die Berliner Kephalaia aber vollständig auf uns gekommen sind, oder ob am Schluss noch Seiten fehlen werden, wird sich nur schwer feststellen lassen. Zu vermuten ist aber, dass noch eine grössere Anzahl von Blättern verlorengegangen ist, denn ein weiteres Kephalaiabuch konnte ich unter den im Besitz von Chester Beatty befindlichen Manibüchern feststellen. Während nun die letzte, sichtbare Kapitelzahl in den Berliner Kephalaia 200 ist, konnte ich auf einer Seite der Londoner *Kephalaia* das Kapitel 333 deutlich lesen. Da noch eine Anzahl von Seiten vorausgehen, die ich noch nicht restaurieren konnte, kann man mit Sicherheit annehmen, dass die Londoner Kephalaia im jetzigen Zustand mit Kapitel 300 begonnen haben. Es fehlen also zwischen den Berliner

the London *Kephalaia* roughly 100 chapters, which would call for about 240 pages or 120 leaves. But there is hardly room for a further volume between the two that are in hand, so that we must initially assume that the missing 120 leaves were lost either from the end of the Berlin or rather from the beginning of the London *Kephalaia*. After all, it is not impossible that each volume of the *Kephalaia* contained 750 pages. Given the very thin papyrus material, the book block would have measured hardly more than 3–4 cm. A tiny fragment still attached to the upper margin of the last leaf along with other uninscribed fragments, and showing vestiges of the pagination ϕιΔ = 514, also proves to us that pages were lost in the case of the Berlin *Kephalaia* at the end of the extant part.

und den Londoner Kephalaia rund 100 Kapitel, die etwa 240 Seiten oder 120 Blätter ergeben würden. Für einen weiteren Band zwischen den beiden vorhandenen ist aber kaum Platz, so dass wir vorerst annehmen müssen, dass die fehlenden 120 Blätter entweder vom Schluss der Berliner, oder vom Anfang der Londoner Kephalaia verlorengegangen sind. Immerhin ist es nicht unmöglich, dass jeder Band der Kephalaia etwa 750 Seiten umfasst hat; bei dem sehr dünnen Papyrusmaterial würde der Buchblock kaum mehr als 3–4 cm gemessen haben. Dass bei den Berliner Kephalaia am Ende des erhaltenen Teils Seiten verlorengegangen sind, beweist uns auch ein winziges Fragment, das noch auf dem oberen Rand des letzten Blattes mit anderen unbeschriebenen Fragmenten festsass and Reste der Pagina ϕιΔ = 514 zeigte.

It is difficult to correlate the seven acquisitions Ibscher here reports with Schmidt's report to the effect that he acquired the bulk as his first purchase in 1930 and two smaller parts in the spring of 1931.

The remains of pp. 311–30 belonging to Vienna must have been sent to Berlin, conserved there by Hugo Ibscher, and then returned to Vienna. Schmidt and Polotsky had reported concerning the Vienna material that "Ibscher recently saved fragments of two leaves from this junk heap," which reference corresponds roughly to Ibscher's allusion to "a few more pages." The material currently in the *Österrreichische Nationalbibliothek* bears the inventory number K 11010. It consists of four glass containers, containing three leaves and a number of fragments. The leaves are identified as pp. 311–16. The leaves 313/314 and 315/316 are most nearly complete, and relate to each other in terms of fiber directions as like (in this case vertical fibers) facing like. The

small remnant of a leaf assigned the numeration 311/312 has been rotated 90 degrees rather than having been glassed right side up, to judge by the alignment of its profile. The surface labeled page 312 shares roughly the profile of pp. 313 and 315, suggesting that p. 312 should be given an odd number. But it could not be p. 311, since then (in terms of fiber directions) like would not face like. For p. 313 and the page labeled p. 312, that should be an odd-numbered page, both have horizontal fibers but would not face each other. In fact, the profile of the page labeled 312 is at places closer to that of p. 315 than to that of 313. Hence, one may postulate that what is labeled as page 312, which has horizontal fibers, is actually p. 317, 321, 325, or 329, all of which one would expect to have horizontal fibers. What is labeled p. 311 would then be p. 318, 322, 326, or 330. The chapter number Ibscher detected, 132, would then fall on page 318, 322, 326, or 330. Since chapter 140 begins on p. 343, one may estimate that a chapter averages two-and-a-half pages, in which case chapter 132 would fall at about p. 323, or, among the actual options, at p. 322. Hence one may quite tentatively postulate that the leaf labeled "311/312" is pp. 321–322. One of the five fragments glassed with "311/312" is identified as "oben links v. 312" ["above left from 312,"] and it would indeed increase the similarity of profile with page 315 if so placed on page 321. The other five fragments in this glass and the some eight fragments in a fourth glass are not identified. It is perhaps more probable that the material between pages 311 and 330 that survived belonged closely together, as a single pad, rather than widely scattered through this spectrum of ten leaves. Hence, the unidentified fragments may be largely from pages 317/318 and 319/320, since the extant leaves are pp. 313/314, 315/316 and probably 321/322.

The *Kephalaia* began to appear in fascicles in 1935; in 1940 the first ten fascicles were published as Volume 1, containing pp. 1–244.[3]

---

3. Polotsky and Böhlig, *Kephalaia*. Manichäische Handschriften der Staatlichen Museen Berlin, Band 1, herausgegeben im Auftrage der Preussischen Akademie der Wissenschaften unter Leitung von Prof. Carl Schmidt, 1. Hälfte (Lieferung 1–10); Böhlig, "Die Arbeit," 183, n. 1 states: "Die Namen der wirklichen Editoren fehlen auf dem Titelblatt aus folgendem Grund: Der Name von H. J. Polotsky sollte in der NS-Zeit im Anschluss an die Rassengesetzgebung nicht auf dem Titelblatt erscheinen; die Nennung meines Namens allein habe ich aber abgelehnt." ["The names of the real editors are missing from the title page for the following reason: The name of H. J. Polotsky was not supposed to appear on the title page in the Nazi time because of the racial legislation. But I turned down the naming of my name alone."] Böhlig reports,

Hugo Ibscher had referred to "over 400 pages" having been conserved. It is unlikely that more was conserved during the war. For Rolf Ibscher reported in 1964–1965 that "already in 1937" his father had stopped working "regularly" on the materials,[4] and in 1955 that "during the war this minutely detailed work ... came to a complete halt."[5] The *Inventarbuch* was at Rolf Ibscher's disposal while the material itself was in the east following the war.[6] It was during this time that the entry was added, perhaps by him, to the effect that there were "ca. 200 leaves." This hardly reflects a new inventory, since the material was inaccessible, but is no doubt merely an imprecise allusion to the 1940 report of "over 400 pages." Thus the exact number of leaves conserved by Hugo Ibscher is not known.

After the war Rolf Ibscher resumed the conservation work his father had not completed. He spoke in 1955 of "the attempt to separate and impregnate a residue of very fragmented leaves of the *Kephalaia*, which my father had designated as 'insoluable.' These leaves should be definitively glassed by this winter, at the beginning of 1956."[7] This material had been taken to the Ibscher home before or during the time of the war and thus had not been taken to Leningrad. Its presence in the home is explainable in terms of the fact that from the age of sixty, i.e., from 1934 on, Hugo Ibscher was permitted to work three days a week at home.[8] In the archive of the Chester Beatty Library there is a black loose-leaf folder entitled: "Papyrus. Biblical Manichaean Hieratic Greek etc. General Catalogue." In the section entitled "Manichaean Pap." there is a note dated May 1940 that reads: "Mr. Allberry said that Dr. Ibscher had the remainder of Mr. Beatty's papyrus at his house in the country, at Klein Machnow (see letter from Allberry)." At the death of Hugo Ibscher it was put in the concrete bunker at the Zoo.

---

183, that Polotsky edited Coptic pages 1–102, and that Böhlig himself edited Coptic pages 103–244. Allberry, *Manichaean Psalm-Book, Part 2*, "Preface," reported that fascicles 1–8 had appeared in 1935–37.

4. Ibscher, "Über den Stand," 50.

5. Ibscher, "Das Konservierungswerk," 2.

6. This is apparent from allusions to it by Rolf Ibscher in letters to Carsten Colpe of August 7, 1957, and August 14–15, 1957, and has been confirmed by Wolfgang Müller.

7. Ibscher, "Das Konservierungswerk," 5.

8. Böhlig reports this in a letter of February 10, 1986.

Böhlig's presentation of 1960/68 reported as follows concerning this material left in Berlin:[9]

> Of the material in Berlin only a very small part has always remained in Berlin. It was the last 20 leaves of the Berlin *Kephalaia* book. They were conserved by Rolf Ibscher in the years 1952 and '53.

Böhlig has explained this ambiguous formulation as follows:[10]

| | |
|---|---|
| It [Böhlig's statement "last 20 leaves"] merely means that Rolf Ibscher in these years conserved the last = the only leaves that were still in Berlin, which belonged to the *Kephalaia* and were still there, i.e., had not been put in security (they survived the war in the Ibscher house). It was indeed 20 pieces. I did not express any opinion as to what page numbers of the book were to be assigned to these leaves, and indeed I could not, since that would have been pure speculation (when the page numbers, as in this case, were no longer preserved on the leaves). For of course I did not know which and how many leaves of the *Kephalaia* had come to the USSR. | Sie [Böhlig's statement "last 20 leaves"] besagt nämlich einfach, dass Rolf Ibscher in diesen Jahren die letzten = die einzigen noch in Berlin befindlichen Blätter, die zu den Kephalaia gehörten und noch vorhanden, d.h. nicht sichergestellt waren (sie überstanden den Krieg im Hause Ibscher), konserviert hat; das waren eben 20 Stück. Mit welcher Seitenzahl des Buchs diese Blätter zu belegen waren, darüber habe ich mich überhaupt nicht geäussert, konnte es auch gar nicht, da es reine Spekulation gewesen wäre (wenn die Seitenzahl, wie hier, auf den Blättern nicht mehr erhalten war); denn ich wusste ja nicht, welche und wieviele Blätter der Kephalaia in die UdSSR gekommen waren. |

The reference to 20 leaves conserved by Rolf Ibscher apparently goes back to his presentation of 1954 (see above), where he referred to conserving a "remainder of some 20 leaves" that had not gone to Leningrad. He there said he conserved them in 1951 after his first trip to London. But his return from London was delayed during the Christmas holidays by a layover at Schondorf on Ammer Lake to visit his wife's family. Hence the actual date of this conservation was no doubt the beginning of 1952, which thus overlaps Böhlig's dating of

---

9. Böhlig, "Die Arbeit," 182.
10. Böhlig in a letter of February 5, 1986.

the conservation as 1952–1953. In 1964/1965 Rolf Ibscher dated this conservation "between 1951 and 1955." But in the published summary of his speech, Rolf Ibscher refers to having conserved a "remainder of the *Kephalaia*, ca. 25 leaves or ca. 50 pages of the text." Thus the exact number seems to have been uncertain, which is of relevance in seeking to interpret the fact that Beltz's catalogue listed the number of plates still in Berlin as 30 (see below). One of these leaves was "atomized" by Rolf Ibscher's sneeze. Since he listed 20 as extant or 25 as conserved by himself, one may assume that this now-missing leaf is not included in his figures.

Böhlig also reported on plans for the continuation of the publication:[11]

| | |
|---|---|
| The double fascicle of the second volume, prepared by me already during the war and embracing pp. 245–92, has not yet been printed by the publisher Kohlhammer, as a result of the lack of specialized typesetters, and after the war as a result of the unclarity that prevailed as to the continuation of the project. Hence I presented the German translation, for the sake of interested persons, in ["Die Arbeit an den koptischen Manichaica,"] *Wissenschaftliche Zeitschrift der Martin-Luther-Universität Halle-Wittenberg* [5 (1956) 1067–84]. This double fascicle should now be printed as the first of the second volume of the *Kephalaia*, and the following ones will be continually added. [Footnote 3, added when the essay was reprinted in 1968: This double fascicle has been worked over still another time by me and in the meantime has appeared in print (1966). The Institut für Byzantinistik of the University of Halle will care for the further | Die noch im Kriege von mir fertiggestellte, die Seiten 245–92 umfassende erste Doppellieferung des 2. Bandes wurde vom Verlag Kohlhammer infolge des Mangels an Spezialsetzern und nach dem Kriege infolge der Unklarheit, die über die Fortführung des Unternehmens herrschte, noch nicht gedruckt. Die deutsche Übersetzung legte ich deshalb um der Interessenten willen 1956 in der Wissenschaftlichen Zeitschrift der Martin-Luther-Universität Halle-Wittenberg vor ["Die Arbeit an den koptischen Manichaica," 5 (1956) 1067–84]. Diese Doppellieferung soll nun als erste des 2. Bandes der Kephalaia gedruckt werden, die weiteren werden sich laufend anschliessen. [Footnote 3, added when the essay was reprinted in 1968: Diese Doppellieferung ist von mir noch einmal überarbeitet worden und inzwischen im Druck erschienen (1966); die weitere Edition wird das Institut für |

---

11. Böhlig, "Die Arbeit," 182.

| | |
|---|---|
| editing through a co-worker [Peter Nagel]. Also an index should be added to the second volume of the *Kephalaia*. The collections prepared along with the editing were lost in the war and must be prepared anew. [Footnote 4: At my request Dr. Dr. P. Nagel of the Institut für Byzantinistik of the University of Halle has produced anew the index for the first volume. It is not yet clear whether it is to appear separately or only together with the index of the second volume at the conclusion of the total edition.] | Byzantinistik der Universität Halle durch einen Mitarbeiter [Peter Nagel] besorgen lassen.] Dem 2. Bande der Kephalaia sollte auch ein Index angefügt werden. Die mit der Edition angefertigten Sammlungen hierfür sind im Kriege verlorengegangen und müssen neu erstellt werden. [Footnote 4: Auf meine Anregung hin hat Herr Dr. Dr. P. Nagel vom Institut für Byzantinistik der Universität Halle den Index für den 1. Band neu erstellt. Es ist noch nicht geklärt, ob er gesondert oder erst zusammen mit dem des 2. Bandes am Ende der Gesamtausgabe erscheinen soll.] |

The first two fascicles of a second volume of the Berlin *Kephalaia*, fascicles 11–12, were published in German translation only in 1956 (pages 245–92), and then in 1966 with Coptic text and revised German translation, but omitting page 292, which was added in 1985.[12]

The Vorwort to the 1966 edition explains the circumstances of the delay:

| | |
|---|---|
| After it was possible to complete the first half of the *Kephalaia* in the year 1940, the second half, including the indices for both halves, was to follow without interruption in further double fascicles. Unfortunately however the editing work had to be interrupted as a consequence of the war and its effects. The double fascicle 11–12 that is here presented was basically | Nachdem die 1. Hälfte der "Kephalaia" im Jahre 1940 abgeschlossen werden konnte, sollte die 2. Hälfte einschliesslich der Indices für beide Teile in weiteren Doppellieferungen laufend folgen. Leider musste die Editionsarbeit aber dann infolge des Krieges und seiner Auswirkungen unterbrochen werden. Die jetzt vorliegende Doppellieferung 11/12 war im |

---

12. Böhlig, "Aus den Manichaischen," 1067–84; *Kephalaia*, 244–91; Böhlig, "Die Arbeit," 183, reported inexactly that the double fascicle contained Coptic pages 245–92. In fact, the last page could not be included for technical reasons within the limits of the double fascicle. Hence Coptic pp. 290, 29–292, and 32 were published with an extensive interpretation by Böhlig, "Ja und Amen," 59–70.

completed in the year 1943, transcriptions of further pages were complete and the indices were supplemented as we went along. Yet the publisher W. Kohlhammer found himself unable, due to the lack of specialized typesetters, to undertake the printing of the double fascicle still during the war. The transcriptions of further pages and the indices became a victim of the air attacks. Finally it was especially the displacement of the papyri, which returned to Berlin only in 1958 and were accessible again in 1960, that made a continuous publication of the edition impossible . . .

Dr. Nagel will also continue the edition in the future.

wesentlichen im Jahre 1943 fertiggestellt, Abschriften weiterer Seiten waren angefertigt und die Indices laufend ergänzt warden. Doch der Verlag W. Kohlhammer sah sich aus Mangel an Spezialsetzern ausserstande, den Druck der Doppellieferung noch während des Krieges vorzunehmen. Die Abschriften weiterer Seiten und die Indices wurden ein Opfer der Fliegerangriffe. Schliesslich machte vor allem die Verlagerung der Papyri, die erst 1958 nach Berlin zurückkehrten und 1960 wieder zugänglich waren, ein kontinuierliches Weitererscheinen der Edition unmöglich . . .

Herr Dr. Nagel wird auch die Edition in Zukunft fortsetzen.

Wolfgang Müller had already reported in 1964 "dass die Kephalaia P. 15[9]96 vollständig erhalten sind und jetzt nach erfolgter Umkonservierung von P. Nagel/Halle weiter ediert werden" ["that the *Kephalaia* P. 15[9]96 are completely extant and now, after their successful reconservation, are being further edited by P. Nagel of Halle."] Similarly Rolf Ibscher reported in 1965/66 that the *Kephalaia* "jetzt erneut nach dem Tode Schmidts und Weggang Böhligs in Halle durch Dr. Dr. Nagel kollationiert und weiter ediert wurden und werden" ["now will be collated and further edited anew after the death of Schmidt and the departure of Böhlig in Halle by Dr. Dr. Nagel."][13]

In August 1985 Nagel confirmed that he had formally submitted his withdrawal, so as not to block the Material from being reassigned. Thus the editing of the material has reverted to the supervision of its repository, the Ägyptisches Museum in Berlin, rather than being still under the care of the Institute that Nagel himself has directed.

Beltz's catalogue reported as follows on this codex:

---

13. Ibscher, "Mani und kein Ende," 219.

I 605 P¹⁵⁹⁹⁶. Codex from the Mani find, P¹⁵⁹⁹⁶ contains the Manichaean *Kephalaia*. The whole codex is glassed. In Berlin are pp. 1–446, 455–56. Pp. 447–54 are at present in Warsaw. Furthermore there are 30 more plates with fragments of various sizes of the same codex in Berlin. On the nature of the codex see the introduction to the edition: Manichäische Handschriften der Staatlichen Museen Berlin, Vol. I, *Kephalaia*. First half prepared by H. J. Polotsky and A. Böhlig (pp. 1–243); second half prepared by A. Böhlig (pp. 244–91). Stuttgart, 1940; 1966.

I 605 P¹⁵⁹⁹⁶; Codex aus dem Manifund, enthält P¹⁵⁹⁹⁶ die manichäischen Kephalaia. Der ganze, Codex ist verglast. In Berlin befinden sich die S. 1–446, 455–56. Die Seiten 447–454 befinden sich z. Z. in Warschau. Ferner sind noch 30 Platten mit Fragmenten unterschiedlicher Grösse vom selben Codex in Berlin. Zur Beschaffenheit des Codex siehe die Einleitung zu der Edition: Manichäische Handschriften der Staatlichen Museen Berlin, Bd. I, Kephalaia. 1. Hälfte bearbeitet von H. J. Polotsky u. A. Böhlig (S. 1–243); 2. Hälfte bearbeitet von A. Böhlig (S. 244–291). Stuttgart 1940; 1966.

Günter Poethke, Custos of the Greek manuscripts in the Papyrus-Sammlung of the Ägyptisches Museum, visited Warsaw in September and October of 1971 and saw there four leaves of the Mani material. On February 23, 1972, he submitted a report preserved in the archives of the Ägyptisches Museum to the effect that in the Kathedra Papirologii of the University of Warsaw four Manichaean leaves were present, for which he listed the numbers 451/2, 453/4, 447/8, 499/500. Beltz saw the leaves on June 2, 1976, and identified them for the first time as belonging to P¹⁵⁹⁹⁶. Subsequently, two additional leaves of the Manichaica have been located at the university.[14]

Wincenty Myszor reported as follows on the materials at the Warsaw University, on July 12, 1986:

There are here 6 glassed leaves. Of these, 5 plates are 36 cm high and 23.5 broad, and 1 plate is 24.5 cm high and 18.5 cm broad. This last plate also has a different glassing. It is smaller and is supplied with dark red adhesive ribbon. The 5 plates have the pp. 447/448;

Hier befinden sich 6 verglaste Blätter. Davon sind 5 Platten 36 cm hoch und 23,5 cm breit und 1 Platte ist 24,5 cm hoch und 18,5 cm breit. Diese letzte Platte hat auch eine andere Verglasung. Sie ist kleiner und mit dunkelrotem Klebeband versehen. Die 5 Platten

14. According to a letter dated December 23, 1985, from Wlodzimierz Godlewski.

449/450; 451/452; 453/454 and 499/500. The plates 447/448 and 449/450 have P$^{15996}$; the plate 499/500 has P$^{14997}$. Also the smaller sixth plate has P$^{15997}$. The other two plates are without P. On June 2, 1976, W. Beltz opened the glass of the leaf 453/454, as is indicated by a piece of paper pasted at the cracked place (with a signature). The 5 leaves seem to belong to the same codex. The state of preservation of the leaves is very bad. The worst is however the sixth leaf with the other glassing. This leaf with P$^{15997}$ (the last digit is not quite clear; it can also be 96!) belongs very certainly to different codex from the plate 499/500 with a quite clear P$^{15997}$, and hence different from the other 5 leaves.

haben die Seiten 447/448; 449/450; 451/452; 453/454 und 499/500. Die Platten 447/448 und 449/450 haben P$^{15996}$; die Platte 499/500 hat P$^{15997}$. Auch die kleinere sechste Platte hat P$^{15997}$. Die anderen beiden Platten sind ohne P. Die Verglasung des Blattes 453/454 hat W. Beltz am 2. Juni 1976 geöffnet, wie ein aufgeklebtes Papier (mit Unterschrift) an der angebrochenen Stelle zeigt. Die 5 Blätter scheinen zu demselben Kodex zu gehören. Der Erhaltungsgrad der Blätter ist sehr schlecht: Am schlechtesten aber ist das sechste Blatt mit der anderen Verglasung. Dieses Blatt mit P$^{15997}$ (die letzte Ziffer ist nicht ganz deutlich; kann es auch 96 sein!) gehört ganz bestimmt zu einem anderen Kodex als die Platte 499/500 mit ganz deutlichem P$^{15997}$, also als die anderen 5 Blätter.

This would indicate that Poethke's report of the labeling 499/500 being in Warsaw and Beltz's report of 449/450 being in Berlin are not conflicting reports about the labeling of the same plate, as has been previously assumed, but are both accurate reports about different plates. The fact that the plate labeled 499/500 is listed as P$^{15997}$ rather than as P$^{15996}$ must be regarded as an error in labeling. For Myszor's conclusion that it is from the same codex as the 4 leaves with pages 447–54, the identity in the size of the glass frame with that of the 4 leaves, and the pagination reaching such a high figure as 500, all point toward the *Kephalaia*, and not toward the *Acts*. For in the case of the *Acts*, no page numbers have been assigned to its few conserved leaves, and the plates are much smaller.

On September 11, 1986, Wolf-Peter Funk examined the five plates, and on November 15, 1986, he wrote a report that brings further clarity to the situation. "Apart from the mystery of the one glass frame of smaller size, there can be no doubt about the assignment of

the leaves to codices: the five glasses clearly belong to P¹⁵⁹⁹⁶ because they actually contain portions of *Kephalaia* text." Concerning the individual leaves, he reports:

> 447/448: "Leaf in extremely bad condition, on both sides only small parts of papyrus *surface* extant . . ." P. 447(with vertical fibres): A label, apparently old, reads 447. Though nothing was transcribed, regular lines, but no chapter heading, could be detected throughout. P. 448, (with horizontal fibres): "'Readability' only slightly better than P. 447." Each of the letters of the pagination of P. 447 is uncertain. Only up to four letters on a line were transcribed from lines 1–4. "No chapter heading visible (but not entirely excluded)."
>
> 449/450: "Leaf in extremely bad condition, on both sides only small parts of papyrus *surface* extant." P. 449 (with horizontal fibres): Nothing was transcribed. No chapter heading is visible. P. 450 (with vertical fibres): A recent label reads "449/450 P¹⁵⁹⁹⁶." In the top left-hand corner of the page is the pagination 450, though the first letter is uncertain. There are 29 or 30 lines, the last seven of which are part of a new chapter, vestiges of whose heading follow upon line 19. The chapter number is legible only as ..5. Only a few letters were transcribed.
>
> 451/452: P. 451 (with vertical fibers): The page number 451 is legible in the upper right-hand corner, as is much of the running title. Twenty-one lines are visible, but no chapter heading. P. 452 (with horizontal fibers): A label reads 451/452. The page number 452 and the complete running title are legible. After line 26 there is the chapter number 1.6; the title follows on the next three lines, followed by the first two lines of the chapter, all only partly legible.
>
> 453/454: There is a label, apparently old, reading "453/454." A "large paper strip across broken glasses on both sides" reads: "Schutzverklebung 2. Juni 1976 / Beltz," ". . . durch WALTER BELTZ Berlin." ["Protective pasting June 2, 1976, Beltz," ". . . by Walter Beltz Berlin."] "Both pages make difficult reading except upper part of recto. Apparently no chapter headings." P. 453 (with horizontal fibres): The running title and the central segment of lines 1–4 were transcribed. P. 454 (with vertical fibers): The uncertain letters of pagination 45. as well as the running title and a couple of words from each of the first two lines were transcribed.
>
> 499/500: The leaf is thus labeled. P. 499 (with vertical fibers): A few words of lines 2–3 were transcribed. Then after line 3 there is what looks like a chapter number reading 2 . . . , where what is taken to be perhaps the second digit looks like a small raised lambda). Two lines

of title follow, of which only a word on each was transcribed. P. 500 (with horizontal fibers): Very occasional letters or words were transcribed. After what may be line 12, 13, or 14, there is a straight clear line drawn horizontally under the line of text, after which there follow lines with only scattered letters legible.

From this wealth of previously unavailable scattered detail there emerges a problem, which Funk analyzes as follows:

> To me, another problem of a different nature arose when I compared what I think I read in Warsaw on the fifth leaf, with Ibscher's statement about the last surviving leaf of *Kephalaia* (Volume One) containing pp. 501/02 and *showing the chapter number c = 200*. If I am not mistaken, the leaf identified as pp. 499/500 contains a chapter heading whose top number is extant (but not the right- or left-hand side numbers): the first figure in this number is clearly S, but apparently followed by other figures (illegible to me), which means that the number must be higher than 200. If this is correct, the partly destroyed chapter numbers on pp. 450 and 452 could be restored as [19]5 and 1[9]6, respectively (which would be in accordance with the average length of chapters in the first 12 quires of the codex). Otherwise they would have to be 185 and 186, assuming that the length of chapters considerably increases after p. 292. This latter question can probably be decided after examining the preceding pages at Berlin.
>
> P. 389 bears the chapter number 156, p. 395 the chapter number 158, p. 397 the chapter number 159, and p. 429 the chapter number 172. Hence it would seem more likely that p. 450 would bear the chapter number [18]5 and p. 452 the chapter number 1[8]6.

These considerations have led Funk to put a question mark beside the numeration 499/500, with which the leaf is labeled. For if Ibscher were correct in detecting on the leaf 501/502 the chapter numeration 200, a chapter numeration beyond 200 could not occur on the leaf 499/500 but of necessity would be a leaf paginated in the 500s.

One may also wonder if the discrepancy may not be due to some error in Ibscher's way of ascertaining that the pagination of the last leaf that survives is 501/502. For he concedes that no pagination is extant; his reasoning is based on unspecified "circumstances of the find." It is not clear how such matters would establish the precise pagination. In any case, the leaf to which Ibscher referred, if other than

the Warsaw leaf labeled 499/500 with a chapter number 2[00], has not been located.

An inventory was carried out in 1985–1986 of the Manichaean material stored in the *Magazin* of the Papyrussammlung of the Ägyptisches Museum in the basement of the Pergamonmuseum on the Museumsinsel. There one finds 21 cardboard boxes, each containing slots for ten glassed leaves, labeled "Kephalaia Seite 1–20" ["*Kephalaia* page 1–20"], etc., through pp. 421–40, which must represent the last complete set of ten leaves that Hugo Ibscher conserved.

A card in the box labeled "Seite 21–40" ["page 21–40"] reports: "Blatt 35/36 fehlt" ["leaf 35/36 is missing"]. Pages 35–36 are in fact missing, though the leaf was published in *Kephalaia*, volume one. A card in the box labeled "Seite 61–80" ["page 61–80"] reads: "61/62 fehlt" ["61/62 is missing"]. Pages 61–62 are in fact missing, though the leaf was published in *Kephalaia*, volume one.

The leaf 217/18 was on display in 1986 in the papyrus gallery of the Egyptian section of the Bode Museum (upstairs, on the left) in Berlin-Hauptstadt der DDR. The leaves 291/92, 293/94, 295/96, 297/98, and 299/300 were in 1986 in the Lesesaal of the Egyptian Museum in the basement of the Pergamon Museum, but may well have been returned to the *Magazin*.

One box is labeled "Seite 301–340," ["page 301–40"] with the comment "311–330 in Wien" ["311–30 in Vienna"]. Pages 311–30 are in fact missing from the box, but one may conclude from the Vienna photographs (see above) that of the twenty pages 311–30 much of 6 pages (pp. 313–16 and perhaps 321–22 plus fragments) survives.

A card in the box labeled "Seite 381–400" ["page 381–400"] reports: "383/84 385/86 fehlen" ["383/84 385/86 are missing."] Pages 383–86 are in fact missing.

A card in the box labeled "Seite 401/420" ["page 401–20"] reads: "415/16 fehlt; 419/20 fehlt" ["415/16 is missing; 419/20 is missing"]. Pages 415/16 and 419/20 are in fact missing. In the list of acquisitions published in 1940 by Hugo Ibscher (see above), the pp. 415–20 are not listed, but he reported: "Thus between the pages 414 and 421 there are only paltry remains of the missing leaves, which can hardly be identified." Thus the only extant leaf (actually only part of the bottom half of a leaf), assigned the numeration 417/18, may in fact be all that is left of pp. 415–20 (if one is not to conjecture that it might be the missing bottom half of pp. 413/14).

In his report of 1965, Rolf Ibscher had stated (see above): "Likewise six leaves of the *Kephalaia* are missing, as has now become apparent from the reglasing . . . I explain the six missing *Kephalaia* leaves as still slumbering somewhere in a drawer, having missed the return trip."

These 6 missing leaves can no doubt be identified as pp. 35/36, 61/62, 383/84, 385/86, 415/16, and 419/20, since similar cards in the hand of Rolf Ibscher's assistant Otto W. Luke identify precisely these six leaves as missing. But since the 1940 listing of acquisitions omitted pp. 415-20, and since Hugo Ibscher had spoken of only "paltry remains" between p. 414 and p. 421, there is little reason to assume leaves 415/16 and 419/20 ever were conserved. Thus one may infer that only four leaves (two of which were unpublished and hence presumably permanently inaccessible to scholarship) were lost in the process of being taken into safekeeping to Leningrad and returned to Berlin. For it is known that some material was in fact lost in transit: pp. 447-54, 499-500, have subsequently been identified in Warsaw.

Thus the boxes labeled pages 1-440 actually contain (including those leaves present elsewhere at the Museum) only pages 1-34, 37-60, 63-310, 331-82, 387-414, 417-18, and 421-40, a total of 418 pages = 209 leaves. To this may be added six pages = three leaves in Vienna, a total of 414 pages = 207 leaves, and ten pages = five leaves in Warsaw. This fits rather well Hugo Ibscher's 1940 reference to "over 400 pages." (At that time two of the leaves now missing, pp. 35/36 and 61/62, must also have been extant, since they were published.) Beltz's listing of all pp. 1-440, as in Berlin, must hence be taken merely as a global statement, overlooking the various missing materials among these pages.

Some leaves of the *Kephalaia* are glassed but not in a box. Like the leaves of the other Manichaean codices, which also are not in boxes, they lie on the wooden shelves in the *Magazin*, on which the boxes also lie. The glasses in the boxes are 23 cm wide by 36 cm high. The glasses not in boxes vary in size, 23 to 25 cm wide by 35 to 35.5 cm high. The tape sealing the glasses of all the Manichaica varies from light to dark brown; brown is the color used to distinguish Coptic papyri from other papyri. In the case of the glasses not in boxes, the tape is so sticky that the glasses adhere to each other. Hence they are to be stacked in a staggered pattern that keeps tape from bonding to tape.

Although there are no leaves labeled as pp. 441–46, which Beltz reported as present, there is extant the last glass he reported, labeled 455/456. Since he did not itemize any material as missing prior to page 440, one may assume he did not itemize any material as missing in pp. 1–456 (except for the leaves he had identified in Warsaw, pp. 447–54). Thus, one need hardly postulate that pp. 441–46 were identified in Berlin at the time of Beltz's inventory and only subsequently became lost. Their presence may simply have been inferred on the basis of the presence of the leaf labeled pp. 455/456.

There are also 30 other glass containers, numbered 1–30, i.e., by leaf or glass container rather than by page, each with a label (on one side only) reading "Kephalaia Nr. 1" ["*Kephalaia* Number 1,"] etc. These glasses numbered 1–30 are no doubt the same thirty glasses that Beltz characterized as containing "fragments of various sizes," e.g., number 23 is more a scattering of unplaced fragments than a leaf. The lack of labeled pagination may in part be due to their not having been definitively conserved and labeled by Hugo Ibscher, with the result that Rolf Ibscher left them unidentified. The increasingly fragmentary nature of the latter part of the codex may account for the unidentified status of the leaves.

Since there is no reason to assume that material prior to p. 440 would be among these 30 leaves, they would be expected to fall in the area of pp. 441–46 and 457–502 (except for pp. 499–500, if that is in fact its pagination, in Warsaw), a total of 25 leaves. Thus one may suspect that some of the thirty leaves belong after p. 502 or before p. 440, or may not in fact belong to $P^{15996}$.

In the case of "Kephalaia $P^{15996}$ Nr. 29" ["*Kephalaia* $P^{15996}$ Number 29"], the number is on an unusually large round label, which also bears the marked-out number 361 (and, marked out on the back, 362), and (also marked out) "zu 15998" ["to 15998"], thus identifying the leaf as once having been ascribed to the *Letters*. Rolf Ibscher had reported (see above) in connection with the leaves provisionally preserved by his father and confusingly labeled, "from Codex B," and "Letters": "But there is also among these leaves one with the number 361. To what does that belong?" Obviously, it has subsequently been reassigned to $P^{15996}$, but with what justification remains unclear. Pages 361–62 are extant at their proper place in the box where they belong, so this marked-out numeration can hardly be responsible for ascribing the

leaf to $P^{15996}$. Yet since such high numbers occur only in the case of the *Kephalaia*, one might have been tempted to assign such a leaf to that codex if one did not look to see if it were absent from the proper box.

The glass container labeled "Kephalaia 15996 Nr. 30" ["*Kephalaia* 15996, Number 30"] actually contains two leaves that were apparently never separated from each other. The surface of the typed label is scraped off, except for "P.," with "15996" and "Nr. 30" added in ink.

The reidentification of these two containers as belonging to $P^{15996}$ was apparently carried out by Walter Beltz when he was preparing his inventory, published in 1978, since Günter Poethke has identified the handwriting as that of Beltz. Hence, they may be three of the leaves previously ascribed to $P^{15998}$ (the *Letters*) that currently are missing (see below).

Two glasses are labeled "Kephalaia o. Nr." ["*Kephalaia* without number."] But these were stacked, when the inventory was begun in 1985, along with 13 other leaves that were labeled $P^{15998}$, in a group accompanied by a piece of paper with a note in Günter Poethke's hand. The note read: "Wahrscheinlich zu $P^{15998}$ gehörig (s. Vortrag von Böhlig in Moskau: 'Schweren Herzens'). 15 Platten. 26.7.72" ["Apparently belonging to $P^{15998}$ (see the lecture by Böhlig in Moscow [that begins] 'With heavy heart...'). 15 glasses. July 26, 1972."] Since the labels were not changed to fit the note, one may wonder if these two plates were originally counted among the 15. Perhaps the two containers whose labels apparently Walter Beltz changed to read "$P^{15996}$ 29 and 30" were among the fifteen classified in 1972 as belonging to $P^{15998}$. Since Beltz does not refer to those fifteen plates in his catalogue, he may well not have been aware of their existence. These two plates from among the 15 may have lain apart by themselves at the time, been seen by Beltz, and been included by him in the large stack that was already ascribed to $P^{15996}$. In that case, when their labels were changed to $P^{15996}$, the number of plates ascribed to $P^{15998}$ would have been reduced from 15 to 13, without the note referring to fifteen plates having been corrected. At some juncture the two plates labeled "Kephalaia without number" would have been stacked with the thirteen to produce the total of fifteen, to fit the note stating there were fifteen leaves. It would seem probable that by some such procedure the thirty plates mentioned in Beltz's catalogue as belonging after page 456 have now become thirty-two, bearing the designation *Kephalaia*, though his catalogue refers

only to thirty. The relabeling of two plates and the removal of two others from the stack of thirty (P$^{15996}$) to the stack of fifteen (P$^{15998}$) functioned, in effect, as a trade. Yet any such solution of the confusion must remain very speculative.

One may hence tentatively assume that there are twenty-nine extant leaves of the *Kephalaia* without assigned pagination (plates 1–22 and 24–28, not counting plate 23 that contains only fragments, plus two leaves "without number"). One may seek to correlate these twenty-nine leaves with the twenty or circa 25 reported to have been conserved by Rolf Ibscher after the war. Since approximately seven or twelve leaves more are extant than his figures would lead one to expect, the question arises whether some of these extra leaves correspond to those that have been identified as missing. They would not be the six leaves Rolf Ibscher mentioned as already missing when he reconserved the codex, and which have been identified from what is currently missing as pp. 35/36, 61/62, 383/84, 385/86, 415/16, 419/20. Nor would they be the missing pp. 311–20, the remains of which are in Vienna. Nor would they be those in Warsaw—pp. 447–54, 499–500. Since the leaf 501/02 was mentioned as the last extant leaf of the codex at an earlier time, the twenty-five leaves composing pp. 441–46, 457–98, 501–2 would be the only leaves unaccounted for. This minimal number should be reduced to twenty-four, to take account of the leaf atomized by a sneeze. This figure is nearer to Rolf Ibscher's figure of c. twenty-five than to his figure twenty. But it tends to suggest that not all the material that Beltz listed as extant in Berlin and not all the material currently labeled as P$^{15996}$ does in fact belong to P$^{15996}$, unless one is to assume that there were an indeterminate number beyond p. 502.

Ibscher presents the *Kephalaia* as consisting codicologically of quires of six sheets (twelve leaves, twenty-four pages). The table below lays out the page ranges and center pages of the *Kephalaia*'s various quires; the chart assumes only complete sheets (i.e., no half sheets plus stubs).

## *Kephalaia* Quires

| Quire Number | Page Range | Center Pages |
|---|---|---|
| 1 | 1–24 | 12–13 |
| 2 | 25–48 | 36–37 |
| 3 | 49–72 | 60–61 |
| 4 | 73–96 | 84–85 |
| 5 | 97–120 | 108–9 |
| 6 | 121–44 | 132–33 |
| 7 | 145–68 | 156–57 |
| 8 | 169–92 | 180–81 |
| 9 | 193–216 | 204–5 |
| 10 | 217–40 | 228–29 |
| 11 | 241–64 | 252–53 |
| 12 | 265–88 | 276–77 |
| 13 | 289–312 | 300–301 |
| 14 | 313–36 | 324–25 |
| 15 | 337–60 | 348–49 |
| 16 | 361–84 | 372–73 |
| 17 | 385–408 | 396–97 |
| 18 | 409–32 | 420–21 |
| 19 | 433–56 | 444–45 |
| 20 | 457–80 | 468–69 |
| 21 | 481–504 | 492–93 |
| 22 | 505–28 | 516–17 |

Since Hugo Ibscher reported a fragment containing the pagination 514 to have been attached to the last extant leaf[15] (pp. 501/02), from which he inferred that "the work must have included in the papyrus codex more than 520 pages = 260 leaves," one may assume that quire 22 concluding with page 528 is the last quire of the codex, at least the last of which there has been any evidence. Thus, pp. 503–28, 26 pages = 13 leaves, were presumably not acquired by Schmidt (except

---

15. Hugo Ibscher, *Kephalaia*, vii.

for the fragment with the pagination), and the pp. 441–502, 62 pages = 31 leaves, have not, with the exception of the leaf labeled 455/456, been identified in Berlin in the inventory of 1985–1986.

Hugo Ibscher reported as follows regarding the fiber directions of the codices of Medinet Madi, where his information was based primarily on the Berlin *Kephalaia* and on Sir Chester Beatty's Codex A, the Psalms:[16]

| | |
|---|---|
| It is interesting, and corresponds to the distinguished character of our Mani books, that the arrangement of the leaves is such that the horizontal and vertical fibers always came to lie on each other. In this way the opened book attained a much more pleasant appearance, since the surface lying before the beholder was not disturbed by the varying fiber directions. This arrangement is unpleasant only for the person who today must separate the leaves from each other. For the fibers have now become so intertwined with each other through the effect of dampness that the leaves can be separated from each other only with the greatest of care and patience. | Interessant und dem vornehmen Charakter unserer Mani-Bücher entsprechend ist auch die Anordnung der Blätter, die so erfolgte, dass immer die horizontalen und vertikalen Fasern aufeinander zu liegen kamen. Dadurch gewann das aufgeschlagene Buch ein weit gefälligeres Aussehen, weil die vor dem Beschauer liegende Fläche nicht durch die verschiedene Faserun gestört wurde. Unangenehm ist diese Anordnung nur für den, der heute die Blätter auseinanderlösen muss, haben sich doch durch die Einwirkung der Feuchtigkeit die Fasern jetzt derart ineinander verfilzt, dass nur mit der grössten Sorgfalt and Geduld die Blätter voneinander zu bringen sind. |

The inventory of the *Kephalaia* of 1985–1986 has shown that this fiber pattern does characterize the codex. To be sure, this pattern is somewhat obscured by the fact that in the glassing by Hugo Ibscher or in the reglassing by Rolf Ibscher, some labels were incorrectly placed. But in the process of preparing the inventory, such plates have been supplemented with correct labels. This could be determined by the profiles of what is extant, by the postulated fiber patterns, by the running heads in some cases, and perhaps by an occasional pagination. Leaf 431/32 consists of a series of fragments, presumably from this leaf, two of which are conserved with the wrong surface up.

16. Hugo Ibscher, "Ein Mani-Fund," 85.

One may wonder just what degree of reliability is to be accorded to the pagination ascribed to all the identified leaves, once the minor suggestions here made have been taken into consideration. This is all the more problematic given Hugo Ibscher's view that the sheets were not cut from rolls, which permits the identification of the sequence of sheets. For he argued "that the papyrus material for the present codices was not cut from a roll, but that the leaves were manufactured especially for our Mani books."[17] This phenomenon is otherwise unattested. To make such a claim, he would have had to establish that there are no *kolleseis* (a point which, to judge by the leaves that have been examined, would indeed seem to be accurate). But since *kolleseis* could have been trimmed off at the margin by a careful stationer preparing a deluxe codex, Ibscher would have had to verify that there is no continuity of fibers from sheet to sheet. Since he does not refer to this negative criterion, it is unknown whether he examined the codex from this point of view. Hence, this needs to be verified to be certain that this criterion for establishing the sequence of the sheets, and hence of the pages, is not available. If Hugo Ibscher is correct, then missing is the main codicological criterion for establishing the sequence of sheets in a codex lacking much of the Coptic pagination and the continuity of text from leaf to leaf, namely the continuity of horizontal fibers (or, in rare instances such as Nag Hammadi Codex XIII, the vertical fibers) from sheet to sheet in the quire. In the case of the *Kephalaia*, chapter numbers are sporadically extant in the text itself, so that in general the assigned pagination may indeed be reliable.

The verification of quires in terms of conjugate leaves needs to be carried through systematically to provide a relative confirmation of the page sequence.

Eight smaller plates that seem to involve the remainder of fragments from the conservation of the *Kephalaia* were located in the *Magazin*. For a card accompanying the fragments states that they are "bestimmte and unbestimmte Mani-Fragmente (farblos gerändert)—8 Platten" ["defined and undefined Mani fragments (colorlessly framed)—8 plates"].

---

17. Ibid., 84: "dass das Papyrusmaterial für die vorliegenden Kodices nicht aus einer Rolle geschnitten ist, sondern dass die Blätter . . . eigens für unsere Mani-Bücher angefertigt worden sind."

Plate 1: A label reports in pencil "S. 479" ["p. 479"] and in ink "zu Kephalaia" ["to *Kephalaia*"]. One fragment does have the numeration 479/48[0], another 47[], another 4[ ].

Plate 2: A label reports 459/60. The plate contains about 9 fragments. This pagination was not noted.

Plate 3: A label records *Kephalaia* and the pagination "503/4??." The plate contains about 18 fragments. This pagination was not noted.

Plate 4: A label reports in Greek ink *Kephalaia* and the numbers ⳨κγ/⳨κδ i.e., 423/424. This leaf is extant in its proper box, though the pagination was not noted on it. Nor was this pagination noted on the some 12 fragments in plate 4.

Plate 5: It contains about 11 small fragments.

Plate 6: It contains about 6 fragments, two of which seemed to consist of more than one leaf.

Plate 7: It contains uninscribed pads and one small inscribed fragment.

Plate 8: It contains about thirteen fragments, three of which contain waved decorations such as may have been at the end of the codex; the back of these fragments is uninscribed.

These eight plates are to be classified as fragments and hence are not included in the following assessment of the number of extant leaves.

Since the 146 leaves = 292 pages that have been published present pp. 1–292, of which 144 leaves = 288 pages are still extant, there remain in Berlin yet to be published among the extant leaves assigned a pagination: pp. 293–310, 331–82, 387–414, 417–18, 421–40, 455–56, i.e. 61 leaves = 122 pages, plus 29 unboxed but glassed extant leaves without assigned pagination, i.e. 58 pages, a total of 90 leaves = 180 pages; three leaves = six pages plus fragments out of the fragmentary pages 311–30 (K 11010) in Vienna's *Österreichische Nationalbibliothek*; and pp. 447–54, 499–500, (i.e., five leaves = ten pages), in Warsaw—a total of 98 unpublished leaves = 196 unpublished pages of the *Kephalaia*

that are presumably extant. Thus, there would seem to be a total of 242 extant leaves = 484 pages. (This does not include the second volume of *Kephalaia* belonging to the Chester Beatty Library, see below.)

Such a listing of unpublished but extant leaves may be somewhat misleading. For although the size of the lacunae is relatively small in many cases, that is to say, although most of the papyrus is usually extant, the amount of extant ink varies considerably, and the resultant legibility of many pages is disappointingly small. Hence, a rough classification of extant ink may give a clearer picture of what one may expect. On a scale of 0 to 5: 0 = no ink is visible; 1 = some ink but probably no letters are visible; 2 = some letters but probably no words are legible; 3 = some words but probably no sentences are legible; 4 = some sentences but probably less than half the page is legible; 5 = probably more than half the page is legible. The 122 unpublished but paginated extant pages in Berlin have been classified in the chart that follows:

### Berlin *Kephalaia* Paginated Leaves

| Category | Total pages in category | Individual page numbers |
|---|---|---|
| Some ink visible | 6 | 422, 424, 431, 432, 435–36. |
| Some letters visible | 12 | 309–10, 331–32, 394, 417–18, 421, 423, 427, 433–34. |
| Some words visible | 29 | 306–8, 333–36, 339, 340, 362, 382, 387, 393, 403–9, 413–14, 425–26, 428–30, 438, 440. |
| Some sentences visible | 42 | 297, 299, 300, 304–5, 337–38, 341–42, 345–46, 351–52, 355, 357, 359–61, 364, 368–70, 372–74, 377, 378, 380, 381, 388, 390, 392, 398, 399, 401, 410–12, 437, 439, 455–56. |
| More than half the page visible | 33 | 293–96, 298, 301–3, 343–44, 347–50, 353–54, 356, 358, 363, 365–67, 371, 375–76, 379, 389, 391, 395–97, 400, 402. |

The unpaginated extant leaves 1–28 in Berlin can be classified as follows (the labeled side is cited as a, the side without the label as b): In category 1, 21b. In category 2, 18b, 19a, 21a, 22b, 23b, 24ab, 25ab, 26a, 27b. In category 3, 2ab, 3ab, 4ab, 5ab, 6ab, 7b, 8ab, 9ab, 10ab, l2ab, 13ab, 14ab, 15ab, 16ab, 17ab, 18a, 19b, 20ab, 22a, 23a, 26b, 27a, 28ab. In category 4, lab, 11ab.

Some transcriptions by H. J. Polotsky are in the Archives of the Chester Beatty Library.[18] They include pp. 25, 26, 30, 34–40, 51, and 54 published in *Kephalaia* and pages 375–76 published in Schmidt and Polotsky's initial essay,[19] and the unpublished pages 343, 344, 353, 354 and 366, with German translations by Polotsky of pp. 353, 354, and 366, and English translations by Sir H. Thompson of pp. 343 and 344. This work is dated from July 1931 to May 18, 1932. There are also holdings in the Griffith Institute in the Ashmoleon Museum in Oxford and at the Academy of Sciences in Berlin (see above).

Reinhold Merkelbach[20] has remarked that chapter 138, extant in Polotsky's German translation, is lost:[21] "Der koptische Text ist verlorengegangen, es existiert nur noch die deutsche Übersetzung." ["The Coptic text is lost, there still exists only the German translation."] However an examination of the papyri in the Papyrus-Sammlung

---

18. Crum, *A Coptic Dictionary*, vi, reports: "As regards the lesser dialects, reference must first be made to the great increase in material resulting from the discovery and gradual publication of the Manichaean papyri, acquired by Mr. Chester Beatty and the Berlin Museum. These we have been able to use, thanks to the permission of their owners and to copies of the unpublished portions kindly sent by Dr. Polotsky and Mr. Allberry. But this advantage has been ours only since reaching the letter P."

Crum, *Coptic Dictionary*, xii, lists:

Mani I = copies of Chester Beatty's unpublished Manichaean papyri by H. J. Polotsky and H. Thompson.

Mani II = copies of sim. papyri at Berlin by Polotsky.

The Crum Archive of the Ashmoleon Museum and the Archive of the Academy of Sciences in Berlin contain material that supplements the incomplete file at the Chester Beatty Library.

19. Schmidt and Polotsky, "Ein Mani-Fund," 45, for the German translation of p. 375, p. 87, in "Anhang Nr. III," for the Coptic text of p. 375, p. 42 for the German translation of p. 376, and p. 86, in "Anhang Nr. II," for the Coptic text of p. 376.

20. Merkelbach, *Mani und sein Religionssystem* (Rheinisch-Westfälische Akademie der Wissenschaften, Geisteswissenschaften, Vorträge: G 281; Opladen: Westdeutscher Verlag, 1986), 18 n. 9.

21. Schmidt and Polotsky, "Ein Mani-Fund," 70–71.

of (East) Berlin on July 13, 1988, tended to indicate that the papyri containing this chapter are in fact not lost. Chapter 136 begins on p. 337, chapter 137 on p. 338, chapter 138 on p. 340, chapters 140 and 141 both on p. 343. The leaf labeled 341/342 is also extant, on which the continuation and conclusion of chapter 138 (and the beginning of chapter 139) presumably take place. Yet the identity of the leaf in question seemed at first unclear, for the labels reading 339/340 and with the chapter numeration 138 were affixed in such a way that when the labels were at the top of the page, the writing was upside down, so that the leaf needed to be returned to its upright position. Nor did the fiber directions conform to the pattern of like fiber directions on facing pages. But if the side labeled 339 is relabeled 340, and that side labeled 340 relabeled 339, then the fiber pattern becomes normal. Furthermore, only on the basis of these corrections do the profiles of this leaf and that of the preceding and following leaves conform to each other. Thus once these corrections were made, the codex seemed at this point to be intact, though the text is less legible than it was half a century ago, to judge by the extant German translation.

In 1986 Wolf-Peter Funk began transcribing the first unpublished leaves, pp. 293–95, 11, here concluding with the numeration and title of chapter 123.

# — 11 —

## $P^{15997}$: *Acts*

SCHMIDT AND POLOTSKY'S BASIC report made it clear that $P^{15997}$ (*Acts*) was acquired in the spring of 1931. Their report concerning this specific codex is as follows:[1]

| | |
|---|---|
| [p. 27] I can be very brief in the case of the third papyrus book, which when acquired lay in the original condition between two wooden covers as remains of the binding. It too belongs to the Berlin holdings. An idea of the desolate condition of the preservation may be gotten from the accompanying photograph (see plate 2). Also there are only a few leaves of this pile that have been separated for the sake of determining the character of the work. Thus it has become clear [p. 28] that it is a work of historical content . . . [p. 29] To judge by [p. 30] the external size, it must have been a work of at least 250 leaves. | [p. 27] Ganz kurz kann ich mich fassen bei dem dritten Papyrusbuch, das bei der Erwerbung noch in dem ursprünglichen Zustand zwischen zwei Holzdeckeln als Reste des Einbandes lag and ebenfalls zum Berliner Bestande gehört. Eine Vorstellung von dem desolaten Zustande der Erhaltung wird die beigefügte Photographie (s. Taf. 2) geben. Auch von diesem Haufen sind nur einige Blätter bisher behufs Feststellung des Charakters des Werkes abgehoben worden. Dabei hat es sich als ein Werk historischen Inhalts heraus- [p. 28] gestellt . . . [p. 29] Nach [p. 30] dem äusseren Umfang zu urteilen, muss es ein Werk von mindestens 250 Blättern gewesen sein. |

---

1. Schmidt and Polotsky, "Ein Mani-Fund," 27–30.

Wilhelm Schubart recorded in the *Inventarbuch* of the Papyrus-Sammlung of the Ägyptisches Museum of East Berlin in black ink for P[15997]: "Koptischer Papyruskodex" ["Coptic Papyrus Codex"]. The column regarding "Art der Erwerbung" ["Nature of the Acquisition"] reads "dsgl" ["the same] as P[15995], i.e., "acquired through Prof. Carl Schmidt in Cairo, 1931, gift of Mr. August Pfeffer 1933." Further notes added in pencil report: "Historischer Text" ["historical text"], "z. T. verglast" ["partially glassed"], "8 Blätter" ["8 leaves,"] "Schrank 5" ["cupboard 5"], "z. Zt. Papyrussammlung Regal" ["at present Papyrus Collection shelf"]. A purple carbon note reports "nach dem Osten sichergestellt" ["put in safety to the east"], to which is added in black ink "8 Blätter sind zurück. Codex nicht! [Rolf] Ib[scher]." ["8 leaves are back. Codex [is] not! [Rolf] Ib[scher]."] That is to say, all 8 glassed leaves were at the time thought to have been returned, but the book block that had not been separated into leaves and individually glassed was not returned. A rubber stamp reading "1958 vorhanden" ["1958 present"] records the return of the leaves from Leningrad in that year. The stamp is followed by 8 counting marks. Another rubber stamp reading "1972 vorhanden" ["1972 present"] records that the leaves were present at the time of the inventory of holdings made that year by Ulrich Luft, then a member of the Museum staff.

Böhlig reported in 1960/68:[2]

| | |
|---|---|
| The codex P[15997] is unfortunately lost except for the 8 leaves that were conserved already before the war. It contained historical reports about Mani and the later time of the church. The loss of this text is so regrettable because one could expect from it, as is already visible from the few remains, both materials on the history of Manichaeism and such as had to do with the history of the Sassanid kingdom and its western neighbors. Whether or not the book formed an inner unity is difficult to say. At the top of a few pages, scarcely legible and hardly interpretable superscriptions are | Der Codex P[15997] ist leider bis auf die 8 Blätter, die bereits vor dem Kriege konserviert waren, verlorengegangen. Er enthielt historische Berichte über Mani und die spätere Zeit der Kirche. Der Verlust dieser Schrift ist deshalb so zu beklagen, weil wir in ihr, wie schon aus den geringen Resten ersichtlich ist, zugleich mit Materialien zur Geschichte des Manichäismus auch solche zur Geschichte des Sassanidenreiches und seiner westlichen Anlieger zu erwarten hatten. Ob das Buch eine innere Einheit gebildet hat, ist schwer zu sagen. Über einigen Seiten sind kaum lesbare und |

---

2. Böhlig, "Die Arbeit," 183–84.

| | |
|---|---|
| present. Schmidt's claim that it [p. 184] had to do here with names of Mani's disciples must be based on an oversight. The handwriting does not have the calligraphic beauty of that of the *Kephalaia*, but rather has angular and awkward-looking forms. Also the inscribed column is not as carefully divided. If at the end of the page there is less room, one made the letters and the space between lines smaller. Of course this does not contribute especially to the text's beauty. | deutbare Überschriften vorhanden. Die Behauptung Schmidts, es [p. 184] handle sich dabei um Namen von Jüngern Manis, dürfte auf einem Versehen beruhen. Die Schrift besitzt nicht die kalligraphische Schönheit wie die der Kephalaia, sondern hat eckigere, ungelenker wirkende Formen. Auch der Schriftspiegel ist nicht so sorgfältig eingeteilt; wenn am Ende der Seite der Raum weniger wird, macht man die Buchstaben und den Zeilenabstand kleiner; das trägt natürlich nicht gerade zur Verschönerung bei. |

It is unclear on the basis of what information Böhlig reported that the 8 leaves were conserved before the war. It may be based on no more than the reference in the *Inventarbuch* to "8 leaves." But the penciled note in the *Inventarbuch* is not dated and hence could have been entered after the war, as a deduction from 8 leaves having been returned from Leningrad conserved in glass panes all of the same size, the others of which were labeled $P^{15997}$. In that case, the only information one would have as to how many leaves had been conserved would be the vague reference in the basic report to "only a few leaves." And even this reference to only a few leaves may be out of date, since further leaves could have been conserved after that report, as in the case of $P^{15998}$, where 4 leaves were reported to have been separated by the time the initial report was published, whereas Hugo Ibscher separated and glassed a total of 6 leaves, and a good number of others were separated but not permanently conserved or glassed (see below). Although the discussion will continue on the assumption that there were only 8 leaves conserved, the possibility that an indeterminate number have been conserved should not be lost from sight.

Wolfgang Müller's preliminary inventory of 1964–1965 reported: "$P^{15997}$: historical content, 8 leaves in Berlin, the rest is lost."[3]

Beltz's catalogue of 1978 reported:

---

3. $P^{15997}$ historischer Inhalt, 8. Bl. in Berlin, Rest verloren.

I 605 P¹⁵⁹⁹⁷. 8 leaves of a codex from the Mani find. The average height of the leaves is 22–25 cm, the average width 8–11 cm. There are about 36–40 lines per page, poorly preserved. The codex is probably a *Vita* of Mani. On the text, see R. Ibscher, *Akten des XXIV. Internationalen Orientalistenkongresses* (Munich, 1957), pp. 226–29, and in *Koptologische Studien in der DDR, Wissenschaftliche Zeitschrift der Universität Halle-Wittenberg* 1965, Sonderheft, pp. 50–64. In Warsaw there is at present a leaf from this codex at the University. The remainder of the codex is lost. R[ecto] line 1: ⲘⲀⲐⲎⲦⲎⲤ; line 11: ⲞⲨⲤ ⲚⲔⲀⲦⲀⲢⲈⲨ ⲈⲀⲚ.

I 605 P¹⁵⁹⁹⁷; 8 Blätter eines Codex aus dem Mani-Fund. Die durchschnittliche H. der Blätter 22–25, die durchschnittliche B. 8–11. Pro S. etwa 36–40 Z., schlecht erhalten. Der Codex ist vermutlich eine Vita Manis. Zum Text siehe R. Ibscher, Akten des XXIV. Intern. Orientalistenkongresses, München 1957, S. 226–29, und in Kopt. Studien in der DDR, WZU Halle-Wittenberg 1965, Sonderheft, S. 50–64. In Warschau befindet sich z. Z. ein Blatt aus diesem Codex in der Universität, der Rest des Codex ist verloren, R. Z. 1: ⲘⲀⲐⲎⲦⲎⲤ Z. 11: ⲞⲨⲤ ⲚⲔⲀⲦⲀⲢⲈⲨ ⲈⲀⲚ.

The transcribed words have not been located on the papyri in Berlin themselves.

This report could readily lead to the assumption that a total of nine leaves are extant. Thus Michel Tardieu reported:[4] "P Berol. 15997 (= I 605 Beltz), of which 8 leaves are in East Berlin and 1 in Warsaw. The rest of the codex has been lost or destroyed during the Second World War."

Wincenty Myszor reported on July 12, 1986, that there are at the Institute for Papyrology of Warsaw University 6 glassed plates. One numbered 499/500 is labeled "with a quite clear P¹⁵⁹⁹⁷," but seems nonetheless to belong to P¹⁵⁹⁹⁶ (see above). It is conserved, as are the 4 leaves of P¹⁵⁹⁹⁶, in glasses 36 by 23.5 cm. Myszor concludes: "These 5 leaves seem to have belonged to the same codex." But the sixth leaf at the University is from another codex. It is conserved in glass panes 24.5 by 18.5 cm, and is sealed with a different, red tape. It is labeled P¹⁵⁹⁹⁷, though the last digit "is not quite clear—it can also be 96!" Its "degree of preservation" is "the worse" among the 6 leaves at

---

4. Tardieu, "Les Manichéens en Égypte," 6. "P.Berol. 15997 (= I 605 Beltz), dont subsistent 8 feuillets a Berlin-Est et 1 a Varsovie. Le reste du codex a été perdu ou détruit durant la second guerre mondiale."

the University. Myszor concludes that it "belongs quite certainly to another codex than ... the other 5 leaves." The Warsaw leaf that Beltz ascribed to $P^{15997}$ may have been the leaf numbered 499–500 and labeled $P^{15997}$, though actually belonging to $P^{15996}$ (see above), for Beltz did not list this leaf for $P^{15996}$. There would be no reason to ascribe the smaller sixth leaf to $P^{15997}$ other than the indistinct label that may read either $P^{15997}$ or $P^{15996}$, and the apparent need to ascribe this leaf to some other codex than $P^{15996}$. The dimensions of the glass panes (24.5 by 18.5 cm) do not correspond to those of $P^{15997}$ in Berlin (32 by 21 cm).

On September 11, 1986, Wolf-Peter Funk examined the smaller plate, and on November 15, 1986, wrote a report that brings further clarity to the situation:

> The one glass frame of unusually smaller size (Myszor: 24.5 x 18.5 cm) and unusually coloured tape (red) has—if my records are complete—two labels: one (on recto? [right-hand page]) at the bottom, reading "Dr. Kohlhammer" (ink, old), above which is written in blue pencil "P. 1599[.]" (part of paper broken off); the other on the verso side of the glass [left-hand page], of recent origin (Beltz's hand?) "zu $P^{15997}$" ["to $P^{15997}$"].
>
> The glass contains a narrow strip of papyrus, inscribed on both sides, with an appearance very similar to the other Manichaean leaves. The writing is Coptic at least. But the scribe's hand is clearly different from the *Kephalaia* codex (and, I think, also different from the *Letters* and *Synaxeis* codices), though the general style is similar. (The letters appear to be slightly more heavy, or more uncial, than those of the other hands.) I consider it possible that an extremely patient and imaginative person might be able to identify several Coptic words on the recto (approximately one third of each line preserved, the rest is only fibers/debris), but hardly more than isolated letters on the verso.
>
> I can only speculate about the reasons which prompted my predecessor to attach a label "zu P. 15997" ["to $P^{15997}$"] (similarity of the hand? or the peculiar mode of conservation?), because I have not seen the glasses of $P^{15997}$ at the Berlin Museum so far.

The two labels that Funk notes seem to include the indistinct label read variously as $P^{15997}$ and $P^{15996}$ by Myszor, and as $P^{1599}[.]$ by Funk, and a clear label reading $P^{15997}$, apparently not noted by Myszor. This raises the question as to whether this clear label was added subse-

quently, conceivably by Myzsor on the basis of a query I posed to him as to whether a leaf of $P^{15997}$ were in Warsaw; this query could have led him or someone else in Warsaw to make such a conjectural identification. Funk's impression that the hand is not that of $P^{15996}$, and, less certainly, not that of $P^{15995}$ or $P^{15998}$, would, by a process of elimination, tend to identify it as $P^{15997}$, since a conservation of $P^{15999}$ seems not to have ever even begun; yet such an identification on the basis of hands (uncertain as this would of necessity have been without leaves of $P^{15995}$ or $P^{15998}$ available for comparison) would be far from conclusive. Since Kohlhammer paid for $P^{15999}$, one may wonder if his name on the plate suggests this was, after all, a sample from that codex.

An inventory carried out in 1986 of the 8 leaves currently in Berlin that are labeled $P^{15997}$ has raised the question as to whether one of the Berlin leaves does not belong to another codex. It bears a printed label "$P^{15998}$," with the 8 marked out and replaced in blue ink by 7. Günter Poethke, Custos of the Greek manuscripts of the Papyrus-Sammlung in East Berlin, reports this to be the work of Rolf Ibscher's assistant, Otto Werner Luke. This would suggest that the leaf was previously attributed to the *Letters* and only at some later time reassigned to the *Acts*. It also has a separate label, similar to those numbering the leaves of $P^{15997}$, reading in ink 36, with the 6 marked out and replaced in pencil by 2. This Arabic leaf numeration diverges from that typical of $P^{15997}$, since Roman numerals, ranging from I to IX (I–V and IX plus an unlabeled leaf), are all that are employed. But in the case of $P^{15998}$, the Arabic numeration of leaves not assigned a pagination reaches 25, which included 6 leaves glassed by Hugo Ibscher (including Nr. 25) and about 22 that he left half conserved, a total of about 28 leaves. One may recall the similar numeration by glass container rather than by page for the half-conserved leaves of the *Kephalaia*, where the Arabic numeration reached 30, with 29 (and perhaps 30) secondarily shifted from $P^{15998}$ to $P^{15996}$, just as here a leaf originally assigned to $P^{15998}$ and numbered 35 was secondarily shifted to $P^{15997}$ and the number 32.

The reason why this leaf was reassigned to $P^{15997}$ may have been that it is conserved, as are the 7 leaves originally labeled $P^{15997}$, in glass frames 32 cm high by 21 cm broad, whereas the 6 leaves of $P^{15998}$ that Hugo Ibscher glassed measure 35.6 by 23 cm, and those of $P^{15998}$ that Rolf Ibscher glassed were 35 by 25 cm. The smaller format may have been used for the single leaf under discussion because the leaf itself is

smaller than is typical for P$^{15998}$. But this does not mean that the dimensions of the leaf fit those of P$^{15997}$. The profile of the leaf is not like that of the leaves of P$^{15997}$. Indeed the frayed edges of the leaf stand in some contrast to the relatively clean edges of the leaves of P$^{15997}$. Thus, in spite of the comparable size of the glass frame, the leaf itself would not seem to belong to P$^{15997}$.

This leaf in the smaller glass frame may have been packed with the equally small glasses of P$^{15997}$ at the time of the war. When it was returned from Leningrad in 1958, it would presumably have been still packed with the 7 leaves of P$^{15997}$ that were returned. Since at the time, it was not known that one leaf (the one in Warsaw) was missing, it could readily have been assumed that the 8 leaves recorded in the *Inventarbuch* as separated from the book block of P$^{15997}$ were the 8 leaves glassed in frames of the same size, and hence stacked together, even though only 7 of these similarly glassed leaves may actually have belonged to P$^{15997}$.

In the second volume of the facsimile edition of the Chester Beatty Library Manichaean texts, there has been published "a single sheet with historical information":[5]

> The two pages have a text with some historical information, and this can be identified with similar information reported by C. Schmidt from a leaf in Berlin (C. Schmidt, *Ein Mani-Fund in Ägypten*, 1933, pp. 28–29). Exactly the same persons are mentioned: Thadamor, Amaro, Sapores the hyparch, Narsaph, Hormezd, Innaios, Abiesus and others. This must either be a parallel text to that mentioned by C. Schmidt, or the leaf must physically be the same. Parallel texts are well known from other papyri, e.g., in the Nag Hammadi texts the two very close long versions of the *Apocryphon of John*, and the two versions of the *Gospel of Truth*.

Yet there is no indication in any reports concerning the discovery from Medinet Madi of there being a duplicate copy of the *Acts*. There are two volumes of *Kephalaia*, a first volume in Berlin and the second in Dublin, a two-volume work rather than a case of duplication. And there were two parts of the *Homilies* codex, the published part in

---

5. Giversen, *Homilies and Varia*: The facsimiles are plates on pp. 99–100, the quotation from p. vii. Subsequent quotations are from pp. viii–ix. Note the Errata on p. x, to the effect that the fiber directions are reversed on pp. 99–100: Plate 99 actually has horizontal fibers, plate 100 vertical fibers.

Dublin and the unpublished part ($P^{15999}$) of Berlin, now lost. But this had to do with two parts of one codex, not of duplicates. Hence there are no known instances of duplication in the library of Medinet Madi (nor is there duplication of the sublibraries among the Nag Hammadi Codices, for that matter). The overwhelming probability is that "the leaf must physically be the same."

Giversen poses the problem of the reports by Böhlig (1968), Müller (1965), and Beltz (1978) cited above, to the effect that all 8 leaves were in Berlin. For a label on the glass initialed by the librarian of the Chester Beatty Library, J. V. S. Wilkinson, is dated "October 1956," and Giversen can report of the leaf that "in 1977 it could be studied in Dublin." He hence speculates: "It is possible that this leaf was not included in the eight pages but was one of the other leaves mentioned by C. Schmidt, and that later on it was transferred to the Chester Beatty collection. In that case it is hard to explain why it was transferred." But Schmidt did not mention "other" leaves than the 8 mentioned in the *Inventarbuch*; rather he spoke of "only a few leaves," a comment that provides no reason to assume there were more than 8 leaves. But in view of the recognition (see above) that only 7 of the 8 Berlin leaves actually belong to $P^{15997}$, it is not necessary to postulate more than 8 leaves.

Wilkinson's label read: "This sheet seems to belong to the *Homilies*, but is not included in Polotsky's publication." Giversen compares the two, noting similarities and divergences, only to conclude: "But despite the similarities, the general impression is that the writing on pp. 99 and 100 is by another hand." But upon quoting Böhlig's description of the awkward hand, Giversen comments:

> This description [p. ix] does not, however, match with the writing of pp. 99 and 100, and if these pages were once a part of the manuscript mentioned by C. Schmidt, this could be the reason why they were separated. If it is true that their handwriting was closer to that of the Chester Beatty *Homilies* than to the manuscript mentioned by C. Schmidt, such an alteration would be understandable.

Giversen then reports from the Archives of the Chester Beatty Library that in May 1932 there were references in correspondence between Sir Chester Beatty and Sir Alan Gardiner to the *Homilies* as consisting of 50 leaves:

> Neither Alan H. Gardiner nor A. Chester Beatty in these two letters use the expression "about 50 leaves", but clearly "*the* 50 leaves" [emphasis Giversen's].

The 50 leaves could be the 49 leaves (48 sheets plus the glass containing the fragments) plus the leaf on pp. 99 and 100. On 19 May 1931 Hugo Ibscher sent A. Chester Beatty an invoice for the preservation and placing under glass of papyri, among others "10 Blatt Manitexte" ["10 leaves of Mani texts"]—probably the first Mani papyri H. Ibscher restored for A. Chester Beatty. An invoice dated 17 June 1934 charges A. Chester Beatty for several Mani pages, the first of them "Manichäische Homilien: 49 Bältter" ["Manichaean Homilies: 49 leaves"]. Afterwards the three codices, A, B, and C, are mentioned. If the leaf on pp. 99 and 100 is included with these papyri mentioned in the invoices, it could be among the "10 Blatt Manitexte" ["10 leaves of Mani texts"], which are not specified, and if this leaf was among the 50 leaves that Polotsky was permitted to publish, the reason it was not included in the publication was probably that it differed too much in appearance from the pages bearing the *Homilies*.

Giversen concludes:

> Because of the doubts about its identity, it has been hard to decide whether this leaf should be included in this edition. Since nobody besides myself has raised such questions until now, and it is stated repeatedly in the two catalogues of the German collection that all eight leaves mentioned above are kept in Berlin, it has been agreed to include the leaf here. If however the two catalogues are wrong, it remains possible that the two texts are identical. In any case I shall continue to investigate the history of the leaf.

It seems that the question has in fact already been clarified. Only 7 leaves of P$^{15997}$ are in Berlin (see above). A Berlin leaf was by mistake taken to London and Dublin, and its absence, though detected by Böhlig and explained by Rolf Ibscher, was lost sight of due to an eighth leaf being erroneously ascribed to P$^{15997}$, until inferred again in Berlin in 1986.

Since this codex was acquired "in the original condition between two wooden covers," one might assume that the "few leaves of this pile that have been separated for the sake of determining the character of

the work"[6] are a more ordered sequence than in the case of codices that dealers have already separated into smaller batches. One might thus speculate that the leaves were taken from the front of the book, (since this might be assumed to provide a clearer indication of its character) in an effort to arrive at a preliminary identification of the codex. But one could also speculate that the codex was first opened elsewhere, or that leaves from different parts of the codex were conserved first, in order thus to achieve an overview. In fact nothing is known about the selection of leaves to be conserved as the initial sample.

The 7 leaves in East Berlin not only bear the number $P^{15997}$. They are also numbered with Roman numerals I–V, with one leaf unnumbered and one numbered IX. Since only 8 leaves are thought to have been separated from the book block, the number IX seems out of place. One may at best wonder if the 8 leaves returned from Leningrad and classified as $P^{15997}$ (and the subsequent report of a leaf in Warsaw) are responsible for the numeration system leading to IX, which would hence be a relatively recent numeration. Such a speculation would not explain why the Berlin leaves were given the specific numeration each has. Indeed one would think that the natural thing to have done would have been to consider the Berlin leaves I–VIII and the Warsaw leaf IX, since there was no possibility to compare them side by side and to establish their relative position in the original codex as a basis for a more useful numeration system.

Schmidt and Polotsky reported, primarily on the basis of the Berlin *Kephalaia* and the London *Psalms*, that the fiber directions on facing pages were always the same. This pattern would seem to apply also to $P^{15997}$, since when leaves are so stacked in the sequence of the Roman numerals, there is continuity of extant profiles. But in order to retain the pattern of the fiber directions being the same on facing pages, the leaf numbered IX could not follow directly upon leaf V. Yet the pattern is retained if the unnumbered leaf is placed between V and IX, a sequence supported by the fact that the profile of IX is nearest to that of the unnumbered leaf. Hence the unnumbered leaf is tentatively assigned the number VIII.

The leaves have labels on one side only, listing the codex number and the Roman numeral; this side of the leaves was apparently intended as the side with horizontal fibers, since only plate I is an exception.

---

6. Schmidt and Polotsky, "Ein Mani-Fund," 27.

Small labels with letters "a" and "b" were found in 1976 on 4 of the 7 plates to distinguish a "front" from a "back," however that may have been understood. Only leaf IV has "a" on the side with the main label and "b" on the other side. In the cases of leaves III, V, and IX, the side with the main label is designated as "b," with the other side identified as "a." (Stephen Patterson in 1987 found these small labels extant only on leaves III and IV.) This conscious effort to identify a first and a second side does not conform consistently to horizontal and vertical fiber directions (IV), or to vertical and horizontal fiber directions (III, V, IX). The lettering may have been intended to identify the first (right-hand) and second (left-hand) side of the leaf, since in the present hypothetical reconstruction, it does in all four cases happen to fall into this pattern.

$P^{15997}$ has no extant page numbers. Whereas $P^{15996}$ had its original pagination, $P^{15998}$ seems not to have been paginated, or at least Schmidt and Polotsky found no extant page numbers. They observed of $P^{15997}$:[7] "ob das Ganze paginiert war, wird sich erst bei der weiteren Konservierung erweisen" ["Whether the whole was paginated will become clear only with the further conservation"]. Since such a further conservation never took place, the question remains unresolved.

A sequence of leaves or pages cannot be inferred from the text itself. For not only does the absence of the papyrus or the illegibility of the text at the tops and bottoms of pages render impossible an argument about the continuity of text from one leaf to the next; even a vague sequence of the train of thought seems unattainable today (in contrast to the trains of thought that Schmidt and Polotsky reported), given the largely illegible status of the ink today. Hence the pagination to be assigned to the 7 leaves in Berlin must be based on such circumstantial considerations as those here indicated, and will lack any real assurance of corresponding to the original pagination or even to the right page sequence. It is also not known whether the pages were an unbroken sequence. The four passages that Schmidt and Polotsky summarized do not suggest a continuous sequence but rather widely separated texts. The numeration by leaf rather than by page, and in Roman numerals, may indicate an interest to avoid attempting a pagination. Stephen Patterson has drawn attention to the pieces of twine pressed into the surface of the papyrus on the horizontal sides

---

7. Schmidt and Polotsky, "Ein Mani-Fund," 30.

of leaves II and IV, without any impressions of these pieces of twine visible on the facing pages of leaves I and III, which might suggest that these are not in fact the original facing pages. It is not even certain that it has been correctly determined which margins were at the spine and which margins were at the leading edge. The use of square brackets [ ] will indicate that the pagination is not legible on the papyrus, and the use of an asterisk (*) will indicate that the pagination is relatively arbitrarily assigned. The pagination should clearly be considered no more than a convention.

In the case of codices with the same fiber directions on facing pages, it was customary that the first page of each quire would have horizontal fibers, the second page vertical fibers, the third vertical, the fourth horizontal, and so on. However, in the case of the present material, leaf I has vertical fibers on the side with the main label (with no labeling of sides as "a" and "b"). One may conjecture that the lack of such letters means that the main label is on the surface facing the front of the book (rather than considering, e.g., the position of the main label as irrelevant, or that the small labels with the letters have in some cases been rubbed off, either of which alternatives is quite possible). The problem of the first page's not having horizontal fibers could be explained in several ways. The codex could simply be atypical. Or the assumptions as to which page is the right-hand page and which the left-hand page (i.e., the assumption about which margin is at the spine and which is at the leading edge) could be reversed. Or the first leaf may be missing. If one may postulate an uninscribed and hence unconserved front flyleaf, then the fiber directions of leaf I (as the second leaf) are as they should be. These are the assumptions, admittedly far from compelling, that have led to the provisional pagination of the seven leaves. It is to be hoped that more solid criteria may emerge as a result of subsequent study.

The following table is intended to identify the pages thus numbered [1*]–[10*], [11*]–[14*] in terms of the labels they already bore:

𝔓 15997: *Acts*  237

| Leaf | Side with main label | Label a or b | Conventional numeration | Horizontal or vertical fibers |
|---|---|---|---|---|
| I | X | | [1*] | Vert. |
| I | | | [2*] | Hor. |
| II | X | | [3*] | Hor. |
| II | | | [4*] | Vert. |
| III | X | a | [5*] | Vert. |
| III | X | b | [6*] | Hor. |
| IV | X | a | [7*] | Hor. |
| IV | | b | [8*] | Vert. |
| V | | a | [9*] | Vert. |
| V | X | b | [10*] | Hor. |
| [VIII] | X | | [11*] | Hor. |
| [VIII] | | | [12*] | Vert. |
| IX | | a | [13*] | Vert. |
| IX | X | b | [14*] | Hor. |

The size of the writing columns and of the leaves is hard to determine. The faded condition of the ink makes measurements of the columns uncertain, in that faint ink traces and darker fibers tend to become indistinguishable, and a completely faded-out area can be mistaken for a margin. The absence of the original edges of the papyrus makes measurements of the original leaf impossible. Even measurements of the extant leaf are imprecise, in that isolated fibers may often extend a measurement by a centimeter or so. In such cases, it may at times be an arbitrary decision how much to include and what to exclude as a stray fiber. The extant writing columns average in height about 20.5 cm.:

    p. [1*] 20.8; p. [2*] 20.6; p. [3*] 20.8; p. [4*] 20.5; p. [5*] 20.7; p. [6*] 20.2; p. [7*] 20.6; p. [8*] 20.3; p. [9*] 20.4?; p. [10*] 20.4?; p. [11*] 20.5; p. [12*] 20.6; p. [13*] 20.5; p. [14*] 20.5?

The top margins have in the cases of pp. [5*], [6*], and [8*] running heads that are up to 1.0 cm high, beginning about .5 cm from the extant top edge of the leaf. These captions are not included in the statistics listed above for the height of the writing columns. The largest

measurement of an extant width of a writing column is 11.5 cm for plate 99 in the facsimile edition of Dublin. The extant top margins reach a height of 3.4 cm (p. [7*]) or 3.0 cm (p. [8*]); the extant bottom margins only .8 cm (p. [4*] and p. [6*]), .7 cm (p. [8*] and p. [14*]), or .6 cm (p. [2*] and p. [3*]). The extant dimensions of the leaves reach 24 by 12 cm ([7*]/[8*]), where the width increases by an extension of the top margin on the opposite edge of the leaf from that with some side margin still extant.

Schmidt, Polotsky, and Hugo Ibscher do not give any dimensions for the book block or the wooden covers. That no dimensions are given for the wooden covers is all the more regrettable in that the covers would have provided the only reliable guide to the original dimensions prior to the fraying of the papyrus edges. By comparison, Hugo Ibscher gives the dimensions of $P^{15996}$ as 31.5 by 18 cm, with the following breakdown: the writing column is 22 by 13 cm, the top margin 4, and the bottom margin 5.5 cm, the inner margin 2 cm and the outer margin 4 cm (*sic!*). The corresponding dimensions of the *Psalms* is a leaf of 27 by 17.5 cm with the following breakdown: the writing column 17.5 by 11 cm, top and bottom margins 3.5 and 5.5 (*sic!*), the inner and outer margins 2 and 4.5.

The only dimension of $P^{15997}$ that seems to be that of the original codex, and relatively certain, is the height of the writing column, some 20.5 cm. This dimension is about midway between that of $P^{15996}$ (22 cm) and the *Psalms* (17.5 cm). This would suggest a basis for conjecturing comparable median dimensions for the width of the writing column and the size of the margins and of the leaves: e.g., a writing-column width of 12 cm, top margins of 3.75 cm, bottom margins of 5.5 cm, inner margins of 2 cm and outer margins of 4.25 cm, producing a leaf dimension of 29.75 by 18.25 cm. When one considers the extant dimensions of the leaves ranging in height from 20.9 ([11*]/[12*]) to 24 ([7*]/[8*]), the estimated loss in height would be 5.75 to 8.85 cm. This would seem to be an excessive estimate of loss, when compared to Plate 2 of the article by Schmidt and Polotsky. For the leaves do not seem quite this much shorter than the covers (if indeed one may assume the photograph displays the height of the codex). Perhaps the conservation process involved loss in the margins.

On October 31, 1986, Günter Poethke confirmed that the two wooden boards of the cover of this codex, mentioned by Schmidt and

Polotsky but omitted in the *Inventarbuch* and by Böhlig and Beltz, are not among the three Coptic book bindings listed by Wolfgang Müller as still extant in the museum.[8] Hence the covers must be considered lost.

The information about the contents of this codex must be derived primarily from Schmidt and Polotsky's report. For the seven leaves in Berlin-Hauptstadt der DDR have on a first scanning produced no more than isolated letters and words, much less than the continuing phrases or sentences or trains of thought such as Schmidt and Polotsky report. This may be the result of the conservation process itself. For if Polotsky transcribed each successive page on the top of the book block before it was removed, he may well have transcribed much more text from the exposed side that could have been read after the leaf was removed. This would mean, of course, that the back of each leaf would in his (no longer extant) transcription present less text than the front. When in the case of $P^{15998}$, one compares the relatively large amount of text legible on the two exposed surfaces of a pair of never-separated leaves with the text legible on individual, separated leaves from the same codex, one can get some impression of the loss involved in rendering the hidden inner surfaces accessible. And the top surface on the lost book block may have been more legible (though the exposed surface on the extant book block of the *Synaxeis* codex is not markedly more legible that the conserved leaves). Yet Schmidt and Polotsky referred explicitly to what could be read "auf den konservierten Blättern" ["on the conserved leaves"], so that their information is presumably derived from the extant leaves.[9] Of course there may well have been fading over the intervening half century. The amount of flaking that would have been caused not only by the normal handling but especially by the transportation to the Zoo Bunker, by repercussions from exploding bombs and from antiaircraft fire, and by the railroad tracks to and from Leningrad in 1945–1946 and 1958, can be sensed from the quantity of dust and minor fragments littering the inside of the glasses. Yet the published leaves of the *Kephalaia* do not display such a marked contrast between what was read then and what can be read now.

---

8. Müller, "Die koptischen Handschriften," 66.
9. Schmidt and Polotsky, "Ein Mani-Fund," 28.

Böhlig has challenged as an "oversight" the concluding detail of Schmidt and Polotsky's report[10]: "Auf den oberen Rändern standen die Namen der Verfasser." ["In the upper margins stood the names of the authors."] Since one must assume the published summaries from the codex are based on actual readings of the text, one should also assume the superscriptions of pages were more legible then than now. Since Böhlig did not record an alternate reading, it is doubtful he has been able to make them out to read differently, given their present illegibility. Schmidt and Polotsky had just noted[11] that the two disciples whose names they had found in the text of $P^{15997}$ occurred as authors in the superscriptions of the pages of $P^{15999}$, so that to make a similar inference concerning perhaps already minimally legible vestiges in the upper margins of $P^{15997}$ would not be unreasonable, although the degree to which their statement was a conjecture can hardly be determined. The fact that the Cologne Mani Codex documents the names of Salmaios and Kustaios in its headings (see below) would tend to support this interpretation.

Beltz's statement that "the codex is probably a *Vita* of Mani" seems based not on new information, but simply on his interpretation of Schmidt and Polotsky's report. However, Schmidt and Polotsky did not refer to it as a *Vita*, but rather as "a work of historical content." The nearest Schmidt and Polotsky came to a discussion of the literary genre of the text is at the conclusion of their summary:

| | |
|---|---|
| Since the master put so much weight on the "book," as we will see, an active writing process developed also among the successors. Of course this writing concerned itself vigorously with the life of the religion's founder, especially with his last blows of fate. Early on, the "Martyrdom" was the object of sketches to be read on the day of his death, on the day of the Bema festival, and to serve as source material for cultic actions | [p. 30] Da der Meister so grosses Gewicht auf das "Buch" legt, wie wir noch sehen werden, hat auch unter den Epigonen eine rege Schriftstellerei eingesetzt. Naturgemäss hat sich diese Schriftstellerei mit dem Leben des Religionsstifters lebhaft beschäftigt, besonders mit seinen letzten Schicksalen. Frühzeitig ist das "Martyrium" Gegenstand der Aufzeichnungen gewesen, um am Todestage, am Tage des Bema-Festes, verlesen zu werden und den |

---

10. Ibid., 30.

11. Ibid., 29, where the codex in question is not identified. But from page 30, the identity is clear.

| | |
|---|---|
| and hymns. From such a historical work, Arabic historians such as An Nadim have drawn their chronological data. Fragments of narrative content have also been found among the Turfan texts. Hence it need not surprise us if also the Egyptian Manichaean incorporated a historical work about his religion into his library. | Kulthandlungen und den Hymnen zur Unterlage zu dienen. Aus einem derartigen Geschichtswerke haben arabische Historiker wie An Nadim ihre chronologischen Angaben bezogen. Auch unter den Turfantexten sind Fragmente erzählenden Inhalts gefunden worden. Daher darf es uns nicht überraschen, wenn auch der ägyptische Manichäer ein historisches Werk über seine Religion in seine Bibliothek aufgenommen hat. |

But Schmidt and Polotsky rejected Alfaric's suggestion that a previously known allusion to a "Book of Apomnemoneumata" should be interpreted as a "Vie du Maître" ("Life of the Master"). For such a reference is very vague and could equally well refer to the *Kephalaia*. Thus the title *Vita* is hardly a valid inference from Schmidt's interpretation. Rather the combination of a Martyrdom with subsequent stories about the original disciples after the founder's death would seem to fit better the genre of apocryphal Acts. To be sure, the Martyrdom of the founder is less obviously part of such Acts, perhaps because in early Christianity the genre of Gospel tended to absorb the Martyrdom into it, with of course the Apostle's martyrdom comprising a worthy conclusion (but not beginning) for apocryphal Acts.

If it were correct to assume that the few pages separated from the book block were from the beginning of the codex and composed some 3.2 percent of the codex (8 out of the some 250 leaves that Schmidt and Polotsky estimated), of which only part contained the Martyrdom, then obviously the whole codex should no more be titled after this prelude than should the canonical Acts of the Apostles be named after the ascension with which it begins. But since one does not know whether the conserved leaves were all from the beginning of the codex, or whether they represent a sampling of different parts of the codex, such an argument cannot be pressed.

To be sure, the almost contemporary *Life of Pachomius* included the administrations of his immediate successors, as abbots of the

Pachomian order, all of whom had been his disciples. But this is hardly a relevant parallel, since the *Life of Pachomius* began with his own call and composed primarily his adult life of leadership of the order, with the period of his immediate successors representing more of an appendix, or continuation of his administration.

Ludwig Koenen has suggested[12] that P$^{15997}$ "seemingly showed the same literary structure and probably was part of the same work" as the Cologne Mani Codex. Schmidt and Polotsky had reported:[13] "Our historical work obviously did not flow from the pen of a single author, but rather was a collection made up of different smaller essays and reports that were put together here under the names of the authors in question." To this Koenen remarks:[14] "This description suits the C[ologne]M[ani]C[odex] perfectly. Headings in the Coptic Codex furnish the names of Ammos, Salmaios, and Kustaios as authors of the articles and reports. Having the same function, the names of Salmaios and Kustaios occur in the headings of the CMC." Although Schmidt and Polotsky did not make clear that Kustaios is mentioned in this codex and did not specify just which names appear in superscriptions, mentioning only Ammos as occurring in a subscription, Koenen's observation is nonetheless quite relevant.

Koenen further conjectures that "the whole work was a history of the Manichaean church, and it consisted of several codices."[15] This conjecture is supported by the note: "To judge from the space which the C[ologne] [Mani] C[odex] needed to deal with the early years of Mani, it seems that the history originally was comprised of several volumes." Although the last suggestion must remain quite speculative, the relation of the Cologne Mani Codex to P$^{15997}$ as that of the Gospel of Luke to the Acts of the Apostles does suggest itself in terms of literary genres, though there is hardly any evidence of its having been composed as a two-volume (or multivolume) work.

---

12. Koenen, "Augustine and Manichaeism," 164.

13. Schmidt and Polotsky, "Ein Mani-Fund," 29: "Unser historisches Werk war offensichtlich nicht aus der Feder eines einzigen Schriftstellers geflossen, sondern ein Sammelband aus verschiedenen kleineren Aufsätzen und Berichten, die unter den Namen der betreffenden Autoren hier zusammengestellt sind."

14. Koenen, "Augustine and Manichaeism," 164 n. 37.

15. Ibid., 165, and n. 38.

It is no doubt Koenen's view that has led Michel Tardieu to characterize the Coptic codex largely in terms of the Greek codex:[16]

> 2) On the Birth of His Body
>
> Allusion to Mani's struggles of youth and to the birth of the Manichaean church... The complete Greek version of this text is known by means of the CMC.

Yet the Cologne Mani Codex does not contain a complete Greek version (if one were to assume the two codices overlap) for there is no material that is shared between the codices, to the extent that they are known. Only the Cologne codex alludes to Mani's struggles of youth, and some allusion to the birth of the Manichaean church may be found in the reports that follow, which is all that is known about the contents of P$^{15997}$.

A summary of the contents of the conserved leaves provided by Schmidt and Polotsky will tend to confirm the orientation of P$^{15997}$ to apocryphal Acts. Four passages are summarized, the second and third introduced as "ein anderes Stück" ["another piece"], the fourth as "ein weiteres Blatt" ["a further leaf"]. It is unclear whether Schmidt and Polotsky present them in the order in which they occur in the codex. To judge by their content, the chronological order might well be 2, 1, 4, 3. Their summary of the four passages, in their order, is as follows:[17]

| | |
|---|---|
| On the conserved leaves we read brief narrations about Mani's death, e.g., a narrative about the dialogue of the imprisoned Mani with the guard of the prison, which according to the subscription is attributed to a certain teacher (ⲤⲀϨ) named Ammôs; furthermore a narrative about the visit of a female catechumen named Anûschak to the imprisoned Mani, who is extremely worried that, if Mani were to forsake | [p. 28] Auf den konservierten Blättern lesen wir kurze Erzählungen über Manis Tod, so z. B. eine Erzählung über die Unterredung Manis im Gefängnis mit dem Wächter des Gefängnisses, die auf einen gewissen Lehrer (ⲤⲀϨ) mit Namen Ammôs nach der Unterschrift zurückgeführt wird; ferner eine Erzählung über den Besuch einer Katechumenin namens Anûschak beim gefangenen Mani, die höchst betrübt darüber |

---

16. Tardieu, "Les Manichéens en Égypte," 6: 2) *Sur la naissance de son corps* Évocation des conflits de jeunesse de Mani et de la naissance de l'Église manichéenne... La version grècque complète de ce texte est connue par le CMC.

17. Schmidt and Polotsky, "Ein Mani-Fund," 28–29.

the world, the catechumens would be robbed of their "father" and come into danger of being lost. Mani consoles her with the observation that his *nous* remains in the church.

[p. 28] In another piece we hear that the day of the arrest was a sabbath, and that as a result of his arrest great weeping and mourning arose among the elect, the catechumens and the brethren. There follows a judgment scene before the king. The Μαγουσαῖοι, who, as is well known, staged the agitation against Mani, come forward with the accusation: "Manichaios has taught contrary to our law (νόμος)."

[p. 28] Another piece leads us into a later time of Manichaeism. Here we meet a quantity of unknown persons, such as the Queen Thadamor (ⲐⲀⲆⲀⲘⲰⲢ), the king Amarô (ⲀⲘⲀⲢⲰ), the hyparch Sapôres, Malôp, the son of Adb[jesu], the teacher Abiêsu (ⲀⲂⲒⲎⲤⲞⲨ), Yachias, the leader Sethel (ⲤⲎⲐⲎⲖ), Abira, etc. One has to do here apparently with events that take place within the Persian Empire. There are mentioned the ⲬⲰⲢⲀ ⲚⲞⲌⲈⲞⲤ and the ⲬⲰⲢⲀ ⲚⲦⲀⲚⲆⲀⲒⲦ ⲆⲆⲞⲨⲢⲂⲀⲖⲀⲄⲀⲚ. Further, one has to do with the position of the provincial governments toward the Manichaean religion, some of which are disposed in a friendly way, especially Amarô, who is designated as "great patron" of the Manichaeans, since they can enjoy his support. One of the heads of the Manichaeans turns to him

ist, dass, wenn Mani die Welt verlassen sollte, die Katechumenen ihres "Vaters" beraubt sind und in Gefahr des Verlorenseins kommen. Mani tröstet sie mit dem Hinweis, dass sein Nus in der Kirche verbleibe.

[p. 28] Wir hören in einem andern Stück, dass der Tag der Gefangennahme ein Sabbat war, und dass ob seiner Gefangennahme grosses Weinen und Trauern unter den Electi, den Katechumenen und den Brüdern entstand. Es folgt eine Gerichtssitzung vor dem König, Die Μαγουσαῖοι, die bekanntlich die Hetze gegen Mani inszeniert haben, treten mit der Anklage auf: "Manichaios hat gegen unser Gesetz (νόμος) gelehrt."

[p. 28] In eine spätere Zeit des Manichäismus führt uns ein anderes Stück. Hier tritt uns eine Fülle von unbekannten Personen entgegen, wie die Königin Thadmor (ⲐⲀⲆⲀⲘⲰⲢ), der König Amarô (ⲀⲘⲀⲢⲰ), der Hyparch Sapôres, Malôp, der Sohn des Abd[jesu], der Lehrer Abiêsu (ⲀⲂⲒⲎⲤⲞⲨ), Yachias, der Leiter Sethel (ⲤⲎⲐⲎⲖ), Abira usw. Es handelt sich offenbar hier um Ereignisse, die sich innerhalb des Persischen Reiches abspielen. Es werden genannt die ⲬⲰⲢⲀ ⲚⲞⲌⲈⲞⲤ und die ⲬⲰⲢⲀ ⲚⲦⲀⲚⲆⲀⲒⲦ ⲆⲆⲞⲨⲢⲂⲀⲖⲀⲄⲀⲚ. Es handelt sich weiter um die Stellung der Provinzialregierungen zur manichäischen Religion, von denen die einen freundlich gesinnt sind, vor allem Amarô, der als "grosser Patron" der Manichäer bezeichnet wird, da sie sich dessen Unterstützung zu erfreuen haben. Eines der Häupter der Manichäer wendet sich deshalb an ihn mit der Bitte um Fürsprache für

for this reason with the request to intercede for the persecuted believers [p. 29] in Persia with the king Narsaph, i.e., Narses (293–302). Amarô assumes this responsibility and sends letters to the main king, which are crowned with success in that the persecutions cease. In these negotiations a certain ΙΝΝΔΙΟC surfaces, who is apparently the transmitter of the letters of Amarô to the king. He has a discussion with King Narses, the result of which is that the oppressions and persecutions of the teacher and believers are suspended on the command of the king... [Evidence for Innaios as a disciple of Mani from other sources is listed.] According to the Berlin papyrus the tranquility under Narses continued up to his death. Under his successor Ormizd II (ϨⲰⲢⲘⲎⲌⲆ), the son of Narses, the agitation of the Mages resumed; as a result there were new persecutions. From these notes we see that the work contained precise historical records about the development of the Manichaean movement in the Persian Empire after the death of Mani from the pen of a Manichaean, and one may suspect that we will also receive important information about Mani and his times.

die verfolgten Gläu-[p. 29]bigen in Persien beim König Narsaph, d.i. Narses(293–302). Amarô übernimmt diese Aufgabe und sendet Briefe an den Oberkönig, die von Erfolg gekrönt sind, indem die Verfolgungen aufhören. Bei diesen Verhandlungen taucht ein gewisser ΙΝΝΔΙΟC auf, der wahrscheinlich der Überbringer der Sendschreiben des Amarô an den König ist. Er hat eine Unterredung mit König Narses, deren Resultat ist, dass die Bedrückungen und Verfolgungen der Lehrer und Gläubigen auf Befehl des Königs sistiert werden ... [Evidence for Innaios as a disciple of Mani from other sources is listed.] Nach dem Berliner Papyrus hat die Ruhe unter Narses bis zu seinem Tode angehalten. Unter seinem Nachfolger Ormizd II. (ϨⲰⲢⲘⲎⲌⲆ), dem Sohne des Narses, hat die Hetze der Magier wieder eingesetzt; die Folge sind erneute Verfolgungen gewesen. Aus diesen Notizen ersehen wir, dass das Werk genaue geschichtliche Aufzeichnungen über die Entwicklung der Manichäerbewegung im Persischen Reiche nach dem Tode Manis aus der Feder eines Manichäers enthielt, und man darf vermuten, dass wir auch wichtige Aufschlüsse über Mani und seine Zeit empfangen werden.

Given the fact that the book block is presumably permanently lost, and in view of the deplorable condition of the seven leaves in Berlin, this last hope must of course be given up.

Søren Giversen in a separate article[18] has provided a translation of some of this leaf, though without making the identification. Yet in light of the language used to describe the leaf in the facsimile edition, the language introducing the translation makes it clear that he has in view the same leaf.

> The last example is taken from the Addenda et Varia. It is a sheet, damaged, but not too bad[ly]. This sheet [h]as some historical informations [sic]. The handwriting reminds very much on [sic] that in the *Homilies*, published by H. J. Polotsky. But this text is not published, and for some reasons I think, that it was not restored together with the Homilies, because the glass and a black buckram frame is quite different from that of the *Homilies*. I am for the moment becoming more convinced that it has had its own history.
>
> This sheet mentions persons we know from other Manichean texts: Innaios and Sapores. I shall shortly give you a small part of it:
>
> (X, 11); . . . He told us [that] the king had arrived into the neighbourhood of our shepherd Innaios, together with the noble Persians [who were] his assistants. He spoke to him . . . He asked him to go to the king. He achieved mercy for us from him [and he] stopped our destruction. The king together with the noblemen [sic], who were many . . . [In]naios, shall I raise . . . Innaios went into [. . .] of the king. Sapores . . .
>
> This was only to give you a little glimpse. Innaios (Zabed's brother in CMC 74, also mentioned in the great formula PG 1; 1468) is mentioned in connection with king Sapores. When the two pages are fully deciphered a more detailed definition of the text and where it comes from, can presumably be given.

The identification of the leaf need not await further decipherment; it is clearly the Berlin leaf reported upon by Schmidt and Polotsky.

Schmidt and Polotsky's report concluded with the summary of another leaf:

---

18. Giversen, "The Unedited Chester Beatty Mani Texts," 1985/1986, 179–80.

[p. 29] A further leaf takes us in fact back into the time of the beginnings, for here, as mentioned above, the ARXHGOS Sisinnios is named, and a certain Salmaios, who bears the honorary title ASKHTHS. Also this Salmaios belongs, as does Sisinnios, to the first generation, for we find his name *Salmaios* among the disciples of Mani in the great abjuration formula. According to An Nadim in the Fihrist under Nr. 64 there is a letter of Mani directed to a certain Salam and Ansara. Besides, his name occurs on the top margins of a papyrus book [P$^{15999}$] alongside of that of Kustaios, so that he himself must have left written material. Our historical work obviously did not flow from the pen of a single author, but was a collection of various smaller essays and reports that have been put together here under the names of the authors in question.

[p. 29] Ein weiteres Blatt führt uns nämlich in die Anfangszeit zurück, denn hier wird, wie erwähnt, der ARXHGOS Sisinnios genannt und ein gewisser Salmaios, der den Ehrentitel ASKHTHS führt. Auch dieser Salmaios gehört wie Sisinnios zu der ersten Generation, denn wir finden seinen Namen *Salmaios* unter den Schülern des Mani in der grossen Abschwörungsformel. Nach An Nadim im Fihrist unter Nr. 64 ist ein Sendschreiben des Mani an einen gewissen Salam und Ansara gerichtet. Ausserdem erscheint sein Name auf den oberen Rändern eines Papyrusbuches [P$^{15999}$] neben dem des Kustaios, so dass er selbst auch Schriftliches hinterlassen haben muss. Unser historisches Werk war offensichtlich nicht aus der Feder eines einzigen Schriftstellers geflossen, sondern ein Sammelband aus verschiedenen kleineren Aufsätzen und Berichten, die unter den Namen der betreffenden Autoren hier zusammengestellt sind.

This codex, thus represented today by seven (or eight) largely illegible leaves in Berlin, 1 part of a leaf in Warsaw, and 1 more legible leaf in Dublin, a total of 9 (or 10) leaves = 18 (or 20) pages has not been published beyond the facsimiles of the leaf in Dublin and the part of this leaf published in English translation by Giversen. Stephen Patterson prepared a preliminary transcription of the leaves in Berlin during three trips there in 1987, and of the leaf in Dublin on the basis of the facsimiles in Claremont in 1988.

Photographs of both sides of the leaf without Roman numeration (here tentatively numbered [VI] 11*/12*) are on file at the Papyrus-Sammlung. One copy of each side was donated to the Manichaean Archives of the Institute for Antiquity and Christianity.

## — 12 —

## 𝑃 ¹⁵⁹⁹⁸: *Letters*

THE BASIC REPORT OF Schmidt and Polotsky had stated:[1]

We now turn to the second papyrus book of the Berlin Manichaica. This can raise the indisputable claim to be an original work of Mani, for it has to do with the collection of his *Letters*. Unfortunately, thus far only 4 leaves have been separated from the pile and put under glass, but there can be no doubt of the fact itself, for again the papyrus transmits the title on the verso side and the name of the addressee on the recto side. Also in the text itself the whole title is repeated as a superscription. The papyrus book hence corresponds outwardly to the *Kephalaia*, except that it does not seem to be paginated. At least no numbers have thus far been found on the conserved leaves. As superscriptions there have been read ⲦⲘⲀϨⲚⲦⲈ ⲚⲈⲠⲒⲤⲦⲞⲖⲎ on the verso, and on the recto Ⲛ̄ⲤⲒⲤⲒⲚⲚⲒⲞⲤ, and

Wir wenden uns nun zu dem zweiten Papyrusbuch der Berliner Manichaica. Dieses kann den sicheren Anspruch erheben, Originalwerk des Mani zu sein, handelt es sich doch um seine Briefsammlung. Leider sind bis jetzt nur 4 Blätter von dem Haufen abgehoben und unter Glas gebracht worden, aber an der Tatsache selbst kann kein Zweifel bestehen, denn wiederum überliefert der Papyrus den Titel auf der Versoseite und den Namen des Adressaten auf der Rektoseite. Auch im Texte selbst ist der ganze Titel als überschrift wiederholt. Das Papyrusbuch entspricht also äusserlich den Kephalaia, nur scheint es nicht paginiert gewesen zu sein, wenigstens sind keine Zahlen auf den konservierten Blättern bisher gefunden worden. Gelesen sind als Überschriften ⲦⲘⲀϨⲚⲦⲈ ⲚⲈⲠⲒⲤⲦⲞⲖⲎ auf dem Verso, auf dem Rekto Ⲛ̄ⲤⲒⲤⲒⲚⲚⲒⲞⲤ,

---

1. Schmidt and Polotsky, "Ein Mani-Fund," 24–27. The quotations are from pp. 24 and 27.

ⲦⲘⲀ2ⲰⲀⲘⲦⲈ ⲚⲈⲠⲒⲤⲦⲞⲖⲎ
on the verso, and on the recto
ⲚⲤⲒⲤⲒⲚⲚⲒⲞⲤ; i.e., "the second
letter (ἐπιστολή) of Sisinnios"
and "the third letter (ἐπιστολή)
of Sisinnios." Actually one should
translate "to Sisinnios." ... Hence
we can with great expectation put
this discovery of the collection
of *Letters* worthily along side the
discovery of the *Kephalaia* and
welcome it as an important source
for history contemporary with
Mani.

und ⲦⲘⲀ2ⲰⲀⲘⲦⲈ ⲚⲈⲠⲒⲤⲦⲞⲖⲎ
auf dem Verso, auf dem Rekto
ⲚⲤⲒⲤⲒⲚⲚⲒⲞⲤ, d. h. "der zweite Brief
(ἐπιστολή) des Sisinnios" und
"der dritte Brief (ἐπιστολή) des
Sisinnios." In Wahrheit muss man
übersetzen: "an Sisinnios."
... Wir können also diesen Fund
der Briefsammlung dem der
Kephalaia würdig an die Seite
stellen und als eine wichtige
Quelle für die Zeitgeschichte des
Mani mit grossen Erwartungen
begrüssen.

Wilhelm Schubart recorded in the *Inventarbuch* of the Papyrus-Sammlung of the Ägyptisches Museum of Berlin-Hauptstadt der DDR in black ink for P[15998] the entry: "Koptischer Papyruskodex" ["Coptic Papyrus Codex"]. The column regarding "Art der Erwerbung" ["Nature of the Acquisition"] reads "dsgl." ["the same"] as P[15995], i.e., "acquired through Prof. Carl Schmidt in Cairo, 1931, gift of Mr. August Pfeffer 1933." Further notes added in pencil report "z. T. zwischen Glass" ["in part between glass"], "6 Blätter" ["6 leaves"], "s. Schrank 24" ["see cupboard 24"] "(Briefsammlung?)" ["(collection of letters?)"], "ähnlich 15995" ["similar to 15995"]. A rubber stamp reading "1958 vorhanden" ["1958 present"] records the return of the material from Leningrad. The stamp is followed by 6 counting marks. A faint purple carbon note reports "z. Zt. in Schondorf" ["at present in Schondorf"], and, in darker purple, "6 Blätter nach dem Osten" ["6 leaves to the east"], to which is added in black ink: "sind zurück. Codex nicht! [Rolf] Ib[scher]." ["[they] are back. Codex [is] not! [Rolf] Ib[scher]"]. Thus is recorded both the assumed fact that this codex, or, more precisely, the remains of the book block that had not yet been conserved by separating and glassing the leaves, was thought to be in Schondorf, whereas the 6 separated and glassed leaves had been taken east and were returned, as well as the contradictory assumption that the book block ("codex") was not returned from Leningrad, which seems to suggest that by now Rolf Ibscher or someone had realized that it too had been taken east. Another stamp reading "1972 vorhanden" ["1972 present"] records that 6 leaves were present at the time of the inven-

tory of holdings made that year by Ulrich Luft, then of the Museum staff.

Böhlig reported as follows about this codex in 1960/68:[2]

3. Nobly written in very large format in decorative script is the codex P¹⁵⁹⁹⁸, which unfortunately has also become a sacrifice of the war, except for a small residue. At the time of the report of the discovery, 4 leaves had been brought under glass, from which one could see that it had to do with the collection of Mani's letters. As page superscriptions the following were read at that time: "The Second Letter to Sisinnios" and "The Third Letter to Sisinnios." I have not found leaves with these page superscriptions now in looking through the material, but I have found a leaf with the following chapter superscription and the beginning of a letter: "The Seventh Letter to Ktesiphon on the *pannychismoi* (Vigils): Mani the apostle of Jesus Christ and Sisinnios and the believing elect who are with me . . ." Of this book are to be found in Berlin, put under glass already in the pre-war period, 6 leaves with the preliminary numbers 12, 13, 21, 23, 24, and 25, and about 22 leaves in half-conserved condition. The folders in which they lay were numbered, and supplement the numbers of the glassed leaves: 1–11, 14–20, 22. It is worth noting that the leaves 17–21 present an appreciably larger, quite differently arranged script, and that leaf 16 is perhaps uninscribed. Incidentally,

3. Herrlich geschrieben auf sehr grossem Format in zierlicher Schrift ist der Codex P¹⁵⁹⁹⁸, der leider ebenfalls bis auf einen kleinen Rest ein Opfer des Krieges geworden ist. Zur Zeit des Fundberichtes waren 4 Blätter unter Glas gebracht, aus denen zu ersehen war, dass es sich um die Briefssammlung Manis handelte. Als Seitenüberschriften wurden damals gelesen: "Der 2. Brief an Sisinnios" und "der 3. Brief an Sisinnios." Blätter mit diesen Seitenüberschriften habe ich jetzt bei der Durchsicht nicht gefunden, wohl aber ein Blatt mit folgender Kapitelüberschrift und Briefbeginn: "Der 7. Brief an Ktesiphon über die *pannychismoi* (Vigilien): Mani, der Apostel Jesu Christi, und Sisinnios und die gläubigen Electi, die mit mir sind . . ." Von diesem Buch befinden sich in Berlin, noch in der Zeit vor dem Kriege unter Glas gebracht, 6 Blätter mit den vorläufigen Nummern 12, 13, 21, 23, 24, und 25 und ungefähr 22 Blätter in halbkonserviertem Zustand. Die Folien, in denen sie lagen, waren numeriert und ergänzen die Zahlen der verglasten Blätter: 1–11, 14–20, 22. Merkwürdig ist dabei, dass die Blätter 17–21 eine wesentlich grössere, ganz anders geartetete Schrift aufweisen, Blatt 16 vielleicht unbeschriftet ist. Die Blattzählung bedarf übrigens der

---

2. Böhlig, "Die Arbeit," 184.

| | |
|---|---|
| the numeration of leaves needs to be corrected, for a leaf treated as an unseparated pair turns out to be triplets, and 2 leaves that were still unnumbered, with the note "Codex B from the volume of *Letters* of Mani," have to be given a place between 21 and 23. | Korrektur, da ein als ungelöster Zwilling betrachtetes Blatt sich als Drilling erweist und noch 2 ungezählte Blätter mit der Notiz "Codex B aus dem Bande Briefe Manis" zwischen 21 und 23 untergebracht werden müssen. |

To judge by the similarity of language, it is apparently to these "half-conserved" leaves that Böhlig had referred earlier in his report of 1960/68, without identifying the codex involved (though it is distinguished from the 20 leaves of the *Kephalaia* that had remained in Berlin, since they are reported in the preceding text to have been conserved in 1952–1953):[3]

> The urgently needed reglasing of all the pieces that had been glassed by Hugo Ibscher and that returned to Berlin in 1958 was undertaken by Rolf Ibscher beginning in June of this year (1960), along with the conservation of a few half-conserved leaves that Ibscher Sr. had at first put to one side as too difficult, doubtlessly correctly, for it had to do usually with double or triple leaves.

It must also be these leaves that are intended in the confused statement of Rolf Ibscher in 1964–1965 quoted above:

> [p. 63] ... a sizable number of leaves separated last, quite provisionally, by my father, with an entry on the paper cover that protected them which really creates puzzles: "from Codex B," i.e. then Chester Beatty [*Synaxeis*] or ?—and with the addition put in parentheses "*Letters*" i.e., then again Codex Nr. 15[9]98. What is one to make of that? But there is also among these leaves one with the number 361. To what does that belong?

The references by Böhlig and Rolf Ibscher are quite similar: "about 22 leaves" or "a few ... leaves" / "a sizable number of leaves"; "half-conserved condition" or "half-conserved leaves" / "quite provisionally"; "folders" / "paper cover."

Müller's preliminary inventory of 1964–1965 listed for P[15998] "Briefsammlung, 6 Bl. in Berlin, Rest verloren" ["Collection of Letters, 6 leaves in Berlin, the rest lost"]. Here the 22 folders that created the

---

3. Ibid., 182.

confusion have apparently not been identified with the *Letters*. They are in fact not mentioned at all in Müller's report. They may have been still in the Ibscher home.

The same omission is in Beltz's catalogue of 1978, which reported about the *Letters* without reference to the 22 folders as follows:

| | |
|---|---|
| I 606 P$^{15998}$. 6 leaves of a codex from the Mani discovery. 2 leaves of this codex are in Warsaw in the National Museum. The average height is 30 cm and an average width 17.5 cm. On an average there are 35–36 lines per page. The corpus of Mani's *Letters*. The state of preservation of the leaves is as poor as in the other Mani texts in Berlin. The remainder of the codex must be regarded as lost. Glass 13, recto, lines 4–8: ⲈⲔⲔⲀⲎⲤⲒⲀ ⲈⲦⲈ . . . ⲰⲞⲠⲚ / ⲚⲀⲀⲒⲚ ⲚⲀⲄⲄⲈⲖⲞⲤ ⲚⲈⲒ ⲈⲦⲰⲞⲠⲚ ⲦⲞⲨ ⲀⲞⲈ . . . / ⲒⲰ . . . ⲀⲀⲚⲞⲨⲀⲚ ⲚⲒⲘ Ⲉϥ . . . / ⲚϥⲚⲀ2Ⲧ ⲈⲢⲀⲤ ⲈⲤⲀⲰⲰⲠⲈ ⲀⲀⲚ . . . | I 606 P$^{15998}$; 6 Blätter eines Codex aus dem Manifund, 2 Blätter dieses Codex befinden sich in Warschau im National-Museum. Die durchschnittliche H. 30 and eine durchschnittliche B. 17,5. Durchschnittlich 35-36 Z., Briefkorpus des Mani. Der Erhaltungsgrad der Blätter ist so schlecht wie bei den übrigen Mani-Texten in Berlin. Der Rest des Codex muss als verloren angesehen werden. Pl. 13, R. Z. 4-8: ⲈⲔⲔⲀⲎⲤⲒⲀ ⲈⲦⲈ . . . ⲰⲞⲠⲚ / ⲚⲀⲀⲒⲚ ⲚⲀⲄⲄⲈⲖⲞⲤ ⲚⲈⲒ ⲈⲦⲰⲞⲠⲚ ⲦⲞⲨ ⲀⲞⲈ . . . / ⲒⲰ . . . ⲀⲀⲚⲞⲨⲀⲚ ⲚⲒⲘ Ⲉϥ . . . / ⲚϥⲚⲀ2Ⲧ ⲈⲢⲀⲤ ⲈⲤⲀⲰⲰⲠⲈ ⲀⲀⲚ . . . |

Günter Poethke, Custos of the Greek manuscripts in the Papyrus-Sammlung of the Ägyptisches Museum in Berlin-Hauptstadt der DDR began on September–October, 1971, saw these materials in Warsaw, and on February 23, 1972, submitted a report preserved in the Archives of the Ägyptisches Museum to the effect that the two leaves are "(1/2; 3/4)." This is apparently an allusion to the two plates numbered 1 and 4, with the assumption that these are page rather than leaf numbers, and hence that the side of these leaves without a label could be numbered 2 and 3. Since he did not see the leaf numbered 3, such an assumption would have been possible, though apparently not correct. Beltz's information is based on what he saw in his own visit to Warsaw, recorded in his "Aktennotiz für die Papyrus-Sammlung der Staatlichen Museen zu Berlin" ["Memorandum for the Papyrus Collection of the State Museums in Berlin"] preserved in the same Archives. There he, following Poethke, listed "zwei Platten, die vermutlich die Seiten 1–4 enthalten" ["two plates that presumably contain the pages 1–4"].

*P 15998: Letters*    253

On December 23, 1985, Wlodzimierz Godlewski reported that 3 Manichaean leaves are at the National Museum in Warsaw. Wincenty Myszor reported on July 12, 1986, as follows on the material at the National Museum:

| | |
|---|---|
| In the National Museum in Warsaw there are three plates that could belong to a Mani codex. All three are without number and at present only have the number of the National Museum [MN]. Two have 140 160 MN A and B and with the number 1 and 4 on the verso, one has the number 200 611 MN and with the number 3. W. Beltz has certainly seen the first two plates [cf. his catalogue]. The third plate [200 611 MN] has the same size and the same ductus, and so could, in terms of externals, belong to the same codex. On the recto the glass is cracked horizontally, but without damage to the text and the leaf. The leaf is in the same state of preservation as the two others. One can make out about 29 or 30 lines; but perhaps the text continues to 32 lines. But only traces of them survive. At the level of lines 7–8 on the verso the papyrus fibers are destroyed, so that one cannot read the text; on the recto on the other hand the fibers are preserved and hence the text is legible. On the edge a few papyrus parts are pushed [out of place]; the bottom margin of the leaf is completely destroyed except for individual fibers. | Im National-Museum in Warschau befinden sich drei Platten, die zu einem Mani-Kodex gehören könnten. Alle drei sind ohne Nummer und haben jetzt nur die Nummer vom National-Museum [MN]. Zwei sind mit 140 160 MN A und B und mit Ziffer 1 und 4 auf der Verso-Seite, und eine mit Nummer 200 611 MN und mit Ziffer 3 versehen. Die ersten zwei Platten hat bestimmt W. Beltz gesehen [vgl. seinen Katalog]. Die dritte Platte [200 611 MN] hat dieselbe Grösse und denselben Schriftductus: könnte also von aussen gesehen zu demselben Kodex gehören. Auf der Rectoseite ist die Verglasung horizontal angebrochen, aber ohne Schaden für den Text und das Blatt. Das Blatt ist in demselben Erhaltungsgrad wie die zwei anderen. Man kann circa 29 bis 30 Zeilen ausmachen; vermutlich aber geht der Text bis 32 Zeilen. Davon sind jedoch nur Spuren erhalten. In der Höhe der Zeilen 7–8 sind auf der Verso-Seite die Papyrusfasern zerstört, so dass man den Text nicht lesen kann; an der Recto-Seite dagegen sind die Fasern erhalten und ist also der Text lesbar. Am Seitenrand sind einige Papyrusteile verschoben; der untere Rand des Blattes ist bis auf einzelne Fasern ganz zerstört. |

The third leaf, which has only recently been mentioned, has been in part transcribed by Myszor, which will help to clarify the identification and the nature of the text.

On September 11, 1986, Wolf-Peter Funk examined the 3 plates (and on October 29, 1986 measured the plates themselves: 35.5 to 35.7 cm by 23.0 cm), and on November 4, 1986, wrote a report that brings further clarity to the situation: The small labels with the numbers 1, 3, and 4 (as well as the Warsaw Museum labels) are on one side only, that with horizontal fibers, which is what Myszor hence meant by recto. If however one would use recto to refer to the right-hand page, as does Funk, the situation is as follows: Since broader margins are usually in the Manichaean codices not at the spine but at the leading edge, and broader margins on one side characterize the leaves in Warsaw, one can distinguish the right-hand page (Funk's recto), whose right edge would be broad, from the left-hand page (Funk's verso), whose left *edge* would be broad. On this basis one can determine the fiber directions of the 4 leaves (right-hand page / left-hand page) as follows: 1, vertical / horizontal; 3, vertical / horizontal; 4, horizontal / vertical. This would suggest that the numeration of the leaves could reflect the correct sequence of the leaves in relation to each other, i.e. the sequence in which they were successively separated from the book block (though it would not be clear whether the conservation took place from front to back or from back to front). For the numeration conforms to the pattern of like fiber directions facing each other as one turns the pages, i.e., the left-hand page of leaf 3 has horizontal fibers, and the facing right-hand page of leaf 4 also has horizontal fibers (or, if the conservation progressed from back to front, the left-hand page of leaf 4 has vertical fibers, which would face the right-hand page of leaf 3, which also has vertical fibers). If the missing leaf 2 had fiber directions like those of leaf 4, then leaf 2 would present like fiber directions on the side facing leaf 1 as well as on the side facing leaf 3.

This identification of which side is the left-hand page and which the right-hand page is continued by page superscriptions in the top margins. For on the left-hand page of leaves 1 and 4 is an ordinal number, and on the right-hand page of leaf 4 is a personal name, so that the page superscriptions would follow the pattern: The x-th Letter / of (or to) X. Schmidt and Polotsky already identified these page superscriptions. For on the left-hand page of leaf 1 there occurs ⲦⲘⲀϨⲰⲀⲘ, and on the left-hand page of leaf 4 there occurs ⲦⲘⲀϨ . . . ⲉ ⲚⲈⲠⲒⲤⲦⲞⲖⲎ . . . The three letters not transcribed could be, in Funk's opinion, ⲤⲚⲦ, though, not having the passage in Schmidt and Polotsky before him,

he did not actually examine the papyrus with these letters in mind. Thus the left-hand page of leaf 1 contains "The thir[d . . .]," the left-hand page of leaf 4 "The [second] Letter." Leaf 4 has on the right-hand page ⲚⲤⲒⲤⲒⲒⲚⲚⲒⲞⲤ. Though this would not be the continuation of the superscription read on the left-hand pages of leaves 1 and 4, but of the leaf next to leaf 4, it would nonetheless indicate the pattern of the superscriptions. This would seem to identify leaves 1 and 4 as those whose running titles Schmidt and Polotsky transcribed, even though they read the complete title. Perhaps merely because they did not indicate lacunae, as Funk expects on the basis of their complete transcription of running titles of the *Synaxeis* codex that are today and probably always have been fragmentary. It may well be that Schmidt and Polotsky did not actually see the page superscriptions on the right-hand facing pages to leaves 1 and 4, but only inferred from the pattern they had established what it may have been. They based preliminary codicological inferences regarding $P^{15998}$ upon their broader experience with $P^{15996}$ as they themselves state: "The papyrus book hence corresponds outwardly to the *Kephalaia*, except that it does not seem to be paginated."

Thus the left-hand page of leaf 4 would have contained part of a second letter, and the left-hand page of leaf 1 part of a third letter. This would suggest that the sequence of the numeration of the leaves is the reverse of their order in the codex. Leaf 4 could have been the first leaf of the codex only if one were to assume a first letter of less than two pages terminated and the second letter began on the left-hand page of that leaf. The second and/or third letters, present on the left-hand page of the first leaf (number 4, in the ordering of the leaves 4, 3, 2, 1) and the left-hand page of the fourth leaf (number 1), a total of nearly seven pages, would have been longer.

It is hence not surprising that Böhlig reported that after World War II he did not find in Berlin the pages with the superscriptions that Schmidt and Polotsky listed. His report to the effect that there were six already-glassed leaves together with the penciled notes in the *Inventarbuch* that six leaves were glassed and returned to Berlin would lead to the normal assumption that the four leaves that Schmidt and Polotsky reported as already glassed would be among these six. But now this would not seem to be the case. The fact that Böhlig listed the numbers on these six glasses as 12, 13, 21, 23, 24, and 25 would also

tend to suggest that the 6 he located did not include the first four that Schmidt and Polotsky reported as glassed.

The inventory carried out in 1985–1986 did not locate what Rolf Ibscher referred to as "the paper cover that protected them" i.e., that protected "a sizable number of leaves." The paper contained the comments "from Codex B" and "*Letters*," which seemed to Rolf Ibscher confusingly contradictory, in that one reference seemed to point to Dublin (Codex B = *Synaxeis*), one to Berlin (*Letters* = $P^{15998}$). If the "paper cover" is the same as the "folders" to which Böhlig referred, then one would no doubt have to do with the usual file folders in which papyri may well have been stored before being put in glass. They would have been left in such folders by Hugo Ibscher, since his conservation was only provisional, and would have been transferred into glass by Rolf Ibscher, even though the conservation was never adequately completed, in that in some instances parts of two leaves are still glassed together. The folders with the confusing information on them would then have been discarded.

But some of the information on the discarded paper cover has apparently been preserved on labels. The glassed but unboxed leaf labeled "*Kephalaia* 15996 Nr. 29" has inscribed on its label, though marked out, the numeral 361 (and on the back, also marked out, 362) as well as "zu 15998" ["to 15998"] (also marked out). Rolf Ibscher had reported in connection with the leaves provisionally preserved by his father and confusingly labeled "from Codex B" and "*Letters*": "But there is also among these leaves one with the number 361. To what does that belong?" Obviously the leaf has subsequently been reassigned to $P^{15996}$, but the reason remains unclear. For the numeration 361/62 should not lead to such an assignment, since that leaf of $P^{15996}$ is present at its correct position in the appropriate box. Yet such high numerations are known only in the case of $P^{15996}$, and this could have led to assigning the plate to $P^{15996}$ if the relevant box were not checked. In any case, one has here clear evidence that at least this one leaf among those that Rolf Ibscher thought might belong either to "Codex B" (the Dublin *Synaxeis*) or to the Berlin *Letters* ($P^{15998}$) is currently assigned by its label to neither, but rather to the *Kephalaia*.

More extant leaves are currently assigned to the *Kephalaia* than one is required to postulate are from that codex. For there are only twenty-five leaves missing between the last bound leaf, pp. 439/440, and the last attested leaf, pp. 501/502. For the extant leaf pp. 455–56

is clearly identified as extant by its label, and the leaves pp. 447–54, 499/500 are in Warsaw. One leaf was atomized by a sneeze by Rolf Ibscher. This leaves a total of 24 leaves missing. Yet there are 32 leaves labeled $P^{15996}$ (not counting plate 23, since it consists only of fragments, but recognizing that plate 30 contains 2 leaves). Up to eight leaves with this label may well belong to the *Kephalaia*, after p. 502, or to other codices. The leaf labeled "*Kephalaia* number 29," reassigned to $P^{15998}$, might well belong there.

This may help to explain another instance, which, however, is less clear due to the fact that the earlier assignment is scraped off. This is a pair of leaves glassed together and labeled by hand "*Kephalaia* 15996 Nr. 30." This plate, like the one numbered 29, may originally have been assigned to the *Letters*.

When the inventory was begun in 1985, a stack of fifteen leaves (separate from the six leaves regularly listed as present) was found accompanied by a piece of paper with a note in the hand of Günter Poethke that read: "Wahrscheinlich zu $P^{15998}$ gehörig (s. Vortrag von Böhlig in Moskau: 'Schweren Herzens'). 15 Platten. 26.7.72." ["Apparently belonging to $P^{15998}$ (see the lecture of Böhlig in Moscow [that begins] 'With heavy heart . . .'). 15 glasses. July 16, 1972."] Poethke has explained the note as simply a pragmatic way to dispose administratively of the matter rather than as the result of new research on his part, which would account for the cautious term "apparently." The reference to Böhlig's paper of 1960/68 would no doubt have in view the passages cited above:

> . . . the conservation of a few half-conserved leaves that Ibscher Sr. had at first put to one side as too difficult, doubtlessly correctly, for it had to do usually with double or triple leaves . . .
> Of this book one finds in Berlin, put under glass already in the prewar period, 6 leaves with the temporary numbers 12, 13, 21, 23, 24, and 25, and about 22 leaves in half-conserved condition. The folders in which they lay were numbered, and supplement the numbers of the glassed leaves: 1–11, 14–20, 22. It is worth noting that the leaves 17–21 present an appreciably larger, quite differently arranged script, and that leaf 16 is perhaps uninscribed. Incidentally, the numeration of leaves needs to be corrected, for a leaf treated as an unseparated pair turns out to be triplets, and 2 leaves that were still unnumbered, with the note "Codex B from the volume of *Letters* of Mani," have to be given a place between 21 and 23.

Each plate in the stack of fifteen leaves is labeled $P^{15998}$, except for two plates labelled "*Kephalaia* o. Nr." "*Kephalaia* without number." This nomenclature recalls Böhlig's reference to "2 leaves that were still unnumbered, with the note 'Codex B from the volume of *Letters* of Mani.'" Since a folder was already numbered 22, there were no unoccupied digits between 21 and 23. This would account for the two leaves not having been numbered, pending a renumeration of all the leaves of $P^{15998}$, which apparently never took place. By some rather inexplicable transaction(s) they would, according to this conjecture, seem to have then been labeled *Kephalaia* rather than *Letters*, but nonetheless stored with the 13 leaves labeled $P^{15998}$, with the appended note to the effect that there were 15 leaves of $P^{15998}$. One may suspect that originally the two plates labeled *Kephalaia* 29 and 30, if in fact they had been previously assigned to $P^{15998}$, may have been included in the stack of 15 plates of $P^{15998}$. Once they had become (re)assigned to $P^{15996}$, they might have been replaced in the stack of 15 by those labeled "*Kephalaia* without number."

The ascription to the *Letters* of the six leaves (12, 13, 21, 23, 24, and 25) singled out by Böhlig as glassed by Hugo Ibscher, has never been questioned. Since what remains of the "about 22 leaves in half-conserved condition" is no longer in "folders" but has now been glassed, the distinction between the two groups can no longer be made in terms of what is glassed and what is in folders. But the 6 leaves always ascribed to the *Letters* can nonetheless be identified. When first seen on October 28–29, 1985, they were stacked separately. Böhlig's numbers largely confirmed this physical separation. Five bear the numbers 12, 21, 23, 24, 25, and the one lacking a label can be identified from the transcription of a few phrases of a leaf numbered 13 in Beltz's catalogue. These phrases do in fact occur, with but minor deviations from Beltz's transcription, on this leaf, which has hence been labeled in 1986 as number 13.

There is, however, a glass not stacked with the six that nonetheless is numbered 12, which thus repeats a number occurring on one of the 6 leaves that Hugo Ibscher conserved. The distinction of two stacks in which the two glasses numbered 12 lie is a weak criterion to distinguish which is among the 6 glassed by Hugo Ibscher, since the place where a glass is stacked can be so readily changed. But the 6 glasses stacked together measure 23 cm wide and 35.5 to 36.6 cm high, whereas the others assigned to $P^{15998}$ measure 25 by 35 cm. And

whereas the others are framed in sticky reddish-brown tape, the 6 are framed in tan plastic tape that readily comes loose, exposing narrower white paper tape beneath. (The tan plastic tape was removed, and Gesa Schenke covered the underlying tape with Filmoplast P$^{90}$ on February 11, 1986.) Furthermore, those conserved by Hugo Ibscher have brown labels with the number prefaced by B (except for number 13 that had lost its label), and only one of the two leaves numbered 12 includes the letter B. For these reasons, the leaf labeled B 12 is clearly the leaf conserved by Hugo Ibscher.

Böhlig's report that he could not find on the 6 leaves the page superscriptions "The Second Letter to Sisinnios" and "The Third Letter to Sisinnios" that Schmidt and Polotsky quoted has been confirmed by a fresh examination of the leaves in Berlin. But these superscriptions were identified as among those in Warsaw (see above). Yet Böhlig did report finding a chapter titled, "The Seventh Letter to Ktesiphon on the *pannychismoi* (vigils)," which letter began: "Mani the apostle of Jesus Christ and Sisinnios and the believing elect who are with me ..." This text, though less legible than this smooth translation suggests, is on leaf 24, the side with horizontal fibers. The title (set off from the text by horizontal lines above and below) is on extant lines 8–9, and the quotation from the opening of the text on the next two lines.

According to Böhlig, the group of about twenty-two leaves were in folders bearing the numbers 1–11, 14–20, and 22, a total of 19 numbers, 3 less than the total of about 22. Also when one adds the 6 leaves under glass and about 22 in half-conserved condition, one reaches a total of about 28 leaves, which, however, were conserved in glasses and folders numbered up only to 25, where again the discrepancy of 3 digits occurs. But this discrepancy could be explained in terms of Böhlig's observation that one folder contained 3 rather than the previously assumed 2 leaves, and that there were 2 unnumbered leaves labeled "Codex B from the volume of *Letters* of Mani" that belonged somewhere between 21! and 23.

Actually, the only glasses with numbers among the fifteen are the nine numbered 8–12, 14–16, and 18. All these numbers except number 12, which in Böhlig's list referred only to a leaf glassed by Hugo Ibscher and hence not to a folder, may be assumed to be the material from the folders with those numbers listed by Böhlig. The assumption is that one glass was by error given the number 12 when it was transferred from a folder that did not bear this number.

Number 10 has on its label, "Mani-Blatt gebleicht Nr 10" ["Mani leaf bleached No 10"]. The leaf is considerably lighter than the others, while the ink is dark. It is unclear why the bleaching technique, if successful, was discontinued. Perhaps concern for negative long-range effects was involved.

The numbers 1–7, 17, 19, 20, and 22 are all absent from the 15 glasses. This makes a total of 11 numbers, which would be over half of the 19 folders, or half of the original list of some 22 leaves. If one of these missing numbers may be assumed to be the glass inaccurately numbered 12, others of the missing material may be found among 4 glasses without numeration:

One unnumbered glass is labeled "Zwillingsblatt von No 8 abgelöst. Dr. I[bscher]." ["Twin leaf separated from Number 8. Dr. I[bscher]."] This label is in the same red ink as the notation on label 8 that reads "Zwillingsblatt zwischen Glas" ["Twin leaf between glass"]. The extant profile, when placed so that like fiber directions face each other, suggests they may indeed have been adjoining leaves.

One unnumbered glass is labeled (in English!) "Twins," no doubt reflecting Rolf Ibscher's (Germanic) English that he acquired in London, which is documented in his English letters. Its shape would suggest that it might have been part of Number 9, which still has part of a second leaf conserved with it. Especially the excess papyrus (covering the right edge of lines 5–10 of the side of the "Twins" that touches the horizontal fibers of leaf 9 when the contours are aligned) seems to correspond to a lacuna on leaf 9. The fact that leaf 9 is considerably smaller than the "twins" would indicate that as a single leaf, it was weaker, and when stuck would tend to lose papyrus to the stronger "twins." Thus we may have to do with what Böhlig described: "a leaf treated as an unseparated pair turns out to be triplets."

Since leaves 8 and 9 have similar profiles, one may conjecture that Hugo Ibscher separated two adjoining layers: one containing two leaves, the other three; and that Rolf Ibscher separated each layer again, producing a total of 4 plates with 5 leaves. On the assumption that like fiber directions faced each other, one could reconstruct the order as: "Twin leaf separated from number 8," with horizontal fibers facing up; followed by leaf 8, with vertical fibers facing up; followed by the twins, where horizontal fibers are visible on both sides, and hence the side facing up is determined by the extant profile; followed by leaf 9 with horizontal fibers facing up.

One unnumbered glass lacks a label. It too contains two leaves, and hence may be assumed to fall within the category of half-conserved twins in P$^{15998}$. Since faint traces of large letters seem to be visible, the pair could be the missing leaves 19–20 or the unnumbered two leaves belonging between 21 and 23. The extant profile is, however, so dissimilar as to make an identification difficult.

One unnumbered glass has a label that records: "Mittelteil ohne Schriftspüren, völlig zerstört, deshalb entfernt. Umbettung am 18. III. 1970." ["Middle part without traces of writing, completely destroyed, hence removed. Reconservation on 18 iii 70."] Günter Poethke has identified the handwriting as that of Rolf Ibscher's assistant, Otto Werner Luke (deceased).

Of the about 22 leaves put in folders by Hugo Ibscher and between glass by Rolf Ibscher, one may thus probably account for most of them:

- 8 folders numbered 8–11, 14–16, 18, may be presumed to be, the 8 leaves in 8 glasses with the same numbers.
- 1 leaf in a glass numbered 8 may be assumed to come from one of these folders also.
- 6 leaves are conserved in 4 unnumbered glasses, since in 2 of the 4 glasses there are 2 leaves each.

3 leaves currently labeled *Kephalaia* may have come from P$^{15998}$:

1. 1 labeled as 29
2. 2 leaves in one glass container labeled as 30 (2 in 2 glass containers listed as without number are here assumed to belong to the *Kephalaia*.)

Böhlig conjectured that some of this codex was by mistake taken to London, on the erroneous assumption that the leaves belonged to Chester Beatty's Codex B, the *Synaxeis*:[4]

| | |
|---|---|
| [p. 186] The question as to the situation regarding the last Chester Beatty codex, Codex B, is very problematic. In London there are 13 leaves, already glassed by Hugo | [p. 186] Sehr problematisch ist die Frage, was es mit dem letzten Chester-Beatty-Codex, dem Codex B, auf sich hat. In London liegen 13 Blätter, noch von Hugo |

---

4. Böhlig, "Die Arbeit," 186–87.

Ibscher, unfortunately without any note as to content or titles that may have been read. Rolf Ibscher could only tell me that it has to do with an unusually large format. Thus far it has not been possible to take a look at these plates for myself. [Footnote 1: Unfortunately it is precisely their conservation that has not yet been completed; they still lie between *paper and glass*, so that one cannot read them without removing glass and paper. But Sir Chester Beatty has not permitted that, out of concern for the condition of the papyri.] However, with all due caution on the basis of minimal indications, I would nonetheless like to present an effort at a solution ...

As has also been conjectured by C. Colpe, we will then indeed, in the case of the Göttingen manuscript, have to do with Codex B of the Chester Beatty collection. What then is the situation with the 13 leaves that are in London as Codex B? They ought to have been 13 leaves of the Göttingen manuscript that were the first separated and glassed by Hugo Ibscher. But if, as Rolf Ibscher recalls, they have an especially large format, that cannot be the case. I would hence like, with all due reservations, to conjecture that they were once brought to London by mistake. They are designated as Codex B. For it could perhaps be possible that Hugo Ibscher, who also designated the Berlin corpus of *Letters* as Codex B, once by mistake brought to London the plates, from the mass of the

Mani manuscripts that were in the process of being worked on, but that they in reality belong to the corpus of *Letters*. For especially large format occurs only in the corpus of *Letters*. Besides, I was not able to find in Berlin the page superscriptions read by Schmidt on 4 glassed leaves of the corpus of *Letters*. But such reflections are actually idle—a glance at the London leaves should suffice to solve all these problematic questions with one blow.

der in Bearbeitung befindlichen Manihandschriften [p. 187] nach London gebracht hatte, sie aber in Wirklichkeit zum Briefcorpus gehören. Denn besonders grosses Format liegt nur beim Briefcorpus vor; ausserdem konnte ich ja die von Schmidt gelesenen Seitenüberschriften auf 4 verglasten Blättern des Briefcorpus in Berlin nicht finden. Aber solche Überlegungen sind eigentlich müssig ein Blick auf die Londoner Blätter dürfte genügen, um alle diese problematischen Fragen mit einem Schlage zu lösen.

The simplest way to have identified the leaves now in Copenhagen with $P^{15998}$ would have been to identify on them the missing page superscriptions that Schmidt and Polotsky reported. But now that these missing materials would seem to have been located in Warsaw, other criteria would have to be used to identify leaves in Copenhagen as belonging to $P^{15998}$.

The 6 leaves that Hugo Ibscher conserved are labeled, in distinction to those that Rolf Ibscher glassed, with the letter B (but no codex number) preceding the number of the leaf. This may be a vestige of the designation of $P^{15998}$ as Berlin Codex B. Böhlig has reported:

The division according to capital letters A, B, etc. is in fact not the division of the Museums. It is a division that Hugo Ibscher used privately for himself. I have still seen with Rolf Ibscher file folders in which things were sorted according to such letters. It is not a claim by me that Hugo Ibscher proceeded this way also for the German parts, but here I repeat information from Rolf Ibscher from the year 196[4].

Die Einteilung nach grossen Buchstaben A, B usw. ist in der Tat nicht die Einteilung der Museen; das ist eine Einteilung, die Hugo Ibscher für sich privat benutzte. Ich habe bei Rolf Ibscher noch Verordner gesehen, in denen nach solchen Buchstaben sortiert war. Dass Hugo Ibscher das auch für die deutschen Teile so gemacht hat, ist nicht eine Behauptung von mir, sondern ich gab damit Informationen von Rolf Ibscher aus dem Jahr 196[4] wieder.

Yet this reference from the year 196[4] is precisely what is in need of clarification. For here Rolf Ibscher senses a problem that would not exist if he recognized B as the Ibscher designation for the *Letters*. The only other reference located thus far to the possibility that Hugo Ibscher designated as Codex B both the Berlin codex P$^{15998}$, the *Letters*, and Chester Beatty's *Synaxeis* is the confused statement of Rolf Ibscher to the effect that a sizable number of leaves separated last by his father (specified by Böhlig as "about 22") were in a paper cover; Ibscher's statement refers to them as "from Codex B" and "(*Letters*)." Rolf Ibscher's confusion here would seem to indicate that he was completely unaware of what Böhlig describes as his father's practice of designating the Berlin Codex P$^{15998}$, the *Letters*, as Codex B. For Rolf Ibscher's perplexity presupposes that the Berlin *Letters* were not designated Codex B. If he had known of such a practice, there would have been nothing confusing or contradictory in the two labels. Both would have affirmed that the leaves in question belong to the Berlin Codex B, P$^{15998}$, the *Letters*. Rolf Ibscher should not have hesitated to add these 22 leaves to the list of 6 leaves of the *Letters* still extant in Berlin, rather than leaving them unidentified.

Böhlig took Rolf Ibscher's reference to "an especially large format" of the 13 leaves as pointing to the *Letters* rather than to the *Synaxeis*. But this reasoning is unclear, since the format of the two codices is similar. The dimensions that Beltz gives for the extant leaves of P$^{15998}$, the *Letters*, is some 30 cm high by 17.5 cm wide. Leaf 18 actually measures 31.5 by 17.0, leaf 23 31.0 by 16.0, leaf 24 30.0 by 17.0, leaf 25 29.5 by 17.5 cm. This is considerably larger than the dimensions Beltz gives for P$^{15995}$, the *Synaxeis*, averaging 18–20 cm high by 11–16 cm wide. But here Beltz is basing his measurements no doubt on the 31 leaves in the Staatliche Museen of Berlin, which are approximately this size. But the book block in Berlin (*West*) measures 30 cm high (or even 31.8 cm when fringes of fiber are included) by 19 cm wide. Neither the *Synaxeis* nor the *Letters* is of unusually large format. P$^{15996}$, The *Kephalaia*, measures according to Hugo Ibscher 31.5 cm high by 18 cm wide.[5] Hugo Ibscher also lists the measurements of Sir Chester Beatty's *Homilies* (= P$^{15999}$) as 31.5 cm high by 18 cm wide.[6] Hugo Ibscher provides there the confusing observation:

---

5. Hugo Ibscher, in Polotsky and Böhlig, *Kephalaia*, xi.
6. Hugo Ibscher, in Polotsky, *Manichäische Homilien*, xiii.

| | |
|---|---|
| With the exception of the *Psalms* from the collection of Mr. Chester Beatty, which has a height of 27 cm and a breadth of 17.5 cm [measurements repeated by Ibscher in his introduction to the *Psalms*[7]], all the rest of the books are 31.5 cm high and 18 cm wide. | Mit Ausnahme des Psalmenbuches aus der Sammlung von Mr. Chester Beatty, das bei einer Höhe von 27 cm eine Breite von 17.5 cm besitzt [measurements repeated by Ibscher in his introduction to the *Psalms*[7]], sind alle übrigen Bücher 31.5 cm hoch and 18 cm breit. |

For Hugo Ibscher seems, in this generalizing statement, to have overlooked $P^{15997}$, the *Acts*, which Beltz reports as averaging 22–25 cm high by 8–10 cm wide. Leaf IV measures 24.0 cm high by some 12.0 cm high. The leaf labeled $P^{15998}$ and 36, both changed to $P^{15997}$ and 32, is 24.9 cm high by 13.0 cm wide. It would seem that an "especially large format" would not dissociate the 13 leaves from the *Synaxeis* with which it had been initially associated, but only from the *Psalms* and the *Acts*, and would not associate it with any particular one of the other codices such as $P^{15998}$, the *Letters*. It would hence require other criteria to identify more precisely the 13 leaves.

The facsimile edition of 1986[7] presents the plates in natural size, reaching to a height only of 28.5 cm (plates 101/02, 111/12). The width reaches 17.5 cm once (plates 103/04), and, thanks to a fragment less than a centimeter in diameter at the end of a few apparently attached fibers, reaches 18.7 cm once (plates 115/16). The designation "especially large format" hence seems inappropriate, since the height lies between the smaller and larger codices, in fact nearer that of the smaller ones, and the width, which in any case varies only half a centimeter between large and small codices, in this case (with the one exception) only once reaches as much as the smaller dimension.

Tito Orlandi reported as follows on the material in Dublin in 1976:[8]

| | |
|---|---|
| On another of the same shelves (to the right of the entrance) there are 16 numbered glasses that could represent the part of Codex B restored before the war by H. | Sur une autre des mêmes étagères (a droite de l'entrée), il y a 16 verres numérotés, qui pourraient representer la partie du Cod. B restaurée avant la guerre par H. |

---

7. Giversen, *Homilies and Varia*, ix–x of the Introduction and the plates on pp. 101–26.

8. Orlandi, "Les manuscrits coptes de Dublin," 324–25.

| | |
|---|---|
| Ibscher; the other part of Codex B, [p. 325] according to Böhlig, is in Germany (the codex of West Berlin, formerly at Göttingen). They are not of large format, according to what I could determine. This assures us that the fragments do not belong to the codex of *Letters* (= Berlin, Codex 3). | Ibscher; l'autre partie du Cod. B, [p. 325] selon Böhlig, se trouverait en Allemagne (codex de Berlin ouest, jadis a Goettingue). Its ne sont pas d'un grand format, d'après ce que j'ai pu constater: ce qui nous assure que les fragments n'appartiennent pas au codex des *Lettres* (= Berlin, Cod. 3). |

Although Orlandi only states that these leaves are numbered, one may assume they are also labeled as Codex B, since Rolf Ibscher and, following him, Böhlig presuppose such an identification. The number of leaves that Rolf Ibscher had reported to Böhlig and that Böhlig had published was 13, not 16, as Orlandi reports. But Orlandi seems to have these 13 in view, in that he identifies the plates as Codex B, and in that he explicitly draws attention to the fact that the format is not large, as a correction of Rolf Ibscher's recollection that it was large. Orlandi takes this as evidence that the 16 leaves are not from the *Letters*, thus correcting the conjecture of Böhlig. Unfortunately, references to larger or smaller formats in this discussion are not accompanied by measurements, so that the base of comparison remains imprecise.

One must thus use all due caution with regard to Böhlig's conjecture that leaves of $P^{15998}$ are to be found in Copenhagen. Hence one should tentatively assume only that there survive of the codex of Mani's *Letters*: 6 leaves conserved by Hugo Ibscher, in the Staatliche Museen zu Berlin, 3 in the National Museum in Warsaw, and 15 leaves in 13 glass containers in Berlin listed in 1972 as belonging to this codex, 3 in two containers numbered 29 and 30 reassigned to the *Kephalaia*, and 1 reassigned to the *Acts*. This would make a total of 28 leaves or 56 pages that survive in whole or in part that are tentatively assigned to the *Letters*.

This codex has not been published.

In 1986 a facsimile edition was published[9] of the 13 leaves that Böhlig had discussed as perhaps belonging to this codex, though in Dublin. Giversen reports that those still in their original glass covers

---

9. Giversen, *Homilies and Varia*, ix–x of the Introduction and the plates on pages 101–26.

bear the label "Codex B," which may have been the basis of the confusion. The pages had also been labeled 51–76, corresponding in the facsimile edition to pages 101–26, in such a way that facing pages have similar fiber directions. A division into two quires, each consisting of "four double leaves" is ascribed to Hugo Ibscher (with the first leaf of the first quire and the last two leaves of the second quire missing). The problem of the identity of the codex is stated, but no solution is indicated:

> The identity of this codex—or poor remnants of a codex—has been widely discussed, for example in the article by A. Böhlig cited above and in a series of other articles, as has the identity of the Mani codex in West Berlin, once called the Schondorf[f] papyrus.
>
> Since this edition should not pre-empt the results of a later critical edition, it has been decided to publish the pages in question in order to promote the work of identifying the papyrus with as little delay as possible. I have therefore refrained from offering any solution, preferring instead to provide some facts which together with the facsimiles should assist in this task.
>
> Not only are the glasses inscribed Codex B, but the frames also are marked "Kephalaia. Codex B." These labels are clearly in Hugo Ibscher's handwriting. The text in most cases is readable, although not easily.
>
> A precise description of the character and content of the text must wait until a critical edition can provide the text in full.

The labeling by Hugo Ibscher as *Kephalaia* would seem to suggest a still further identification than previously envisaged, either with the first volume of *Kephalaia* in Berlin (P[15996]) or with the second volume of *Kephalaia* in Dublin, Codex C, published as Volume I of the facsimile edition.[10] But Giversen does not enter further into the problem of the identification of the material, but contents himself with observing that "important subjects are clearly dealt with" and transcribing a few words.

Photographs of both sides of leaf 13 are on file at the Papyrus-Sammlung of Berlin. One copy of each side was donated to the Manichaean Archives of the Institute for Antiquity and Christianity.

---

10. Giversen, *Kephalaia*.

## — 13 —

## $P^{15999}$: *Homilies (Berlin Part)*

SCHMIDT AND POLOTSKY REPORTED as follows:[1]

| | |
|---|---|
| The papyrus book most recently added to the corpus of Berlin Manichaica could not yet be subjected to any further investigation. This much seems however to be certain, that it contains a collection of so-called λόγοι of different authors. The names of authors from the circle of disciples of Mani crop up on the upper margins, such as Koustaios, Salmaios. | Das jüngst zum Corpus der Berliner Manichaica gekommene Papyrusbuch konnte noch keiner weiteren Untersuchung unterzogen werden. So viel scheint aber festzustehen, dass es eine Sammlung von sogenannten λόγοι verschiedener Autoren enthält. Es tauchen auf den oberen Rändern die Autorennamen aus dem Kreise der Jüngerschaft des Mani auf, wie Koustaios, Salmaios. |

Wilhelm Schubart recorded in the *Inventarbuch* of the Ägyptisches Museum of Berlin-Hauptstadt der DDR in black ink to P[15999]: "Koptischer Papyruskodex. Erworben durch Herrn Prof. Carl Schmidt, in Cairo 1932. Geschenk des Herrn Dr. W. Kohlhammer." ["Coptic Papyrus Codex. Acquired through Prof. Carl Schmidt in Cairo 1932. Gift of Dr. W. Kohlhammer."] A further note added in pencil reports under the "Standort" ["location"]: "ausgestellt" ["displayed"]. A similar hand in pencil reads "Mani." A purple carbon note reads "z. Zt. in Mo[skau]" ["at present in Mo[scow]"].

---

1. Schmidt and Polotsky, "Ein Mani-Fund," 30.

Rolf Ibscher has reported that Kohlhammer paid 5,000 Marks for this part of a codex.[2]

Böhlig reported in 1960/68[3]:

| | |
|---|---|
| 4. P$^{15999}$, not yet made accessible, is also lost. Whether this loss is so great can be doubted. For the condition of the manuscript was so desolate that among the collaborators of the papyrus collection it was generally designated as the "wig." Schmidt could determine on the basis of the captions at the top of the pages that it must have had to do with *logoi* of disciples of Mani. | 4. Die noch nicht erschlossene Handschrift P$^{15999}$ ist ebenfalls verlorengegangen. Ob dieser Verlust so schwer ist, kann man bezweifeln. Denn der Zustand der Handschrift war so desolat, dass sie unter den Mitarbeitern der Papyrussammlung allgemein als die "Perücke" bezeichnet wurde. Schmidt konnte nach Seitenüberschriften feststellen, dass es sich dabei um *logoi* von Jüngern Manis handeln musste. |

Beltz's catalogue omits P$^{15999}$, since none of it in Berlin in 1978.

This part of a codex in Berlin has not been published. But in fact it is part of the *Homilies* codex that is among Sir Chester Beatty's codices, which has been published (see below). Michel Tardieu[4] incorrectly refers to the Dublin *Homilies* as: "Codex complète de 48 feuillets conservé à Dublin (codex D)." ["Complete codex of 48 leaves conserved at Dublin (Codex D)."] He makes no reference to P$^{15999}$.

2. Rolf Ibscher, in a letter of August 29, 1957, to Carsten Colpe.
3. Böhlig, "Die Arbeit," 184.
4. Tardieu, "Les Manichéens en Égypte," 6.

Part Four

The Dublin Holdings

— 14 —

## The Wooden Covers

From the Archives of the Chester Beatty Library the story of the acquisition that Schmidt and Polotsky reported has been augmented (above) with the information that on March 23, 1930, Beatty purchased from Maurice Nahman two bindings at £40 each, on the condition that if the British Museum decided they were later than the sixth century, they could be returned. This was the same acquisition that included two Coptic manuscripts on approval, which turned out to be part of the *Psalms*, which Beatty acquired, and part of the *Homilies*, which Beatty did not acquire, but which Schmidt did in 1932 ($P^{15999}$). But the two covers were paid for on March 23, 1930—there is a dated signed receipt from Nahman in the Archives. Yet a small ring binder that seems to have served in the early years as a kind of accessions book for Beatty's library records for July 30, when Nahman visited London to settle accounts with Beatty: "Sent by Nahman, belonging to him. Papyrus, with 1 cover. *Safe B.* (Ibscher 1930)." The reference to "Ibscher 1930" suggests this was with the Second Part of the *Psalms* taken in 1930 to Berlin. This suggests that one cover was associated with the manuscript on which Beatty had an option, what was to become $P^{15999}$, perhaps because the manuscript lay on the cover. A note in another hand reads: "Given to Dr. Ibscher for Nahman." This apparently refers to Beatty's releasing in 1932 his option for the part of the *Homilies* that he had on approval since 1930 and, on instructions from Nahman dated March 15, 1932, turning it over to Sir Alan Gardiner on May 10, 1932 for Ibscher to take to Berlin to be acquired there ($P^{15999}$). These notes would seem to indicate that one cover went with the manuscript to Berlin. Since Beatty had already paid for the cover,

it would presumably have been an oversight on his or his staff's part to include it in what was sent of Berlin to be purchased from Nahman.

In April 1931 Beatty again acquired two manuscripts, one listed in the ring binder as "Manichaean Hymns," that is to say, the first part of the *Psalms* codex, and the other as "Manichaean Ritual Laws," which is an early designation for what in fact was the other part of the *Homilies* codex, the part published by Polotsky. In the same record were listed "3 wooden covers."

Whereas the two covers acquired in 1930 have not been located at the Chester Beatty Library (or at the Egyptian Museum in Berlin), there is at the Chester Beatty Library a large paper envelope with a handwritten note on it stating "purchased Spring 1931," containing three wooden boards, two complete, one only partially so, each apparently a front or back cover of a codex.

Schmidt and Polotsky had reported about the wooden covers of the Manichaean codices as follows (see above):[1]

> In the process, a papyrus book [$P^{15997}$, *Acts*] emerged that lay in the original condition as when found, between two bare wooden covers, since one had risked no further handling . . .
>
> My man of confidence must have had the whole discovery before his eyes, for, according to a passing comment that he just now made to me on my visit in March 1932, the papyrus books, each surrounded by bare covers in wood, lay in a wooden box that was found in what had been a dwelling house.

In his more popular presentation of 1933, Schmidt had written: "The box contained a series of papyrus books, each surrounded by rough wooden covers."[2]

There was even a published photograph of the edges of two such boards. For Schmidt and Polotsky had reported concerning $P^{15997}$, the *Acts*:[3]

> Very briefly I can turn to the third papyrus book, which when acquired lay in the original condition between two wooden covers as remains of the binding. It too belongs to the Berlin holdings. A concept of the desolate condition of the preservation is given in the accompanying photograph . . .

---

1. Schmidt and Polotsky, "Ein Mani-Fund," 7, 9.
2. Schmidt, *Neue Originalquellen des Manichäismus aus Aegypten*, 4.
3. Schmidt and Polotsky, "Ein Mani-Fund," 27.

Wolfgang Müller listed three Coptic book bindings as still extant in 1964/65.[4] But Günter Poethke confirmed on September 31, 1986, that no Manichaean covers are included among them. There are also no references to Manichaean covers in the *Inventarbuch* (at least not at $P^{15995-15999}$) or in the reports by Böhlig and Beltz, though they may be tacitly included in references to $P^{15997}$ and $P^{15999}$. Thus the two wooden covers to $P^{15997}$ that apparently came from Egypt to Berlin and the cover of $P^{15999}$ that apparently came to Berlin via London must be assumed to be lost.

In the case of $P^{15996}$, the Berlin *Kephalaia*, by the time of the acquisition, the covers had apparently been ripped off of the book block, according to the report by Hugo Ibscher:[5]

| | |
|---|---|
| Of a binding nothing more could be discovered, since the covers had been undoubtedly removed with raw force, whereby along with the binding also at the same time any and every connection of the double leaves had been lost at the spine. | Von einer Heftung war nichts mehr zu entdecken, weil die Einbände unzweifelhaft mit roher Gewalt entfernt worden sind, wobei mit der Heftung auch gleichzeitig sämtliche Zusammenhänge der Doppelblätter am Rücken verlorengegangen sind. |

The existence of simple wooden boards, rather than ornate leather covers, initially posed a problem. For it had been assumed that the Manichaean codices were deluxe copies, for which ornate covers would be expected. In the initial report Hugo Ibscher had stated:[6]

| | |
|---|---|
| It stands beyond question that such elegantly furnished books must have also possessed valuable covers. The wooden covers without any decoration that lay along with the discoveries can never be looked upon as remainders of covers, at least not of our Mani books. It is possible that these extant wooden covers were once covered with leather. But one finds | Dass derart vornehm ausgestattete Bücher auch kostbare Einbände besessen haben müssen, steht ausser jedem Zweifel. Niemals können die bei den Funden gelegenen Holzdeckel ohne jedwede Verzierung als Einbandreste angesprochen werden, wenigstens nicht für unsere Mani-Bücher. Möglich ist es, dass diese vorhandenen |

---

4. Müller, "Die koptischen Handschriften," 66.

5. Hugo Ibscher, "Die Handschrift," in *Kephalaia*: 1. Hälfte (Lieferung 1–10), xi.

6. Hugo Ibscher, "Die Handschriften," 85.

no trace of such. But that they served the purpose of covers is proven by the extant holes and the furrows present on the long side, which was intended to receive the cord that binds the book block to the cover. It is after all well known that the Manichaeans decorated their books especially elegantly, which was on occasion turned into a reproach by their enemies. That the Copts were capable of producing precious covers is seen from the remains of covers that the Berlin Museum like the British Museum and Vienna's National Library possess. A rich collection of Coptic manuscripts with covers is also in the Pierpont Morgan Library. Even though all extant covers belong to the eighth to the tenth centuries A.D., one still does not need to doubt that 400 years earlier the Manichaeans were capable of producing even more expensive covers, which would mean for their divine works both protection and decoration. One may hope that the sand of Egypt will some day provide us attestation of this bookbinding art, of the greatest importance for the study of bookbinding.

Holzdeckel einmal mit Leder überzogen gewesen sind. Nur findet man hiervon keine Spur. Dass sie aber Einbandzwecken dienten, beweisen die vorhandenen Löcher und die längsseitig vorhandene Rille, die zur Aufnahme der Verschnürung des Buchblockes an den Deckel bestimmt war. Es ist ja bekannt, dass die Manichäer ihre Bücher besonders prunkvoll ausgestattet haben, was ihnen von ihren Feinden gelegentlich zum Vorwurf gemacht wurde. Dass die Kopten fähig waren, kostbare Einbände herzustellen, ersieht man aus den Einbandresten, die das Berliner Museum wie das British Museum und die Wiener Nationalbibliothek besitzen. Eine reiche Kollektion koptischer Manuskripte mit Einbänden birgt auch die Pierpont Morgan Library. Gehören alle vorhandenen Einbände auch dem 8. bis 10. Jahrhundert n. Chr. an, so braucht man nicht daran zu zweifeln, dass die Manichäer 400 Jahre früher in der Lage waren, noch kostbarere Einbände herzustellen, die für ihre göttlichen Werke Schutz und Zierde zugleich bedeuteten. Hoffentlich gibt uns der Boden Agyptens auch einmal Zeugen dieser Einbandkunst, die für die Einbandforschung von allergrösstem Werte wären.

In the introduction to Charles Allberry's edition of *A Manichaean Psalm-Book Part II*, Hugo Ibscher had conjectured:[7]

---

7. Hugo Ibscher, "Die Handschrift," in *A Manichaean Psalm-Book. Part II*, xvii–xviii.

## The Wooden Covers  277

No doubt there lay along side this one, as well as by a few other volumes of the find, raw wooden covers, and, as the dealers explained, the individual books had always lain between two such wooden covers. Here too it is regrettable that the expert could not be on hand as the treasure was dug out. In any case I doubt very much that in this condition the raw wooden covers could ever have been the cover for these valuable books. It is for me certain that the original covers have been removed by force from the book block. Whether this took place already in antiquity, or first after the discovery by the dealers, is left open. I personally assume that the destruction took place already in antiquity, perhaps by a later owner, who either used the valuable bindings for other works, or wanted to make money out of the precious stones and metals that had been used for the decoration of the holy books. Otherwise it cannot be explained that it is precisely at the spine of the books that the destruction appears so strongly. If the books had not been ripped out of the cover, the firm spine of the cover would have protected the book block at this place from harm [p. xviii], and the sewing would have been preserved for us. It is lucky for us that the scribe has left at the spine of the book about 2 cm of free space, otherwise much more line beginnings would have been lost by the brutal ripping out of the book block from the cover. On

Es lagen wohl bei diesem, wie auch bei einigen anderen Bänden des Fundes rohe Holzdeckel dabei, und wie die Händler erklärten, hätten die einzelnen Bücher immer zwischen zwei solchen Holzdeckeln gelegen. Es ist auch hier wieder zu bedauern, dass der Fachmann nicht zur Stelle sein konnte, als der Schatz gehoben wurde. Jedenfalls be-zweifele ich sehr, dass die rohen Holzdeckel in diesem Zustande jemals den Einband für diese kostbaren Bücher abgegeben haben. Fest steht für mich, dass die ursprünglichen Einbände mit Gewalt vom Buchblock entfernt worden sind. Ob dies schon im Altertum oder erst nach der Auffindung durch die Händler geschehen ist, sei dahingestellt. Ich persönlich nehme an, dass die Zerstörung bereits im Altertum, vielleicht durch einen späteren Besitzer erfolgte, der die kostbaren Einbände entweder für andere Werke verwendete, oder aber die zur Ausschmückung der heiligen Bücher verwendeten Edelsteine und Edelmetalle zu Geld machen wollte. Anders ist es nicht zu erklären, dass gerade am Rücken der Bücher die Zerstörung so stark in die Erscheinung getreten ist. Wären die Bücher nicht aus dem Einband gerissen worden, so hätte gerade der feste Rücken des Einbandes den Buchblock an dieser Stelle vor Scha- [p. xviii] den bewahrt, und die Heftung wäre uns erhalten geblieben. Ein Glück für uns, dass der Schreiber am Rücken des Buches etwa 2 cm freien Raum gelassen hat, sonst wären noch weit mehr Zeilenanfänge durch das brutale Herausreissen des Buchblockes aus dem Einband verlorengegangen. Auf der beigefügten

the appended picture one can still clearly recognize the violent destruction on the spine of the book.

If the covers really were of wood, and the dimensions of the two covers found with the *Psalms* book justify this conjecture, then Greek binding artists must have been at work, who already in very early times knew of the use of wood for covers. All early Coptic covers that have cropped up in Egypt—from the 6th to the 8th centuries A.D.—consistently present covers that have been constructed from the remains of the papyrus stalk, or in which the covers were pasted together from old cartonnage. It would have been very nice to come to know here for once old covers from the beginning of the 4th century A.D., which would have advanced considerably our knowledge in the area of research into book binding, since the earliest covers come from the 6th century A.D.

Abbildung kann man die gewaltmässige Zerstörung am Buchrücken noch gut erkennen.

Sollten die Einbanddeckel wirklich aus Holz bestanden haben, und die Grösse der beiden mit dem Psalmenbuch gefundenen Decked rechtfertigen diese Vermutung, dann müssen hier griechische Einbandkünstler am Werke gewesen sein, die die Verwendung von Holz zu Einbanddeckeln schon in sehr früher Zeit kannten. Sämtliche bisher in Ägypten aufgetauchten frühen koptischen Einbände—aus dem 6. bis 8. Jahrhundert n. Chr.—zeigen durchweg Deckel, die aus Abfällen von der Papyrusstaude hergestellt sind, oder bei denen die Deckel aus alter Makulatur zusammengeklebt wurden. Es wäre erfreulich gewesen, hier einmal alte Einbände aus dem Ausgang des 4. Jahrh. n. Chr. kennenzulernen, die unsere Kenntnis auf dem Gebiete der Einbandforschung ungemein gefördert hätte[n], da die frühesten Einbände aus dem 6. Jahrh. n. Chr. stammen.

In 1938 Charles Allberry was no doubt following Ibscher in conjecturing the bindings were ripped out in antiquity:[8]

> When the dealers divided each book up they had to tear the parts asunder. The books seem to have been ripped out of their bindings in antiquity and in consequence one margin has disappeared, so that on alternate pages for the most part the beginning and the end of the lines are more often than not destroyed.

Hugo Ibscher reported further about the luxurious covers of Manichaean codices in 1940:[9]

8. Allberry, "Manichaean Studies," 341.
9. Hugo Ibscher, "Die Handschrift," in *Kephalaia: 1. Hälfte (Lieferung 1–10)*, vii–viii.

| | |
|---|---|
| The fact that the Mani manuscripts have come down to us in codex form does not mean in and of itself anything new, but is actually quite a matter of course. For also the manuscripts of the Manichaean primitive community that may have served as a *Vorlage* for the Coptic scribes usually already had this book form. Although [p. viii] according to the discoveries in Dura, in the region of the Euphrates, papyrus writing material was not unknown, in contrast to the Mani manuscripts from Egypt the writing material used for the manuscripts of the primitive community will have been parchment. This is clearly and unambiguously shown from the many reports of the Arabic writings, according to which, in burning the Mani writings in the time of persecution, "precious stones fell out and gold flowed out." Both were materials that were used only to decorate codex covers, but never for the protective coverings for papyrus rolls. Just so Augustine also as a fanatical opponent of the Manichaeans called on his followers in his polemical writings, "burn all those parchment manuscripts and those expensive leather covers." | Dass die Manihandschriften in Kodexform auf uns gekommen sind, bedeutet an und für sich nichts Neues, sondern ist eigentlich ganz selbstverständlich. Denn auch die Handschriften der Manichäischen Urgemeinde, die den koptischen Schreibern als Vorlage gedient haben mögen, trugen sicher schon diese Buchform. Obgleich [p. viii] nach den Funden in Dura im Euphratgebiet der Papyrus-Beschreibstoff nicht unbekannt gewesen ist, wird aber im Gegensatz zu den Manihandschriften aus Agypten der für die Handschriften der Urgemeinde verwendete Beschreibstoff Pergament gewesen sein. Dies geht klar und eindeutig aus den vielen Berichten der arabischen Schriftsteller hervor, wonach bei der Verbrennung der Manischriften in der Verfolgungszeit "Edelsteine herausfielen und Gold herausfloss." Beides Materialien, die nur zur Ausschmückung der Kodexeinbände Verwendung fanden, niemals aber bei den Schutzhüllen für die Papyrusrollen. Ebenso forderte auch Augustin als fanatischer Gegner der Manichäer in seinen Streitschriften seine Anhänger auf, "verbrennt alle jene Pergament-Handschriften und jene kostbaren Ledereinbände." |

Such assumptions about luxurious Manichaean covers do not provide a solid basis for putting in question that these simple boards were in fact the original covers of these Manichaean codices. There are no grounds for further speculation implying something like a rebinding in antiquity, which of course could take place (P. Bodmer XIV–XV), but should not be conjectured merely as an inference from secondary literature.

To judge by the similar position of the holes in two of the three Dublin boards and their similar overall dimensions and irregularities, these two belonged to the same codex. The two covers measure 34 cm high by 19.4 (at the top) to 19.8 cm (at the bottom) wide. The third board, presumably from a different codex, is incomplete, having a vertical break resulting in dimensions of 32.7 to 33.0 cm high by 12.5 to 14.4 cm wide. If one may calculate that the relative dimensions of the two codices would have been about the same, one may assume that the original width of the broken board would have been only slightly less than that of the other two boards, indicating an original size for it of about 33 by 19 cm.

These dimensions of the covers are slightly larger than the dimensions of any of the leaves, which reach to about 31.5 cm in height ($P^{15996}$, Volume 1 of the *Kephalaia*; $P^{15998}$, the *Letters*; the *Synaxeis* book block, Codex B; and the Dublin part of the *Homilies*, Codex D), with widths reaching 19 cm for the book block of the *Synaxeis*. But if one may assume that the covers would normally be slightly larger than the leaves, the measurements of the covers could correspond to any of these four codices. $P^{15997}$, the *Acts*, that Beltz reported to average 22–25 by 13.0 cm wide, was still between its wooden covers when Schmidt acquired it, and so does not come in question. The *Psalms*, Codex A, 27 by 17.5 cm, was also sufficiently smaller that one might doubt that the extant covers belonged to it, even though apparently acquired in the same transaction as that involving the front part of the *Psalms*. To be sure, Ibscher used "the size of the two covers found with the *Psalms* book" to justify the conjecture that the codices actually had wooden covers. But these covers would not seem to be the covers of the *Psalms* codex, but rather of the *Homilies*, parts of which were sold in each of the transactions (1930 and 1931) involving parts of the *Psalms* codex, or even to another of the Manichaean codices, given the jumbling of the material in the hands of middlemen, and the fact that both Schmidt and Beatty bought from Nahman.

The two completely extant boards at the Chester Beatty Library do have vestiges of leather on each side, with traces of tooling marks of circles and lines on the outside surfaces. There are a series of holes through the boards at positions near three edges of the boards, positioned on the two boards so that they correspond to each other. Two pegs are still in a hole each on one board, and one peg in a hole on the other, all three on the head and foot sides of the covers. These holes

are no doubt near enough the lips of the covers that pegs or thongs could have passed through both covers to hold the codex closed without having to pass through the quires themselves. On the long side without holes, an indention some 2 cm wide and .5 cm deep has been chiseled out for the length of this side. This indention may have been intended to be covered with a leather band functioning as the flexible spine, to hold the two covers together. As to the four corners of each board, those at the end of the long chiseled edge are pointed; whereas those at the end of the long side with holes are rounded.

Since no covers are extant in Berlin, further information about the Manichaean covers is apparently limited to the three boards at the Chester Beatty Library. Unfortunately, the several publications by Berthe van Regemorter on the book bindings of the Chester Beatty Library do not seem to have made reference to such unpretentious boards.[10] Yet they are so dissimilar from the covers of the Nag Hammadi Codices and of the Disnha (Bodmer) Codices (though rather near in time and space), that a detailed analysis might result in the kind of new insight into the history of bookbinding that Ibscher had envisaged, in his appeal to the Greek tradition to explain them.

---

10. Van Regemorter, "Le Codex relié depuis son origine jusqu'au Haut Moyen-Age," 1–26; Van Regemorter, *Some Early Bindings from Egypt in the Chester Beatty Library*; Van Regemorter, *Some Oriental Bindings in the Chester Beatty Library*.

## — 15 —

## *Codex A: Psalms*

SCHMIDT AND POLOTSKY LIST in first place among Sir Chester Beatty's holdings the *Psalms*:[1]

One has to do in the London collection with a large papyrus book. The individual psalms were numbered. The highest number that has been read thus far is 230. If we could assume for the individual psalms an average length of (at least) 2 pages, this would require an extent of 460 pages = 230 leaves. Hence one does not go wrong in calculating that the whole book, as in the case of the *Kephalaia*, consisted of over 250 leaves. Unfortunately the individual leaves are not paginated, and there are no running heads on the upper margins. The individual psalms are simply distinguished by the numbers. Thus far about 50 of the extant leaves have been brought under glass, so that our knowledge of the content is still quite limited.

Es handelt sich in der Londoner Sammlung um ein umfangreiches Papyrusbuch. Die einzelnen Psalmen waren numeriert. Die höchste Zahl, die bis jetzt gelesen wurde, ist 230. Würden wir für die einzelnen Psalmen eine durchschnittliche Länge von (mindestens) 2 Seiten annehmen, würde dies einen Umfang von 460 Seiten = 230 Blättern erfordern. Deshalb geht man nicht fehl, das ganze Buch wie bei den Kephalaia auf über 250 Blätter zu berechnen. Leider sind die einzelnen Blätter nicht paginiert und finden sich keine Titelüberschriften auf den oberen Rändern; die einzelnen Psalmen sind einfach nur durch die Nummern unterschieden. Von den vorhandenen Blättern sind bisher nur etwa 50 unter Glas gebracht, so dass unsere Kenntnis des Inhalts noch beschränkt ist.

---

1. Schmidt and Polotsky, "Ein Mani-Fund," 30, 34. The quotation is from 34.

## Codex A: Psalms

C. R. C. Allberry published in 1938 the last half of the *Psalms*, which had been purchased and hence conserved first.[2] In the Preface he reported:

> What is presented here, in the same format as the *Homilies* and the *Kephalaia*, is the *Psalm-book* (see *Mani-Fund*, pp. 33ff. [actually 30–34]), or rather the second part of the *Psalm-book*: for before it appeared in the Cairo market the codex had already been split up into several blocks, and on the largest and least mutilated of these, together with a smaller block preceding it, the two forming approximately one half of the codex, Dr. Hugo Ibscher, the Papyruskonservator in the Berlin Egyptian Museum, began his work of reconstruction, and succeeded between 1931 and 1934 in separating and glassing about one hundred and twenty consecutive leaves. These are published here with an English version and a minimum of annotation.

In the Crum Archives of the Griffith Institute in the Ashmolean Museum in Oxford, there is a file of transcriptions (sometimes with translations and/or notes) by H. J. Polotsky. (Its classification in terms of published, inventory numbers II.28.1 ff. on the back of each leaf, and unpublished, II.30.1 ff., is inexact.) Some are pages published by Allberry, but others are unpublished:

- II.30.1 (= II.28.138, with Polotsky's English translation at II.28.142), with the Psalm numeration 213 and the comment that it precedes page 1 of Allberry, i.e., that it is from the unpublished first part of the *Psalms* (Allberry's volume began with the last 3 lines of Psalm 218)
- II.30.2 (= II.28.140)
- II.30.3 (= II.28.140)
- II.30.4 (= II.28.136)
- II.30.5 ( = II.28.139)
- II.30.6 ( = II.28.137), with II.30.7 representing a second transcription and a second hand (Allberry?) and
- II.30.10

Unpublished transcriptions or translations of the Chester Beatty holdings have not been located in the Chester Beatty Archives.

---

2. Allberry, *A Manichaean Psalm-Book, Part II*.

Torgny Säve-Söderbergh soon published an important comparison of the *Psalms* with Mandaean hymnody.[3]

Böhlig presented this first codex of Sir Chester Beatty as follows[4]:

1. The *Psalms* (Codex A) was edited in 1938 in its second part (115 [read: 117] leaves) by C. R. C. Allberry. It contains various types and collections of psalms and became the most noted work of the Manichaean discovery, especially since religious feeling came here more strongly to expression and addressed one's own religious feeling more than was the case in the rationalistic style of the *Kephalaia*. The remaining leaves, a total of 56, were conserved by Rolf Ibscher after the war. They have been awaiting editing for years.

1. Das Psalmbuch (Codex A) wurde in seinem 2. Teil (115 [read: 117] Blätter) von C. R. C. Allberry 1938 ediert. Es enthält verschiedene Typen und Sammlungen von Psalmen und wurde zum beachtesten Werk des manichäischen Fundes, insbesondere weil das religiöse Gefühl hier stärker zum Ausdruck kam und angesprochen wurde als durch den logizistischen Stil der Kephalaia. Die restlichen insgesamt 56 Blätter wurden von Rolf Ibscher nach dem Kriege konserviert. Sie harren seit Jahren der Edition.

Since none of this codex is in Berlin, it is not included in Beltz's catalogue. However, Tito Orlandi published a report on Coptic manuscripts in the Chester Beatty Library in 1976, where he reported:[5]

---

3. Säve-Söderbergh, *Studies in the Coptic Manichaean Psalm-Book*.

4. Böhlig, "Die Arbeit," 185. The typescript of the 1960 address that is in the Archives of the Chester Beatty Library has been corrected by hand to read 117 rather than 115 leaves, though the text of Böhlig's address published in 1968 was not so corrected. There are in fact 234 Coptic pages that Allberry published, which would support the correction to 117 leaves. Böhlig's comment about the greater popularity of the Psalms is a reflection of Torgny Säve-Söderbergh, *Studies in the Coptic Manichaean Psalm-Book*, especially p. 1:

> Whereas the *Kephalaia*, edited by Schmidt, Polotsky and Böhlig, consist chiefly of a rather dry and dull systematization of the Manichaean dogma and the *Homilies*, edited by Polotsky, are unfortunately very fragmentary, the rather well preserved *Psalm Book* not only have an interesting content, but are also composed in a most charming poetical form.

5. Orlandi, "Les manuscrits coptes de Dublin, du British Museum et de Vienne," 324.

During our visit we were able to verify that the already-edited manuscripts have been carefully separated from the fragments that are still unedited. They are also readily recognizable, leaf by leaf, by comparing them with the editions that one has. In effect we have noted that the part of Codex A edited by Mr. Allberry (*Psalms* Part II) is perfectly conserved in 9 little wooden boxes, in which the glasses containing the leaves are arranged in vertical position ...

Let us now come to the unpublished materials. The first part of Codex A (*Psalms*), which had been conserved soon after the war, and which, according to Böhlig, included 56 glasses, consists in fact of 106 glasses (of which some conserve two fragments), arranged in their turn in 9 little boxes equal to those of the second part. On the shelves to the right of the entrance (where the unpublished leaves restored after the war by R. Ibscher are put) there are also 49 glasses numbered in relation to the *recto* and *verso* of the fragments (each glass hence has two numbers). They bear no identification. But, given the characteristics of some titles, of the hand and of the format, they must comprise a third part of the *Psalms*, [a part] whose existence seems unknown up to the present.

Pendant notre visite, nous avons pu verifier que les manuscrits déjà édités ont été soigneusement separés des fragments encore inédits; ils sont aussi aisément reconnaissables, feuillet par feuillet, en comparaison avec les éditions que l'on possède. En effet, nous avons constaté que la partie du Cod. A éditée par M. Allberry (*Psaumes*, IIe partie) est parfaitement conservée dans 9 petites caisses en bois, dans lesquelles les verres contenant les feuillets sont ranges en position verticale ...

Venons-en maintenant aux inédits. La I$^e$ partie du Cod. A (*Psaumes*), qui avait été restaurée peu après la guerre, et qui selon Böhlig comprenait 56 verres, se compose en fait de 106 verres (dont certains conservent deux fragments), rangés a leur tour dans 9 petites caisses, égales a celles de la II$^e$ partie. Sur les étagères a droite de l'entrée (ou sont placés les feuillets inédits restaurés après la guerre par R. Ibscher) ii y a en outre 49 verres, qui sont numerotés par rapport au *recto* et *verso* des fragments (chaque verre a donc deux numéros); ils ne portent aucune indication; mais, étant donné les caractéristiques de certains titres, de l'écriture et du format, ils devraient former une III$^e$ partie des *Psaumes*, dont l'existence parait jusqu'a maintenant inconnue.

Thus one would be led to infer that there are 155 glasses containing unpublished leaves or fragments of Codex A.

The typed page in the Chester Beatty Library titled "Manichean Papyri on Loan to Royal Library, Copenhagen," dated January 13,

1984, lists under "Psalm Book" 9 boxes containing a total of 106 glasses, which is presumably the material that Orlandi listed as labeled as belonging to the *Psalms* but unpublished. The list of material taken to Copenhagen then itemizes folios numbered 219–308, 369–78, a total of 50 glasses; numbers 387–404, 9 glasses, marked as fragments; leaves numbered 51–76, a total of 13 glasses, marked as Codex B; and 6 glasses marked fragments and numbered x1–x12. The 13 glasses marked Codex B can safely be identified with plates 101–26 of the second volume of the facsimile edition.[6]

Søren Giversen explained in a telephone conversation of September 4, 1985, that the material taken to Copenhagen included the 13 unidentified leaves that Böhlig had conjectured might belong to the Berlin *Letters*, P[15998] (that in fact probably belong to the *Synaxeis*), as well as leaves that, according to the Dublin records, were not listed as from the *Psalms* but which, since Giversen detected in them psalms, might belong to the *Psalms*. This would lead one to conclude that the 50 unidentified leaves taken to Copenhagen include the 49 unidentified leaves that Orlandi ascribed to the *Psalms*. The remaining unidentified leaf in Copenhagen may be that of P[15997].

Søren Giversen published in 1986 an English translation of parts of two Psalms from Part One of the *Psalms*. He introduced the first with the comment: "From notes and decipherment from 1931, I can see, that something has gone [sic] lost since then, especially at the beginning of lines 30–33."[7] One must infer that this is an allusion to a transcription and/or translation and notes by H. J. Polotsky, such as he provided in 1931–1932 to Sir Herbert Thompson to translate into English and supply to Beatty, though Polotsky's Coptic transcription, translation, and/or notes have not yet been located in the Crum or Chester Beatty Archives. It is unclear why such a use of Polotsky's scholarship would not be clearly stated.

The other Psalm that Giversen translates is numbered 119 and entitled "Psalms on the Lord's Day."[8] From the work of Polotsky (recognizable by his abbreviated signature in the bottom right-hand corners: "P-y") preserved in the Griffith Institute, there is a page in his handwriting that he numbered "C.B.i, 'II'a" (Crum Mss II.30.2)

---

6. Giversen, *Homilies and Varia*, ix–x, 101–26.
7. Giversen, "The Unedited Chester Beatty Mani Texts," 376.
8. Ibid., 378–79.

with the title 'CALMOI THS KYRIAK' and the numeral RIQ, followed by 8 lines of text. Polotsky also provided a typed German translation (Crum Mss II.28.85 = Crum Mss II.28.7). Giversen, after quoting the title and numeral, presents, as "a," 8 lines of text in English translation corresponding to Polotsky's 8 lines, followed by "b," introduced with the comment "plus or minus 7 lines almost illegible" and then an English translation of lines 8–33. These lines correspond to those on the page that Polotsky numbered "C.B. i, 'II' b" (Crum Mss II.30.3 in Coptic transcription and Crum Mss 11.28.86 and Crum Mss II.28.8 in German translation). Since Giversen refers in the case of the first Psalm that he translates to the "notes and decipherment from 1931," it is hard to avoid the conclusion that the other English translation of a Psalm that he presents is also based at least in part on Polotsky's transcription and German translation. But it is very difficult to understand why, in that case, appropriate acknowledgement to Polotsky is not given: all the more so when one recalls that due to racist legislation in the Third Reich, the first volume of the *Kephalaia* could not carry Polotsky's name, so that the co-editor Böhlig left off his own name as well, and explained the lamentable situation after World War II, when the publication of the first double-fascicle of the second volume appeared. One would think that with such a background, one would be scrupulous to give Polotsky due credit for his excellent work. Only when the facsimile edition of the *Psalms* appears will it be possible to see to what extent the papyrus itself is still as legible as it was in Polotsky's day, and to what extent we all, including Giversen, are dependent on Polotsky for rescuing text subsequently lost, as Giversen indirectly concedes in the case of the first Psalm that he translates.

— 16 —

## Codex B: Synaxeis

SCHMIDT AND POLOTSKY REPORTED as follows: A third papyrus book, that surely had a size of 250 leaves, seems to belong together with the *Living Gospel* of Mani. Also a bundle from this papyrus, to the extent of 31 leaves, was brought under glass by Dr. Ibscher. Already there has been a brief report about the titles that were read (see above, P[15995]). The book would be of great importance for Mani research, if some kind of commentary to the *Gospel* of Mani would be hidden there.[1]

Thus Codex B of Sir Chester Beatty is identified as the bulk of the codex of which 31 leaves are in Berlin. For Schmidt and Polotsky had reported (see above) that these 31 leaves "were acquired in the Fayyum and without doubt belong to the London Mani pieces." For in the description of their acquisition, it was stated that "the antiquities dealer in the Fayyum had sold his manuscripts exclusively to Mr. Chester Beatty." The 31 leaves are an exception, for "one had removed the top and bottom layers of papyrus, which had suffered to an especial extent against the covers of the binding . . . , to give the whole a better appearance." In the spring of 1931, after Sir Chester Beatty had acquired the three codices of the Fayyum dealer, Schmidt "found such outwardly unimpressive remains, which doubtlessly belong to the pa-

---

1. Schmidt and Polotsky, "Ein Mani-Fund," 34. "Ein drittes Papyrusbuch, das sicherlich einen Umfang von 250 Blättern gehabt hat, scheint mit dem 'lebendigen Evangelium' des Mani zusammenzuhängen. Auch von diesem Papyrus ist ein Konvolut im Umfang von 31 Blättern von Dr. Ibscher unter Glas gebracht. Über die gelesenen Überschriften ist vorhin kurz berichtet [see above, P[15995]]. Das Buch wäre für die Mani-Forschung von grosser Wichtigkeit, wenn irgendeine Art von Kommentar zum 'Evangelium' des Mani sich dahinter verbergen würde."

pyrus books acquired by Mr. Chester Beatty in the Fayyum, and . . . acquired them for a cheap sum, since the dealer already had his great reward in his pocket." Thus only the 31 leaves from the *Synaxeis* that Schmidt acquired are inventoried in Berlin as P$^{15995}$, and the rest of the codex, to the extent extant, comprises Codex B of Sir Chester Beatty.

Rolf Ibscher reported to Sir Chester Beatty that Codex B had by mistake been left in the anti-aircraft tower at the Zoo, rather than having been taken with Sir Chester Beatty's other codices to Schondorf, and that hence it had been taken to Leningrad along with the Berlin holdings. Rolf Ibscher maintained that the codex that was left in Schondorf when the others there were returned to Sir Chester Beatty was P$^{15998}$, the *Letters*, a codex belonging to Berlin. But once the scholarly study of the Schondorf codex was undertaken in Göttingen by Colpe and Böhlig, it became obvious that this codex was the *Synaxeis* Codex B, belonging to Sir Chester Beatty.

Böhlig presented in 1957 at the 24th International Orientalists' Congress in Munich a report to this effect:[2]

| | |
|---|---|
| During the war, along with the codices belonging to Sir Chester Beatty, a Manuscript was stored outside into the territory that is now the Bundesrepublik. This text is at present in Göttingen for conservation. In 1957, while looking through the leaves that have thus far been separated (which are in an unusually bad condition), I thought I could reconstruct from individual words the same running head. [Footnote 3: For the possibility of being permitted to see the codex I am indebted to the friendliness of the Göttingen Egyptologist S. Schott, who was in charge of the undertaking. I also owe special thanks to C. Colpe and R. Ibscher, who occupied | Im Kriege wurde zusammen mit den Sir Chester Beatty gehörigen Codices eine Handschrift in das jetzige Gebiet der Bundesrepublik ausgelagert; dieser Text befindet sich gegenwärtig in Göttingen zur Konservierung. Bei einer Durchsicht der bisher abgehobenen Blätter, die sich in einem ausserordentlich schlechten Zustand befinden, im Jahre 1957 glaubte ich, aus einzelnen Wörtern die gleiche Überschrift rekonstruieren zu können. [Footnote 3: Die Möglichkeit, den Codex ansehen zu dürfen, verdanke ich der Freundlichkeit des Göttinger Agyptologen S. Schott, der das Unternehmen betreute. Besonderen Dank schulde ich auch C. Colpe und R. Ibscher, die sich um die Restaurierung und Abschrift be- |

---

2. Böhlig, "Synaxis = Homilie," 485–86; "Zu den Synaxeis des Lebendigen Evangeliums," 229–30. The full text of this address is published in *Mysterion and Wahrheit*, 222–27. The quotation is from 222–23.

themselves with the restoration and transcription.] On one leaf one could read "the first" in a page's running head, as the only surviving remnant at the top left, on another leaf in the middle *synaxis*, on a third leaf to the left above, *logos*. These readings could be combined with two chapter titles that for their part could not be completely recognized. One reads: "The [p. 223] *synaxis* of the [1]9th *logos*." Though *synaxis* is here hardly legible, it is nonetheless confirmed by a second chapter title, in which *synaxis* is to be recognized without doubt as the first word. Through these readings the same title can be assumed for the running heads of the book, as C. Schmidt also read in one of the 31 leaves mentioned above. The running heads of the pages would hence be divided as follows on verso and recto: "The 1st *Synaxis* of the 1st *logos* of the *Living Gospel*." Thus one can assume, as also C. Colpe thinks, that the vestige of a codex in Berlin discussed by C. Schmidt forms with this codex a unity of contents but not of ownership.

mühten.] Auf einem Blatt war als Seitenüberschrift als einziger Rest links oben "die erste" zu lesen, auf einem anderen Blatt in der Mitte *synaxis*, auf einem 3. Blatt links oben *logos*. Diese Lesungen konnten mit zwei Kapitelüberschriften kombiniert werden, die ihrerseits auch nicht vollständig zu erkennen waren; die eine lautet: "Die [p. 223] *synaxis* des [1]9. *logos*"; ist dabei *synaxis* kaum lesbar, so wird es doch bestätigt durch die 2. Kapitelüberschrift, in der SYNAXIS als erstes Wort einwandfrei zu erkennen ist. Durch diese Lesungen kann für die Überschriften des Buches derselbe Titel angenommen werden, wie ihn auch C. Schmidt auf einem der oben erwähnten 31 Blätter gelesen hat. Die Seitenüberschriften würden sich auf Verso und Recto folgendermassen verteilen: "Die 1. *synaxis* des 1. / *logos* des Lebendigen Evangeliums." Damit kann man annehmen, wie auch C. Colpe meint, dass der von C. Schmidt besprochene Berliner Restcodex mit diesem Codex eine inhaltliche, aber keine besitzmässige Einheit bildet.

Böhlig in 1960/68 reaffirmed this position:[3]

Carl Schmidt, in his report on the discovery, listed as belonging to the English acquisition a book that has to do with Mani's *Living Gospel*. He considered the Berlin remnant of a codex consisting of 31 leaves (P[15995]), which we

Carl Schmidt hat in seinem Fundbericht zum englischen Besitz gehörig ein Buch angeführt, das es mit Manis Lebendigem Evangelium zu tun hat. Als Teil von ihm und von den Händlern abgetrennt betrachtet er den

---

3. Böhlig, "Die Arbeit," 186.

listed above as the fifth book of the Berlin collection, to be a part of it separated off by the dealers. The manuscript that is now in Göttingen, and was considered as belonging to Berlin at the time of its rescue from the anti-aircraft tower in 1944, turned out, in the superscriptions identified by me in 1957 and confirmed by C. Colpe, to belong with the 31 Berlin leaves, what now also, on seeing the 31 leaves, is confirmed by the format. So we have to do indeed, as is also conjectured by C. Colpe, in the case of the Göttingen manuscript, with Codex B of the Chester Beatty collection.

Berliner Restcodex von 31 Blättern (P$^{15995}$), den wir oben als 5. Buch der Berliner Sammlung genannt haben. Die jetzt in Göttingen befindliche und bei der Bergung aus dem Flakturm 1944 als Berliner Besitz angesehene Handschrift erwies sich in den von mir im Jahre 1957 identifizierten und von C. Colpe bestätigten Überschriften als mit den 31 Berliner Blättern zusammengehörig, was jetzt auch bei In-Augenschein-Nahme der 31 Blätter das Format bestätigte. Wir werden es also in der Tat, wie auch von C. Colpe vermutet, bei der Göttinger Handschrift mit dem Codex B der Chester-Beatty-Sammlung zu tun haben.

Rolf Ibscher in 1964/65 (see above) conceded that the Schondorf-Göttingen–West Berlin codex is the same codex from which the 31 leaves P$^{15995}$ come:

> Carsten Colpe, who worked for a time on the leaves that had been won up until then, brought into play in Munich at the International Orientalists' Congress [1957] the thesis that the manuscript does not belong to Berlin at all, but is identical with the 13 leaves of Codex B in Dublin . . . Böhlig on the other hand maintained that the 31 leaves of the Berlin codex Nr. 15995 belong, in view of the shared titles on the pages (SYNAXIS), together with the Göttingen codex, whereas he had earlier held it to be codex Nr. 15998 . . . What is then the situation with the 31 leaves in Berlin, that after all are identical with those of the codex in Göttingen?

Rolf Ibscher also raised the question as to whether leaves still in Berlin might belong to the Chester Beatty Library's Codex B, the *Synaxeis*:

> . . . a sizable number of leaves separated last, quite provisionally, by my father, with an entry on the paper cover that protected them, which really creates puzzles: "from Codex B," i.e., then Chester Beatty [*Synaxeis*]or ?—and with the addition put

in parentheses "Letters," i.e., then again Codex Nr. 15[9]98. What is one to make of that?[4]

These leaves are currently in the Ägyptisches Museum in Berlin, where they are classified as belonging to $P^{15998}$. They present no running heads or chapter titles like those of the *Synaxeis* codex.

Rolf Ibscher had sought to maintain that the Schondorf-Göttingen codex belonged to the Berlin Museum on the grounds that it was part of $P^{15995}$, either ignoring or ignorant of the fact that the Berlin acquisition, $P^{15995}$, consisted only of 31 leaves. But here he seems indirectly to concede that the Schondorf-Göttingen codex belongs to Sir Chester Beatty by leaving open the question, presumably the question of the ownership, of the 31 leaves in Berlin. He does not seem to have accepted the fact of divided ownership. Carsten Colpe, in a Berlin interview of 1986, attributes this dangling uncertainty in Rolf Ibscher's interpretation to an intentional obscuring of the situation, an obfuscation useful in Rolf Ibscher's perennial efforts to secure German funding for his conservation work on this codex, in view of the fact that there were no papyri left in Berlin to conserve and that his wife pressured him constantly for more money.

Wolfgang Müller's preliminary inventory of 1964/65 had added, in reporting on $P^{15995}$, the 31 leaves of the *Synaxeis*: "The rest in Göttingen." Beltz's catalogue had reported similarly on $P^{15995}$, though by this time (1978) the rest was in West Berlin, at the Ägyptisches Museum in Charlottenburg: "The remainder of the codex is to be found for the time being in West Berlin ... A. Böhlig and C. Colpe have defined the codex as "*Synaxeis* to the *Living Gospel* of Mani." This identification of the Schondorf-Göttingen–West Berlin codex with Sir Chester Beatty's Codex B has thus over the past generation had the support of Böhlig, Colpe, Ibscher, Müller, and Beltz, and has in fact not been contested. The most telling evidence is a list of eleven section titles collected by Colpe, in which the word SYNAXIS is in part or in its entirety preserved, occurring in at least the three more legible cases in the formula "The [e.g.] Fourth SYNAXIS of the [e.g.] First Logos of the Gospel" (on a page he identified as "1957 / 17 V" ( = 19.2.2.66 vert.).

---

4. Rolf Ibscher, "Über den Stand der Umkonservierung der Manipapyri" (1964–65), 52.

Rolf Ibscher's report on his conservation activities had referred to "ca. 145 leaves" that he had separated from the book block, which "still has about 100 to 120 unseparated leaves." Hence Müller's preliminary inventory had reported: "Here 145 leaf units separated, about 100-120 leaves still on the book block." Beltz had reported: "Since 1945, 145 new leaf units have been separated and conserved. The remainder of the book block is not yet conserved." Michel Tardieu continues to refer to 145 leaves.[5]

The inventory of the holdings in the Ägyptisches Museum in Charlottenburg in West Berlin in 1985–1986 located, in addition to the book block, 125 labeled leaves, plus 5 glass frames containing fragments. Thus the figure "ca. 145 leaves" would seem to be an inflated estimate, unless some material has been misplaced.

The combination of 125 conserved leaves in West Berlin and 31 in East Berlin makes a total of 156 leaves. This would mean 312 pages. But the top page of the book block is also accessible, making a total of 313 pages accessible to scholarship.

Such a listing of unpublished but extant leaves may be somewhat misleading. For although the size of the lacunae is relatively small in many cases, that is to say, although a large part of the papyrus is usually extant, the amount of extant ink varies considerably, and the resultant legibility of many pages is disappointingly small. Hence a rough classification of extant ink may, imprecise though it is, give a clearer picture of what one may expect. Each page is graded on a scale of 0 to 5: 0 = no ink is visible; 1 = some ink but no letters are legible; 2 = some letters but probably no words are legible; 3 = some words but probably no sentences are legible; 4 = some sentences but probably less than half the page is legible; 5 = probably more than half the page is legible.

---

5. Tardieu, "Les Manichéens en Égypte," 6.

**Codex B:** *Synaxeis*

| Category | Total pieces in category | Page numbers and fiber directions |
|---|---|---|
| No ink is visible | No pages can be listed. | No pages can be listed. |
| Some ink, but no letters are legible | 11 pages and 4 fragment plates | 2.2.3.5 (vert.); 3.2.2 [8 1/2] (vert. and hor.); 6.1.2.B (vert.); 13.1.1.85 (hor.); 13.1.1.2.86 (vert.); 13.2.3.90 (hor. and vert.); 14.1.3.93 (hor.); 17.2.1.59 (vert.); 18.2.2.115 (hor.); the fragmentary plates 9.1.3.96 (hor. and vert.); 21.2.3 (hor. and vert.); 22.1.2 (hor. and vert.); 22.1.3 (hor. and vert.) |
| Some letters but probably no words are legible | 60 pages | 2.1.2.4 (hor. and vert.); 2.2.2.4 (hor. and vert.); 2.2.3.5 (hor.); 3.1.2.2 (hor. and vert.); 3.1.3.6 (hor. and vert.); 3.2.1.8 (hor. and vert.); 3.2.3.9 (hor. and vert.); 4.1.2.117 (vert.); 5.2.3.16 (vert.); 6.1.2.A (hor. and vert.); 6.1.2.B (hor.); 6.2.2 (hor. and vert.); 7.2.25 (vert.); 8.1.2.39 (hor.); 8.1.3.40 (hor. and vert.); 8.2.1.41 (hor. and vert.); 9.1.1 (hor. and vert.); 9.1.2.95 (hor. and vert.); |

| | | |
|---|---|---|
| Some letters but probably no words are legible (*cont.*) | 60 pages | 9.2.1.97 (hor.); 10.1.100 (vert.); 11.2.2.77 (vert.); 12.1.1.79 (hor. and vert.); 12.1.3.81 (hor.); 13.1.2.86 (hor.); 13.2.1.88 (hor. and vert.); 13.2.2.89 (hor. and vert.); 14.1.1.91 (hor. and vert.); 14.1.2.92 (hor. and vert.); 14.1.3.93 (vert.); 14.1.4.94 (vert.); 14.2.1.106 (hor.); 14.2.2.107 (hor.); 15.2.1.111 (hor.); 16.2.1.48 (hor.); 17.1.2.52 (hor. and vert.); 17.1.3.53 (hor. and vert.); 17.2.1.59 (hor.); 17.2.3.61 (hor.); 18.2.2.115 (vert.); 21.1.2.55 (hor. and vert.) |
| Some words, but probably no sentences are legible | 144 pages | 1.1.1.30 (hor. and vert.); 1.1.2.33 (hor. and vert.); 1.1.3.32 (vert.); 1.2.1.31 (hor. and vert.); 1.2.2.124 (hor. and vert.); 1.2.3.123 (hor. and vert.); 2.1.1.27 (hor. and vert.); 2.1.3.29 (hor. and vert.); 2.2.1.3 (hor. and vert.); 3.1.1.1 (hor. and vert.); 3.1.4.7 (hor. and vert.); 3.2.4.10 (hor. and vert.); 4.1.1.116 (hor. and vert.); 4.1.2.117 (hor.); 4.1.3.118 (hor. and vert.); |

| | | |
|---|---|---|
| Some words, but probably no sentences are legible (*cont.*) | 144 pages | 4.2.3.13 (hor.); 5.1.1.119 (hor. and vert.); 5.1.2.34 (hor. and vert.); 5.1.3.35 (hor. and vert.); 5.1.4.36 (hor. and vert.); 5.2.1.14 (hor. and vert.); 5.2.2.15 (hor. and vert.); 5.2.3.16 (hor.); 6.1.1.17 (hor. and vert.); 6.1.3.18 (hor. and vert.); 6.2.1.19 (hor. and vert.); 6.2.3.21 (hor. and vert.); 7.1.1.20 (hor. and vert.); 7.1.2.22 (hor. and vert.); 7.1.3.23 (hor. and vert.); 7.2.1.24 (hor. and vert.); 7.2.2.25 (hor.); 7.2.3.26 (hor. and vert.); 8.1.1.38 (hor. and vert.); 8.1.2.39 (vert.); 8.2.2.42 (hor. and vert.); 8.2.3.43 (hor. and vert.); 8.2.4.44 (hor. and vert.); 9.2.1.97 (vert.); 9.2.3.99 (hor. and vert.); 10.1.1.100 (hor.); 10.1.2.101 (vert.); 10.1.3.102 (hor. and vert.); 10.2.1.103 (hor. and vert.); 10.2.2.104 (hor. and vert.); 11.1.3.75 (hor. and vert.); 11.2.1.76 (vert.); 11.2.2.77 (hor.); 11.2.3.78 (hor. and vert.); 12.1.2.80 (hor.); 12.1.3.81 (vert.); |

| | | |
|---|---|---|
| Some words, but probably no sentences are legible (*cont.*) | 144 pages | 12.2.1.82 (hor. and vert.); 12.2.2.83 (hor. and vert.); 12.2.3.84 (hor. and vert.); 13.1.1.85 (vert.); 13.1.3.87 (hor. and vert.); 14.1.4.94 (hor.); 14.2.1.106 (vert.); 14.2.2.107 (vert.); 14.2.3.108 (vert.); 15.1.2.110 (vert.); 15.2.1.111 (vert.); 15.2.2.112 (hor. and vert.); 16.1.2.37 (vert.); 16.1.3.47 (hor. and vert.); 16.2.1.48 (vert.); 16.2.2.49 (hor. and vert.); 16.2.3.50 (hor. and vert.); 17.1.1.51 (hor.); 17.2.3.61 (vert.); 18.1.1 113 (hor.); 18.1.2.121 (hor. and vert.); 18.2.1.114 (hor. and vert.); 19.1.2.63 (hor.); 19.1.3.64 (hor.); 19.2.1.65 (hor. and vert.); 19.2.2.66 (hor.); 19.2.3.67 (hor. and vert.); 20.1.1.68 (hor.); 20.1.2.69 (hor. and vert.); 20.1.3.70 (hor. and vert.); 20.2.1.71 (hor.); 21.1.1.54 (hor. and vert.); 21.2.1.56 (hor. and vert.); 21.2.2.57 (hor. and vert.); and the fragmentary plate 22.1.1 (hor. and vert.) |

| | | |
|---|---|---|
| Some sentences are legible; half the page is illegible | 34 pages | 1.1.3.32 (hor.); 4.2.3.13 (vert.); 9.2.2.98 (hor. and vert.); 10.1.2.101 (hor.); 10.2.3.105 (hor. and vert.); 11.1.1.45 (hor. and vert.); 11.1.2.74 (hor. and vert.); 11.2.1.76 (hor.); 14.2.3.108 (hor.); 15.1.1.109 (hor. and vert.); 15.1.2.110 (hor.); 16.1.1.46 (hor. and vert.); 16.1.2.37 (hor.); 17.1.1.51 (vert.); 17.2.2.60 (hor. and vert.); 18.1.1.113 (vert.); 19.1.1.62 (hor. and vert.); 19.1.2.63 (vert.); 19.1.3.64 (vert.); 19.2.2.66 (vert.); 20.1.1.68 (vert.); 20.2.1.71 (vert.); 20.2.2.72 (hor. and vert.); and 20.2.3.73 (hor. and vert.) |
| More than half the page is legible | 1 page | 12.1.2.80 |

This produces a total of 250 pages (not counting material that should be more accurately considered fragments), graded roughly as follows: 1:11; 2:60; 3:144; 4:34; 5:1. Thus there are hardly more than 35 pages from which one might hope to recover coherent text. This is a much more sober assessment of the quantity of conserved material than simply a list of the total number of conserved leaves.

Tito Orlandi reported as follows on the material in Dublin in 1976[6]:

---

6. Orlandi, "Les Manuscrits coptes de Dublin," 324–25.

| | |
|---|---|
| On another of the same shelves (at the right of the entrance) there are 16 numbered glasses that could represent the part of Codex B restored before the war by H. Ibscher. The other part of Codex B, [p. 325] according to Böhlig, would be in Germany (the codex of West Berlin, formerly at Göttingen). They are not of a large format, from what I was able to ascertain. This assures us that the fragments do not belong to the codex of *Letters* (= Berlin, Codex 3). | Sur une autre des mémes étagères (a droite de l'entrée), it y a 16 verres numérotés, qui pourraient representer la partie du Cod. B restaurée avant la guerre par H. Ibscher; l'autre partie du Cod. B, [p. 325] selon Böhlig, se trouverait en Allemagne (codex de Berlin ouest, jadis a Goettingue). Its ne sont pas d'un grand format, d'après ce que j'ai pu constater: ce qui nous assure que les fragments n'appartiennent pas au codex des *Lettres* (Berlin, Cod. 3). |

Here Orlandi apparently is here correcting Bohlig's conjecture that the 13, or 16, leaves come from the Berlin *Letters*, since these leaves do not have a large format such as does the codex of *Letters* (see above). But the format of the *Synaxeis* book block in West Berlin is comparable to the larger size, 30 (or with fringes 31.8) cm high by 19 cm wide. Beltz had listed the size of the 31 leaves of $P^{15995}$, the *Synaxeis*, in East Berlin, as 18–20 cm high and 11–16 cm wide, which is apparently what Orlandi has in view. But a smaller format for an extant leaf does not necessarily mean that the whole codex was smaller. In this regard, the report of a smaller format is not as decisive for identifying material as the report of a larger format, since a codex is as large in format as the largest leaf, but not as small as the smallest extant leaf, given the fragmentary nature of much of the material. The 31 East Berlin leaves were, after all, the worn outside leaves that the middlemen had discarded. The conserved leaves in West Berlin vary in size down from the maximum represented by the book block. The smaller format that Orlandi reported would of course open the question as to whether the leaves might belong to a smaller codex, the *Psalms* (or the *Acts*?). Since there is no reason to assume that leaves of the Berlin *Acts* would be in the Chester Beatty Library, it is possible that the 16, or 13, leaves belong to the Dublin Psalms, Codex A, and were erroneously labeled Codex B. But it is not necessary to conjecture such an error.

Michael Tardieu[7] refers to "16 feuillets" ["16 leaves"] of the *Synaxeis* being in Dublin, apparently dependent on Orlandi.

---

7. Tardieu, "Les Manichéens en Égypte," 7.

This codex has not been published.

The second volume of the facsimile edition[8] has reproduced the 13 (not 16) leaves labeled so confusedly "Codex B," which Rolf Ibscher sought to ascribe to $P^{15998}$ (see above). Søren Giversen has commented in his introduction:

> The identity of this codex—or poor remnants of a codex—has been widely discussed, for example in the article by A. Böhlig cited above and in a series of other articles, as has the identity of the Mani codex in West Berlin, once called the Schondorff [read: Schondorf] papyrus.
>
> Since this edition should not pre-empt the results of a later critical edition, it has been decided to publish the pages in question in order to promote the work of identifying the papyrus with as little delay as possible. I have therefore refrained from offering any solution, preferring instead to provide some facts which together with the facsimiles should assist in this task.
>
> Not only are the glasses inscribed Codex B, but the frames also are marked "Kephalaia. Codex B." These labels are clearly in Hugo Ibscher's handwriting. The text in most cases is readable, although not easily.

The arguments that have been advanced to identify these 13 leaves with $P^{15998}$ have proven to be without force. A comparison of the facsimiles with the leaves of the *Synaxeis* indicates that the hand is so similar that the 13 leaves could well belong to the *Synaxeis* codex, though no chapter titles have been identified to confirm such an identification. The labeling is misleading insofar as the reference to *Kephalaia* is incorrect, but the labeling as Codex B, the Dublin designation of the *Synaxeis* codex, may well be correct. Giversen's allusion in this connection to "the Schondorf papyrus," which Rolf Ibscher identified as $P^{15998}$ (but is in fact the *Synaxeis*), indirectly suggests this identification.

Giversen reports that "the leaves were divided by [Hugo] Ibscher into two sections (quires)." Each quire consists of four sheets or eight leaves. The first leaf of the first quire and the last two leaves of the second quire are missing. Orlandi's report of 16 leaves may be due to having in view 2 quires but overlooking the absence of 3 leaves. Facing pages have like fiber directions, with the first page of each quire hav-

---

8. Giversen, *Homilies and Varia, Facsimile Edition*, ix–x, 101–26.

ing vertical fibers. The first quire is reproduced on pages 101–14, the second on 115–26.

Giversen comments: "The sheets are marked from 51 to 76, the equivalent of this edition's 101–126." The document dated January 13, 1984, on the letterhead of the Chester Beatty Library, entitled "Manichean Papyri on Loan to Royal Library, Copenhagen," lists "Codex B 51–76 13 glasses." Thus it is clear that these 13 leaves of the *Synaxeis* were in Copenhagen.

The Ägyptisches Museum in Berlin gave to the Manichaean Archives of the Institute for Antiquity and Christianity older photographs of pages 1.1.1.30 (hor.), 1.2.2.124 (hor.), 1.2.3.123 (vert.), and 4.1.1.116 (hor.); and newer photographs made at the Ägyptisches Museum itself of pages 1.1.1.30 (hor. and vert.), and 10.1.2.101 (hor. and vert.).

Carsten Colpe put at the disposal of a team that began to form in 1984 transcriptions he had made of the conserved leaves when they had been at Göttingen. In August 1985 Karen L. King made transcriptions in West Berlin of 16.1.2 (hor.), 16.2.3 (hor. and vert.), 17.1.1 (vert.), 18.1.1.113 (hor.), and, in August 1986, of 19.1.3.64 (vert.); and, together with Stephen Patterson, in July and August 1986, of 12.1.2.8 (vert.), 18.1.1.113 (vert.), and 19.2.2.66 (vert.). Wolf-Peter Funk provided draft translations of some of the material in April 1988.

From May to August 1987, Paul Allan Mirecki transcribed the following leaves in West Berlin: 4.2.3.13; 12.1.2.80; 14.2.3.108; 19.1.2.63; 19.1.3.64; 19.2.2.66; 20.1.1.68; and 20.2.1.71. He presented a preliminary report on his work under the title "The Coptic Manichaean Synaxeis Codex: Observations on the Ordinal System of the Synaxis Sections" at the First International Conference on Manichaeism held from August 5–9, 1987 at the University of Lund, Sweden.[9]

In August 1986 King received on loan from the Ägyptisches Museum, for study at the library of Occidental College in Los Angeles, 10 leaves: 9.2.2.98; 10.2.1.103; 10.2.3.105; 11.1.1.45; 11.1.2.74; 15.1.1.109; 16.1.1.46; 17.2.2.60; 19.1.1.62; and 20.2.3.73. King tran-

---

9. Mirecki, "The Coptic Manichaean Synaxeis Codex: Descriptive Catalogue of Synaxis Chapter Titles," 135–45. This is an expansion of part of the paper presented at the conference. An expansion of another part, entitled "The Coptic Manichaean Synaxeis Codex: Indicators for Codicological Reconstruction," was presented at the Consultation on Manichaeism at the Society of Biblical Literature convention at Chicago November 19–22, 1988.

scribed in November 1987 10.2.1.103 (hor.), and on November 18, 1987, 19.1.1.62 (hor.) On November 7, 1987, Wolf-Peter Funk transcribed at Occidental College lines 18–19 of 10.2.1.103 (hor.), 11.1.1.45 (hor. and vert.), 16.1.1.46 (hor. and vert.), and 20.2.3.73 (hor. and vert.). On November 13, 1987, he transcribed at Claremont 11.1.2.74 (hor. and vert.) and 15.1.1.109 (hor. and vert.). In March 1988 he made partial draft translations of 10.2.1.103 (hor.), 11.1.1.45 (hor. and vert.), 11.1.2.74 (hor. and vert.), 15.1.1.109 (hor. and vert.), 16.1.1.46 (hor. and vert.), and 20.2.3.73 (hor. and vert.). The leaves were brought to the Institute for Antiquity and Christianity in Claremont for a concentrated teamwork period from June 13 to 23, 1988. There Harold W. Attridge, Charles A. Bobertz, Stephen Patterson, and Gesine Schenke Robinson transcribed as follows:

9.2.2.98 [Bobertz];

10.2.1.103 (hor.) [Robinson, Attridge], (vert.) [Attridge];

10.2.3.105 (hor. and vert.) [Bobertz, Attridge, Patterson];

11.1.1.45 (hor. and vert.) [Bobertz];

11.1.2.74 (hor. and vert.) [Patterson, Attridge];

15.1.1.109 (hor. and vert.) [Bobertz, Attridge];

16.1.1.46 (hor. and vert.) [Patterson];

17.2.2.60 (hor. and vert.) [Patterson];

19.1.1.62 (hor. and vert.) [Robinson and Bobertz]; (vert. only) [Patterson and Attridge];

20.2.3.73 (hor. and vert.) [Robinson, Attridge].

The leaves, though mostly among the better ones in terms of legibility, are nonetheless so obscure that the transcriptions are very far from complete and at best are provisional.

# — 17 —
# Codex C: Kephalaia, Volume Two

THE FOURTH CODEX OF Sir Chester Beatty presented by Schmidt and Polotsky, though unidentified, is described as follows[1]:

| | |
|---|---|
| A last and fourth papyrus book, which seems to be rather completely preserved—here too it is possible to assume about 250 leaves—has thus far been subjected to no conservation, so that a deep darkness still lurks over its content. | Ein letztes and viertes Papyrusbuch, das ziemlich vollständig erhalten zu sein scheint—auch hierfür wird man etwa 250 Blätter annehmen können—ist bis jetzt noch keiner Konservierung unterzogen, so dass noch ein tiefes Dunkel über dessen Inhalt lagert. |

This codex has been identified as *Kephalaia*, though with chapters bearing higher numbers than those in the Berlin *Kephalaia*, so that one might think of this as a second volume, rather than as "la seconds partie du codex" ["the second part of the codex"] P[15996].[2] Böhlig described it as follows:[3]

| | |
|---|---|
| 2. Already before the war Hugo Ibscher began the work of conservation on the text of Codex C, which was still completely unconserved at the time of the report of the discovery, so that by | 2. An dem nach dem Fundbericht noch vollkommen unkonservierten Text Codex C begann schon vor dem Kriege Hugo Ibscher die Konservierungsarbeit, so dass sich bei Kriegsausbruch bereits 34 ver- |

---

1. Schmidt and Polotsky, "Ein Mani-Fund in Agypten," 34.
2. Tardieu, "Les Manichéens en Égypte," 6. This error may account for the problem of referring to "sept titles" ["seven titles"] and then listing only six.
3. Böhlig, "Die Arbeit," 185.

| | |
|---|---|
| the time the war broke out already 34 glassed leaves were in London. One hundred forty five more leaves could be separated by Rolf Ibscher after the war. Whereas already at the beginning of the conservation the book could be recognized as *Kephalaia* with appreciably higher chapter numerations than the Berlin *Kephalaia* show, now a still-further surprise emerged, in that perhaps another text had been laid inside the book. This is not yet identified, since for this book as well still no arrangements for an edition have been made. | glaste Blätter in London befanden. Weitere 145 Blätter konnte Rolf Ibscher nach dem Kriege ablösen. Hatte man schon bei Beginn der Konservierung das Buch als *Kephalaia* mit wesentlich höheren Kapitelzahlen, als sie die Berliner *Kephalaia* aufweisen, erkennen können, so fand sich nun noch eine Überraschung dadurch, dass in das Buch vielleicht ein anderer Text hineingelegt worden war. Dieser ist noch nicht identifiziert, da auch für dieses Buch noch keine Anstalten einer Edition gemacht wurden. |

Beltz's catalogue does not mention this codex, since it is not in Berlin. But Tito Orlandi reported in 1976 on the material at the Chester Beatty Library as follows[4]:

| | |
|---|---|
| Finally, the most important piece in the collection, in my opinion, is Codex C, which contains the second part of the *Kephalaia* and another, unknown text. It consists today (a) of 30 glasses [in a footnote Orlandi presents this as a correction of Böhlig's figure 34] numbered in terms of *recto* and *verso* (hence two numerals per glass) up to the number 60; these are obviously the pieces restored before the war, which are now put on two sets of shelves (numbered 1 and 2). (b) After them are to be found the fragments conserved between plexiglass, more recently restored, which are numbered in the same way; nonetheless their numeration begins again with | Finalement, la pièce la plus importante du recueil est, a mon avis, le Cod. C, qui contient la deuxième partie des *Kephalaia* et un autre texte inconnu. Il consiste maintenant (a) en 30 verres [in a footnote Orlandi presents this as a correction of Böhlig's figure 34] numérotés par rapport au *recto* et *verso* (donc deux numéros par verre) jusqu'au numero 60; ce sont évidemment les pièces restaurées avant la guerre, qui sont maintenant placées sur deux étagères (numérotóes I et II). (b) Après eux, se trouvent les fragments sous plexiglas, restaurés plus récemment, qui sont numérotés de la même façon; toutefois leur numérotation recommence par le no 1. Comme |

---

4. Orlandi, "Les manuscrits coptes de Dublin," 325.

number 1. Since they were stacked pell-mell on the shelves, I put them all back in order, and I verified at the same time that no glass is lacking. They are in fact 368 numbers and hence 184 fragments, divided among 18 shelves (shelves 3 to 20). The 20th shelf contains 8 fragments without numeration, in very bad condition, which nonetheless seem to belong to Codex C; they are marked: Cl, C2, C3, C4, C20, C24, C25, C96 [C26?].

It is necessary to draw attention to the fact that the numeration of the part described under (b) is juxtaposed to a preceding numeration that seems to represent the primitive classification given at the time that the leaves were detached from the ensemble of the codex, in separating each quire, beginning with the last. The numeration of the quires (in Roman numerals) is hence the reverse of the new order; however the numeration of the pages inside the quires follows the same order. We give an example:

"new numeration" = "other" numeration

31/32 . . . to 45/46 = C VIII 120 . . . to 127

47/48 . . . to 61/62 = C VII 113 . . . to 119 [?]

As much as we were able to determine, no other piece of the Manichaean collection is conserved at the Chester Beatty Library.

ils étaient déposés pêle-mêle dans les étagères, je les ai tous remis en ordre, et j'ai contrôlé en méme temps qu'aucun verre ne manque. Ils sont en fait 368 numéros, donc 184 fragments, partagés entre 18 étagères (étagères III a XX). La 20e étagère contient 8 fragments hors numérotation, en très mauvais état, qui toutefois semblent appartenir au Cod. C; ils sont marqués: Cl, C2, C3, C4, C20, C24, C25, C96 [C26?].

Il faut signaler que la numérotation de la partie décrite sous le par. (b) est juxtaposée a une numérotation précedente, qui parait representer la classification primitive, donnée au moment où les feuillets ont éta détachés de l'ensemble du codex, en separant chaque cahier, a partir du dernier. La numérotation des cahiers (en chiffres romains) est donc contraire au nouvel ordre; cependant la numérotation des pages a l'interieur des cahiers suit le même ordre. Nous en donnerons un example:

"nouvelle numérotation" = "autre" numérotation

31/32 . . . jusqu'a 45/46 = C VIII 120 . . .jusqu'a 127 47/48 . . . jusqu'a 61/62 = C VII 113 . . . jusqu'a 119 [?]

Pour ce que nous avons constaté, aucune autre pièce de la collection manichéenne n'est conservée à la Chester Beatty Library.

This codex has not been published.

The first volume of the facsimile edition[5] has published 354 plates.

In the preface (pages xi–xii) Søren Giversen indicates the limited objective of the edition:

> It was evident from the state of the papyri that if they were to be published in the foreseeable future, it would be necessary initially to abandon all thought of perfection. What was needed was first to establish the correct order of the unpaginated sheets, so far as this was possible within a reasonable time, and then [page xii] to publish a facsimile edition without delay. Once this was published, every interested scholar would have plenty of time and opportunity to work on the texts.

Thus plate 339 has the note: "Collocatio paginarum 339–354 incerta," ["the ordering of the pages 339–354 is uncertain."] But even plates 1–338 are not to be taken as pagination of the original codex. Thus when the Introduction refers to the plates as pages, what is meant is pages in the facsimile edition itself, not in the codex. This is clear from the comment (p. xvii) "... missing pages not being counted," and for the fuller observation (p. xxi):

> It must however be emphasized that the continuous numbering does not show the many lacunae which occur in the quires, and little can be said about the loss of perhaps one or more quires, for example between C.VI and C.B.

---

5. Giversen, *The Manichaean Coptic Papyri in the Chester Beatty Library, Vol. 1, Kephalaia, Facsimile Edition*, i–xxvi, 1–354. The title page reports that the edition is "Published under the Auspices of the Trustees of the Chester Beatty Library with the Support of the Carlsberg Foundation and under the Responsibility of the International Committee for the Publication of the Manichaean Coptic Papyri from Medinet Madi Belonging to the Chester Beatty Library (Søren Giversen, Rodolphe Kasser, Martin Krause)." The Preface, p. xii, reports concerning the facsimile edition: "Once this was published, every interested scholar would have plenty of time and opportunity to work on the texts." But it is also reported: "This committee ... is also responsible for the critical edition of the texts." At the meeting of the Association francophone de Coptologie in Paris on May 23, 1986, Rodolphe Kasser circulated an announcement concerning the committee "qui repartira cette tache [les éditions critiques] entre les divers coptisants" ["who will distribute this task {the critical editions} among the various Coptologists."] "Seuls seront invités a participer aux editions princeps manichéennes coptes Chester Beatty ceux qui n'ont pas déjà obtenu cette faculté en ce qui concerne les éditions princeps manichéennes coptes des fragments de Berlin oû de Vienne." ["Only they will be invited to participate in the *editio princeps* of the Chester Beatty Coptic Manichaica who have not already received this privilege regarding the of the Coptic Manichaica of Berlin or Vienna."]

One should also note the disclaimer on page xvii:

> Both Hugo and Rolf Ibscher found the task of reconstructing the leaves and fragments in the right order extremely difficult, and as we are not in possession of all the observations made by the two conservators during their work, it is today perhaps impossible for us to so reconstruct them—or it will take a very long time and will probably necessitate the deciphering of the texts in some detail. According to the wishes of the committee, I have therefore chosen to publish the results of my work so far in the hope that these will be of use to scholars. Any improvement that they make will naturally be a pleasure to me.

The problem is partly ascribed to ambiguities on the part of Rolf Ibscher (p. xix):

> Rolf Ibscher later gives different figures for the number of leaves restored by his father. Sometimes he said that Hugo Ibscher had restored 34 leaves from Codex C, sometimes 36 and sometimes 47 . . . Rolf Ibscher perhaps added to the 34 leaves from Codex C the 13 leaves which Hugo Ibscher had already restored in 1934 and which are also mentioned in the letter quoted above as belonging to Codex B. This is borne out by the fact that on the frames of the glasses which contain these 13 leaves is written "Kephalaia. Codex B."

Thus Giversen concludes (page xvii) that Hugo Ibscher conserved only 34 leaves. But Rolf Ibscher is quoted (pages xviii–xix) as listing at times 136, at times 139 as the number of leaves he himself had conserved. Since there are 346 plates, one would assume the figure 139 to be correct (since 139 plus 34 equals 173 leaves, = 346 pages). This calculation admittedly, does not account for plates 347–54, of which it is said, p. xxvi: "The following pages or fragments are in such poor condition that it will be very difficult to locate their original position." Though they seem uninscribed, they are not just fragments—a characterization that actually only fits 347–48—but in three cases leaves (in one case hardly more than the vertical fibers), which must be assumed to have been consistently omitted from numerations (unless the figure 36 was reached by adding 2 from this group to the figure 34).

The confusion is augmented by Giversen's explanation (pages xix–xx):

The sheets restored by Hugo Ibscher were marked la–4b and 1–60, and Rolf Ibscher has arranged them into quires. The sheets which Rolf Ibscher restored are marked first according to codex with a C, then according to section (quire), so that indications are as follows: C.1–C.8, C.OI, C.I–C.X. To this a number is added, so that the sheets are numbered from 1 to 140. This last numbering was presumably given when Rolf Ibscher succeeded in rescuing the sheets, and as he sometimes had to work on the papyri from different ends this numbering does not always follow the order of the sheets in the codex. To this must be added the fact that the codex was in some disarray when it reached the conservators' laboratory. There is yet another numbering system to be mentioned. This may have been given when the sheets were photographed, or to indicate which of the papyri were restored by Rolf Ibscher. This system, however practical [page xx] it may have been for its special purpose, is now useless and possibly confusing for anyone who is not aware of its meaning, since it does not give any information about the reconstruction of the codex or the real order of the sheets. In my attempt to arrange the order of all the sheets in the collection which is called Codex C I have therefore not used this numbering at all.

The way to account for 139 sheets being numbered 1–140 is to note that the numbers 1, 2, 97, and 111 occur twice, whereas the numbers 91, 92, and 96 are missing, leaving a balance of one more number than there are sheets.

The hope is expressed (page xxi): "This introduction will, I hope, provide some background information until a much more detailed account is made available as a result of this facsimile edition."

# — 18 —
## Codex D: Homilies (Dublin Part)

THIS CODEX IS PART of the Berlin codex $P^{15999}$. Schmidt and Polotsky report:[1]

| | |
|---|---|
| A second papyrus book contains a collection of *Homilies* (*logoi*) of various contents and by different authors. Here we have before us a completely faithful report about the last days of Mani, which must have come from the pen of an eye witness . . . 48 leaves of this papyrus book have been brought under glass and are to be published separated by Dr. Polotsky. As I mentioned above, a large part of this book has come to Berlin. | Ein zweites Papyrusbuch enthält eine Sammlung von Homilien (*logoi*) verschiedenen Inhalts und von verschiedenen Verfassern. Da haben wir vor uns einen ganz getreuen Bericht über die letzten Tage des Mani, der aus der Feder eines Augenzeugen geflossen sein muss . . . Von diesem Papyrusbuch sind 48 Blätter unter Glas gebracht und sollen von Dr. Polotsky separat publiziert werden. Von diesem Buche ist, wie ich oben erwähnt habe, ein umfangreicher Teil nach Berlin gekommen. |

Polotsky's transcriptions of pages 8, 11, 12, 27–30, 44, 60, 69, 76, 78, 79, 82–84, 91, and 93 from 1931–1932 are in the Archives of the Chester Beatty Library. Polotsky published Beatty's part of the *Homilies* in 1934.[2]

Tito Orlandi's 1976 report of the material in the Chester Beatty Library noted:[3]

---

1. Schmidt and Polotsky, "Ein Mani-Fund," 34.
2. Polotsky, *Manichäische Homilien*, Band I.
3. Orlandi, "Les manuscrits coptes de Dublin," 324.

| | |
|---|---|
| Indeed we have noted that the part of Codex A edited by Mr. Allberry (*Psalms, Part II*) is perfectly conserved in 9 little wooden boxes, in which the glasses containing the leaves are arranged in vertical position. The part of Codex A [read: D] edited by Polotsky (*Homilies*) has been arranged in the same way. | En effet, nous avons constaté que la partie du Cod. A éditée par M. Allberry (*Psaumes*, IIe partie) est parfaitement conservée dans 9 petites caisses en bois, dans lesquelles les verres contenant les feuillets sont ranges en position verticale. La partie du Cod. A [read: D] éditée par Polotsky (*Homilies*) a été rangée de la même façon. |

Since in early reports the part of the *Homilies* codex that Sir Chester Beatty acquired was found with the *Psalms* codex, Orlandi lists the Dublin leaves of the *Homilies* also as A. But since these letters designate codices, and the leaves of the *Homilies* come from a different codex than those of the *Psalms*, the leaves of the *Homilies* should not be given the same codex designation as those of the *Psalms*. Rolf Ibscher hence introduced the letter D for the leaves of the *Homilies*, which is used in the present report.

Michael H. Browder has prepared an English translation of the published *Homilies* in machine-readable form.[4]

A facsimile edition of the *Homilies* of the Chester Beatty Library was published in 1986.[5] The glass panes could not be opened to make minor adjustments in the positioning of already-placed fragments, since the panes are stuck to the papyrus. But some have been "repositioned photographically" on pages 19–20, 25–26, and 97–98, while tiny fragments needing to be repositioned could not, "for technical reasons" be adjusted, "for example on pp. 3–4 and 49–50." A facsimile of page 29 published in the 1934 edition lacks a fragment present in the facsimile edition but also present in the transcription of page 34 in the 1934 edition, due presumably to the 1934 published photograph's being made prior to the placement of the fragment, which however, took place prior to the completion of the 1934 edition. Such

---

4. Browder, *A Manichaean Anthology: A New English Translation of the Manichaische Homilien*, 1985, unpublished.

5. Giversen, *Homilies and Varia*, vii–viii for the Introduction, from which the quotations come; and 1–96, plates corresponding to the pagination of Polotsky's edition, with pp. 95–96 reproducing the unplaced fragments that Polotsky did not publish.

photographs made early in the conservation procedure would serve as a record "if some smaller, fragile pieces perhaps went missing in the process of conservation." Thus pages 41–42, "where some lines are now lost." Polotsky omitted pages 65–66 since so little text survived, but they are included in the facsimile edition.

Eleven fragments not placed by Polotsky are published on pages 97–98, still unidentified. "They will presumably be placed when the much needed critical study has been carried out." In view of the fact that the critical edition has already been published, it is unclear what occasion is envisaged for "the much needed critical study," if the publication of the facsimile edition itself did not provide such an occasion.

Michel Tardieu[6] has incorrectly stated: "Codex complet de 48 feuillets conservé à Dublin (codex D)." ["Complete codex of 48 leaves conserved at Dublin (Codex D)."] This is only part of the codex of which $P^{15999}$ was also a part, no doubt the major part.

---

6. Tardieu, "Les Manichéens en Égypte," 6.

# Scholars, Collectors, Dealers, and Others

CHARLES R. C. ALLBERRY (1911–1943). British Coptologist and Fellow of Christ's College, Cambridge. He was editor of the *Journal of Egyptian Archaeology* from 1939–43. He translated and edited the first edition of *A Manichaean Psalm-Book*, Part II in 1938.

HUGH MURRAY BAILLIE (1916–1982). A British officer, who after World War II remained in Germany as a member of the Fine Arts Commission of the British Zone.

SIR A. CHESTER BEATTY (1875–1968). Major collector of manuscripts and papyri. He founded the Chester Beatty Library. Born in the U.S., he became a naturalized citizen of Great Britain, and was an honorary citizen of Ireland. He made his fortune mining copper in the U.S. and around the world.

ALEXANDER BÖHLIG (1912–1996). German Coptologist and Byzantinist, who taught first at the University of Halle and after 1963 at the University of Tübingen, where he was eventually emeritus. At Halle he was director of the Institut für Byzantinistik.

WILLIAM M. BRASHEAR (1946–2000). Papyrologist and curator of the Papyrus-Sammlung of the Ägyptisches Museum in Berlin-Charlottenburg.

CARSTEN COLPE (1929–2009). German professor of Iranian studies, first at the University of Göttingen and then at the University of Berlin.

**WALTER EWING CRUM** (1865–1944). British Coptologist and Egyptologist. He edited the monumental reference work, *Coptic Dictionary*, and catalogued the Coptic manuscripts in the John Rylands Library and the British Museum.

**SIR I. E. S. EDWARDS** (1909–1996). Egyptian Egyptologist and leading expert on the pyramids. He became the Assistant Keeper in the Department of Egyptian and Assyrian Antiquities at the British Museum in 1934. He was the Keeper of Egyptian Antiquities from 1955 to 1974.

**OTTO FIRCHOW** (b. 1912). Director of the Ägyptisches Museum and Papyrus-Sammlung in Berlin.

**WOLF-PETER FUNK**. Coptologist and Research Associate at the Université Laval in Quebec. He is the editor of the series Manichäische Handschriften der Staatlichen Museen zu Berlin.

**SIR ALAN GARDINER** (1879–1963). One of the leading Egyptologists of the twentieth century.

**SØREN GIVERSEN** (1928–2009). Danish New Testament scholar and Coptologist who taught at Aarhus University. He was the president of the International Committee for the Publication of the Manichaean Coptic Papyri from Medinet Madi Belonging to the Chester Beatty Library.

**HUGO IBSCHER** (1874–1943). Papyrus conservator from Kleinmachnow, near Berlin, who worked for Chester Beatty.

**ROLF IBSCHER** (1906–1967). Son of Hugo Ibscher, who took over papyrus conservation for Beatty after his father's death.

**RODOLPHE KASSER** (b. 1927). Swiss Coptologist and archaeologist. He was Professor at the University of Geneva until becoming emeritus in 1998. He is a member of the International Committee for the Publication of the Manichaean Coptic Papyri from Medinet Madi Belonging to the Chester Beatty Library and head of the archaeo-

logical excavations of the Swiss Mission of Coptic Archaeology in the Kelia, Lower Egypt.

MARTIN KRAUSE (b. 1930). German Coptologist and Professor at the University of Münster. He was the first President of the International Association for Coptic Studies. He is a member of the International Committee for the Publication of the Manichaean Coptic Papyri from Medinet Madi Belonging to the Chester Beatty Library.

WILFRID LOCKWOOD. Librarian and Director of the Chester Beatty Library.

OTTO WERNER LUKE. Assistant and then successor to Rolf Ibscher.

PAUL ALLAN MIRECKI. Coptologist and historian of religion at the University of Kansas.

WOLFGANG MÜLLER (1922–2012). Papyrologist and ancient historian. He became Director of the Ägyptisches Museum in Berlin as well as overseer of the Papyrus-Sammlung.

WINCENTY MYSZOR. Professor of Papyrology at the Institute for Papyrology at Warsaw University.

MAURICE NAHMAN (1868–1948). The leading Cairo antiquities dealer prior to World War II, who showed H. O. Lange Manichaean manuscripts in 1929. He sold Manichaean manuscripts to Chester Beatty and Carl Schmidt in the 1930s.

TITO ORLANDI. Italian Coptologist and Professor at La Sapienza University, Rome. He was President of the International Association for Coptic Studies (2000–2004). He is Director of Corpus dei Manoscritti Copti Letterari.

GÜNTER POETHKE (b. 1939). Custos of the Greek manuscripts in the Papyrus-Sammlung of the Ägyptisches Museum in Berlin and Professor of Papyrology at the Humboldt-Universität zu Berlin.

**Hans Jakob Polotsky** (1905–1991). German-born Israeli Egyptologist, Coptologist, and Semitist. He was professor at the Hebrew University, Jerusalem.

**Berthe van Regemorter.** Belgian bookbinder.

**Gesine Schenke Robinson.** New Testament scholar, Coptologist, and Director of the Coptic Texts Editing Project at the Institute for Antiquity and Christianity.

**James M. Robinson** (b. 1924). Professor of New Testament and Coptologist at Claremont Graduate University (emeritus). He is the founding Director of the Institute for Antiquity and Christianity, Director of the Coptic Gnostic Library Project, and the editor of the Nag Hammadi Library.

**Carl Schmidt** (1868–1938). German New Testament scholar, church historian, and papyrologist; his mentor was Adolf von Harnack. He discovered and published numerous ancient gnostic and Manichaean texts.

**Wilhelm Schubart** (1873–1960). German papyrologist, professor of ancient history, and Director of the Papyrus-Sammlung of the Ägyptisches Museum in Berlin-Charlottenburg.

**Michel Tardieu** (b. 1938). French Coptologist, historian of religion, and professor at the Collège de France, Paris. He became emeritus in 2008.

**Sir Herbert Thompson** (1859–1944). British Egyptologist and Coptologist who represented Chester Beatty beginning in 1931.

**J. V. S. Wilkinson** (d. 1957). After working in the Department of Oriental Manuscripts at the British Museum (1924–46), he became Librarian of the Chester Beatty Library in 1946.

# Bibliography

Allberry, C. R. C., editor. *A Manichaean Psalm-Book. Part II*. Manichaean Manuscripts of the Chester Beatty Collection 2. Stuttgart: Kohlhammer, 1938.
———. "Manichaean Studies." *JTS* 39 (1938) 337–49.
Beltz, Walter. "Katalog der koptischen Handschriften der Papyrus-Sammlung der Staatlichen Museen zu Berlin." *APF* 26 (1978) 57–119; 27 (1980) 121–222. The Manichaean codices are catalogued in 26 (1978) 97–98.
Böhlig, Alexander. "Die Arbeit an den koptischen Manichaica." WZUH *Gesellschafts und Sprachwissenschaftliche Reihe* 10 (1961) 157–61. Reprinted in *Mysterion und Wahrheit*. Also published in *Actes du XXVe Congrès International des Orientalistes*, Moscou 9–16 aut 1960, 1 (Moscow, 1962) 535–41.
———. "Aus den Manichäischen 'Kephalaia des Lehrers,'" *Wissenschaftliche Zeitschrift der Universität Halle-Wittenberg* 5 (1956) 1067–84 (translation of pages 244–92, 6th double fascicle).
———. *Gnosis und Synkretismus: Gesammelte Aufsätze zur spätantiken Religionsgeschichte*. 2 vols. WUNT 47–48. Tübingen: Mohr/Siebeck, 1989.
———. "Ja und Amen in manichäischer Deutung." *ZPE* 58 (1985) 59–70.
———. *Kephalaia*. Manichäische Handschriften der Staatlichen Museen Berlin herausgegeben im Auftrag der Deutschen Akademie der Wissenschaften zu Berlin, zweite Hälfte, (Lieferungen 11/12 = Coptic pages 244–91). Stuttgart: Kohlhammer, 1966.
———. *Mysterion und Wahrheit: Gesammelte Beiträge zur spätantiken Religionsgeschichte*. Arbeiten zur Geschichte des späteren Judentums und des Urchristentums 6. Leiden: Brill, 1968. Reprints, revised. "Die Arbeit an den koptischen Manichaica," 177–87. The text has been copyedited, but not altered, in terms of the typescript of the address of 1960 in the Archives of the Chester Beatty Library.
———. "Neue Initiativen zur Erschliessung der koptisch-manichäischen Bibliothek von Medinet Madi: James M. Robinson zum 65. Geburtstag gewidmet." *ZNW* 80 (1989) 240–62.
———. "Neue *Kephalaia* des Mani." *BSAC* 18 (1965/66) 5–22.
———. "Synaxis = Homilia?" *WZUH* 6 (1957) 485–86.
———. "Zu den Synaxeis des Lebendigen Evangeliums." In *Mysterion und Wahrheit: Gesammelte Beiträge zur spätantiken Religionsgeschichte*, 222–27. Arbeiten zur

Geschichte des späteren Judentums und des Urchristentums 6. Leiden: Brill, 1968. Originally delivered at Akten des Vierundzwanzigsten Internationalen Orientalisten-Kongresses München 28 August bis 4 September 1957. Wiesbaden: Deutsche Morgenländische Gesellschaft, 1959.

———. "Zu den Synaxeis des Lebendigen Evangeliums," pp. 222–27. The text is enlarged (see above, 1957). "Neue Kephalaia des Mani," 252–66.

Browder, Michael H. "Al-Biruni as a Source for Mani and Manichaeism." PhD diss., Duke University, 1982.

———. *A Manichaean Anthology: A New English Translation of the Manichäische Homilien*. Floppy Disc, 1985.

Crum, W. E. *A Coptic Dictionary*. 1939. Reprinted with a new foreword by James M. Robinson. Ancient Language Resources. Eugene, OR: Wipf & Stock, 2005.

Fackelmann, Michael. *Restaurierung von Papyrus und anderen Schriftträgern aus Ägypten*. Studia Amstelodamensia ad Epigraphicam, Jus Antiquum et Papyrologicam Pertinenta 24. Zuphen, The Netherlands: Terra, 1985.

Gardner, Iaian. *Coptic Theological Papyri II Edition, Commentary, Translation: With an Appendix "The Docetic Jesus."* Mitteilungen aus der Papyrussammlung der Österreichischen Nationalbibliothek [Papyrus Erzherzog Rainer], n.S. 21 MPER XXI. Vienna: Österreiche Nationalbibliothek bei Verlag Brüder Hollinek, 1988.

Giversen, Søren. *The Manichaean Coptic Papyri in the Chester Beatty Library*. Vol. 1, *Kephalaia*. Facsimile edition. Cahiers d'Orientalisme 14. Geneva: Cramer, 1986.

———. *The Manichaean Coptic Papyri in the Chester Beatty Library*. Vol. 2, *Homilies and Varia*. Facsimile edition. Cahiers d'Orientalisme 15. Geneva: Cramer, 1986 [1987].

———. *The Manichaean Coptic Papyri in the Chester Beatty Library*. Vol. 3, *Psalm Book Part 1*. Facsimile edition. Cahiers d'orientalisme 16. Geneva: Cramer, 1988.

———. *The Manichaean Coptic Papyri in the Chester Beatty Library*. Volume 4, *Psalm Book, Part 2*. Facsimile edition. Cahiers d'orientalisme 17. Geneva: Cramer, 1988.

———. *The Manichaean Papyri of the Chester Beatty Library*. Proceedings of the Irish Biblical Association 11. Dublin, 1988.

———. "The Manichaean Texts from the Chester Beatty Collection." In *Manichaean Studies: Proceedings of the First International Conference on Manichaeism August 5–9 1987; Department of History of Religions—Lund University Sweden*, edited by Peter Bryder, 265–72. Lund Studies in African and Asian Religions 1. Lund: Lund University plus Ultra, 1988.

———. "The Unedited Chester Beatty Mani Texts." In *Codex Manichaicus Coloniensius: Atti del Simposio Internazionale (Rende-Amantea 3–7 settembre 1984)*, edited by Luigi Cirillo with Amneris Roselli, 371–80. Cosenza: Marra, 1986.

Ibscher, Hugo. "Die Handschrift." In *Kephalaia*, edited by H. J. Polotsky and Alexander Böhlig, v–xiv. Stuttgart: Kohlhammer, 1940.

———. "Die Handschriften." In *A Manichaean Psalm-Book. Part II*, edited by C. R. C. Allberry, i–xxiii. Manichaean Manuscripts in the Chester Beatty Collection 2. Stuttgart: Kohlhammer, 1938.

Ibscher, Rolf. "Das Konservierungswerk an den Manichäischen Papyruscodices: Vortrag, gehalten auf dem VIII. Internationalen Papyrologen-Kongress in Wien 1955." Unpublished typescript.

―――. "Mani und kein Ende." In *Atti dell'XI Congresso Internazionale di Papirologia, Milano 2-8 Settembre 1965*, 218-24. Milan: Istituto Lombardo di Scienze e Lettere, 1966.

―――. "Über den Stand der Umkonservierung der Manipapyri." In *Koptologische Studien in der DDR: Wissenschaftliche Zeitschrift der Martin-Luther Universität Halle-Wittenberg 1965, Sonderheft*, 50-64. Originally presented December 14-15, 1964.

―――. "Wiederaufnahme und neuester Stand der Konservierung der Manichäischen Papyruscodices." In *Proceedings of the Twenty-third International Congress of Orientalists. Cambridge, 21st-28th August, 1954*. London: The Royal Asiatic Society,- 1956. Abstract, pp. 359-360. Zusammenfassung des auf dem Internationalen Orientalisten-Kongress gehaltenen Berichts, typescript, 4 pp. [Cited according to the complete text in typescript, 12 pp., unless otherwise indicated.]

Ibscher, Rolf, Carsten Colpe, and Alexander Böhlig. "Der Mani-Fund." In *Akten des Vierundzwanzigsten Internationalen Orientalisten-Kongresses München, 28. August bis 4. September 1957*. Wiesbaden: Deutsche Morgenländische Gesellschaft, 1959.

Kasser, Rodolphe. "Projet international pour la publication des manuscrits manichéens coptes de Medinet Madi appartenant à la Chester Beatty Library (premier communiqué)." *Newsletter of the International Association for Coptic Studies* 19 (1986) 6-7.

King, Karen. "A Progress Report on the Editing of the Manichaean *Synaxeis* Codex." In *Actes du IVe congrès copte, Louvain-la-Neuve, 5-10 Septembre 1988*, edited by Marguerite Rassart-Debergh and Julien Ries, 281-88. Publications de l'Institut orientaliste de Louvain 40. Louvain: Université Catholique de Louvain, 1992.

Koenen, Ludwig. "Augustine and Manichaeism in Light of the Cologne Mani Codex." *Illinois Classical Studies* 3 (1978) 154-95.

Krause, Martin. Review of *The Facsimile Edition of the Nag Hammadi Codices: Introduction*. ZDMG 138 (1988) 378.

Kühnel-Kunze, Irene. *Bergung—Evakuierung—Rückführung: Die Berliner Museen in den Jahren 1939-1959*. Jahrbuch Preussicher Kulturbesitz, Sonderband 2. Berlin: Mann, 1984.

Lewis, Patricia K. *G. Charles Allberry: A Portrait*. Cambridge, UK: Plumridge, 1984.

Luke, Otto Walter. "Die Umkonservierung des Berliner Kephalaia-Kodex." *Staatliche Museen Berlin: Forschungen und Berichte* 12 (1970) 151-52.

Maugham, W. Somerset. *The Razor's Edge*. Introduction by Anthony Curtis. Penguin Twentieth-Century Classics. New York: Penguin, 1992.

Merkelbach, Reinhold. *Mani und sein Religionssystem*. Rheinisch-Westfälische Akademie der Wissenschaften. Geisteswissenschaften. Vorträge: G 281. Opladen: Westdeutscher Verlag, 1986.

Mirecki, Paul Allan. "The Coptic Manichaean *Synaxeis* Codex: Descriptive Catalogue of Synaxis Chapter Titles." In *Manichaean Studies: Proceedings of the First International Conference on Manichaeism August 5-9, 1987; Department of History of Religions, Lund University, Sweden*, edited by Peter Bryder, 135-45. Lund Studies in African and Asian Religions 1. Lund: Lund University plus Ultra, 1988.

Müller, Wolfgang. "In memoriam Rolf Ibscher (18.9.1906—5.2.1967)." *APF* 20 (1970) 207.

———. "Die koptischen Handschriften der Berliner Papyrussammlung." In *Koptologische Studien in der DDR*, 65-85. Wissenschaftliche Zeitschrift der Martin-Luther-Universität Halle-Wittenberg 1965, Sonderheft. Halle: Institut für Byzantinistik der Martin-Luther-Universität Halle-Wittenberg, 1965. [The meeting at which the paper was presented took place December 14-15, 1964.]

Orlandi, Tito. "Les manuscrits coptes de Dublin, du British Museum et de Vienne." *Le Muséon* 89 (1976) 323-38.

Polotsky, H. J. *Manichäische Homilien*. Manichäische Handschriften der Sammlung A. Chester Beatty 1. Stuttgart: Kohlhammer, 1934.

Polotsky, H. J., and Alexander Böhlig, editors. *Kephalaia*. Manichäische Handshhriften der staatlichen Museen Berlins, herausgegeben im Auftrage der Preussischen Akademie der Wissenschaften unter Leitung von Prof. Carl Schmidt, 1. Hälfte (Lieferung 1-10). Stuttgart: Kohlhammer, 1940.

Putt, S. Gorley. "Charles Allberry and Roy Calvert." *Encounter* 69 (1987) 70-76.

Regemorter, Berthe van. "Le codex relié depuis son origine jusqu'au Haut Moyen-Age." *Le Moyen Age* 61 (1955) 1-26.

———. *Some Early Bindings from Egypt in the Chester Beatty Library*. Chester Beatty Monographs 7. Dublin: Hodges Figgis, 1958.

———. *Some Oriental Bindings in the Chester Beatty Library*. Dublin: Hodges Figgis, 1961.

Robinson, James M. "International Committee for the Manichaean Codices of Medinet Madi." *Newsletter of the International Association for Coptic Studies* 19 (1986) 3-4.

———. "Organizational Meeting and First Work Session: International Committee for the Manichaean Codices of Medinet Madi." *Newsletter of the International Association for Coptic Studies* 19 (1986) 5.

Säve-Söderbergh, Torgny. *Studies in the Coptic Manichaean Psalm-Book: Prosody and Mandaean Parallels*. Arbeten utgivna med Understöd av Vilhelm Ekmans Universitetsfond, Uppsala 55. Uppsala: Almqvist & Wiksells, 1949.

Schenke, Hans-Martin. "Gnosis-Forschung 1984-1988." Paper presented at the Fourth International Congress on Coptic Studies of the International Association for Coptic Studies. Louvain-la-Neuve, Belgium, 5-10 September 1988.

Schmidt, Carl. *Neue Originalquellen des Manichäismus aus Ägypten*. Stuttgart: Kohlhammer, 1933.

Schmidt, Carl, and H. J. Polotsky, with a contribution, "Die Handschriften," pp. 82-85, by Hugo Ibscher. "Ein Mani-Fund in Ägypten: Originalschriften des Mani und seiner Schüler." In *Sitzungsberichte der Preussischen Akademie der Wissenschaften zu Berlin, philosophisch-historische Klasse*, 4-90. Berlin: Akademie, 1933.

Snow, C. P. *The Light and the Dark*. Strangers and Brothers. New York: Scribner, 1947.

*Strangers and Brothers*. Original release date, January 11, 1984 by the British Broadcasting Corporation. Distributed by *Masterpiece Theatre*. Directed by Jeremy Summers and Ronald Wilson. Written by Julian Bond, based on novels by C. P. Snow.

Tardieu, Michel. "Les Manichéens en Égypte." *BSFE* 94 (1982) 5-19.

## GUIDES

Brashear, William, Joachim Selim Karig, and Jürgen Settgast. *Ägyptisches Museum Berlin: Staatliche Museen Preussicher Kulturbesitz*, 1982.
[In the pocketbook series *Museum*. Braunschweig: Westermann, 1981, reprinted 1984. This material is summarized in more or less detail in the hardback booklet published by the Ägyptisches Museum der Stattlichen Museen, Preussicher Kulturbesitz, Berlin (West) in German, English, and French: Kniese, Sigrid and Liselotte Robbel. *Ägyptisches Museum Berlin* (1983). Fay, Biri. *Egyptian Museum Berlin* (1982, revised 1984); Alte, Monique. *Musée Égyptien Berlin* (1984).
Geismeier, Willi. *Die "Museumsinsel." Die kleine Berolina-Reihe*. Berlin Hauptstadt der DDR: Berlin-Werbung Berolina, n.d. (1961?)
Hühns, Erik. "Zur Geschichte der Staatlichen Museen zu Berlin." In *Schätze der Weltkultur*, 8–28. Berlin-Hauptstadt der DDR: Staatliche Museen zu Berlin, and Berlin-Information, 2. Überarbeitete Auflage, 1981.
Müller, Wolfgang. "Einleitung." Kleiner Führer durch die Ausstellung des Ägyptischen Museums, 5–7. Berlin-Hauptstadt der DDR: Staatliche Museen zu Berlin, Ägyptisches Museum, 1981.
Wipprech, E. *Schloss Berlin-Friedrichsfelde: Der Bau und seine Wiederherstellung*. "Vorwort" by H. Dathe, J. Schuchardt, and L. Deiters. Berlin-Hauptstadt der DDR: Magistrat, n.d.
Zauzich, Karl-Theodor. "Die Papyrussammlung." In *Kunst der Welt in den Berliner Museen: Ägyptisches Museum Staatliche Museen Preussicher Kulturbesitz*, 10–12. Stuttgart: Belser, 1980.

# Index of Names

Allberry, Charles R. C., xi, 2, 3, 8, 25, 47–48, 59, 60, 66, 83, 86, 87, 91, 110–12, 126, 170, 175–76, 178, 187, 204, 223, 276, 278, 283–85, 310, 313
Anthes, Rudolf, 9, 113, 125, 133–34, 187
Attridge, Harold W., 20, 302

Baker, Stanley, 16–17, 131
Beatty, A. Chester, Sir, xi–xiii, 2–5, 7–8, 10–19, 22–27, 30–31, 37–38, 43–46, 52, 54–59, 61–79, 82–83, 86–87, 89–102, 104–11, 122–29, 131–35, 147–50, 165–66, 172, 175–78, 180–87, 194, 196, 201, 204, 219, 223, 232–33, 251, 261–62, 264–65, 269, 273, 280, 282, 284, 286, 288–89, 291–92, 303, 309–10, 313–16
Bell, Harold I., Sir, 61, 182
Beltz, Walter, 2, 40, 41, 190, 196, 206, 208–11, 214–17, 227–29, 232, 239–40, 252–53, 258, 264–65, 269, 275, 280, 284, 292–93, 299, 304, 317
Berfelde, Lothar, 33
Bobertz, Charles A., 20, 302

Böhlig, Alexander, xiii, 6–11, 18, 26, 30, 33–34, 36–38, 41–42, 44–48, 83–84, 87, 90, 110, 122, 124–27, 134–35, 141–42, 144, 155, 157, 159, 167, 170–71, 174–75, 179–81, 187, 189, 195–96, 203–9, 216, 226–27, 232–33, 239–40, 250–51, 255–61, 263–64, 266–67, 269, 275, 284–87, 289–92, 299–300, 303–4, 313, 317–20
Brashear, William, xii, 19, 313, 321
Browder, Michael H., 310, 318
Bryder, Peter, 318–19

Cirillo, Luigi, 318
Colpe, Carsten, xii, 18–19, 44, 59, 84, 174–75, 178–79, 181, 194, 196, 204, 262, 269, 289–92, 301, 314, 319
Corble, J. W., 61, 63, 65, 68, 99
Crum, W. E. xi, 22, 24–28, 30, 37, 57, 66, 92–93, 96, 98, 111–12, 223, 283, 286–87, 314, 318

Dathe, H., 136, 321
Deiters, L., 321
Diakonov, Prof., 129

## Index of Names

Doering, Wolf Henry, xii, 9, 123, 182
Dolt, Pater, 151
Donlon, Pat, 1
Dube, Wolf-Dieter, 19

Edwards, I. E. S., 9, 16, 61, 125, 128–35, 186–87, 314

Fackelmann, Michael, 172, 318
Firchow, Otto, 7, 16–17, 128–34, 314
Forsdyke, John, Sir, 11–12
Francis, F., 12
Funk, Wolf-Peter, ix, xii, xiv, 7, 20–22, 32, 34–35, 40–42, 197, 199, 210, 212, 224, 229–30, 254–55, 301–2, 314

Gardiner, A. H., 4–5, 10, 12–14, 24, 26, 57, 64–68, 70–72, 74, 78, 92–93, 95–97, 105–10, 182, 232–33, 273, 314
Gardner, Iaian, 32, 318
Geiler, Karl, 165, 171, 175
Geismeier, Willi, 321
Giversen, Søren, xi–xiv, 1–3, 5–7, 17–18, 20, 22, 27–31, 38–39, 42, 47, 60, 78, 112, 124, 231–33, 246–47, 265–67, 286–87, 300–301, 306–7, 310, 314, 318
Glanville, Stephen, 182
Godlewski, Wlodzimierz, 209, 253
Grapow, Hermann, 129–30
Grohmann, Adolf, xiv, 32, 55, 148
Guber, Prof., 129

Harnack, Adolf von, 45, 52, 70, 316
Hayes, R. J., 9, 46, 125, 129–31, 133–35, 186
Heilmeyer, Prof., 19
Henchey, Patrick, 18

Holan, Gisela, 19
Holl, Karl, 2
Hühns, Erik, 118, 321

Ibscher, Hugo, xi–xiv, 1, 3–5, 7–9, 13–14, 17, 22, 24–26, 30, 32, 34–35, 41–44, 47, 51, 62, 79–92, 125, 127, 132–34, 143, 148, 156, 159, 187, 194, 199–202, 204, 213–15, 218–20, 227, 230, 233, 238, 251, 256, 258–67, 275–76, 278, 283, 300, 303, 307–8, 314, 318, 320
Ibscher, Rolf, x, xii–xiii, 10–16, 18–20, 34–35, 38, 40–47, 59, 79, 81–84, 88–90, 121, 123–28, 132–34, 136, 147–89, 194–96, 204–6, 208, 214–15, 217, 219, 226, 230, 233, 249, 251, 256–57, 260–64, 266, 269, 284, 289, 291–92, 300, 304, 307–8, 310, 314–15, 318–19
Irmscher, Johannes, 16, 46

Karig, Joachim Selim, 19, 113, 116, 141, 321,
Kasser, Rodlophe, xiii, 5–6, 22, 30, 306, 314–15, 319
King, Karen L., 20–21, 301, 319
Kingsford, Joan. *See* Joan Kingsford Wood
Klimkeit, Hans-Joachim, ix–x
Kniese, Sigrid, 114, 321
Koenen, Ludwig, 242–43, 319
Kohlhammer, Walter, 43–44, 48, 59, 72–73, 85, 87, 91, 206, 208, 229–30, 268–69
Krause, Martin, xiii, 5–7, 22, 30, 306, 315, 319
Kühnel-Kunze, Irene, 319
Kümmel, General Director, 9–10, 123–24

Lange, H. O., 2, 45, 60, 315
Lewis, Patrica K. G., 47, 319
Lockwood, Wilfrid, 5, 17, 20, 315
Lubowski, E., 53
Luft, Ulrich, 195, 199, 226, 250
Luke, Otto Werner, 34, 40, 42, 160, 214, 230, 261, 315

Manteuffel, J. von, 33, 141–43
Maugham, W. Somerset, 47, 319
McGilligan, Miss, 135
Merkelbach, Reinhold, 36, 223, 319
Merton, Mr., 186
Michalowski, K., 33, 143
Millar, Eric G., 61
Mirecki, Paul Allan, xii, 20–21, 32, 301, 315, 319
Moritz, Privy Councillor, 54,
Müller, Wolfgang, 15, 19, 40, 121, 135–36, 159, 189–90, 194, 196–97, 204, 208, 227, 232, 239, 251–52, 275, 292–93, 320–21
Myszor, Wincenty, 33, 40, 142, 209–10, 228–29, 253–54, 315

Nagel, Peter, 47, 159, 162, 199, 207–8
Norris, Christopher, 12–13

Orlandi, Tito, 265–66, 285–86, 298–300, 304, 309–10, 315, 320

Patterson, Stephen J., 20, 40–41, 235, 247, 301–2
Pfeffer, August, 31, 52, 57, 73, 195, 199, 226, 249
Plenderleith, Harold, 150, 168
Poethke, Günter, 38, 40, 42–43, 143, 209–10, 216, 230, 238, 252, 257, 261, 275, 315

Polotsky, H. J., xi, xiii–xiv, 1–2, 4, 18, 22, 25–34, 36–40, 42, 44–45, 47–48, 51, 57, 59, 66, 72–73, 78–80, 83, 91–92–101, 103–11, 148, 170, 187, 189, 193–94, 196, 198, 202–4, 209, 223, 225, 232–35, 238–43, 246, 248, 254–56, 259, 263–64, 268, 273–74, 282–84, 286–88, 303, 309–11, 316, 318, 320
Putt, S. Gorley, 47, 320

Rassart-Debergh, Marguerite, 319
Regemorter, Berthe van , 281, 316
Ries, Julien, 319
Robbel, Liselotte, 114, 321
Robinson, Gesina Schenke, xii, 20, 31, 197, 302, 316
Robinson, James M., 7, 316, 318, 320
Roeder, Günther, 133, 186
Roselli, Amneris, 318

Säve-Söderbergh, Torgny, 284, 320
Schäfter, Heinrich, 113
Schellenberg, Prof., 165
Schenke, Gesa, 259
Schenke, Gesina. *See* Gesina Schenke Robinson
Schenke, Hans-Martin, 36–37, 40, 320
Schmidt, Carl, xi–xiv, 1–2, 4, 18, 22–26, 31–32, 34, 37–45, 47, 51–60, 63–68, 70–74, 76–78, 80, 82, 84, 90–94, 96–106, 109–11, 148, 167, 170, 176, 178–79, 181, 188–89, 193–96, 198–99, 202–3, 208, 218, 223, 225–27, 231–32, 234–35, 238–43, 246, 248–49, 254–56, 259, 263, 268–69, 273–74, 280, 282, 284, 288–90, 303, 309, 315, 316, 320

## Index of Names

Schott, Siegfried, 289
Schubart, Wilhelm, 24, 31, 64, 72, 92, 95–99, 104–8, 189, 194, 199, 226, 249, 268, 316
Schuchardt, J., 321
Seeberg, Erich, 52
Seidel, P., xii, 9–11, 15, 124–25
Settgast, Jürgen, 114, 321
Skeat, T. C., 46
Snow, C. P., 47, 320
Struve, Prof., 129

Tardieu, Michel, 16, 128, 228, 243, 269, 293, 299, 303, 311, 316, 320
Thompson, Herbert, Sir, 10, 24–28, 43, 57, 59, 66, 71, 76, 78, 92–102, 105–11, 223, 286, 316
Till, Walter, 187

Wiessner, Gernot, ix
Wilkinson, J. V. S., 8, 11–14, 30, 186, 232, 316,
Wipprech, E., 321
Wood, Joan Kingsford, 5, 8, 10, 13–14, 30, 69, 93, 101
Wooderson, John, 61, 65, 67–69, 72
Weymes, Mr., 132

Zauzich, Karl-Theodor, 117, 321
Zuckerman, Bruce, 21
Zuckerman, Kenneth, 21

www.ingramcontent.com/pod-product-compliance
Lightning Source LLC
Chambersburg PA
CBHW030432300426
44112CB00009B/972